THE JPS B'NAI MITZVAH
TORAH COMMENTARY

The Jewish Publication Society expresses its gratitude for the generosity of the following sponsors of this book:

Wendy Fein Cooper and Leonard J. Cooper, in honor of Noah, Nathaniel, Adam, Rafaella, Ariella, and Liora Cooper.

Rabbi Barry and Debby Schwartz, in appreciation to Gittel Hilibrand and David Lerman for their leadership of JPS.

University of Nebraska Press
Lincoln

THE JPS B'NAI MITZVAH TORAH COMMENTARY

Rabbi Jeffrey K. Salkin

The Jewish Publication Society
Philadelphia

Library of Congress Cataloging-in-Publication Data
Names: Salkin, Jeffrey K., 1954–author. | Jewish
Publication Society.
Title: The JPS b'nai mitzvah Torah commentary /
Rabbi Jeffrey K. Salkin.
Description: Lincoln: University of Nebraska
Press, [2017] | Series: JPS Study Bible |
Includes bibliographical references.
Identifiers: LCCN 2016051243 (print)
LCCN 2016051983 (ebook)
ISBN 9780827612525 (pbk.: alk. paper)
ISBN 9780827613294 (epub)
ISBN 9780827613300 (mobi)
ISBN 9780827613317 (pdf)
Subjects: LCSH: Bible. Pentateuch—Commentaries—
Juvenile literature. | Bar mitzvah—Juvenile literature.
| Bat mitzvah—Juvenile literature.
Classification: LCC BS1225.53 .S3414 2016 (print) |
LCC BS1225.53 (ebook) | DDC 222/.107—dc23
LC record available at https://lccn.loc.gov/2016051243

Set in Iowan Old Style by Rachel Gould.

CONTENTS

Acknowledgments   xiii

Introduction   xv

PART 1 ❖ The Torah

1. GENESIS   3

Bere'shit 1:1–6:8   3

Noaḥ 6:9–11:32   7

Lekh Lekha 12:1–17:27   12

Va-yera' 18:1–22:24   16

Ḥayyei Sarah 23:1–25:18   21

Toledot 25:19–28:9   25

Va-yetse' 28:10–32:3   30

Va-yishlah 32:4–36:43   34

Va-yeshev 37:1–40:23   38

Mikkets 41:1–44:17   43

Va-yiggash 44:18–47:27   48

Va-yeḥi 47:28–50:26   52

2. EXODUS   59

Shemot 1:1–6:1   59

Va-'era' 6:2–9:35   63

Bo' 10:1–13:16   68

Be-shallaḥ 13:17–17:16   72

Yitro 18:1–20:23   77

Mishpatim 21:1–24:18   82

Terumah 25:1–27:19   87

Tetsavveh 27:20–30:10   92

Ki Tissa' 30:11–34:35   96

Va-yakhel 35:1–38:20   101

Pekudei 38:21–40:38   106

3. LEVITICUS   111

Va-yikra' 1:1–5:26   111

Tsav 6:1–8:36   115

Shemini 9:1–11:47   119

Tazria' 12:1–13:59   124

Metsora' 14:1–15:33   129

'Aḥarei Mot 16:1–18:30   132

Kedoshim 19:1–20:27   136

'Emor 21:1–24:23   141

Be-har 25:1–26:2   146

Be-ḥukkotai 26:3–27:34   151

4. NUMBERS   157

Be-midbar 1:1–4:20   157

Naso' 4:21–7:89   161

Be-haʻalotekha 8:1–12:16   166

Shelaḥ Lekha 13:1–15:41   171

Koraḥ 16:1–18:32   177

Ḥukkat 19:1–22:1   182

Balak 22:2–25:9   188

Pinḥas 25:10–30:1   192

Mattot 30:2–32:42   198

Maseʻei 33:1–36:13   202

5. DEUTERONOMY   209

Devarim 1:1–3:22   209

Va-'etḥannan 3:23–7:11   213

'Ekev 7:12–11:25   218

Re'eh 11:26–16:17   223

Shofetim 16:18–21:9   229

Ki Tetse' 21:10–25:19   233

Ki Tavo' 26:1–29:8   239

Nitsavim 29:9–30:20   244

Va-yelekh 31:1–30   250

Ha'azinu 32:1–52   255

Ve-zo't ha-berakhah 33:1–34:12   259

Part 2 ❖ The Haftarot

6. GENESIS   267

Bere'shit: Isaiah 42:5–43:10   267

Noaḥ: Isaiah 54:1–55:5   269

Lekh Lekha: Isaiah 40:27–41:16   271

Va-yera': 2 Kings 4:1–37   273

Ḥayyei Sarah: 1 Kings 1:1–31   275

Toledot: Malachi 1:1–2:7   277

Va-yetse': Hosea 12:13–14:10   279

Va-yishlaḥ: Obadiah 1:1–21   281

Va-yeshev: Amos 2:6–3:8   282

Mikkets: 1 Kings 3:15–28; 4:1   285

Shabbat Hanukkah: Zechariah 2:14–4:7   286

Va-yiggash: Ezekiel 37:15–28   288

Va-yeḥi: 1 Kings 2:1–12   291

7. EXODUS   293

Shemot: Isaiah 27:6–28:13; 29:22–23   293

Va-'era': Ezekiel 28:25–29:21   295

Bo': Jeremiah 46:13–28   297

Be-shallaḥ: Judges 4:4–5:31   299

Yitro: Isaiah 6:1–7:6; 9:5–6   301

Mishpatim: Jeremiah 34:8–22; 33:25–26   303

Terumah: 1 Kings 5:26–6:13   305

Tetsavveh: Ezekiel 43:10–27   307

Ki Tissa': 1 Kings 18:1–39   309

Va-yakhel–Pekudei: 1 Kings 7:40–50   311

8. LEVITICUS   315

    Va-yikra': Isaiah 43:21–44:23   315
    Tsav: Jeremiah 7:21–8:3; 9:22–23   317
    Shemini: 2 Samuel 6:1–7:17   318
    Tazria': 2 Kings 4:42–5:19   321
    Metsora': 2 Kings 7:3–20   323
    'Aḥarei Mot: Ezekiel 22:1–19   325
    Kedoshim: Amos 9:7–15   327
    'Emor: Ezekiel 44:15–31   329
    Be-har: Jeremiah 32:6–27   331
    Be-ḥukkotai: Jeremiah 16:19–17:14   333

9. NUMBERS   337

    Be-midbar: Hosea 2:1–22   337
    Naso': Judges 13:2–25   339
    Be-ha'alotekha: Zechariah 2:14–4:7   341
    Shelaḥ-Lekha: Joshua 2:1–24   343
    Koraḥ: 1 Samuel 11:14–12:22   344
    Ḥukkat: Judges 11:1–33   346
    Balak: Micah 5:6–6:8   348
    Pinḥas: 1 Kings 18:46–19:21   350
    Mattot: Jeremiah 1:1–2:3   352
    Mase'ei: Jeremiah 2:4–28; 3:4   353

10. DEUTERONOMY   357

    Devarim: Isaiah 1:1–27   357
    Va-etḥannan: Isaiah 40:1–26   359
    'Ekev: Isaiah 49:14–51:3   361
    Re'eh: Isaiah 54:11–55:5   363
    Shofetim: Isaiah 51:12–52:12   365
    Ki Tetse': Isaiah 54:1–10   367
    Ki Tavo': Isaiah 60:1–22   369
    Nitsavim–Va-yelekh: Isaiah 61:10–63:9   370
    Ha'azinu: 2 Samuel 22:1–51   372

11. SPECIAL HAFTAROT FOR MAJOR HOLIDAYS 375

    Maḥar Ḥodesh: 1 Samuel 20:18–42 375

    Shabbat Parah: Ezekiel 36:16–38 377

    Shabbat Shekalim: 2 Kings 12:1–17 378

    Rosh Ḥodesh: Isaiah 66:1–24 380

    Notes 383

ACKNOWLEDGMENTS

There are many people who inspired me, and encouraged me, to write this book. Their help and support have been blessings to me, and I raise my voice in gratitude to them.

First, Barry Schwartz and Carol Hupping of the Jewish Publication Society. Ever since Rabbi Schwartz, an old and dear friend, took the reins of this old and venerable publishing company, he has brought new life and vision to its mission. He first suggested this book as part of a larger series of Torah volumes that would focus on different aspects of Jewish life. Without his urging, prodding, and encouragement— and that of Carol Hupping—this book could never have been possible. They were, in many ways, the book's "father" and "mother," and, because the Ten Commandments lists "honor your father and mother" in a very prominent place, I must honor them.

Second, Stuart Matlins, the founder of Jewish Lights Publishing. More than twenty years ago, Stuart got me thinking about the meaning of bar and bat mitzvah, along with the many challenges this popular ceremony faces in American life, and he urged me to write my first books about bar and bat mitzvah. Those efforts produced *Putting God on the Guest List* and *For Kids—Putting God on Your Guest List*. Those books, and the ongoing thought that I have put into bar and bat mitzvah over the years, created the initial spark that became this book. I am ever grateful to him for his encouragement and friendship.

Third, the members of my congregation, Temple Solel in Hollywood, Florida. Although this book was well on its way to completion when I started my rabbinate there, the members of Solel have been most enthusiastic about this project. In particular, I am grateful to my bar and bat mitzvah students, who have used material from this book to create their *divrei Torah* for their ceremonies. Their insights and suggestions were very important to me, and I pray that the lessons contained in this book will remain with them forever.

Fourth, my wife, Sheila Shuster. This book took years of study, preparation, and editing, and she has always been supportive of my need to bring this book to life. She is my partner in all things, as well as a fellow lover of Judaism.

And fifth, to Jewish young people, their parents, and all those who love and study Torah. This book can only exist if it is read. Without that, it is merely pages on a shelf. Your willingness and eagerness to make Torah your own, and to find old and new meanings in its words, makes this book not only necessary, but important. We call Torah an *etz chayyim*, a "tree of life," because it grows with every passing year.

As long as Jews study and learn Torah, the Jewish people will live, thrive, and rejoice. May this book be a modest offering toward that future.

January 19, 2016
9 Shevat 5776

INTRODUCTION

News flash: the most important thing about becoming bar or bat mitzvah isn't the party. Nor is it the presents. Nor even being able to celebrate with your family and friends—as wonderful as those things are. Nor is it even standing before the congregation and reading the prayers of the liturgy—as important as that is.

No, the most important thing about becoming bar or bat mitzvah is sharing Torah with the congregation. And why is that? Because of all Jewish skills, that is the most important one.

Here is what is true about rites of passage: you can tell what a culture values by the tasks it asks its young people to perform on their way to maturity. In American culture, you become responsible for driving, responsible for voting, and yes, responsible for drinking responsibly.

In some cultures, the rite of passage toward maturity includes some kind of trial, or a test of strength. Sometimes, it is a kind of "outward bound" camping adventure. Among the Maasai tribe in Africa, it is traditional for a young person to hunt and kill a lion. In some Hispanic cultures, fifteen year-old girls celebrate the *quinceañera*, which marks their entrance into maturity.

What is Judaism's way of marking maturity? It combines both of these rites of passage: *responsibility* and *test*. You show that you are on your way to becoming a *responsible* Jewish adult through a public *test* of strength and knowledge—reading or chanting Torah, and then teaching it to the congregation.

This is the most important Jewish ritual mitzvah (commandment), and that is how you demonstrate that you are, truly, bar or bat mitzvah—old enough to be responsible for the mitzvot.

What Is Torah?

So, what exactly is the Torah? You probably know this already, but let's review.

The Torah (teaching) consists of "the five books of Moses," sometimes also called the *chumash* (from the Hebrew word *chameish*, which means "five"), or, sometimes, the Greek word Pentateuch (which means "the five teachings").

Here are the five books of the Torah, with their common names and their Hebrew names.

꜔ **Genesis (The beginning), which in Hebrew is Bere'shit (from the first words—"When God began to create").** Bere'shit spans the years from Creation to Joseph's death in Egypt. Many of the Bible's best stories are in Genesis: the creation story itself; Adam and Eve in the Garden of Eden; Cain and Abel; Noah and the Flood; and the tales of the Patriarchs and Matriarchs, Abraham, Isaac, Jacob, Sarah, Rebekah, Rachel, and Leah. It also includes one of the greatest pieces of world literature, the story of Joseph, which is actually the oldest complete novel in history, comprising more than one-quarter of all Genesis.

꜔ **Exodus (Getting out), which in Hebrew is Shemot (These are the names).** Exodus begins with the story of the Israelite slavery in Egypt. It then moves to the rise of Moses as a leader, and the Israelites' liberation from slavery. After the Israelites leave Egypt, they experience the miracle of the parting of the Sea of Reeds (or "Red Sea"); the giving of the Ten Commandments at Mount Sinai; the idolatry of the Golden Calf; and the design and construction of the Tabernacle and of the ark for the original tablets of the law, which our ancestors carried with them in the desert. Exodus also includes various ethical and civil laws, such as "You shall not wrong a stranger or oppress him, for you were strangers in the land of Egypt" (22:20).

꜔ **Leviticus (about the Levites), or, in Hebrew, Va-yikra' (And God called).** It goes into great detail about the kinds of sacrifices that the ancient Israelites brought as offerings; the laws of ritual purity; the animals that were permitted and forbidden for eating (the beginnings of the tradition of kashrut, the Jewish dietary laws); the diagnosis of various skin diseases; the ethical laws of holiness; the ritual calendar of the Jewish year; and various agricultural laws concerning the treatment of the Land of Israel. Leviticus is basically the manual of ancient Judaism.

Ŧ **Numbers (because the book begins with the census of the Isra-elites), or, in Hebrew, Be-midbar (In the wilderness).** The book describes the forty years of wandering in the wilderness and the various rebellions against Moses. The constant theme: "Egypt wasn't so bad. Maybe we should go back." The greatest rebellion against Moses was the negative reports of the spies about the Land of Israel, which discouraged the Israelites from wanting to move forward into the land. For that reason, the "wilderness gen-eration" must die off before a new generation can come into ma-turity and finish the journey.

Ŧ **Deuteronomy (The repetition of the laws of the Torah), or, in Hebrew, Devarim (The words).** The final book of the Torah is, essentially, Moses's farewell address to the Israelites as they pre-pare to enter the Land of Israel. Here we find various laws that had been previously taught, though sometimes with different wording. Much of Deuteronomy contains laws that will be im-portant to the Israelites as they enter the Land of Israel—laws concerning the establishment of a monarchy and the ethics of warfare. Perhaps the most famous passage from Deuteronomy contains the *Shema,* the declaration of God's unity and unique-ness, and the *Ve-ahavta,* which follows it. Deuteronomy ends with the death of Moses on Mount Nebo as he looks across the Jordan Valley into the land that he will not enter.

Jews read the Torah in sequence—starting with Bere'shit right af-ter Simchat Torah in the autumn, and then finishing Devarim on the following Simchat Torah. Each Torah portion is called a parashah (di-vision; sometimes called a *sidrah,* a place in the order of the Torah reading). The stories go around in a full circle, reminding us that we can always gain more insights and more wisdom from the Torah. This means that if you don't "get" the meaning this year, don't worry—it will come around again.

And What Else? The Haftarah

We read or chant the Torah from the Torah scroll—the most sacred thing that a Jewish community has in its possession. The Torah is written without vowels, and the ability to read it and chant it is part of the challenge and the test.

But there is more to the synagogue reading. Every Torah reading has an accompanying haftarah reading. Haftarah means "conclusion," because there was once a time when the service actually ended with that reading. Some scholars believe that the reading of the haftarah originated at a time when non-Jewish authorities outlawed the reading of the Torah, and the Jews read the haftarah sections instead. In fact, in some synagogues, young people who become bar or bat mitzvah read very little Torah and instead read the entire haftarah portion.

The haftarah portion comes from the Nevi'im, the prophetic books, which are the second part of the Jewish Bible. It is either read or chanted from a Hebrew Bible, or maybe from a booklet or a photocopy.

The ancient sages chose the haftarah passages because their themes reminded them of the words or stories in the Torah text. Sometimes, they chose *haftarot* with special themes in honor of a festival or an upcoming festival.

Not all books in the prophetic section of the Hebrew Bible consist of prophecy. Several are historical. For example:

The book of Joshua tells the story of the conquest and settlement of Israel.

The book of Judges speaks of the period of early tribal rulers who would rise to power, usually for the purpose of uniting the tribes in war against their enemies. Some of these leaders are famous: Deborah, the great prophetess and military leader, and Samson, the biblical strong man.

The books of Samuel start with Samuel, the last judge, and then move to the creation of the Israelite monarchy under Saul and David (approximately 1000 BCE).

The books of Kings tell of the death of King David, the rise of King Solomon, and how the Israelite kingdom split into the Northern Kingdom of Israel and the Southern Kingdom of Judah (approximately 900 BCE).

And then there are the books of the prophets, those spokesmen for God whose words fired the Jewish conscience. Their names are immortal: Isaiah, Jeremiah, Ezekiel, Amos, Hosea, among others.

Someone once said: "There is no evidence of a biblical prophet ever being invited back a second time for dinner." Why? Because the prophets were tough. They had no patience for injustice, apathy, or hypocrisy. No one escaped their criticisms. Here's what they taught:

- ϯ God commands the Jews to behave decently toward one another. In fact, God cares more about basic ethics and decency than about ritual behavior.
- ϯ God chose the Jews *not* for special privileges, but for special duties to humanity.
- ϯ As bad as the Jews sometimes were, there was always the possibility that they would improve their behavior.
- ϯ As bad as things might be now, it will not always be that way. Someday, there will be universal justice and peace. Human history is moving forward toward an ultimate conclusion that some call the Messianic Age: a time of universal peace and prosperity for the Jewish people and for all the people of the world.

Your Mission—To Teach Torah to the Congregation

On the day when you become bar or bat mitzvah, you will be reading, or chanting, Torah—in Hebrew. You will be reading, or chanting, the haftarah—in Hebrew. That is the major skill that publicly marks the becoming of bar or bat mitzvah. But, perhaps even more important than that, you need to be able to teach something about the Torah portion, and perhaps the haftarah as well.

And that is where this book comes in. It will be a very valuable resource for you, and your family, in the b'nai mitzvah process.

Here is what you will find in it:

- ϯ A brief **summary** of every Torah portion. This is a basic overview of the portion; and, while it might not refer to everything in the Torah portion, it will explain its most important aspects.
- ϯ A list of the **major ideas** in the Torah portion. The purpose: to make the Torah portion real, in ways that we can relate to. Every Torah portion contains unique ideas, and when you put all

of those ideas together, you actually come up with a list of Judaism's most important ideas.

ᵗ Two ***divrei Torah*** ("words of Torah," or "sermonettes") for each portion. These *divrei Torah* explain significant aspects of the Torah portion in accessible, reader-friendly language. Each *devar Torah* contains references to **traditional** Jewish sources (those that were written before the modern era), as well as **modern** sources and quotes. We have searched, far and wide, to find sources that are unusual, interesting, and not just the "same old stuff" that many people already know about the Torah portion. Why did we include these minisermons in the volume? Not because we want you to simply copy those sermons and pass them off as your own (that would be cheating), though you are free to quote from them. We included them so that you can see what is possible—how you can try to make meaning for yourself out of the words of Torah.

ᵗ **Connections:** This is perhaps the most valuable part. It's a list of questions that you can ask yourself, or that others might help you think about—any of which can lead to the creation of your *devar Torah*.

Note: you don't have to like everything that's in a particular Torah portion. Some aren't that loveable. Some are hard to understand; some are about religious practices that people today might find confusing, and even offensive; some contain ideas that we might find totally outmoded.

But this doesn't have to get in the way. After all, most kids spend a lot of time thinking about stories that contain ideas that modern people would find totally bizarre. Any good medieval fantasy story falls into that category.

And we also believe that, if you spend just a little bit of time with those texts, you can begin to understand what the author was trying to say.

This volume goes one step further. Sometimes, the haftarah comes off as a second thought, and no one really thinks about it. We have tried to solve that problem by including a **summary** of each haftarah, and then a mini-sermon on the haftarah. This will help you learn how these sacred words are relevant to today's world, and even to your own life.

All Bible quotations come from the NJPS translation, which is found in the many different editions of the JPS TANAKH; in the Conservative movement's *Etz Hayim: Torah and Commentary;* in the Reform movement's *Torah: A Modern Commentary;* and in other Bible commentaries and study guides.

How Do I Write a *Devar Torah*?

It really is easier than it looks.

There are many ways of thinking about the *devar Torah.* It is, of course, a short sermon on the meaning of the Torah (and, perhaps, the haftarah) portion. It might even be helpful to think of the *devar Torah* as a "book report" on the portion itself.

The most important thing you can know about this sacred task is: *Learn* the words. *Love* the words. Teach people what it could mean to *live* the words.

Here's a basic outline for a *devar Torah:*

"My Torah portion is (name of portion)_____,
    from the book of _____, chapter
    _____.

"In my Torah portion, we learn that_____
    (Summary of portion)

"For me, the most important lesson of this Torah portion is (what is the best thing in the portion? Take the portion as a whole; your *devar Torah* does not have to be only, or specifically, on the verses that you are reading).

"As I learned my Torah portion, I found myself wondering:

ℶ *Raise a question that the Torah portion itself raises.*

ℶ *"Pick a fight"* with the portion. Argue with it.

ℶ *Answer a question* that is listed in the "Connections" section of each Torah portion.

ℶ *Suggest a question to your rabbi* that you would want the rabbi to answer in his or her own *devar Torah* or sermon.

"I have lived the values of the Torah by
_____(here, you can talk about how the
Torah portion relates to your own life. If you have done a mitzvah project, you can talk about that here).

How To Keep It from Being Boring
(and You from Being Bored)

Some people just don't like giving traditional speeches. From our perspective, that's really okay. Perhaps you can teach Torah in a different
way—one that makes sense to you.

- Write an "open letter" to one of the characters in your Torah portion. "Dear Abraham: I hope that your trip to Canaan was not too
  hard . . ." "Dear Moses: Were you afraid when you got the Ten
  Commandments on Mount Sinai? I sure would have been . . ."
- Write a news story about what happens. Imagine yourself to
  be a television or news reporter. "Residents of neighboring cities were horrified yesterday as the wicked cities of Sodom and
  Gomorrah were burned to the ground. Some say that God was
  responsible . . ."
- Write an imaginary interview with a character in your Torah portion.
- Tell the story from the point of view of another character, or a minor character, in the story. For instance, tell the story of the Garden of Eden from the point of view of the serpent. Or the story
  of the Binding of Isaac from the point of view of the ram, which
  was substituted for Isaac as a sacrifice. Or perhaps the story of
  the sale of Joseph from the point of view of his coat, which was
  stripped off him and dipped in a goat's blood.
- Write a poem about your Torah portion.
- Write a song about your Torah portion.
- Write a play about your Torah portion, and have some friends act
  it out with you.
- Create a piece of artwork about your Torah portion.

The bottom line is: Make this a joyful experience. Yes—it could
even be fun.

The Very Last Thing You Need to Know at This Point

The Torah scroll is written without vowels. Why? Don't *sofrim* (Torah scribes) know the vowels?

Of course they do.

So, why do they leave the vowels out?

One reason is that the Torah came into existence at a time when sages were still arguing about the proper vowels, and the proper pronunciation.

But here is another reason: The Torah text, as we have it today, and as it sits in the scroll, is actually *an unfinished work*. Think of it: the words are just sitting there. Because they have no vowels, it is as if they have no voice.

When we read the Torah publicly, we give voice to the ancient words. And when we find meaning in those ancient words, and we talk about those meanings, those words jump to life. They enter our lives. They make our world deeper and better.

Mazal tov to you, and your family. This is your journey toward Jewish maturity. Love it.

THE JPS B'NAI MITZVAH
TORAH COMMENTARY

PART 1 ❖ The Torah

GENESIS

❖ Bere'shit: Genesis 1:1–6:8

This is how it all starts—with a Torah portion that poses a lot of questions. God creates the world in six days (right, but how long was a day?). God rests on the seventh day, which is how Shabbat gets started. God then creates Adam and Eve and places them in the Garden of Eden.

Things are going great until Adam and Eve disobey God by eating from the Tree of Knowledge of Good and Evil. God kicks them out of the garden. Just when you think things are bad enough, Cain kills his brother, Abel. As punishment, Cain is condemned to wander the earth. And over the next several generations, humanity increasingly descends into violence.

Maybe the whole "humanity" project isn't working out as well as God had planned. Stay tuned for God's solution to the problem.

Summary

ᚻ God creates the universe as we know it in a series of six days. (1:1–29)

ᚻ Human beings are created in the image of God. (1:26–28)

ᚻ The seventh day of creation is a day of rest—Shabbat—and God declares it holy. (2:1–3)

ᚻ Human beings had a special role in the Garden of Eden, and God commands them not to eat from the Tree of Knowledge of Good and Evil. The snake convinces Adam and Eve to disobey God's command, with severe consequences that include expulsion from the garden. (2:4–3:24)

ᚻ Cain kills his brother, Abel, and God confronts him. From there, things go downhill fast and humanity increasingly descends into violence. (4:1–6:8)

The Big Ideas

℔ **The story of creation in Genesis is a moral story, about the nature of the world and of humanity itself.** It contains ethical teachings about the pattern of creation and the meaning of the world itself.

℔ **God created order out of chaos.** We don't know how long a day was, but the most important thing is that there is a rhythm and pattern to creation, and that things do not simply happen in a random way.

℔ **Language is a tool of creation.** That is precisely how God uses language: "Let there be . . ." The words that we say have the power to create worlds, or, if we use words irresponsibly, they can destroy worlds—and people—as well.

℔ **Nature must be respected.** We are not free to do whatever we want to the earth, its living things, and its resources. Because the earth is God's creation, we must respect it and take care of it, which was one of God's commandments to Adam and Eve in the Garden of Eden.

℔ **Special times can be holy.** The first thing declared holy in the Torah is not a place nor a person, but a time. The seventh day is holy and set apart because God rested on that day. When we rest on Shabbat we too make it a holy—a special—day.

℔ **Human beings are responsible for one another.** The Torah tells us that humanity is made in God's image, and one way of interpreting this is that there is a piece of God within us all. In some deep way, we are all connected to each other and to God, and we should treat one other as we want to be treated, and as God would want to be treated.

Divrei Torah

IN GOD'S IMAGE: WHAT DOES IT MEAN?

The last thing that God creates is humanity. The Torah suggests that perhaps God saved the best for last. We are uniquely described as created in God's image: "And God created humankind in the divine image, creating it in the image of God—creating them male and female" (1:27).

This is perhaps the greatest idea that Judaism ever gave to the world—that every person has the spark of divinity within him or her. The great sage Rabbi Akiba recognized that our awareness of this spark makes us even more special: "Beloved are human beings, because they were created in the divine image. But it was through a special love that they became aware that they were created in the divine image."

What does this really mean—"in the divine image"?

On its most basic level, it means that while we are certainly not God, in some way we resemble God. It means that we should try to imitate God. A large part of our human responsibilities flow from the various things that God does in the Torah. Our tradition teaches that as God creates, we can create. As God clothes Adam and Eve, so we can clothe the needy. As God gives life, so we strive to heal the sick.

Being made in God's image means that we have special tasks and opportunities in the world. We have a special responsibility to care for all of God's creation. Because God created the world and all living things within it, we must avoid destruction of the earth and its plant life (*ba'al tashhit*). Because God created *and blessed* animals (1:22), we must avoid cruelty to animals (*tza'ar ba'alei chayyim*). Because God created, blessed, *and* made human beings in the divine image, we must recognize the sacred in all human beings and cherish them. Yes, to avoid destruction, and yes, to avoid cruelty—but also to create ways of helping people through acts of kindness (*gemilut chasadim*).

Note that the Torah teaches that both man *and* woman are made in the divine image. All people are equal in dignity and deserve equal respect and opportunity. In the words of Rabbi Irving (Yitz) Greenberg, in an imitation of the American Declaration of Independence, which also speaks of basic rights: "We hold these truths to be self-evident: that all human beings are created in the image of God, that they are endowed by their Creator with certain fundamental dignities, that among these are infinite value, equality and uniqueness. Our faith calls on all humanity to join in a covenant with God and a partnership between the generations for *tikkun olam* (the repair of the world) so that all forms of life are sustained in the fullest of dignity."

So, that is the Jewish task: to work toward a world where everyone knows that he or she is created in the divine image. And a world where everyone else knows it as well!

WHERE IS YOUR BROTHER?

In one sense, Cain was the first and worst murderer in the world. When he killed his brother, Abel, he essentially wiped out one-quarter of all humanity, because the Torah claims that at that time there were only four people in the world: Adam, Eve, Cain, and Abel.

Both Cain and Abel brought offerings to God. God accepted Abel's offering of a lamb, but rejected Cain's offering of grain. Cain is very jealous, and very angry.

God warned Cain that "sin crouches at the door"—that we have to be careful of our feelings of anger and jealousy. It was too late for Cain to engage in "anger management." Cain killed Abel. God asked Cain: "Where is your brother Abel?" (4:9). To which Cain responded: "I don't know. Am I my brother's keeper?"

Of course, God knew where Abel was. (God is, after all, God, who knows everything.) God simply wanted Cain to own up to what he had done, and to learn the lesson of moral responsibility.

More than this: God wanted Cain to know that he had not only killed Abel. The text says that Abel's bloods (*demei*) cried out from the ground—a strange way of putting it, especially since "blood" is one of those words that has no plural form. A midrash explains it this way: "It is not written, 'Your brother's blood cries out to me from the ground!' but 'your brother's *bloods*'—not only his blood, but also the blood of his descendants."

The tragedy of it all is that Cain not only took his brother's life, but also cut off his brother's line forever, and then evaded responsibility. God spared Cain's life, however, while putting a mark on him. One wonders: Did Cain learn his lesson in any way? As Rabbi Marshall Meyer said: "True hope is born when I learn to scream NO to injustice, to bribery, to corruption; when I scream that I will be involved; when I scream that I won't stay frozen in my ways. True hope is born when I can scream with all my being: YES to honesty; YES, I am my brother's keeper!"

Connections

ß In many places in the United States, people think that schools should teach the biblical version of creation, as well as the theory of evolution. How do you feel about this?

ß Why is Shabbat important to the Jewish people? Is it important to you and your family? How do you make it so? What do you think an ideal Shabbat would be like?

ß What does being created in the divine image mean to you? What are some examples of ways that we can show that people are made in the divine image?

ß What are some of the implications of the way that we are supposed to care for the earth? For animals? Is it a violation of *tza'ar ba'alei chayyim* (avoid cruelty to animals) to experiment on animals for medical research? What about for cosmetic research?

ß We might think of the entire Torah as the answer to God's question to Cain: "Where is Abel your brother?" What are some ways this is so?

❖ Noaḥ: Genesis 6:9–11:32

There is an old comedy bit that includes these famous words: "Hey, Noah—how long can you tread water?" That's a good question for this Torah portion, because it contains the story of Noah and the Flood.

Noah is a good man, living in a terrible time. Everyone's doing corrupt things, except for him. God tells Noah that a great flood is coming that will destroy the world, and Noah should build an ark and take two of every animal, and his own family, into the ark. It rains—for forty days.

After the Flood subsides, Noah and his wife, his sons, and their wives emerge from the ark. Noah's sons become the ancestors of the nations of the ancient world. But things don't get better. People become arrogant, and they build the Tower of Babel, trying in vain to reach the heavens and become famous. God is just about ready to give up on the whole humanity thing.

Summary

ß Because the earth has become corrupt and lawless, God decrees that there will be a flood, and commands Noah to build an ark, and to take his family and animals into it. (6:9–7:5)

ß God unleashes the Flood, which lasts for forty days. When a dove returns to the ark with an olive leaf, Noah knows that the Flood has subsided. God promises never again to destroy the earth. (7:10–8:22)

ⓑ Noah's sons and daughters-in-law have many children and become the ancestors of the nations of the ancient world. (10:1–32)

ⓑ The people of the world, unified by a single language, build the Tower of Babel. (11:1–9)

The Big Ideas

ⓑ **The Bible portrays God as having "human" feelings—disappointment, anger, etc.** God is not detached from creation and from human beings; to the contrary, in this Torah portion and elsewhere in the Bible, God is very much affected by what people do—especially by evil.

ⓑ **God is also "human" because God "changes" and "grows."** God grows from the experience of the Flood and makes a covenant with Noah, in which God promises to never again destroy the earth. The rainbow is the sign of that covenant.

ⓑ **Civilization needs basic ethical laws.** The ancient sages suggest that as a result of the Flood, God demanded that humanity follow certain basic laws: to abstain from blasphemy (misusing God's name), idolatry (worshiping false gods), incest, murder, robbery, and mistreating animals; and to establish courts of law to make sure that these laws are observed. This code of laws is called the Noahide Laws.

ⓑ **All human beings are part of the same "extended family."** Genesis 9 contains the famous "table of nations," which imagines that all the nations of the ancient world are descended from Noah's three sons. While this chapter's geographic understanding of the world is very limited (it doesn't mention the peoples of North America, eastern Asia, or Australia, for example), it demonstrates that all human beings are connected and part of the same huge family.

ⓑ **Multiculturalism is good.** All the nations have their own territories, languages, and cultures. Human diversity is part of God's plan. Then, when the nations gather together, united by one common language, to build the Tower of Babel, it is not only an act of massive chutzpah (building a tower to go into the heavens!); it is also contrary to God's wishes for different languages, and therefore, different and diverse peoples.

Divrei Torah
HOW GOOD WAS NOAH—REALLY?

No doubt about it—Noah was a good person. In fact, the Torah tells us that he was the most righteous person in his generation. But, perhaps that's like praising someone for being the best player on a losing team!

Let's look more closely at Noah.

Noah saved his family and the animals. This is all good. But something is missing. Nowhere do we read that Noah tried to persuade his friends, neighbors, and anyone who would listen to repent and change their ways. He didn't utter a word of concern for all the people who were about to drown in the waters of the Flood. While it's true that God commanded Noah to bring just his family and the animals aboard, you would think he would have argued with God about the death sentence for humanity.

The Hasidic master, Rabbi Menachem Mendel of Kotzk, once referred to a certain rabbi (in Yiddish) as a *tzadik in peltz*—"a righteous person in a fur coat." Here is what he meant: "When it is freezing cold outside, you can build a fire, or you can wrap yourself in a fur coat. If you wear a fur coat, you're the only one who gets warm. But, if you build a fire, everyone else can get warm, as well."

While Noah didn't wear a fur coat during the Flood, he certainly remained content with saving just his family. This is precisely why, in the opinion of many of the sages, even though Noah was a good person, he was not great. When the decree of the Flood came, Noah did as he was told, but didn't intercede on behalf of all those who would lose their lives. As the Torah says simply, "Noah did so; just as God commanded him, so he did" (6:22).

Unlike Noah, Abraham, ten generations later, stands up to God. As soon as God tells Abraham that Sodom and Gomorrah are to be destroyed, Abraham approaches God and famously says: "Will You sweep away the innocent along with the guilty?" (18:23). In a huge debate, Abraham asks God how many innocent people it would take to spare the city. It's all there in 18:16–33. For many sages, God chooses to make Abraham the first Jew precisely because of his concern for others.

Righteous people cannot merely care about themselves and their families; they have to care about others as well. This is why, for example, we honor the righteous gentiles who saved Jewish lives during the Holocaust, often at the risk of their own lives. The greatest heroes in history have been those who have gone beyond their own needs and their own safety to save others.

GOD CARES ABOUT MORE THAN BIG BUILDINGS

Was the Tower of Babel "real?" Maybe, maybe not; but the story has something to teach us. The tower may well have been modeled on the ziggurat, the sacred tower located in Ur, in what is now southwestern Iraq, which according to the Bible was Abraham's birthplace. Some early sages thought that Abraham might actually have seen the ziggurat when he was growing up.

As towers go, it was relatively short—only three stories high. It had monumental staircases, however—reminding us of the *sulam,* the "staircase" (or, as it is usually translated, "ladder") that figured prominently in Jacob's famous dream (Genesis 28). It was constructed from raw bricks surrounded by baked bricks.

It sounds like a great building. What could possibly have been wrong with it?

First, there is something troubling about the project itself. In Genesis 10, the chapter before the building of the Tower of Babel, we read that every nation has its own location—and, presumably, its own language. God wanted every national group to have its own place, its own culture, and its own language. God never needed diversity training; God *invented* diversity!

But instead, what happened with the building of the Tower of Babel? According to the sages, the people ignored their own languages and local cultures. The builders united under one language, but that unity came at a price. As Rabbi Daniel Gordis suggests: "Dispersion is part of the divine plan. It is only thus that human beings may fully realize their own unique potential. The tower builders of Babel sought to sustain uniformity. That is why they had to be stopped."

Second, the building of the Tower of Babel was basically an ego trip on the part of the builders. The Bible makes it very clear that the people wanted to make a "name for themselves" (11:4). They wanted bragging rights for having the biggest, tallest building in the world. They believed that this would make them famous. They may have even thought that it would bring them closer to God. Yet, apparently the builders did not consult God!

But the worst part, according to a midrash, is that the builders became so absorbed in their project that they forgot the rules of a decent society. They neglected their basic responsibilities to other people, and in the process, they lost their humanity: "If a man fell off the tower, they paid no attention to him, but if a brick fell they sat down and wept, and said: "Woe is us! When will another brick come and replace it?"

With people like this, it is no surprise that God decides that in the very place where the tower was built—ancient Ur—a man would be born who would teach the world a new way. That man will be Abraham.

Connections

ᛒ Some people read the story of Noah, the Flood, and the ark and they see a connection between that story and contemporary environmental concerns. What connections can you make between the story and our concern for the environment, such as climate change?

ᛒ A midrash says that the major sin of the generation of the Flood was that people cheated each other for such small amounts of money that the courts could not prosecute them. Why is this a sin?

ᛒ How does the story of the Flood portray God? How can God be disappointed with the world that God created? Why couldn't God have created a perfect world in the first place?

ᛒ How good a man was Noah? Was he "good enough?" Should he have warned people about the Flood? Why or why not?

ᛒ If Noah was so special, why wasn't he the first Jew?

ᛒ What was the sin of the builders of the Tower of Babel? What are some examples of this sin today?

❖ Lekh Lekha: Genesis 12:1–17:27

Things are not working out the way God wanted. Adam and Eve disobeyed the divine order not to eat of the Tree of Knowledge of Good and Evil. Cain killed Abel. People were so bad that God had to bring a flood to the earth. Then, people got arrogant and built a tower in an attempt to reach the heavens. Enough!

God decides to choose one man to become a holy person and be a role model for how humans should really be.

This is how Jewish history begins: God tells Abram (Abraham) to say goodbye to the place where he is living, Haran; to his father; and to everything he knows. Abram and his wife, Sarai (Sarah), wind up in the land of Canaan (Israel)—but as soon as they get there, they go to Egypt to escape famine. Sarai cannot have children, which poses challenges to Judaism's "first family." She comes up with an interesting idea: Abraham should take her slave, Hagar, and have children with her. Hagar gives birth to Ishmael.

Summary

- ꭞ God commands Abram (Abraham) to leave his land and to go to the land that God would show him—the land of Canaan (Israel). (12:1–3)
- ꭞ God tells Abraham that he, and the Jewish people, will be a blessing to the world, and that those who bless the Jewish people will be blessed, and that those who curse the Jewish people will be cursed. (12:1–9)
- ꭞ In Egypt, Abram tries to pass Sarai off as his sister—with dangerous results. (12:10–20)
- ꭞ Abram and his nephew, Lot, cannot get along, and so they divide the land of Canaan between them. (13:1–18)
- ꭞ The Middle East has its first war, and Lot is taken hostage. Even though Abram has big problems with Lot, he goes out of his way to rescue him. (14:1–24)
- ꭞ Abram has a bizarre dream in which God tells him that his people will be "strangers in a strange land"—not only in Egypt, but in many other places as well. (15:1–18)

The Big Ideas

- ꭞ **Adventure is an essential part of life.** Jewish history starts with an adventure: Abram must leave everything that he knows, and go out into the great unknown. That means not only leaving a place; it means leaving old ideas behind, as well.

ᵼ **The mission of the Jewish people is to be a blessing to the world.** While Judaism is the religion of the Jewish people, the Jewish way of life has larger lessons that everyone can learn. This means, among many other things, modeling ethical behavior.

ᵼ **Lying is wrong—at least, most of the time.** Abram and Sarai are trapped in a ticklish situation in Egypt, and Abram feels he has to lie about Sarai and say that she is his sister. He is afraid that the Egyptians would kill him in order to take his wife from him. Sometimes, truth is not the largest value—saving life is.

ᵼ **All Jews are responsible for one another.** Abram has no warm and fuzzy feelings for his nephew, Lot. Still, when Lot is taken hostage, Abram has no choice but to act on his behalf and rescue him—traveling the length of the entire Land of Israel to do so. From this gesture we learn that even though the Jews are a small people, they are a very large family—and family feelings will always prevail. Jews have done this over and over again through the centuries, for example, saving fellow Jews during the Holocaust, Soviet Jews from Russia, and Ethiopian Jews from Ethiopia.

ᵼ **To be Jewish is to know what it means to be a stranger.** That was the essential message of the vision that Abram had—the "coming attractions" of his descendants becoming slaves in Egypt. The experience in Egypt taught the Jews the meaning of what it's like to be a stranger, and from this they learned to treat strangers with dignity.

Divrei Torah

WITHOUT A REBELLIOUS TEENAGER
THERE WOULD BE NO JEWS

If you were going to start a new religion, this might be what you would do: sit around thinking of great ideas and how to get others to believe in those ideas.

But that's not how the Jewish people began. Terah, the father of Abram (Abraham's original name) decided to move his family out of the city of Ur. Ur was the most sophisticated city of its time. It had great architecture, sculpture, and literature. It was the New York and Paris of 1800 BCE.

The family got as far as Haran, in what is today southern Turkey, and they decided to stay there. Then, suddenly, God told Abram that he had to get on the move again. He had to leave his land, and he had to leave his father, and that meant that he had to abandon his father's ways of looking at the world.

Who was Terah? What was he like? A famous legend teaches that Terah was in the idol business. It says that when Abram was thirteen years old he figured out that worshiping idols was wrong. He came up with an amazing realization: you can't make a god, because then you have power over the god that you have created—and then it can't be a god!

What did Abram do? According to a midrash, "Abram seized a stick, smashed all the images, and placed the stick in the hand of the biggest of them. When his father came, he asked: 'Who did this to the gods?' Abram answered: 'A woman came with a bowl of fine flour and said: "Here, offer it up to them." When I offered it, one god said, "I will eat first," and another said, "No, I will eat first." Then the biggest of them rose up and smashed all the others.' His father replied: 'Are you messing around with me? They cannot do anything!' Abram answered: 'You say they cannot. Let your ears hear what your mouth is saying!'"

As Jonathan Sacks, the former chief rabbi of Great Britain, writes: "There are times, especially in adolescence, when we tell ourselves that we are breaking with our parents, charting a path that is completely new."

And so, according to legend, Judaism began with a thirteen-year-old kid challenging the old ways of thinking. Jews challenge old ideas and create new ones. That has been one reason why so many great scientists, writers, and thinkers have been Jews. It has been the key to Jewish survival and creativity over the centuries.

THE JEWISH PEOPLE:
WE ARE ALL IN IT TOGETHER

Let's face it—sometimes there are strange relationships in families.

Consider Abram and Lot. Lot was Abram's nephew, the son of

Abram's brother, Haran (not to be confused with the city of Haran), who had died years before. After Haran died, Abram and Sarai were his only real family. And so, Abram took Lot with him when they began their journey to the land of Canaan (Israel). Abram always felt somewhat responsible for his nephew. He referred to Lot as his "brother," which in biblical times simply meant a close relative (13:8).

But, actually, Abram and Lot didn't get along. They were constantly arguing about who would own the land, and finally they decided to divide the land between them. Abram let Lot choose which land he wanted, and Lot chose the plush, fertile land in the Jordan Valley, near the wicked cities of Sodom and Gomorrah. Being near these places didn't bother Lot that much. His basic attitude toward life seemed to be "Whatever!" Lot and Abram were very different people, and when they physically separated from each other they became emotionally separated as well.

But then, in chapter 14. we find the first recorded war in the Torah. A coalition of four kings stage a rebellion against a coalition of five kings. In the midst of the war, one group of kings invades Sodom and Gomorrah, stealing all their food and taking Lot hostage. Abram gets an army together and pursues the enemy as far away as Damascus, which is very far away from where they were all living at the time. He rescues Lot and brings him back home. Abram already knew what the early sages would say, centuries later: "All Israel is responsible for one another."

Back in the beginning of Genesis, Cain had asked God: "Am I my brother's keeper?" (4:9). Abram knew the answer to that question. It is "yes." Jews don't have to like each other; they just have to care about each other. Abram knew that his responsibility for Lot was more important than his personal feelings for his nephew. According to Rabbi Joseph B. Soloveitchik: "A Jew must feel a duty to save his brother, even if his brother has departed from the righteous path. Loyalty is the first mark of Abraham."

Connections

꠸ The forming of the Jewish people began with the act of going out into the unknown. Have you ever had that kind of experience: mov-

ing to a new house or community; going to a new camp, or a new
school? What was it like? How do you think Abram must have felt?

ᚦ The Torah portion says that those nations that curse the Jewish
people will themselves be cursed. In other words, countries that
are good to the Jews will do well; if they don't, they will do badly.
Is this true? Think of such examples as the Spanish Inquisition,
the Russian pogroms, Nazi Germany, Arab countries' antisemitism. How has this pattern played out in history?

ᚦ Midrash says that Abram broke his father's idols. This means
that Abram had the courage to break with what previous generations thought. How did people like Christopher Columbus,
Charles Darwin, and Rosa Parks demonstrate that kind of courage? How have great Jewish women and men, like Albert Ein-
stein, Hank Greenberg, Gloria Steinem, and Golda Meir, been
courageous? What other names would you add to that list?

ᚦ According to tradition, Abram broke his father's idols at the age
of thirteen, and that was one of the origins of bar mitzvah. This
suggests that thirteen-year-olds are ready to think independently
from their parents. In what ways do you disagree with your parents? How do you demonstrate that? When is it good for children
to rebel against their parents? When is it not so good?

ᚦ Under what circumstances might it be permissible, and even necessary, to lie? Are "white lies" acceptable? For instances, is it
okay to tell someone that you like his or her new shirt (or hair-
cut, or whatever) when, in fact, you don't?

ᚦ How have Jews demonstrated their solidarity by helping other
Jews? Think about such historical moments as the Holocaust and
the rescuing of Jews from Russia and Ethiopia.

❖ Va-yera': Genesis 18:1–22:24

Life gets interesting for Abraham and Sarah. This whole business of
starting a new people and a new way of life has its difficulties. When
Sarah could not have children she urged Abraham to take her slave,
Hagar, and have a child with her. That child is named Ishmael. Sarah
becomes pregnant at the advanced age of ninety. At that point, she

cannot tolerate having Hagar and Ishmael around the camp, so she tells Abraham to kick them out.

Meanwhile, the people of the cities of Sodom and Gomorrah have become increasingly more evil. God decides to destroy the cities and their inhabitants (sounds like the Flood story, right?). Abraham argues with God and implores him to save the cities, which doesn't quite work out. Later, God tells Abraham to offer his son, Isaac, as a sacrifice. But, at the last minute Isaac is saved.

Summary

- ꚃ Abraham and Sarah welcome three visitors, who announce that Sarah, age ninety, will have a child—which is really laughable—and so, Sarah laughs when she hears the news. (18:1–15)
- ꚃ God and Abraham argue over the fate of the wicked cities of Sodom and Gomorrah. Abraham tries to get God to spare the cities, but his pleas are unsuccessful. (18:16–33)
- ꚃ God destroys Sodom and Gomorrah. (19:1–36)
- ꚃ Sarah has a child, Isaac, and at Sarah's insistence Abraham sends Hagar and Ishmael into the wilderness. (21:1–21)
- ꚃ God tells Abraham to sacrifice his son Isaac, which Abraham is ready to do, but, just in the nick of time, an angel prevents the sacrifice from happening; this story is known as *Akedat Yitzchak*, "the Binding of Isaac." (22:1–19)

The Big Ideas

- ꚃ **Hospitality (*hakhnasat orchim*) is an important Jewish value.** The Jewish people began in the desert, where welcoming strangers was particularly important, and that mitzvah continues to this very day. Jews traditionally open their homes to guests and strangers, particularly for Shabbat and holiday dinners.
- ꚃ **Judaism believes that it is sometimes necessary to challenge God.** Challenging God is an ancient tradition, and, in every generation, that tradition appears in Jewish literature. Confronting God is not the same as not believing in God (you cannot confront something that you don't think exists). Rather, the act of confronting God affirms the close Jewish relationship with God. It shows that we take God seriously.

ቴ **Evil societies destroy themselves.** While the biblical text says
that God rained down sulfuric flames on Sodom and Gomorrah,
we might suggest that, in reality, those cities destroyed themselves through their wickedness. People and societies that pursue
evil will eventually harm themselves. It has happened many times
in human history—medieval Spain, Nazi Germany, and Commu-
nist Russia. Oppressive societies eventually simply fall apart.

ቴ **Jews and Arabs are "cousin peoples."** According to tradition, the
Arab nation is descended from Abraham's older son, Ishmael.
Therefore, despite the painful history of Jewish-Arab relations,
there is a deep connection between these two peoples. Hebrew
and Arabic are "cousin" languages. So, too, there are numerous
connections and similarities between Judaism and Islam.

ቴ **Child sacrifice is evil.** The Canaanites and other ancient peoples
practiced child sacrifice in their religious rituals. They believed that
it was the way to show gratitude to God for having children, and to
guarantee future fertility. Judaism found that practice repulsive, and
it broke with that tradition. The story of the Binding of Isaac demonstrates that God does not want children to be killed in God's name.

Divrei Torah

COME ON IN!

Everyone talks about Southern hospitality. No doubt about it; South-
erners are very good at welcoming both friends and strangers into
their homes.

That may be true, but the Jews were the original experts in hospitality.

Abraham offers hospitality to the strangers who have come to announce that Sarah will have a child. Because Abraham (along with
Sarah) welcomed them with an open heart, and made sure that they
were fed, he is a model for the mitzvah of hospitality (*hakhnasat orchim*).

But who are those strangers? To Abraham, they were simply *anashim*,
"men" (18:2). By contrast, when Abraham's nephew, Lot, saw those
same visitors in Sodom, he saw them as *malakhim*, "angels" (19:1).

In the words of a midrash: "To Abraham, endowed with great spiritual qualities, they appeared as men; but to Lot, a man poor in spiritual qualities, they appeared in the form of angels." Who wouldn't

want to welcome angels to their home? For this reason, Lot's offering of hospitality to the "angels" is no big deal. But to welcome "mere" people—that is a true mitzvah.

Perhaps it is because the Jewish people started its history as a people of the desert, where resources are scarce, that they have emphasized hospitality to strangers so much. But how many of us are really that eager to open our doors, and let anyone come in and stay for a meal, or "crash" for the night? Back then it may not have been that risky (though who knows who might come visit you in the desert?). Today—it is not so safe; it can even be dangerous.

Perhaps, then, we should interpret this mitzvah of *hakhnasat orchim* differently. Many synagogues (and other houses of worship) have homeless shelters and soup kitchens where strangers are welcome. But the mitzvah of hospitality is also about how we treat newcomers in our synagogues. When "strangers" come to synagogue, do members make them feel welcome, or are they left standing around with no one to talk to? When people come to services and they are unfamiliar with the rituals and the prayer book, does someone come and help them figure out what is going on? Are our synagogues truly open to everyone—intermarried families, people with disabilities, people of different races, and LGBT people?

Rabbi Judah Loew of Prague teaches: "To welcome a guest into your home and treat him with respect because he is created in the likeness and image of God—this is considered like honoring God." So, like Abraham, when we open our homes and our synagogues—and our lives—to strangers and friends alike, maybe God is present for us and for them.

CHALLENGING GOD: A JEWISH MITZVAH

When God told Abraham that the wicked cities of Sodom and Gomorrah were about to be destroyed, Abraham argued that they should be spared. This is one of the most notable aspects of Abraham's character: he had the courage to challenge God.

The Jewish tradition does not criticize Abraham for doing so; far from it, Abraham is a hero for trying to reason with God! In the words of a midrash: "Abraham said to God: 'Master of the universe, You are in danger of causing embarrassment to Yourself. You don't want people to say that this is the way You operate. You destroyed the generation of the Flood; You destroyed the Tower of Babel. You want people to think that you're still at it?"

Judaism does not believe that we should have blind faith in God; rather, our faith should always be open to questions and challenges. When we question God, or raise challenges to our faith and our traditions, we are not being disloyal. Quite the opposite; such acts show that we are mature enough to take our relationship with God seriously.

Many people simply don't appreciate that Judaism's questioning nature is one of the best things that the religion has going for it. The other two major Western religions—Christianity and Islam—are more focused on absolute faith and true belief. People who question the divinity of Jesus Christ don't always have an easy time of it in their churches. The very word "Islam" means "to surrender one's will to God." To be a good Christian or Muslim, you need to have faith. By contrast, Judaism has always cared more about right action than right belief.

There is a long history of Jewish heroes confronting God. It started with Abraham. Then there's Moses, who challenges God when God wants to destroy the Jewish people at the incident of the Golden Calf. And, in his misery, Job cries out to God and demands to know why he is suffering so terribly. A famous talmudic sage, Elisha ben Avuya, was so upset with God that he actually said: "There is no Judge and there is no justice!" And the tradition goes all the way to Tevye in the musical *Fiddler on the Roof*—"God, I know that we are the Chosen People. But could you choose another people once in a while?"

Just as we challenge God, we must also challenge the evil that occurs in society—even when it seems that it is useless to do so. The writer Elie Wiesel tells this story: "A righteous man came to Sodom and pleaded with the people to change their ways. No one listened. Finally, he sat in the middle of the city and simply screamed. Someone asked him, 'Do you think that will change anyone?' 'No,' said the righteous man. 'But at least, they will not change me.'"

Connections

ᴃ Has anyone ever offered you hospitality? Have you ever offered someone hospitality? What did you most appreciate? What do you think your guests most appreciated? How did it make you feel?

ቴ Does your synagogue do a good job of welcoming people? How can you help your synagogue improve how it does this?

ቴ Do you agree that wicked societies ultimately harm themselves? What are some examples from history? Is Nazi Germany an example of this? Are there societies that have changed for the better? Would that describe what happened in the American South during the civil rights period?

ቴ Have there been times when you have wanted to challenge God? If yes, what did you want to say? What kind of courage did that take?

ቴ Despite the painful history that has existed between Jews and Arabs, there have been deep connections between these peoples. What have some of them been? Do those connections make peace possible? What does it mean that according to tradition the Jews and Arabs can both trace their ancestry back to Abraham?

❖ Ḥayyei Sarah: Genesis 23:1–25:18

Abraham's wife Sarah dies—maybe from a broken heart, thinking that Isaac is dead (remember how Abraham almost offered him up as a sacrifice?). Abraham—devoted husband that he is—buys a burial place for Sarah, outside the future city of Hebron.

With the death of Sarah, Abraham realizes that he's not going to be around forever. He knows that Isaac needs a wife, and so he sends his servant back to Aram-naharaim to find one for him. The servant returns home with Rebekah.

Abraham marries again and has more children. These children drift out of the Jewish story—at least for a while. When Abraham finally dies, his sons Isaac and Ishmael bury him in the cave of Machpelah with Sarah. They don't have anything to say to each other, but at least they are together again. Sometimes, rifts in families can heal.

Summary

ቴ Sarah dies and Abraham is determined to find a proper burial place for her. Abraham pays full price for the burial site. That site—the cave of Machpelah—became the burial place for all the Patriarchs and Matriarchs, with the exception of Rachel, Jacob's wife. (23:1–20)

℔ Abraham wants to keep Isaac close to home, and he doesn't want him to marry a Canaanite woman. And so, his servant goes and finds a wife for him from among Abraham's relatives. (24:1–61)

℔ Rebekah and Isaac meet, and it is love at first sight. (24:62–66)

℔ Abraham takes another wife, and (believe it or not!) has more children. (25:1–6)

℔ Abraham dies, and his sons, Isaac and Ishmael, reunite to bury him. (25:7–11)

The Big Ideas

℔ **Honoring the dead (*k'vod ha-met*) is central to the Jewish way of life.** The way that we treat the dead is one of the greatest tests of our humanity. For this reason, the purchase of land for a cemetery is generally one of the first things a new Jewish community will do.

℔ **The Land of Israel is precious to Jews.** In the Torah portion, Abraham purchases a burial place for Sarah, which will wind up being the burial site for all the Patriarchs and Matriarchs (except Rachel). He paid a lot for that piece of land—far more than it was actually worth. The Land of Israel is so precious to Jews that they have been willing to sacrifice almost anything for it—not only money (early Zionist settlers purchased swampland in Israel for exorbitant rates in the 1800s), but life as well.

℔ **Marrying within the Jewish people is an important Jewish value.** That is why Abraham took great pains to send his servant back to their "home country"—in order to find a member of the extended family for Isaac to marry. Abraham did not want Isaac to marry a Canaanite. This preference for in-marriage has been a Jewish tradition for thousands of years. That is how Jews kept the Jewish people together, and passed values and traditions from one generation to the next. Today, many Jews marry non-Jews; fortunately, many of the children of those marriages are raised as Jews.

℔ **Kindness to animals is an important mitzvah.** The story of Rebekah at the well underscores this value. Abraham's servant knew that the woman for Isaac would be the one who offered to feed and water his camels. You can learn a lot about someone by watching how he or she treats animals. For that reason, having pets is a great way to develop responsibility and character.

- **Families can always heal themselves.** We learn this from the brief passage in which Isaac and Ishmael meet once again to bury their father, Abraham. The brothers had been separated from each other for many years. Often, family celebrations and shared sadness bring people together.

Divrei Torah

THIS LAND IS OUR LAND

This Torah portion is filled with famous "firsts." Sarah is the first Jew to die, and Abraham is the first person in the Torah to cry (at Sarah's death). Later on in the Torah portion, Isaac becomes the first person in the Bible to love a spouse (Rebekah).

There is one more famous "first." When Abraham purchases the cave of Machpelah as a burial place, he becomes the first Jew to purchase property in the Land of Israel.

But wait: hadn't God already promised the Land of Israel to Abraham and his descendants?

Yes, but God's promise wasn't enough. After all, who would believe him—"This land is mine, because God said so"? Abraham needed to stake his own claim to the Land of Israel. He needed to buy his own piece of it. And more than this: the purchase of Machpelah was not going to be a behind-the-scenes, private sale of land. No, it was going to be out in the open, in the sight of all who were gathered there. They needed to see the sale; they needed to hear the sale; they had to be witnesses.

And why? Because Abraham could already predict what people would say in the future—that the Jews had no claim to the Land of Israel. (In fact, they are still saying precisely that.) A midrash says, "Machpelah is one of the places in the Land of Israel that no one can say was stolen."

Abraham not only bought the piece of land for all to see. He also overpaid for it! Scholars have said that with the amount of money that Abraham spent for the cave he could have purchased an entire village. That pattern of overpaying has also continued. In the 1880s, when

Jews started to purchase property in the Land of Israel, it was mostly swampland—and yet, they gladly paid generously for it.

It's not enough for God to promise the Land of Israel to the Jewish people. Abraham needed to make that divine promise into a reality. Jews are still making that promise into a reality, and that is how they have built their people and their connection to the land. In the words of an old Zionist folk song: "We have come to the land, to build and to be rebuilt within it."

In this way, the Land of Israel is like the Torah. Yes, God gave the Torah, but we need to interpret it. God promised the Land of Israel, but we need to build it. That is part of what it means for Jews to be partners with God.

WHY KINDNESS TO ANIMALS MATTERS

We can imagine Abraham's servant (usually assumed to be Eliezer, based on Gen. 15:2), saying to himself: "I cannot believe that I agreed to do this. Yes, I love my master. I would do almost anything for him. But I never should have agreed to this errand—this whole 'find a wife for Isaac' thing. What was I thinking?"

It was bad enough that he had to go all the way back to Aram-naharaim. Eliezer understood that part; Aram-naharaim, or Haran, was the "old family homestead." That's where the extended family lived. There was no way that Abraham was going to want a Canaanite wife for Isaac. Eliezer had to go back to the old country to find a wife for Isaac.

How would he know who the right woman is? It was not as if Abraham had given his trusted servant any explicit instructions or directions. It was not as if Abraham described the ideal woman that he wanted as a wife for Isaac. And so, Eliezer invented a test. He would go to a well, preparing to get water. If a woman came forward and not only offered him water, but also offered water for his camels—that would be the woman who would be the best match for Isaac.

We might have imagined that Eliezer would have said to himself: "Let's see: the woman has to like music, dancing, and living in tents." But that wasn't going to do it. This was to be a character contest. The real test would be: is this a woman who will offer to feed the camels? Is she a kind person—not only to human travelers, but to animals as well?

One of the best tests of a person's character is how that person treats those who need the most care and those who are helpless: animals.

For this reason, a midrash says, God "auditioned" Moses by seeing how well he did as a shepherd. "When Moses tended the flock of Jethro in the wilderness, a little kid escaped from him. When he found it, he said: 'I did not know that you ran away because of thirst; you must be weary.' So he placed the kid on his shoulder and walked away."

Chances are: if you care about animals, then you also care about others. That quality of caring makes for a good wife, and for a good human being as well.

Connections

- Abraham cries when he hears about Sarah's death. What does this say about the way we express our sadness and grief? About the way we react when we lose a person or an animal dear to us?
- Abraham pays an exorbitant amount of money for the burial place. What does this say about the Jewish connection to the Land of Israel? Have you ever paid more than you thought you would pay for something that you wanted?
- How does the way that someone treats animals demonstrate his or her character? Do you have a pet? How has that helped make you a better person?
- What do you think Isaac and Ishmael said to each other at Abraham's funeral? Have you ever had a tense situation with someone where you finally made up? What was it like? What did you learn from that experience?

❖ Toledot: Genesis 25:19–28:9

Welcome to the first major sibling rivalry in the Torah (excluding Cain and Abel, which was short, violent, and one sided). It is not pretty. Jacob forces Esau to sell him his birthright as the firstborn (apparently, you actually could do that back in ancient times).

By doing this, Jacob steals the blessing that was due Esau as the firstborn and, in the process, deceives his elderly, blind father, Isaac—all with the help of his mother, Rebekah. Esau is so angry at Jacob that it looks like he might kill him. How could this possibly end well? It doesn't, and Jacob has to flee.

Summary

ꜩ Isaac and Rebekah struggle with infertility; ultimately, Rebekah conceives and gives birth to twins, Esau and Jacob. They could not be more different from each other. (25:19–26)

ꜩ Esau makes a quick decision that will change Jewish history—he sells Jacob his birthright as the oldest son. (25:27–34)

ꜩ Isaac re-digs the wells that his father, Abraham, had dug, and that the Philistines had maliciously filled in. (26:12–22)

ꜩ Esau marries two Hittite women. His mother, Rebekah, was not happy. (26:34–35)

ꜩ Rebekah shows parental favoritism to Jacob, and gets him to deceive his blind father, Isaac, to obtain the blessing that was intended for Esau. Sibling rivalry gets out of hand. (27:1–46)

ꜩ Jacob fears that Esau will seek revenge against him, so he flees for his life and goes to his extended family in Paddan-aram. (28:1–5)

The Big Ideas

ꜩ **Diversity is important within families.** Jacob and Esau represent two types of opposing characters. Jacob is quiet and studious; Esau is physically strong, active, and sometimes violent. Jews identify with Jacob, and Jewish lore likes to imagine that the enemies of the Jews are actually the descendants of Esau.

ꜩ **There are no perfect people in the Torah.** Jacob is sneaky and deceptive—a trait that he learned from his mother, Rebekah. But even the imperfect people of the Bible have a role in the continuation of the covenant and the Jewish people.

ꜩ **Being original and inventive is not always important.** Isaac really doesn't have much going on in his life. His only real achievement seems to have been digging wells—and these were wells that his father, Abraham, had already dug. Sometimes you don't have to be an innovator; continuing a tradition (symbolized by Isaac re-digging the wells of Abraham) can often be enough.

ꜩ **Honoring parents is a universal human value.** Esau is a tough hunter who doesn't have much to say. But, let us be fair to him. His hunting was for the sole purpose of bringing food to his father, Isaac. Esau is an expert at honoring his father. He is a far better human being than we often give him credit for.

℔ **Age order doesn't always matter.** In the Torah and the Hebrew Bible, the younger child often becomes more important than older siblings. That is how it worked with Jacob, and Joseph, and Moses, and David—they were all younger children. The preference for the younger child over the older is contrary to most ancient (and many modern) cultures. This helps us remember that birth order is not destiny—that a younger child can do just as well, if not better, than older children.

Divrei Torah
WHY DID GOD CHOOSE JACOB?

If you have siblings—even if you have a twin—chances are that you are very different. And why wouldn't you be? Just because you have the same genes as someone doesn't mean that you have to be his or her clone.

The story of Jacob and Esau is a classic story of sibling rivalry—a tale of twins who were pretty un-twinlike. There is Jacob—a quiet man who was most comfortable staying in the tent and close to home. And there is Esau, his older brother—an outdoorsman, a hunter, a tough guy.

When Esau comes home from the hunt, famished and thirsty, Jacob gets him to sell him his birthright, the special status that comes as the older son, in exchange for bread and lentil stew. Without even hesitating, Esau sells it. For the sages, that meant that Esau was reckless and would continue to be so. A midrash claims that Jacob and Esau were thirteen at the time: "For thirteen years Jacob and Esau went to school and came home from school. After this age, Jacob went on to continue studying and Esau went on to worship idols."

And this, by the way, is one reason why bar and bat mitzvah occurs at the age of thirteen. It is the age of choices. Your whole life is ahead of you, but now you are old enough to make intelligent (let's hope!) choices.

Isn't it disturbing that Jacob—a cheat and a thief—was chosen to carry on the covenant of his grandfather Abraham? Rabbi Samuel Karff notes that both Jacob and Esau are flawed human beings: "God must choose between someone who cared so little about the birthright that he was willing to simply throw it away for a quick meal, and someone who cared about it so much that he was willing to cheat in order to get it." Apparently God decided that it was better to care too much than too little.

While the Torah condemns the qualities we see in Jacob, we have to admit that those qualities can actually "work" in our everyday lives. If you have ever been on a sports team or in a play, you will probably agree that it is better to work with people who care a lot, or even a little too much, and sometimes cross the line. You can always calm those people down, and hopefully teach them the importance of honesty and fair play. It is much harder to rev up someone who is apathetic and simply doesn't care. Passion should be channeled, but we can't do without it.

That's the way it is with many people, and that's the way it has been through much of Jewish history. In every generation, there are Jews who care deeply, and there are Jews who care little about Judaism or the Jewish people. Jewish history has gotten this far because of those Jews who are passionate and care about Judaism and the Jewish people—not because of those who are willing to throw it away.

LET'S BE FAIR TO ESAU

If anyone in the Torah gets a bum rap, it's Esau. He sold Jacob his birthright for a bowl of lentil soup, with a little bread on the side. Then Jacob deceived their father, Isaac, and stole the blessing that was intended for Esau as the oldest son.

Esau is big, hairy, and a hunter. This might have been enough to put Esau into the perpetual time-out corner. Hunting (for pleasure) is against Jewish law, because it is considered cruelty to animals. Furthermore, Esau has no self-control; on the spur of the moment, he throws away his future for a bowl of soup. The ancient sages associated Esau with violence, and they imagined that every enemy of the Jews was another version of Esau. (In fact, Haman, the arch-villain of Purim, is descended from Esau).

But, surely, this can't be all there is to Esau. No person is all bad. Doesn't he have any good points?

As it turns out, yes. Esau went out hunting in order to feed his father. Read the entire story and you will see that Esau cares about his father. In fact, the early sages thought that no one in the Torah was better at honoring his father than Esau. "Rabbi Simeon ben Gamaliel said: I usually waited on my father dressed in soiled clothes, but when I went out into the street I put on handsome clothes. It was different with Esau; he wore his best clothes when tending to his father. That is how we learn that Esau was most diligent in honoring his parents."

Esau cared about his parents and their feelings. The Torah tells us that Esau married Hittite women. When he saw that this troubled his parents deeply, he went back to the extended family, and married one of the daughters of his uncle, Ishmael. He really wanted to be a good son.

And when Jacob and Esau finally reunite, Esau readily forgives him and wants to continue their relationship. After what Jacob did to him, that's a big deal. How many of us would be willing to forgive?

So, it's not as if Esau was a total loser. Not at all! Rabbi Mordecai Finley imagines an essay that "Esau Isaacson" would have written as a school assignment: "I come from a very disturbed family. Something very bad happened to my father when he was a kid. I know this will sound like I am crazy or something, but I think my grandfather Abraham tried to kill him in some weird religious thing." Esau is still trying to understand his family dynamics.

It could not have been easy growing up in the Isaac and Rebekah household. It was not easy having Jacob as a twin brother. Esau did as well as he knew how. Let's cut him some slack.

Connections

ቴ If you have a sibling, chances are you're nothing like him or her. Maybe you look alike, but that might be all that you have in common, with the exception of your parents. How do your differences affect your relationship? Have you experienced sibling rivalry in your own life? What has it been like? How have you worked things out?

ቴ Do you agree with the Jewish position on hunting? Do you believe that it is cruel to animals?

ቴ Do you agree that the biblical tradition is unfair to Esau? In what ways was he better than Jacob? In what ways was Jacob better than Esau?

ٮ Who are some other characters in the Torah who are less than perfect? What are their flaws? What about American heroes? What are their flaws? What can we learn from those flaws?

ٮ Have you ever done something totally impulsive, like Esau did when he sold his birthright (though probably nothing as serious as that)? What were the results?

ٮ Do you agree that it is better to care too much about something than to care too little? What examples can you think of—teams, patriotism, religion, etc.?

❖ Va-yetse': Genesis 28:10–32:3

Jacob is not only a little sneaky—disguising himself so that he can steal his father's blessing from Esau. He is also now scared, because Esau has threatened to kill him for doing so. And, so, Jacob runs away—back to his extended family in Haran. On the way, he has a strange dream—of angels ascending and descending a stairway (or ladder). It is one of the most famous dreams in all literature and art (not to mention "Stairway to Heaven" by Led Zeppelin, which might be the most-played song in the history of radio).

When he gets to Haran (or Paddan-aram, or Aram-naharaim—the place has several names), he meets and falls in love with his cousin, Rachel. But Jacob's uncle Laban is no less sneaky than Jacob (in fact, you might say that the extended Abraham family has the "sneaky gene"). He tricks Jacob by switching the older "average-looking" sister, Leah, for the beautiful Rachel. Jacob winds up working seven more years in order to marry Rachel. Rachel, Leah, and their handmaidens, Bilhah and Zilpah, give birth to the children who will ultimately become the ancestors of the tribes of Israel.

Summary

ٮ On his way to Haran, Jacob dreams about a stairway reaching up to the heavens, with angels going up and down. God speaks to Jacob and blesses him and his descendants. (28:10–22)

ঌ Jacob meets Rachel and her father, Laban, who is also Jacob's uncle. Jacob falls in love with Rachel, but Laban has other ideas; he
wants his older daughter, Leah, to marry first. (29:1–35)

ঌ Just as there was a rivalry between Jacob and Esau, there is a rivalry between Rachel, who is childless, and her sister Leah, who
has many children. (30:1–24)

ঌ Jacob tries an experiment in breeding goats and sheep, with interesting results. (30:25–43)

ঌ Jacob and his family flee from Laban. (31:1–54; 32:1–3)

The Big Ideas

ঌ **Dreams have meaning.** Jews have always been fascinated by
dreams and dream interpretation. From ancient times, Jews have
sensed that sometimes dreams can reveal a person's destiny. We
should pay attention to our dreams; they often have something
very important to tell us.

ঌ **The Jews are a wandering people.** Jewish history is the story of
Jews moving from place to place—exiled from the Land of Israel,
from England, Spain, Germany, Russia, and elsewhere. That is
why the story of Jacob is so important. He wanders a lot. He often has to escape from uncomfortable places. Jacob is a model for
the Jewish people throughout history.

ঌ **What goes around, comes around.** Just as Jacob deceived his
brother and his father, he is deceived by his uncle and father-
in-law, Laban. Be careful of what you do—it could come back to
haunt you, or, even better, reward you!

ঌ **Jews knows what it's like to be slaves.** Jacob's years of servitude
to Laban are a sort of dress rehearsal for what it was like for the
Israelites as slaves in Egypt. And the way that Jacob and his family escape from Laban reminds us of the Exodus.

Divrei Torah
WHO WERE THOSE ANGELS, AND WHAT WERE
THEY DOING ON THE LADDER?

Jacob saw angels in a dream. Assume for a moment that angels exist—
symbolically if not literally—as messengers of some kind. The Torah

tells us that angels of God were "going up and down on it [the stairway]." If we further assume that angels came from heaven, why did they start by going *up* the stairway?

The first possibility: The angels symbolize Jacob's transition from childhood to entering adulthood. As Rabbi Solomon B. Freehof writes: "The first group of angels were the angels that had accompanied him from home. But a new group of angels was descending to accompany him further on his journey. Jacob is now going on the journey of life, to be self-reliant and an adult." Jacob's dream, therefore, is a rite of passage from childhood to adulthood—an ancient "bar mitzvah!"

The second possibility: The angels represent Jewish history. An ancient tradition says that Jacob saw angels representing every ancient nation that would conquer the Jews—Assyria, Babylon, Persia, Greece, Rome—going up and coming down again. God invited Jacob, as the ancestor of the Jewish people, to climb up the stairway. God was saying to Jacob: dare to become a world empire! But Jacob refused; he didn't want to risk it. He didn't want the Jewish people to simply become an empire like all the other ancient empires. He didn't want the Jews to be famous just for having military power. He knew that the power of the Jews was in words and what words could teach. He was also afraid that if he went up the ladder, someday his descendants would have to come down the ladder—that his people's future success might only be temporary.

The third possibility: The angels represent Jacob himself—a life filled with ups and downs. The ancient Jewish philosopher Philo said: "Life is comparable to a ladder because of its irregular course. A single day can carry the person who is set on high downward, and someone else upward. None of us remains in the same circumstances." It's like the old board game Chutes and Ladders—you never know when you are going to climb up, or fall down.

Life is, indeed, like a ladder. Our job is to learn how to live with those ups and downs, and to make the best of those opportunities for growth.

LIVING WITH LABAN

Sometimes, the way that the text appears in the Torah scroll itself tells its own story. Every other Torah portion, except this one, appears in the Torah with spaces and "paragraphs." Not this one; it's one large, closed block of text. Why?

The layout of the Torah text is like Jacob himself—and then his family—who became "closed up" and basically imprisoned within the household of his uncle and father-in-law, Laban. Jacob first met Rachel and he immediately fell in love with her. He thought that he was marrying Rachel, but on their wedding night, under the cover of darkness, Laban switched her sister, Leah, for Rachel. Jacob loved Rachel so much that he worked another seven years in order to win her hand in marriage too. Laban made Jacob miserable, changing his wages several times, essentially keeping him as a slave. Finally, in the middle of the night, Jacob and his wives escape from Laban, with Laban chasing after them.

For this reason, Laban is considered one of the villains of the Bible. Here's how he comes off in the Passover Haggadah: "Go out and learn what Laban wanted to do to Jacob our father. Pharaoh wanted to kill only the boys, but Laban sought to destroy Jacob's entire family."

Why is there so much drama between Jacob and Laban? Perhaps because it serves as a sort of "coming attractions" for Jacob's descendants, who will be enslaved in Egypt. We can see Laban as an earlier version of Pharaoh. And the way that Jacob and his family left Laban—in the middle of the night, with Laban chasing them—is exactly the way that the Israelites would leave Egypt, generations later.

But there is more. Jacob had deceived his father, Isaac, by stealing the blessing reserved for his brother, Esau—and Jacob was able to do that because Isaac was blind. In exactly the same way, Laban took advantage of Jacob's "blindness" in the darkness of his wedding night, and he switched Leah for Rachel. The ancient Rabbis called this *middah k'neged middah*, "measure for measure." We would say: what goes around, comes around. It's all payback.

Or, maybe it's not just revenge, and not just payback. Maybe there's a purpose behind it all. Perhaps it's to teach Jacob a lesson—to make him a better person. In the words of Israeli statesman Avraham Burg: "Jacob is the ultimate proof of our claim that the entire Torah is, among other things, the improvement manual for our forefathers' character flaws. It's an improvement process that obligates each and every one of us, all day, every day. Happy is the person who is always improving."

Connections

ᛒ Which interpretation of the identity of the angels on the stairway do you like the most? Why? Do you have any other interpretations?

ᛒ If you could imagine the angels of adulthood speaking to Jacob, what do you think they would say? What would your "angels" say to you?

ᛒ Do you agree with Jacob's fear to go up on the stairway? Why was he afraid to take the risk? What risks have you been willing, or unwilling, to take?

ᛒ Jacob's experience with Laban forced him to confront some of the flaws in his character. Everyone has flaws; which of your flaws or weaknesses do you want to work on? What are you particularly good at doing? How do you want to strengthen your skills and your positive points?

ᛒ What historical figures have had lives like Jacob—filled with ups and downs? Some examples: Abraham Lincoln, Franklin Roosevelt, Mother Teresa, Helen Keller, Oprah Winfrey. Do you have friends or family members who have had ups and downs? What lessons can you learn from their stories?

❖ Va-yishlaḥ: Genesis 32:4–36:43

Jacob realizes that he has a piece of unfinished business to take care of. He has to finally face up to his brother, Esau, and he's afraid that Esau might kill him. The reunion comes off better than Jacob had expected.

But Jacob's troubles are far from over. He winds up wounded from an all-night wrestling match with a mysterious, nameless stranger, and that leaves him with a limp for the rest of his life. And then his daughter, Dinah, gets raped by a Canaanite prince. To top it off, his beloved wife, Rachel, dies in childbirth. It can't get worse. But, of course, it does—and it will.

Summary

ᛒ Jacob brings his family, his animals, and gifts to his brother, Esau. (32:4–22)

ᚬ The night before their meeting, Jacob wrestled with a mysterious stranger, who changed his name to Israel. (Gen 32:23–33)

ᚬ Jacob's fears about his reunion with Esau dissolve when Esau greets him lovingly, and they tearfully reunite. (33:1–17)

ᚬ Jacob's daughter, Dinah, is raped by a Canaanite prince, and her brothers viciously retaliate against the city of Shechem, the place where it happened. (34:1–31)

ᚬ Rachel dies while giving birth to her son Benjamin, and Jacob buries her on the road to Ephrath (now Bethlehem) and builds a pillar over her grave. (35:16–21)

ᚬ The descendants of Esau are listed. (36:1–43)

The Big Ideas

ᚬ **Judaism means wrestling**—with the world, with God, and with yourself. Judaism does not believe that life should be easy; rather, our challenges can be useful to us. That value is found in the very name of the Jewish people—*Yisrael,* which is often translated as "the one who wrestles with God."

ᚬ **Wounds are important.** Most people get "wounded" in life somehow, and our wounds can become ways to grow.

ᚬ **Facing your failings is crucial for moral growth.** It can be very scary to face people whom you have hurt. But when you do, it can be better than you imagined. You can also grow from the experience.

ᚬ **Serious divisions in families need not be forever.** Jacob and Esau eventually put their differences aside and make up with each other. Crises in families can be healed if people make honest efforts to do so.

ᚬ **Extreme violence, even in self-defense, is inappropriate.** While we can understand that Dinah's brothers were furious that she had been raped, their extremely violent act of revenge is simply over-the-top awful. Jacob believes that their actions have brought disrepute to his family, and years later he curses Levi and Simeon for their actions (34:30).

ᚬ **It takes more than Jews to create the Jewish story.** Even though the descendants of Esau are not Jewish, they (and he) are important enough to merit an entire chapter of the Torah (chapter

36). Moreover, the Torah goes out of its way to mention that the Edomites, the descendants of Esau, had kings even before there were any kings in Israel (36:31)—as if to remind the ancient Israelites that they were not the first in the "king department," and to keep them humble.

Divrei Torah
MEETING ESAU AND MAKING WAR

It has been many years since Jacob cheated his brother, Esau—out of his birthright and out of his blessing as the firstborn. Ever since then, Jacob has learned about life the hard way. He fled to his family's homeland in Aram-naharaim, and there his uncle Laban deceived him, giving him Leah as a wife instead of Rachel, for whom he will work an additional seven years. In the ensuing years, Jacob has a family. He becomes rich in flocks and herds. And then comes the moment when he knows that the unfinished business of his life has caught up with him. Jacob is about to reunite with Esau. He knows that he must make peace with him, and he is frightened.

Perhaps that explains why Jacob constantly refers to himself as a "servant." And he keeps referring to Esau as "my lord." Having once dreamed of angels climbing a ladder, it is as if he has suddenly discovered humility. More than that: as he is preparing to meet Esau, he sends him gifts, hoping that he can gain his favor. That's Jacob. He is always practical. He is either taking gifts, such as the birthright from Esau and the blessing from his father, Isaac; or he is giving gifts—now to Esau and later to his son Joseph.

But what is making Jacob really nervous as he prepares to have a reunion with his brother, Esau? The text says: "Jacob was greatly frightened; in his anxiety, he divided the people with him" (32:8). In the words of the great medieval commentator Rashi: "He was afraid that he might be killed, and he was afraid that he would have to kill."

Judaism says that if you have to fight a war, do it—but only if it is absolutely necessary. If you have to use force, only use the amount of force that is absolutely necessary. Soldiers should avoid targeting civilians as much as is humanly possible.

This is especially true of Israel. Former prime minister of Israel

Golda Meir was rumored to have said: "We can forgive the Arabs for killing our children. We cannot forgive them for forcing us to kill their children. We will only have peace with the Arabs when they love their children more than they hate us."

War stinks. If you have to, fight. But don't enjoy it.

WHO WAS THAT MAN?

Jacob's night wrestling is one of the most famous episodes in the entire Torah, and in all literature.

Jacob, on the eve of his reunion with his brother, Esau, who has previously sworn to kill him, sends his family ahead of him across the Jabbok River. (Interesting thing about the Jabbok River: its name is actually a mixed-up way of saying Jacob's name. There's a pun there, as well. In Hebrew, Jabbok sounds like the word *evek*, "wrestling"— which is exactly what Jacob is about to do.)

There, Jacob was left alone, "And a man wrestled with him until the break of dawn" (32:25). Why is this wrestling match happening? We don't know. We have no sense of motives here. Why was Jacob attacked? We don't know.

Who is the wrestling partner? That is something else we don't know. But the possibilities teach us a lot about Judaism, and about ourselves.

The Torah says that it is a man. Was it simply a stranger? Perhaps Jacob's brother, Esau?

Maybe it was a more mysterious being, an angel of some sort. The ancient Rabbis say that "it was the guardian Prince of Esau." In Jewish lore, Esau is the ancestor of all enemies of the Jews. So, the guardian Prince of Esau is the spirit of all those who have wanted to destroy the Jews—sort of like an eternal Darth Vader. At that moment, Jacob started a wrestling match with the forces of evil, and that wrestling match has continued, unbroken, to our own time.

Was Jacob wrestling with God? That's certainly how the tradition understands it; his name becomes Israel, the one who struggled with God. This is huge. To wrestle with God can mean, to some people, wondering whether God really exists, or wondering why God allows certain things to happen. It can also mean wrestling with what our relationship with God should be, with what God wants of us.

Perhaps Jacob was wrestling with himself—the part of himself with big conflicts about all the less-than-wonderful things he has done in his life, like stealing a birthright and a blessing. The "stranger" has to ask Jacob his name because he wants to know if Jacob is going to own up to who he really is. Rabbi Shmuel Klitsner writes: "This night-time being functions as Jacob's own dark side. At the same time, the stranger functions as the divine image within Jacob. If Jacob can be whole, it is by struggling with the human and the divine within himself." Jacob limps away from that all-night wrestling match.

Sometimes, looking at ourselves realistically and critically can hurt. It takes courage to do it. But it is necessary.

Connections

ﭏ What have you struggled with? A bad habit, perhaps? Have you made progress?

ﭏ In what ways could you say you struggle with God?

ﭏ In what ways do we struggle with ourselves?

ﭏ The midrash says that Jacob wrestled with the Prince of Esau, which means that he wrestled with all of the Jews' enemies throughout history. Who are some of those enemies? How have Jacob's descendants—the Jewish people—struggled against them?

ﭏ Have you ever reconciled with someone with whom you had a real disagreement or a deep conflict? What was it like?

❖ Va-yeshev: Genesis 37:1–40:23

Welcome to the longest story in Genesis, and one of the most famous in the entire Bible—the story of Joseph. Joseph is Jacob's favorite child, although he is a bit of a jerk to his brothers. Joseph is constantly bragging to his brothers about his dreams of grandeur, and this really annoys them. Eventually they plot to do away with Joseph, throw him into a pit, and then sell him to some traders who are on their way to Egypt.

Joseph winds up as a slave in Egypt, working for the captain of Pharaoh's guard. He is doing pretty well (for a slave) until a false accusation lands him, once again, into the "pit" of a prison cell. Yes, life is the "pits" for Joseph—until you realize that a pit (like a peach pit) can be the seed of new growth. Joseph will grow up. Stay tuned.

Summary

℔ Jacob's favorite child is his second-youngest son, Joseph. Jacob makes him a special coat, which stirs up jealousy in his brothers. Joseph also has dreams of grandeur, which does not win him any popularity contests with his brothers, either. (37:1–11)

℔ Joseph's brothers get fed up with his bragging, and they sell him to some Midianite traders, who take him to Egypt. And, there, Joseph is sold to Potiphar, the captain of Pharaoh's guard. (37:12–36)

℔ A side story about Judah shows how he wrongs his daughter-in-law, Tamar. Judah has relations with her, and later Judah must publicly admit his wrongdoing. (38:1–30)

℔ In the first case of sexual harassment in the Torah, Potiphar's wife hits on the handsome Joseph. When he resists, he winds up in prison. (39:1–23)

℔ The always-talented Joseph interprets the dreams of his fellow prisoners, but they forget what he did for them. (40:1–23)

The Big Ideas

℔ **Parents should treat their children equally.** Parents should not play favorites. Jacob made it clear to everyone that he loved Joseph best, and this created terrible jealousy within his family.

℔ **Even seemingly "small" actions can have massive consequences.** Jacob spoiled Joseph. While this might have appeared to be a small matter at the time, it had terrible results. It ultimately resulted in the entire Jewish people becoming enslaved in Egypt. The small stuff counts.

℔ **Dreams are important.** Our dreams tell us a lot about what is going on inside our heads, and so we ought to pay attention to them. Often, they represent things that we are worried about. In the Bible they can sometimes even predict the future.

℔ **Being honest with yourself is the mark of maturity.** In particular, the best leaders are those who can own up to their mistakes, apologize, and then move on to do better. Judah's admission that he was wrong is an example of this. Perhaps that is why his tribe became the most important tribe, and why Jews, to this day, bear his name—Judah-ites, which means "Jews."

☙ **Temptation is an ever-present reality.** Temptation always exists, whether it involves cheating, irresponsible sex, stealing or misusing money, or abusing power. It takes great strength and maturity to stand up to those temptations.

☙ **Jews have a role to play in their societies.** Here, Joseph is the historical role model for Jewish engagement in the world, because he devotes his efforts to improving the Egyptian economy. Jews have always brought their talents and their gifts to the countries and societies in which they live.

Divrei Torah
DON'T PLAY FAVORITES!

Here's a story that's all too common: Mother dies—she had been old, and she had lived a good life. One of her sons has always loved the antique dining-room table that used to be the setting for their warm family dinners. That's the only thing of his parents that he wanted. Instead, his mother made it clear before her death that his younger sister would get the dining-room table. He wound up with a simple bookcase. Yes, it is nice—but it is not the same as the antique dining-room table. That table had all the good memories built into it. But, now, it will never sit in his home. It will sit in his sister's house. He is jealous of his sister, and the anger burns inside him.

Sound familiar? It should. It's the story of Joseph, updated for our time. Joseph's brothers may have been jealous about his "amazing technicolor dreamcoat," but what they really wanted was their father's attention and affection.

Why did Jacob favor Joseph? He was born when Jacob was already quite old. Perhaps the mere existence of Joseph reminded him that he was still young enough to produce children! Or, perhaps Joseph looked like Jacob's beloved wife, Rachel, who dies when giving birth to her second son, Benjamin. Jacob had fallen instantly in love with Rachel; every time he saw Joseph, he relived that moment of falling in love.

Parental favoritism is the Genesis family pattern. Remember Sarah favoring Isaac, Rebekah favoring Jacob, and Isaac favoring Esau? It is what we would nowadays call "dysfunctional."

There are two lessons here.

First, when parents play favorites, it breeds deep resentment and anger that can go on for generations.

And the second—our actions can have unintended consequences. "A parent should never single out one child among the others, for on account of a piece of silk, which Jacob gave Joseph in excess of his other sons, his brothers became jealous of him and the matter resulted in our descent into Egypt." Joseph's brothers' jealousy over that one silk coat was the tipping point of the resentment that eventually led not just to their brother's slavery, but that of the entire Jewish people in Egypt.

But wait. Maybe God needed Joseph to be taken to Egypt, so that the Jewish people would wind up in Egypt, and eventually experience the Exodus from Egypt. As Bible scholar Avivah Zornberg writes: "[Joseph's brothers] find themselves in the chaos of a reality whose plot is hidden from them." Could it be that there is a greater reason for what happens to Joseph and his family that they themselves cannot discern?

Maybe this is all part of God's Big Plan. And maybe our actions are as well.

JUDAH AND TAMAR: THE EPISODE THAT CREATED THE JEWISH FUTURE

How did the Jews get their name?

Simple. The word "Jew" comes from the Southern Kingdom of Judah (the Northern Kingdom was Israel)—and, before that, from the tribe of Judah, which got its name from Jacob's son Judah. In Hebrew, the name Judah is Yehudah, which means "thanks" (from the same root as *todah*), because Leah was thankful to God after the birth of her fourth child (Judah).

But what was so special about Judah that the Southern Kingdom of ancient Israel and later the Jewish people were named after him, and that King David and his dynasty should be descended from him?

After the brothers sell Joseph into slavery, Judah wanders off from his troubled family, and marries, and has three sons. He marries the first son to a woman named Tamar; the son dies. He marries the second son to Tamar; he dies as well. There is still a third son waiting in the wings. Judah tells his daughter-in-law to wait around for that third son to grow up so that they can marry.

Why is that important? According to the biblical law known as levirate marriage, if a man dies, a surviving male relative must marry the widow so that they can have children. With two brothers dead and one left, the surviving son should have married Tamar so that they could have children. But Judah didn't give that son to Tamar. Therefore as the only other man in the family, Judah would have had to marry his daughter-in-law so they could have children and continue the family line. But, he doesn't. (And, don't worry: this tradition no longer exists).

Tamar knows that Judah has done wrong by not giving her his third son, or by not marrying her himself. He "owes" her children. And, so, she disguises herself as a prostitute, and she has sex with Judah—in order to get pregnant. Judah doesn't have enough "cash" on hand to pay her, so he leaves some of his belongings behind as a pledge that he will return and pay her later. Tamar, the "prostitute," becomes pregnant. Meanwhile, Judah finds out that his former daughter-in-law, Tamar, is pregnant—and she is unmarried! Big scandal! And here's the big deal—Judah doesn't realize that he has had sex with his own daughter-in-law, and he surely doesn't know that he has impregnated her!

Look at how Tamar handles the situation. She sends Judah's belongings to him, with the message that the man who left those things with her had impregnated her. As Rabbi Geela-Rayzel Raphael teaches: "Tamar refuses to publicly humiliate Judah. She does not report directly that Judah is the father; rather, she sets it up so that he confesses." Judah realizes that he has, by mistake, had sex with his daughter-in-law. He realizes that he should have married Tamar all along. He declares: "She is more in the right than I am!" (38:26). The ancient sages taught: "Why did Judah's descendants deserve to become kings? Because he admitted that he had done wrong."

Yes, when it comes to biblical stories about sex, this story is a little "out there." But Judah's sin is not the most important thing here; it is the way that he owns up to it. Ever since Cain denied moral responsibility for his brother, Abel, God has been waiting for someone to own up, publicly, to doing wrong. Judah is the first person in the Torah to do that. He will do so a second time when he steps forward to Joseph. Our tradition says that's why the Jews are named for Judah— because he could say, "I'm sorry."

Connections

 maqaf Joseph not only bragged to his brothers about his dreams; he also brought bad reports about them to his father. In other words, he was a tattletale. What is this story teaching us about gossip? Have you ever experienced gossip? What was it like?

maqaf Do you know of siblings who are jealous of each other? What are some things in a family that can provoke jealousy? How do you think that parents should deal with this?

maqaf Have you ever been in a situation where you had to own up to something you had done wrong? How did it feel? What did you learn from that? Can you think of historical examples of people who publicly confessed that they were wrong? Why is this trait particularly important in a leader?

maqaf Have you ever faced a particular temptation (taking money, cheating on a test, doing anything that is wrong)? How did you deal with that temptation? Were you successful in resisting it? What does it take to fight temptations?

maqaf Tamar refuses to accuse Judah in public. She does not want to humiliate him. Why is public humiliation so bad? How can it be avoided?

maqaf Have you ever done something for a friend and felt that he or she was not particularly grateful to you? Did you ever feel "forgotten" by that friend? What was that experience like? How did you deal with it? What kind of advice can you offer people who experience this?

❖ Mikkets: Genesis 41:1–44:17

The Joseph drama, part 2. Joseph, the dreamer, morphs into Joseph, the dream interpreter. Pharaoh has a series of troubling dreams, and Joseph is summoned from the dungeon to interpret them. This turns out to be an ideal career move. Joseph becomes second in power only to Pharaoh, and helps Egypt prepare for the coming famine.

His brothers come down to Egypt to buy grain and run into Joseph, but they don't recognize him. Joseph wonders if the brothers have changed, if he can really trust them now, and so he puts them through various (somewhat cruel) trials to test them. Will he reveal his identity? Then what will happen?

Summary

ᶲ Joseph interprets the dreams of Pharaoh, and Pharaoh rewards him by releasing him from jail and inviting him to take charge of the Egyptian economy and to protect the country from famine. (41:1–44)

ᶲ Joseph acquires an Egyptian name and marries into an influential Egyptian family. He and his wife, Asenath, have two sons— Ephraim and Manasseh. (41:45–46,50-52)

ᶲ When the famine hits Canaan, Joseph's brothers come down to Egypt to purchase grain. They don't realize that the powerful man they are dealing with is actually their long-lost brother, Joseph. Joseph imprisons them on trumped-up spying charges. Ultimately, he lets them go—on the condition that they bring his youngest brother, Benjamin, to him. (42:1–17)

ᶲ The famine continues, and the brothers return to Egypt with Benjamin. (43:1–34)

ᶲ As the brothers prepare to return to Canaan, Joseph puts his silver goblet in Benjamin's bag, and accuses the brothers of being thieves. (44:1–17)

The Big Ideas

ᶲ **Assimilation is always a temptation for Jews.** Joseph assimilates in Egypt. In some ways, he becomes like a regular Egyptian. In others, he is still Jewish. He has a foot in two cultures, like modern Jews who are both deeply American (or Canadian, or British) and deeply Jewish.

ᶲ **Actions always have consequences.** Joseph reorganizes the Egyptian economy. But, in doing so, he turns the Egyptian people into slaves to Pharaoh. Years later, this will happen to the Israelites in Egypt as well. As we have already seen: what goes around, comes around.

ᵗᵇ **Life is filled with tests of character.** That was what Joseph was doing to his brothers—seeing if they had really changed (and there may be some pure vengeance going on as well!). Joseph tightens the screws by framing Benjamin. The stakes for all involved have just been raised.

ᵗᵇ **Showing emotion is healthy for everybody.** Joseph shows more emotion than almost anyone else in the Bible. He cries—out of sadness, longing, and even joy. Mature men and women can show their emotions, and it is often good to do so.

Divrei Torah
JOSEPH'S SECRET IDENTITY

Many people do not know that a handful of Jewish men invented the comic-book industry. In fact, the most famous comic-book characters were created by Jews: Superman (by Joe Shuster and Jerry Siegel) and Batman (by Bob Kane).

Perhaps the strangest thing about super heroes is that they have secret identities. Superman is really Clark Kent. Batman is really Bruce Wayne. Ever wonder if they get confused—"who am I really, at this moment?" And, really—how dumb were the people of Metropolis and Gotham City? They couldn't figure out who Superman and Batman really were? Do you think that Batman's mask made a difference? And Superman—who couldn't figure out that Superman and Clark Kent were one and the same person?

That's the way it is with Joseph. When he gets out of prison, he not only sheds his prison garb. He gets a new set of clothing and, with it, a new identity. Pharaoh changes his name to Zaphenath-paneah. To quote a medieval commentator: "If that name is Egyptian, then we don't know what it means! In any case, Pharaoh wanted to honor Joseph by giving him an Egyptian name. If it is Hebrew, then it could mean 'the revealer of secret things.'" Joseph marries Asenath, the daughter of Poti-phera, the high priest of the sun god (not to be confused with Potiphar, who had earlier bought Joseph as a slave).

Did Joseph ever wonder who he really was? Hebrew—or Egyptian?

Sometimes it seems that Joseph is really Egyptian. He looks so Egyptian that his brothers don't recognize him. He marries an Egyptian woman, whose father was a very powerful priest of one of Egypt's main gods. He moves through the corridors of power in Egyptian society. And, during all his years in Egypt, he never "phones home," even to tell his poor father, Jacob, that he is still alive.

And, sometimes it seems that Joseph is really a Hebrew. Yes, he was married to the daughter of a major Egyptian priest, but some ancient writers thought that Asenath converted to Judaism. Yes, Joseph's father-in-law, Poti-phera, was heavily involved with worshiping the sun, but Joseph is never portrayed as following his example. Finally, Joseph reunites with his Hebrew family, travels back to Canaan to bury his father, and names his sons Ephraim and Manasseh—Hebrew names.

Joseph lived in two cultures—Hebrew and Egyptian. He is the forerunner of the modern American Jew, who lives in two cultures at the same time—American and Jewish. To quote Mordecai Kaplan: "Jews live in two civilizations, in their own and in the countries in which they live, and they want those two civilizations to play an equal part in their lives."

So, who is Joseph? In many respects, isn't he like us?

WHY DOES JOSEPH MESS WITH HIS BROTHERS?

We can only imagine Joseph's brothers saying the following under their breaths: "All right, we know that this guy is very important here in Egypt. We got that. But, why is he being such a jerk to us?"

Ever since Joseph recognized his brothers, who had come down to Egypt to buy grain during the famine in the Land of Israel, he has been really messing with their heads. He accuses them of being spies. He demands that they bring their youngest brother, Benjamin, down to Egypt. He ties his brother Simeon up in front of them. When they come back to Egypt to buy food again, he puts his silver cup into Benjamin's bag and accuses them of being thieves. He then demands that Benjamin should remain with him as his slave.

Why is Joseph doing this to his brothers? Was it simply payback for what they had done to him, years before? Or, perhaps he was testing them. He wanted to see if they would stick up for their younger brother, Benjamin. Would they treat him better than they had treated him?

Even though Joseph is clearly in charge here, and even though he is actually bullying his brothers, they don't cry. No—the only one who cries is Joseph—a lot. Is it because he was so moved to see them again, and how they had aged? Was he remembering how he had suffered at their hands? Was he thinking about all the years that they had missed together? Was he pained to see how much anger he still had inside him?

Rabbi Morris Adler suggests that Joseph cries because he realizes how much power he now has, and how easy it is to abuse that power and to become overly arrogant about it. "Privilege is in danger of giving us a sense of personal quality and egotism that puts us far above the common man and feeds our vanity with the most destructive illusions."

Perhaps Joseph is moved to tears because he saw that his brothers had truly repented. They could have given up Benjamin to him, but they didn't. In the words of the great medieval philosopher Maimonides: "What constitutes complete repentance? If someone finds himself in the same situation in which he had previously sinned, and if he could commit the sin again, but he doesn't do it again, then we know that this person has truly repented."

But there is yet another possibility. Perhaps Joseph is moved by how much his brothers demonstrate that they care for each other and for their aged father. It had not always been that way. Joseph had been the victim of their lack of caring, and so had their father.

But his brothers had changed, and that was reason enough for Joseph to cry. This time, in joy.

Connections

- ъ Have you ever had odd or interesting dreams? Have you thought about what they might mean?
- ъ What things that you love to do are Jewish? Which are American? Do you ever feel you need to choose one over the other?
- ъ Has your character ever been tested? When was it tough to decide right from wrong?
- ъ Do you agree that Joseph was bullying his brothers? Could he have handled things differently?

℔ Have you ever been in a situation where you did something wrong, and then chose not to do so again? Or perhaps you did do it again and regretted it?

℔ When is it okay for grownups to cry publicly?

❖ Va-yiggash: Genesis 44:18–47:27

Here we are in part 3 of the Joseph story, the final episode. This is where it all comes together for Joseph, as he reconciles with his family and with his Hebrew past.

Judah finally stands up to his brother Joseph, protesting the way that he and his other brothers have been treated. Joseph totally falls apart and reveals his identity to his brothers. They cannot believe that it is really him; after all, they thought that he was a slave, or that he was dead. But Joseph is very much alive, and he shows himself to be a decent and hospitable person. With the encouragement of Pharaoh, Joseph invites his brothers to settle in Goshen, a section of Egypt. He sends for his elderly father, Jacob, so that the family can be reunited.

Meanwhile, Joseph completely restructures the Egyptian economy. He becomes even more powerful, but in the process he takes the land from the Egyptians, and he essentially turns them into slaves. Hmmn.—do you think that this could be where the Egyptians got the idea of turning the Hebrews into slaves?

Summary

℔ In the longest speech in Genesis, Joseph's brother Judah protests the way that the brothers have been treated. (44:18–43)

℔ Joseph finally reveals himself to his brothers. (45:1–20)

℔ Joseph's brothers return to Canaan to get their father, Jacob, and they bring him down to Egypt to see Joseph. (45:21–46:34)

℔ Joseph presents his father to Pharaoh, and Pharaoh invites them to settle in the region of Goshen—"in the best part of the land." (47:1–12)

℔ Joseph creates land policies that protect Egypt during the famine. (47:13–27)

The Big Ideas

ᚼ **To be a Jew means to take moral responsibility.** When he defends his brothers against Joseph's unreasonable behavior, Judah completes his transformation into a moral person who can take responsibility. As he does that, he shows that he deserves to become the namesake and ancestor of the Jews.

ᚼ **Forgiveness is essential in families.** For families to exist, there must be a way that people can forgive and be forgiven. When Joseph forgives his brothers, he invents the very idea of forgiveness. No one in the Bible had ever done that before.

ᚼ **What we see in front of us is not always the whole picture.** Sometimes it seems as if there is a bigger plan going on behind the scenes, even if we are not sure what it is. That is how Joseph can forgive his brothers for selling him into slavery in Egypt. He believes that it was all part of a huge divine plan, and that it was all for the good.

ᚼ **Jews must be different.** Jewish identity has always required that Jews be a holy people. This has meant that, to some degree, Jews have to be different from their gentile neighbors. That is why Joseph told his brothers to identify themselves as shepherds. The lamb was one of Egypt's main gods, and anyone who worked with sheep, like shepherds, would have been repugnant to Egyptians. Shepherds could not socialize with Egyptians. So that would be how Joseph's brothers would be able to maintain their uniqueness and integrity—what Rabbi Jonathan Sacks, the former chief rabbi of Great Britain, calls "the dignity of difference."

ᚼ **Remember everything—the bad and the good.** When Jews think of ancient Egypt, they often think of despair and slavery. But the story of Joseph reminds us that Egypt was initially welcoming to the Jews. That historical memory is also important.

Divrei Torah
WHO'S WORKING BEHIND THE SCENES?

It's time to learn a great Yiddish word: *bashert*. While it is difficult to translate accurately, it means "meant to be" or "predestined to happen." In life, we often look back, and sometimes it seems that things are just *bashert*; they were meant to happen. That doesn't mean that you have no moral choices about what you do. Of course you do—but it's all part of a larger picture that you might not ever see.

That's the message Joseph gives his brothers. First, he says: "I am Joseph. Is my father still well?" (45:3). And then, immediately, he comforts them. Don't be angry with yourselves, he tells them. It wasn't you who sent me here. It was God. It had to happen so I could save Egypt.

We can imagine that the brothers just stood there with their mouths open. Then after the shock, we might also imagine one brother saying: "I thought we were rid of that dreamer. And yet, here he is, getting all cosmic on us again. Yeah, right—God sent him here. Give me a break."

And, we can also imagine another brother responding: "No. No, this is different. He's not saying that God chose him to save Egypt. He's just saying that it all worked out fine. And maybe that's a sign that God was behind all this, after all."

Make no mistake. The brothers are still guilty of selling Joseph into slavery. As the medieval commentator Isaac Abravanel writes: "True, God used the brothers for the unfolding of the divine plan. But that does not absolve them of responsibility for what they did." And while they appear to have repented, does Joseph still harbor a bit of doubt about their integrity? Do the brothers still wonder if their brother has really forgiven them?

This is the true meaning of something being *bashert*. Sometimes, things just happen and we are not sure why they happen. But they do, and only much later we realize that it was all part of a larger plan. Here is how it could work for you. Perhaps you will suddenly decide to switch classes in school, and you meet someone who will wind up becoming your best friend—for the rest of your life. Or, you try out for a team and don't make it, but you wind up doing something else that you really love.

Sure—we have free will. We are not God's puppets. But there is a script to this great theatrical production that we call "life." We did not entirely write it on our own. There is a Director who is off camera, and in the theater of life we must sometimes simply show up and read the script, do our best, and hope for the best.

That's what Joseph is saying to his brothers: Relax. I forgive you. This all happened because God wanted it to. As the Hasidic sage Za-dok Ha-kohen of Lublin taught: "At its deepest level, faith is the belief that life is meaningful and that things happen for a reason."

Or, to put it in a different way: We get the jigsaw-puzzle pieces, but only God gets the picture on the cover of the box.

WAS JOSEPH REALLY SUCH A NICE PERSON?

The Bible is filled with righteous people. But the ancient sages give only one person in the entire Bible the title of *tzadik*, "a righteous person." And that person would be Joseph.

Really?

Look at what happens. Pharaoh puts Joseph in charge of the Egyptian economy. He needs Joseph to save the land from famine. Yes, Joseph does that, and his careful saving and distribution is no easy feat. But Joseph accomplishes his goal in a rather ugly way. First, Joseph takes all of the Egyptians' livestock and wealth. Then, he takes all the farmlands and makes them the possession of the state, and he sells the people back their food. He reduces the Egyptians to slaves; only the priests are allowed to keep their land.

So, really—how good a person is Joseph? Is he a brilliant manager who rescues Egypt from famine? Or, is he cruel and heartless? Or even a combination of both?

The same Talmud that calls Joseph a *tzadik* also rather surprisingly teaches: "Joseph died before his brothers because he acted as if he were superior to the Egyptians." Joseph is competent. But he is also cruel. He enslaves the Egyptians and, generations later, they "returned the favor." Perhaps that is why we spill ten drops of wine at the seder each year—not just to refrain from showing joy while another suffers (even if the Pharaoh persecuted us) but to show our sympathy with the Egyptians.

Deuteronomy 23:8 states: "You shall not abhor an Egyptian, for you were a stranger in his land." The Jewish experience with the Egyptians was not all bad. In fact, it started out pretty good. Let's remember: the Egyptians welcomed the Jews in a time of famine.

Let's face it. No matter how good Joseph was, he wasn't Moses.

In fact, Moses comes on the scene as the total opposite of Joseph. To quote the contemporary Jewish leader Barry Shrage: "Joseph was the Hebrew who became an Egyptian. Moses was the Egyptian who became a Jew. Joseph was the slave who became an overseer. Moses was the prince who identified with slaves. Joseph was the overseer who enslaved the Egyptians. Moses was the prince who freed the slaves. Joseph worked for a Pharaoh. Moses worked against a Pharaoh."

Yes, Joseph has his good qualities. That is why he is known as a *tzadik*, a righteous man But his flaw is that he doesn't question power. Maybe he is not secure enough to do so. Maybe he does what he thinks is best—for Egypt, and probably most of all for him and his family—and he is blind to some of the consequences.

Joseph is a hero, but a flawed one. He was once weak and poor, but it seems that he forgot where he came from. It would take a Moses to teach the Jews not simply to do what is best for them, but to never forget to "love the stranger, for you were strangers in the land of Egypt."

Connections

- Have you ever had a moment when you realized that you were doing the right thing? What was it like?
- Did you ever forgive someone in your family, or in some other situation in your life? Why? What did it feel like to you?
- Have you ever felt that something was simply meant to be?
- In what ways have Jews been separate and different from other people? Is that still the case? Do you agree that Jews need to be different from other people? Why or why not?
- Do you think that Joseph was righteous, or not so righteous?

❖ Va-yeḥi: Genesis 47:28–50:26

As we come to the end of the book of Genesis, it is truly a time of transition. Two people die: Jacob, and then his beloved son Joseph. Joseph's brothers worry that, with their father dead, all the old family fights will start up again. But Joseph makes them feel better about the way that everything worked out.

As Genesis ends, the children of Jacob are living, happily and comfortably, in the land of Goshen in Egypt. But, as we shall see, "happily" does not mean "happily ever after."

Summary

ᚦ Jacob, on his deathbed, blesses his grandsons, Ephraim and Manasseh, and then he blesses each of his sons. Each son's blessing refers not only to his character and personality, but also to the destiny of the tribe that will descend from him. When Jacob finishes blessing his sons, he dies. (48:1–49:33)

ᚦ Joseph and his brothers take their father, Jacob, back to Canaan for burial, and then they return to Egypt. (50:1–14)

ᚦ Joseph's brothers are afraid that Joseph will now hate them for what they did to him when he was young. Joseph reassures them, however, and tells them that what has happened was all been part of God's plan for him and his family. (50:15–21)

ᚦ As Joseph is about to die, he makes his brothers swear that, when they finally leave Egypt, his bones will be buried in the Land of Israel. (50:22–26)

The Big Ideas

ᚦ **Jacob's blessings of his sons predict the future.** Jacob's words to them refer to their personalities, but, even more so, to the future of the tribes that will descend from them. Jacob's blessings even foresee the future of the territories in the Land of Israel that the tribes will inhabit. A traditional explanation is that God gave Jacob the gift of prophecy. Modern scholars would say that the blessings—and in a few cases, curses—reflect the realities of Israelite tribal history.

ᚦ **Judaism accepts the reality of bodily death.** When Jacob dies, the Egyptians embalm his body, as they do also with Joseph's body. This is the well-known practice of mummification. The ancient Egyptians believed that the body needed to be preserved in order to be reunited with the soul in the afterlife. By contrast, Judaism embraces the finality of the body's death, and does not believe that it needs to be artificially preserved.

ᚦ **The Diaspora (places where Jews live outside of Israel) is an**

historical reality for Jews. When Jacob's sons carry their father's body back to the Land of Israel for burial, they could have stayed there. But, instead, they return to Egypt. They had gotten very comfortable there, and they might even have thought of themselves as Egyptians. In the same way, American Jews tend to think of themselves as Americans; Canadian Jews, as Canadians, etc.

ᛒ **Forgiveness is a central Jewish value.** Joseph refuses to hold a grudge against his brothers. In this way, he demonstrates the Jewish attitude toward grudges—it's best not to carry them.

ᛒ **The Land of Israel is always precious to the Jew—even in death.** Despite the fact that he has lived his entire adult life in Egypt, Joseph is, at heart, a Jew. That is why he wants to be buried in the Land of Israel—which will ultimately happen when the Israelites enter the land. Joseph's deathbed wish emphasizes the Jewish linkage to the Land of Israel.

Divrei Torah
DON'T HOLD A GRUDGE!

This is going to happen to you.

No matter how popular you are, not everyone in school is going to be your friend. Or even like you. Some will actually dislike you; some might even be mean to you. You might know this already.

You'll go to your thirtieth high school reunion, and maybe you'll run into the people who didn't like you back then. They might come up to you, and hug you, and say, "Wow! It is so great to see you after all these years! You look wonderful! What are you doing now?"

You may be tempted to remind them of all that they did to you, way back then. You might want to accuse them of being hypocrites and phonies. But you won't. You will remember the story of Joseph, and how he says to his brothers that he basically forgives them for what they had done to him. That's because Joseph will not carry a grudge.

Maybe those who mistreated you actually want you to be honest with them (after all, it might help them feel better).

Similarly, Joseph's brothers worry aloud: "What if Joseph still bears a grudge against us?" (50:15).

The sentence starts with the word *lu,* which has several different meanings. The commentator Rashi says: "*Lu* can mean 'please' and 'if only'" (Rashi on Gen. 50:15). Rashi is saying that Joseph's brothers are still afraid and insecure, and they want Joseph to take seriously what they had done to him. They want Joseph to hold them responsible for what they did, and not simply sweep it under the rug.

But Joseph doesn't hate them, or bear a grudge. This is the great life lesson of Joseph. Joseph sees his life as a life with cosmic consequences. Stuff happened to him for a reason. He is sure what the reason is: "God sent me here to save life. Your hands did not sell me into Egypt; God did." Imagine having an attitude like that!

Rabbi Lawrence Kushner thinks that grudges are really like a slow-acting poison. "In very small doses, I will poison myself for the rest of my life. I will carry around the injury you caused me. I will watch it and guard it. But I will never tell you."

We've come to the end of Genesis. Cain killed his brother, Abel. Isaac and Ishmael reconciled, but never speak to each other. Jacob and Esau reconciled, and they do speak to each other. Joseph and his brothers reconciled, and speak to each other—and, then, Joseph invited them to live with him. Forgiveness is possible. Healing is possible. Family unity is possible.

THE FIRST TIME ANYONE SAID THE SHEMA

Some people have easy lives, or so we think. Not Jacob.

Jacob was lying on his deathbed. In those final moments, he went over his life. Born as a twin, he struggled in the womb with his brother, Esau. He cheated Esau out of his birthright. He stole his brother's blessing. When his brother sought to kill him, he escaped, stopping for the night at Beth El, where he dreamed of a ladder of angels. He wound up with Leah instead of Rachel, then he married Rachel too. He had a wrestling match with a mysterious stranger that left him with a permanent injury and a new name—Israel, the one who struggles with God.

His daughter, Dinah, was raped. His sons reacted violently. They then sold his son Joseph into slavery in Egypt. For many years, Jacob was bereaved. He thought that his son Joseph was dead. And then, when he was already an old man, he learned that Joseph was still alive. He made the long trip down to Egypt to reunite with Joseph. No wonder that when he met Pharaoh he would say his days had been long and hard.

At the end of his life, Jacob was gripped with fear. Perhaps this covenant that exists between him and God, this covenant that is still in its infancy, this covenant that he has sought so hard to fulfill, in his way—perhaps this covenant will die with him.

A midrash says: "When Jacob was dying, he called his twelve sons and said to them: 'Do you have faith in God?' And they said: 'Hear, O Israel [for that was Jacob's other name] the Lord is our God, the Lord is One.' And Jacob died with these words on his lips: 'Blessed be the name of His glorious kingdom for ever and ever.'" It's a lovely tale about the origin of the *Shema,* but, even more, about who the Jews are—a people that has faith in God

Jacob is like any other Jewish parent. He has worries, dreams, and hopes. He wants to pass his values and his faith to his children and his grandchildren. He wants to perpetuate his people and what is most important to him. He knows he will die, but he wants to live on, like his ancestors before him, in the generations that will come.

Continuing the Jewish people is a major responsibility. But how can you do that, especially as a kid? Steven M. Cohen, one of today's wisest Jewish sociologists, states: "Having Jewish friends in childhood (and later in life) is a good way to predict one's future Jewish identity." The best way to start building a Jewish identity and creating the Jewish future is to create a network of Jewish friends: through religious school, youth group, Jewish summer camp, Israel trips—even social media.

The future of the Jewish people starts with you. And it starts today.

Connections

ᵮ What would you want your parents to say to you when they bless you?

ᵮ Have you ever held a grudge? What examples in world history and Jewish history of grudges can you think of?

ᵮ Are the Jews still holding a grudge against the German people for the Holocaust?

ᵮ Do you agree that Joseph's brothers wanted to be taken seriously, and perhaps not be forgiven so quickly?

ᘐ What do you think was going through the minds of Jacob's sons when he was dying?

ᘐ What do you think your parents' Jewish hopes for you are?

ᘐ In what way have you inherited Judaism from your own parents and grandparents?

ᘐ Do you agree that having Jewish friends is essential to creating a Jewish identity? What other things are important?

EXODUS

❖ Shemot: Exodus 1:1–6:1

When we last saw Jacob's family, they had settled down in the Goshen region of Egypt. Everyone was happy. Everyone was (finally!) getting along. Generations have now passed since Jacob's son Joseph and his brothers have settled in Egypt. The Israelites have grown numerous, and probably prosperous as well. But the new Egyptian king doesn't know, and could care less, about everything that Joseph had done for Egypt. The Egyptians become afraid of the Israelites, and Pharaoh decides to enslave them. Then he embarks upon an even more evil plan: to kill Israelite children.

All seems lost—until a hero emerges: Moses, born into slavery, adopted by Pharaoh's daughter, a man who figures out that the Israelites are his people, and will have the God-given courage to approach Pharaoh and plead for his people's freedom.

Summary

- ♱ Jacob's children and descendants have become comfortable in Egypt. But a new king arises who institutes a program of oppression and enslavement. (1:1–14)
- ♱ Two midwives, Shiphrah and Puah, defy Pharaoh's orders to kill Israelite children, and they become the inventors of civil disobedience. (1:15–22)
- ♱ A Hebrew boy is born. His parents, fearing for his life, send him floating in a basket down the Nile River. Pharaoh's daughter finds him, adopts him, and gives him the name "Moses." (2:1–10)
- ♱ Moses realizes that he is a Hebrew. He fights back against Egyptian oppressors, ultimately fleeing from Egypt to the land of Midian. He marries Zipporah, the daughter of Jethro, a Midianite priest, and they have two sons. (2:11–22)

ᵼ Moses encounters God at a bush that burns but is not consumed by fire. God gives him his mission: to lead the Israelites out of Egypt. (3:1–4:23)

The Big Ideas

ᵼ **Jewish history has a predictable pattern.** The beginning of Exodus establishes the pattern for much of Jewish history: thriving, success, increased vulnerability, and, ultimately, persecution. This pattern has changed, however, in the United States and other places around the world.

ᵼ **Women's roles are crucial in Judaism.** The redemption from Egypt could not have happened without the heroic acts of righteous women: Shiphrah and Puah; Jochebed (Moses's birth mother); Miriam (Moses's sister); and Pharaoh's daughter, who adopted Moses.

ᵼ **It's a mitzvah to protest immoral orders.** In fact, that is how people become moral heroes. Here, the lesson of Shiphrah and Puah is crucial. They silently protested the evil plans of Pharaoh, and they saved the lives of the Hebrew children. They were the "inventors" of civil disobedience.

ᵼ **To be a Jew means taking care of your own people, and other people as well.** That is the lesson of Moses's early life. He begins by intervening when he sees his own people being persecuted (yet, how does he know that these are his people?), and then he intervenes when shepherds are harassing Jethro's daughters. Jews cannot only think and act on behalf of themselves; they have to think and act on behalf of others as well.

ᵼ **The Jews are an eternal people.** God deliberately speaks to Moses out of a bush that burns but is not consumed by fire—which is a symbol of Jewish history. The Jews have often suffered but they have not been consumed by their suffering.

Divrei Torah

THEY SAID, "NO!"

You know how there are "coming attractions" from the next episode at the end of some television shows? That's what the first chapter of

Exodus is—the coming attractions for all of Jewish history. Jewish immigrants in Egypt thrive, just as Jews have thrived in many times and places. A new king forgets what Joseph had done for Egypt; in the past, new governments often forgot previous Jewish contributions to their societies. Increasingly, the Egyptians think of the Israelites as a foreign element. The Egyptians begin to question the Israelites' loyalty to Egypt—just as Jews have often been seen as disloyal foreigners in the lands in which they have lived.

Then: persecution, slavery, mass murder. It's all too familiar.

Enter two of the most extraordinary characters of the Hebrew Bible: Shiphrah and Puah, a pair of midwives, whose job it is to help women give birth. Pharaoh commanded them to kill Hebrew infant boys and to let Hebrew girls live. But they refused to do so.

Shiphrah and Puah were the originators of civil disobedience. They are the first people in the Torah to question and defy authority. When a bus driver in Montgomery, Alabama, told Rosa Parks to sit in the back of the bus, where African Americans were then supposed to sit, she refused. It was as if she were channeling Shiphrah and Puah. Perhaps Reverend Martin Luther King Jr. was thinking of them when he said: "An unjust law is a human law that is not rooted in eternal law." King was sitting in jail because he refused to obey an unjust law, and he urged nonviolent civil disobedience against segregation.

An interesting question: Were these midwives Jews or Egyptians? The text says that they were *m'yaldot ivriot* (Hebrew midwives). But according to an alternative understanding of the Hebrew grammar, you can also read that as "midwives *for the Hebrew women.*"

So, were they Hebrew (Israelite) women? Their names are certainly Hebrew. But would Pharaoh really have had Hebrew women kill their own people? It is far more interesting to believe that they were, in fact, Egyptians who saved Jewish lives. Otherwise, how could Pharaoh have told them to kill Jews? The Roman Jewish historian Josephus says that the midwives were certainly Egyptian: "for this office was, by Pharaoh's orders, to be performed by women who, as compatriots of the king, were not likely to transgress his will."

Shiphrah and Puah were good people who saved Jewish lives. It is easier for people to help save their own kin than people they don't know, and much more difficult for people from the "in" group to help people from the "out" group. Think of the "righteous gentiles" who rescued Jews during the Holocaust. If Shiphrah and Puah were, in fact, non-Israelites, it makes their actions even more courageous.

TIME TO GROW UP

Every kid asks this question, usually right around bar and bat mitzvah time: how do I know that I have really grown up?

Let's ask Moses that question.

Moses is a Hebrew, but Pharaoh's daughter found him and raised him as her own child, in Pharaoh's palace. Moses could have had a very cushy life. But, at a certain point, he figures out that he is a Hebrew. How does he figure that out? The Torah doesn't say.

But we do know this: Moses sees an Egyptian torturing a Hebrew slave, and he kills the Egyptian. It would have been nice if Moses didn't have to do that. When the text tells us that Moses "turned this way and that" before killing the Egyptian, maybe he wasn't looking to see whether there were any witnesses around. Maybe he was looking to see whether there were any other people around who could help. But no, Moses was totally alone, and he had to act with courage and with speed.

The next day, Moses sees two Hebrews fighting, and this time he doesn't respond with force. Rather than letting his fists do the talking, he asks a question. Like all good Jewish questions, it starts with "Why?" "Why do you strike your fellow?" (2:13).

At that moment, Moses's childhood ends. As you journey through your teenage years, and as you approach adulthood, you will figure out that a major part of growing up is learning to ask good questions. That has always been the Jewish way: to ask questions whenever possible, and to act decisively when necessary.

The next stop on Moses's journey to maturity is when he flees to Midian, and he sees shepherds harassing Jethro's daughters at the well. Moses sticks up for the women, and drives the harassers away. Moses has no real responsibility for them; they are not his family or his people. But, at that moment, Moses goes beyond the borders of his own family and people and intervenes for the sake of others.

As I have written: "Bonding yourself with your people; responding to their pain; questioning injustice; responding to the pain of those who are outside your people—these are all essential moments on the journey toward adulthood."

We all need role models who can teach us about standing up for ourselves, and for others. For Jews, Shiphrah and Puah are those role models, and so is Moses.

In the words of the sage Hillel: "In a place where there are no men, strive to be a man." Of course, Hillel didn't just mean "men." He meant that it is everyone's job to stand up, be counted, and make a difference. In a situation when no else is willing to stand out and stand up, making a difference can make all the difference!

Connections

- What actions of Moses do you most admire? What actions of Moses do you wish that you will be able to emulate?
- In what way does chapter 1 of Exodus establish a pattern of Jewish history? In what countries has that pattern existed?
- What Jewish women do you admire most?
- From what people do you think that Shiphrah and Puah came—Egyptian or Hebrew? Does it matter? Why or why not?
- Would you have the courage to defy illegal orders or unjust laws? Would you risk your life to save someone you don't know? In the spirit of these two remarkable women, what can you do for other people who need your help?
- What historical figures have behaved like Shiphrah and Puah?
- Have you ever stuck up for someone who was weaker? What was that experience like?
- How will you know when you have become an adult?

❖ Va-'era': Exodus 6:2–9:35

It was not as if Moses had no experience with the God of the Israelites. He had first met that God in the form of a burning bush. Now it was time for Moses to meet God again. The last time that Moses met God, God was "the God of your father the God of Abraham, the

God of Isaac, and the God of Jacob" (3:6). This time, God has a "new" name—a name that is mysterious and unpronounceable.

God reassures Moses that God has noticed the suffering of the Israelites in Egypt, and that it will be Moses's job to appeal to Pharaoh to let them go. But Moses isn't so sure about that. He tries to get out of this job; he protests that he's got a speech impediment and doesn't talk very well. And so, Moses's brother, Aaron, becomes his spokesperson.

They approach Pharaoh and demand that the Israelites be freed—with a little help from some old-fashioned snake tricks. But Pharaoh isn't impressed; he doesn't get it. He needs a wake-up call. That's how the plagues started—turning the Nile into blood, bringing on frogs, swarms of insects, cattle disease, boils, and hail. Throughout it all, Pharaoh remains stubborn, and refuses to let the Israelites go.

Summary

ᚦ God reveals a new divine name to Moses—YHVH (*Yud Heh Vav Heh*), which Jews now pronounce as "Adonai." (6:2–13)

ᚦ Moses insists that he has trouble speaking, which will make it very difficult for him to lead the Israelites out of Egypt. (6:30)

ᚦ Moses and Aaron get into a war of magical powers with the magicians of Egypt to see who has the most power—the God of the Israelites, or the gods of the Egyptians. (7:8–18)

ᚦ God brings the first plagues upon the Egyptians. The Nile turns to blood; frogs appeared, lice, swarms of insects, cattle disease, boils, and hail. Throughout it all, Pharaoh's heart is "hardened," which means that he is unable to make the wise decision to let the Israelites go—though, at times, he gets pretty close to figuring that out. (7:19–9:34)

The Big Ideas

ᚦ **We can never know God entirely.** God reveals a new name to Moses—*Yud Heh Vav Heh*. But the name is mysterious, and perhaps even unpronounceable. In the ancient world, to know someone's name means to have some kind of power over that person, and you cannot have power over God.

ᚦ **Disability does not mean that you have to be helpless.** Even though Moses has trouble speaking, he's still able to be a leader of his people. Disabilities need not keep people from doing great and important things.

Ƀ **Only God is God.** The plagues were not just nasty acts that God performed against the Egyptians; they were acts aimed against the gods of Egypt. The whole purpose of the plagues was to give Pharaoh a lesson in God's power.

Ƀ **Everyone (except for Pharaoh) has free will.** God "froze" Pharaoh's ability to think for himself, so that he would not let the Israelites go. If he had in fact done so, then Pharaoh would have been the agent of freedom, not God.

Divrei Torah
GOD'S NEW NAME

A teenager (perhaps you) applies for a special summer program. The application asks: "name of father." The kid writes: "Dad."

It's a sweet and understandable error. But, in fact, "Dad" is not your father's name. Well, it is to you. His real name is (let's just say) Harold Schwartz. You call your father Dad, but his boss might call him Harold. The person who works at the bank might call him Mr. Schwartz. Your mother might call him Hal, or at times "honey," "dear," or other affectionate nicknames. His siblings might refer to him by his childhood nickname Hally. So, the truth is: your father has many names—simultaneously. You probably do as well.

In this Torah portion God tells Moses that the Patriarchs knew God as El Shaddai. A midrash says: "God said to Moses: Many times I appeared to Abraham, Isaac and Jacob as El Shaddai, but they never asked My name nor questioned My ways! Yet You ask my name?" In fact, there are many different names for God, and you already know some of them, like Elohim, Adonai—and on the High Holy Days, Avinu Malkheinu.

God's "new" name is YHVH, *Yud Heh Vav Heh.* For two thousand years, Jews have pronounced it Adonai—"my Lord," though some people simply translate this as "the Eternal."

All those "names" for God are just guesses. We don't know how to pronounce God's "real" name; maybe we never knew it. Once a year, on Yom Kippur, the High Priest would enter the Holy of Holies in the ancient Temple and say God's name. But, somehow, the vowels of God's name got lost—along with the real pronunciation of God's four-letter name. Is it pronounced "Yahweh"? Is it Jehovah (as in the Christian missionary group Jehovah's Witnesses)? We not only don't know how to say it; it is considered bad form to even try. That's why some Jews simply refer to God as *ha-Shem* (the Name).

YHVH seems to be related to the Hebrew verb root *heh-vav-heh,* which means "to be." YHVH could mean "that which causes to be," which would be a pretty good way to describe God.

The contemporary theologian Arthur Green believes that YHVH is a simultaneous rendition of the Hebrew root "to be" in its past, present, and perfect tenses: "As though it really was 'Is-Was-Will Be.' It is a verb caught in motion."

So, God's name is something like "iswaswillbe." It is impossible for us to say God's "real" name. As it is impossible to really know God's nature, although we strive to imitate God's ways. That's the problem and the challenge.

MOSES, SPEAK UP!

It's called being tongue tied. Some people call it stuttering. Others call it stammering. Whatever you want to call it, it's difficult and annoying. And yet, many people overcome speech impediments like this one, and they become great leaders.

Take Moses, for example. In fact, Moses has two kinds of speech problems. But they are very different, and they tell us a lot about who Moses really is.

One of these impediments has to do with the way that Moses actually speaks. Moses refers to himself as being *kaved peh* and *kaved lashon* (4:10), which is translated as "slow of speech and slow of tongue." Moses is either not an orator, or he has a speech defect. Just as Jacob was wounded and limps, Moses is also "wounded" and "limps" with his speech.

How did that happen? An ancient legend says that when Moses was an infant, Pharaoh placed before him a gold vessel and a live coal. If he reached for the gold, he would have proven himself to be a future threat. If he went for the coal—no problem. A midrash tells us, "The infant Moses was about to reach forth for the gold when the angel Gabriel came and moved his hand so that it seized the coal, and he thrust his hand with the live coal into his mouth, so that his tongue was burnt, with the result that he became slow of speech and of tongue."

So maybe that is how Moses developed his speech defect. More likely, he was simply born with a problem or failed to develop typical language skills. But the Torah also says that Moses is *aral sefatayim* (6:12). While most translations say that this means "impeded speech," it really means that he has "uncircumcised lips" (or "uncircumcised language").

Uncircumcised *lips*? What? When the Bible says that someone is uncircumcised, it may not mean physical circumcision. To be *arel* or *aral*, "uncircumcised," can also mean that someone is a foreigner. Moses was not really an Israelite. Having grown up in the royal court, Moses would have seemed foreign to the Israelites. They would not have accepted him as their leader. Perhaps Moses is saying that he doesn't know Hebrew because he has been so cut off from his people. That also would have created a problem in communication.

Another interpretation—this one from a Hasidic sage, Yehudah Aryeh Leib of Ger. "As long as there are those who will listen, then there can be those who speak, because the power of the leader issues from the people. For this reason, if the children of Israel listen to Moses, his mouth would be opened, his speech would be fluent, and his words would reach Pharaoh. But if they don't want to listen to him he would be made into one of impeded speech." Moses has a hard time not only getting Pharaoh to listen, but also his very own people to listen.

How often we see this happening! It's not enough for the leader to be able to speak, to be eloquent and forceful. People have to listen. Sometimes that's the hardest part of all.

Connections

፠ Can you think of examples of people who had disabilities or physical challenges and were still able to do great things? What do you think made them successful at what they did?

ᚻ Have you ever been a leader, or tried to lead? What have been some of your challenges in doing so?

ᚻ Were there any times when you had difficulty being understood, or understanding someone else? What was that like? How did you overcome it?

ᚻ Another interpretation of God's Name, YHVH, is that each Hebrew character is "open —*yud* on the left-hand side, *heh* on the bottom (there is a space between the two prongs of the letter), and *vav* on all sides. What are you open to learning, experiencing, and doing?

❖ Bo': Exodus 10:1–13:16

No doubt about it, Pharaoh has a problem. He has got to be one of the slowest learners in all of world history. Because Pharaoh's heart continues to be hardened, and because his stubbornness persists, God continues to bring plagues upon Egypt. This portion features the plagues of locusts, darkness, and, the worst of them all, the death of the firstborn. At that point, Pharaoh finally relents and lets the Israelites go.

God tells Moses and Aaron that they will depart from Egypt in the first month, and that on the tenth day of that month each Israelite household should acquire a lamb. At twilight on the fourteenth day, each household should slaughter their lamb, putting some of its blood on the doorposts so that their houses are spared the plague of the death of the firstborn. The Israelites must also eat unleavened bread (matzah) for seven days.

These observances—the sacrifice of the lamb and the eating of matzah—will become important parts of the festival of Pesach. The Israelites are further told to consecrate their firstborn to God, as a further remembrance of their departure from Egypt.

Summary

ᚻ Pharaoh still stubbornly refuses to let the Israelites go. The final plagues of locusts, darkness, and the death of the firstborn come upon the Egyptians. (10:12–11:10)

ᚻ God commands Moses to establish the festival of Pesach. (12:1–23) ᵽ The Israelites are commanded to tell their children about the meaning of Pesach—which means telling them about the meaning of freedom itself. (12:24–27)

ᵽ God gives Moses the laws of the Pesach sacrifice. (12:43–49)

The Big Ideas

ᵽ **Jews must be a distinct people.** That is why the final act of liberation for the Israelites is to sacrifice a lamb. The lamb was one of Egypt's most important gods. Publicly slaughtering the lamb was how the Israelites would declare that they did not worship that god, and, by doing that, the Israelites had no choice but to leave Egypt.

ᵽ **Rituals help us remember important ideas and keep them alive.** Rituals help us feel that we, personally, are part of Jewish history. Whether or not the biblical account of the Exodus is historically accurate, when we remember it we relearn moral lessons that have shaped human history.

ᵽ **Education is one of Judaism's most important values.** It guarantees that Judaism will be passed down through the generations. Asking questions, as we do at the Passover seder, is the most important part of learning.

ᵽ **When we celebrate, we must remember those who are poor or are without family.** That is why the Torah commands Jews to join together with other families that cannot afford their own lamb for the Pesach sacrifice. Even though we do not sacrifice animals anymore, all our celebrations should remind us that there is a world beyond ourselves.

Divrei Torah

WHY DO YOU HAVE TO KILL THE EGYPTIAN GOD?

As many scholars have noted, the plagues that struck Egypt during the Exodus can be interpreted as being assaults on the various gods of Egypt: the Nile, the sun, even to the firstborn of Pharaoh. But after the "official" plagues have ended, one more Egyptian god will come under assault. "Speak to the whole community of Israel and say that on the tenth of this month [the first month, Nisan] each of them shall take a lamb to a family, a lamb to a household" (12:3). God told the Israelites to acquire a *lamb*—which is not just an animal, but an Egyptian animal god.

In other words, it seems as if God is telling the Israelites to get themselves an Egyptian lamb-god and therefore buy into the Egyptian religious system—which means becoming good Egyptians.

The Israelites must live with their lamb-gods for four days. That's enough time to become comfortable with their new gods. It is also enough time for their Egyptian neighbors to have seen them with their new gods and to have therefore assumed that the Israelites are (finally) prepared to fit into Egyptian life and to stop being outsiders.

Not so fast.

The Israelites then slaughter their lambs. They dab the blood on the doorposts of their houses—in a place where everyone can see it. That is why a midrash portrays God as understanding that "as long as the Israelites worship the Egyptian gods, they shall not be redeemed. Withdraw your hands from idolatry and take a lamb, and therefore slaughter the gods of Egypt and make the Passover."

The slaughtering of the lambs, therefore, did not only symbolize physical freedom and national redemption. It was also an outward manifestation of freedom from Egyptian idolatry—and, with that, the Israelites are ready to truly make their break with Egypt. As Rabbi Lawrence Kushner has written about the ill-fated lamb: "Come tomorrow and its blood is on our door, we leave with Moses, or they will surely kill us. A slave who can kill the master's god is no longer a slave. And if we are afraid to kill the lamb, then we may not leave with Moses."

Today, killing lambs (especially since they are no longer worshiped as gods) is not our idea of a good time, nor is it a symbolic act. But when our ancestors made their courageous break for freedom they had to break with every aspect of their enslavement. This has always been one of the great things about the Jews: the willingness to stand apart and to be different. Why? To make a better world.

DID THE EXODUS REALLY HAPPEN?
DOES IT MATTER?

One of the most famous composers in American history was George Gershwin. He was also Jewish. In one of his most famous songs, we find the words: "The stuff that you're liable to find in the Bible, they ain't neces-sarily so." Gershwin had a good sense of humor. The melody of "It Ain't Necessarily So" sounds very similar to the traditional Torah blessing!

So is it "necessarily so" that the Israelites went forth from Egypt? Did the Exodus really happen? Well, as the song says, not necessarily.

First, the Torah says that six hundred thousand men (not count-ing the women and the children) left Egypt and then wandered across the Sinai Desert to get to the Land of Israel. But archeologists have not found a trace of evidence that anyone was ever there! And, if you put together all those who supposedly came out of Egypt, they would have created a long line of people that would have stretched all the way from Egypt to Israel!

What about in the Land of Israel itself? Here, again, archeologists tell us that there is no evidence for a huge group of people entering the Land of Israel at that time. If that had been the case, then, at the very least, there would have been a sudden, vast increase in the amount of pottery that was made, but archeologists have found no evidence for increased amounts of pottery. So, the general opinion among arche-ologists and historians is that while there were some Israelite slaves who left Egypt, most Israelites lived in the Land of Israel for many generations. They never left and they never had to return.

On the other hand: what nation would ever invent a history of it-self that says that it started out in slavery? In the words of modern scholar Eli Barnavi: "It is highly improbable that a nation would choose to invent for itself a history of slavery as an explanation for its ori-gins." And, as an old saying goes, "The absence of evidence is not ev-idence of absence." A group of nomads, even a large one, could have traveled across the great desert and, after these thousands of years, hardly left a trace.

The Torah is probably not one hundred percent historically accu-rate. But does that really matter? Whether or not it happened just the way that the Torah says, the Exodus from Egypt teaches us about the value of human freedom and of human hope. And not just for Jews. "In every generation, a person [not: "a Jew"] should see himself or herself as if he or she had personally gone forth from Egypt, states the Passover Haggadah.

We are probably not going to come to a definitive answer to the question "Did the Exodus really happen?" That's all right. We can live with not knowing for sure. No matter what the archeologists and historians finally conclude, the Exodus is part of our heritage and how we view our origins and character. The Exodus, our journey from slavery to freedom, politically and spiritually, didn't just happen once in history. It happens within each of us. And it happens all the time.

Connections

ᚦ Do you believe that the plagues were necessary in order for the Israelites to be able to leave Egypt? What alternatives could have been possible?

ᚦ What are the most important questions that you have about Judaism, or about life?

ᚦ How has Jewish education been important to you and your family?

ᚦ What kind of Pesach memories does your family have? Has it been a memorable holiday for you and your family? What does it mean to you?

ᚦ Do you believe that the Exodus really happened? Do you think that it matters if it did or not? In what way have you personally felt that you have gone out of Egypt? What is your Egypt? (For example, breaking a bad habit, overcoming a difficulty at school, etc.)

❖ Be-shallaḥ: Exodus 13:17–17:16

You'd have thought that Pharaoh would have finally understood what was going on. The plagues that had devastated Egypt should have been enough of a lesson in how not to mess with God or the Israelites. But, no. As the Israelites finally escape Egypt, Pharaoh changes his mind and he sends his armies to pursue them.

Coming to the Sea of Reeds (sometimes called the Red Sea), the Israelites are faced with almost certain death, until God splits the sea for them and they walk through the parted waters. The sea closes back on the Egyptian armies and they drown.

This miracle prompts the Israelites to sing the "Song at the Sea" (which is why the Shabbat associated with this Torah reading is also called Shabbat Shirah, the "Shabbat of song"). But this miracle doesn't succeed in making the Israelites happy; soon, they are complaining about the lack of food and water. To make matters worse, the Amalekites attack the Israelites in the desert—a battle that the Israelites actually win.

Summary

- ᵼ There are no shortcuts through the wilderness! God takes the Israelites the long way. Moses carries the bones of Joseph with him, remembering that Joseph's brothers had promised to bury him in the Land of Israel. (13:17–19)
- ᵼ Pharaoh and his armies pursue the Israelites, and they come to the Sea of Reeds (sometimes also referred to as "the Red Sea"). The sea parts, the Israelites march through the parted waters, the waters come back together again to drown the Egyptian soldiers, and the Israelites sing. Moses's sister, Miriam, leads the women in joyous song. (14:10–15:21)
- ᵼ There is a shortage of food, and the people complain. (16:1–11)
- ᵼ God rains manna—a white, flaky substance—on the Israelites. They gather the manna, with a double portion for Shabbat. (16:13–36)
- ᵼ There is a shortage of water, and the people keep complaining. God tells Moses to hit a rock so that it will produce water. It works! (17:1–7)
- ᵼ Amalek attacks the Israelites. They fight the Amalekites, and the Israelites defeat them. (17:8–16)

The Big Ideas

- ᵼ **The road to freedom is rarely short and easy.** It always seems to have twists and turns and even U-turns. This is true not only for the Jews, but also for other groups that have fought for freedom.
- ᵼ **In our personal journeys we always travel with pieces of our past.** That is why the Israelites took the bones of Joseph with them. They knew that his final resting place could not be Egypt, but rather the Land of Israel.
- ᵼ **The parting of the sea was the miracle that "created" the Jewish people.** True—there are scientific explanations for what hap-

pened at the sea; perhaps it was a tidal wave or some other natural occurrence. But its parting is a symbol; it mirrors the moment of creation, when God separates the upper waters from the lower waters. At the moment that God parts the waters, the Jewish people is created.

ᵬ **Women have their own voices in Judaism.** Those voices have always been important and cherished, even when it has seemed that they are barely audible. That is the lesson of Miriam's involvement in the Song at the Sea.

ᵬ **Jews love to complain!** That is true throughout Jewish history and even and especially in Jewish humor. It starts right here. Complaining is a constant theme in the story of the Exodus and the wandering in the wilderness.

Divrei Torah
WHY NOT THE EASY WAY?

Time for an old Jewish joke. "Why did it take the Israelites forty years to go through the wilderness and get to the Land of Israel? Because Moses refused to stop and ask for directions!"

That's sort of how the Torah portion begins. It tells us that God did not lead the people by way of the land of the Philistines, "although it was nearer." Imagine that—if the Israelites had traveled across the land of the Philistines (or, to be more precise, the land that the ancient Philistines would someday occupy), across the top of the Sinai Peninsula, they would have gotten to the Land of Israel in almost no time at all.

So, why didn't God take the Israelites the easy, short way? The text says that the people would have been afraid "when they see war," which probably means that those borders were heavily fortified. Or perhaps it was precisely *because* it was the easy way. That's how Rashi, the great medieval commentator, understood it: "It was easy to return by that road to Egypt." God wanted to teach the Israelites the importance of perseverance. God was afraid that they might return; if they had an easy time of it, it would be more tempting to turn back if things got rough.

When we travel, we usually like going the shortest way; that's why we have a GPS. But that's not the way it is in real life. There's a modern expression that we sometimes use: "No pain, no gain." It is true of athletes, great artists and musicians, and anyone who has had to work for something. If the task is too easy, then we won't value it.

Rabbi Steven Moskowitz writes: "Too often we want the shortcut. Too many students for example read *Spark Notes* rather than reading *Hamlet*. The long, hard work, the struggle, is the greatest lesson and provides the most lasting meaning. You can only appreciate Shakespeare and what he teaches us about life if you read Shakespeare."

What is true about appreciating great literature is certainly true of national liberation movements. Those movements never have it easy. Think of the struggles that the Reverend Martin Luther King Jr. had to endure (and it's a sweet coincidence that this Torah portion often comes right around his birthday). The title of Nelson Mandela's autobiography is *No Easy Walk to Freedom*. It was true of the struggle of Soviet Jews to gain their freedom. And it was definitely true of the story of Israel and Zionism.

And it is almost definitely true of kids who are preparing to become bar and bat mitzvah! It's not easy. It's not meant to be. It probably shouldn't be. Because if it were, how much would we value it?

One last thing: the long way through the wilderness includes stopping at Mount Sinai, where the Israelites will receive the Ten Commandments. The long way includes the encounter with God.

GET READY TO JUMP!

Whenever you think of the meaning of faith, consider this: every time you jump into a swimming pool, you have faith that since the last time you jumped into the pool the laws of physics have not changed. Every time you board an airplane the same thing happens. You have faith that the pilot knows how to fly the plane and that planes can still fly through the air.

But those examples are about things that have already happened in the past. What about those things that you have never encountered yet? Would you have the same kind of faith?

That was precisely what happened when the Israelites got to the shores of the Sea of Reeds. The Egyptians were behind them, the sea was in front of them. Either way they turned, there was the probability of death, either by the sword or by drowning. What should they do?

Here is where the richness of the Jewish tradition comes alive. What happened at the edge of the water? Some ancient sages said that each tribe demanded the privilege of going in first. Others said quite the opposite: each tribe demanded that the others go in first. Like we've already learned, in this Torah portion it would seem that the Israelites discovered the fine art of complaining—and, some say, that is what they all did at the shores of the sea.

Except for one man. As a midrash says, "When Israel stood by the sea, the tribes stood arguing with each other, one saying, 'I will go in first,' and the other saying, 'I will go in first.' At that moment, Nahshon ben Amminadab of the tribe of Judah jumped into the waves of the sea and waded in." And at that moment, the waters parted and the people were able to walk through to safety and freedom.

This is what we sometimes call "a leap of faith." Nahshon chose not to be afraid. Because he jumped, the tradition says that he would be the ancestor of King David, and he would have the honor of being the first person to bring an offering at the dedication of the Tabernacle.

Rabbi Sid Schwarz teaches: "Maybe you don't believe that the miracle happened as the midrash suggests it did. But you don't have to. Every great moment in history, every person who achieves greatness, every person who conquers the fears that may have paralyzed them for years has that Nachshon moment."

Even in an age in which God splits seas, the Torah places tremendous emphasis on human beings taking the first step. God will not save the Israelites unless and until they are willing to go forward into the unknown. The sea will not split until someone is ready to proceed. It is only once the Israelites act, boldly and dauntlessly, that God's miraculous intervention sets in.

Connections

ᵬ What do you think happened at the sea? Was it a miracle, or a natural occurrence? What have been some "miracles" in your life? What were they like?

ᵬ When have you imitated Nahshon? When have you jumped right into something? What were your feelings before you did it? What were your feelings afterward?

- Who are the men or women in your (extended) family who have taken a risk in their lives or in their careers? What did they do and why?
- Who are some people in history who have imitated Nahshon?
- What are some examples of things that have taken time and effort in your life?

❖ Yitro: Exodus 18:1–20:23

Moses never really had a whole lot of father love in his life. He never knew his real father. That is why Moses's relationship with his father-in-law, Jethro, the priest of Midian, is so important. Moses and Jethro reunite, and Jethro is sincerely happy about everything that has happened to the Israelites. Loving father figure that he is, he notices that Moses is working too hard, and he tells him what he must do to "lighten up."

Moses then has another reunion with an old "friend"—God. In one of the most dramatic scenes in the entire Bible, God descends onto Mount Sinai and proclaims the Ten Commandments to the Jewish people. It would be the first, and last, time that God personally reveals teachings to the Israelites.

Summary

- Moses's father-in-law, Jethro, takes great delight in everything that has happened to the Israelites. He then gives Moses some "management advice," telling him to appoint judges to decide small cases and to only judge the big cases himself. In this way, Jethro not only "invents" the ancient Jewish judicial system, the Sanhedrin; he also plants the seeds for the modern Supreme Court system. (18:1–24)
- God tells Moses that the Jewish people must be "a kingdom of priests and a holy nation." This means that they are to have a special role in human history—to teach the world and to model the idea of holiness. (19:3–9)
- In preparation for the revelation of the Ten Commandments on Mount Sinai, God issues a series of instructions about how the

people should prepare, as well as warnings about the sacred nature of Mount Sinai itself. (19:11–14)

ᵗᵇ God reveals the Ten Commandments (*Aseret ha-Dibberot*) to the Israelites. The first five commandments—"I am God," no idolatry, no taking God's name in vain, observing Shabbat, honoring parents—are all about the human relationship to God. (20:1–12)

ᵗᵇ The second five commandments—not murdering, not committing adultery, not stealing, not bearing false witness, and not coveting—are all about the relationship that people have with each other. (20:13–14)

The Big Ideas

ᵗᵇ **True leaders are always open to advice from others.** Moses was perhaps the greatest leader that the Jewish people ever had. And yet, he did not know everything about leadership. He needed his father-in-law, Jethro, to teach him how to improve his leadership practices. In whatever we do, it is important to hear and learn from constructive feedback.

ᵗᵇ **To be the Chosen People entails responsibilities.** Throughout Jewish history, Jews (and others) have wondered about what it means to be God's Chosen People. The Torah portion makes it very clear that the Jews are supposed to be a teaching people and a learning people: to teach ethics and holiness to the world, and to be a model for how a life of holiness can be lived.

ᵗᵇ **Holiness means boundaries.** When God prepares the Israelites for the moment of revelation at Mount Sinai, God tells them (among other things) not to come close to the mountain, and to set boundaries around it. This is a good, basic rule of religious life: everything that is holy has boundaries set around it. The Sabbath is set off from the other days of the week; marriage is different from other relationships.

ᵗᵇ **Religious life is, first and foremost, the way that we relate to God.** That is the meaning of the first five teachings. They are all about the human relationship with God. But "honoring your parents" is among these five—as if to say that when we honor our parents, we simultaneously honor God.

ⓑ **Religious life is also the way that we relate to other people.** The "people" teachings in the Ten Commandments—not murdering, not committing adultery, not stealing, not bearing false witness, and not coveting—form the basis of civil society. Most of these acts are in fact illegal. (Coveting isn't illegal, and it is the only "thought crime" on the list).

Divrei Torah
THE GREATEST TEACHER OF THEM ALL

Here's a great Yiddish word: *mensch*—a decent, ethical human being. Time to meet the greatest mensch of the Torah. He is Jethro, the father-in-law of Moses. And the interesting thing is that he's not even Jewish.

Here is how we meet him: Moses rescues Jethro's seven daughters from some shepherds who are harassing them at a well. They go home and tell their father about it, and he orders them to bring this stranger home for a meal. Moses marries one of Jethro's daughters, Zipporah (2:16–22).

The next time we meet Jethro is in this week's Torah portion. Jethro hears of the wonderful things that God has done for Israel, and so he brings his daughters and his grandsons to Moses. Jethro also brings offerings to God. Some ancient sages, therefore, thought that Jethro had actually joined the Jewish people. The Rabbis in a midrash imagine God saying: "I draw near; I do not drive away. Just as I brought Jethro close and did not drive him away, so, too, when someone comes to you to convert for the sake of heaven, you must bring that person close and do not drive him away."

We don't know if Jethro actually joined the Jewish people. But he was, in fact, Moses's teacher. When he sees Moses judging every legal case on his own, he realizes that Moses is going to burn out, and so he suggests a way of developing a system of lower courts and higher courts—similar to the United States court system. Jethro figures it out on his own—he doesn't need God to tell him how to do it. To quote Rabbi Shai Held: "Just before the revelation of divine guidance for how Israel ought to live, Exodus stops to teach a lesson: there is wisdom among the non-Jews, and there is wisdom to be found through the use of reason to evaluate a situation and the needs of the moment."

But there is still one big question about the relationship between Moses and Jethro. What was the secret of their bond?

Moses never really knew his real father, Amram. And as for Pharaoh, his adopted grandfather (remember, Pharaoh's daughter had adopted Moses)—he probably wasn't the most fun father in the world.

Jethro was the father figure in Moses's life. The Torah keeps referring to Jethro as "Moses's father-in-law." This is quite possibly the most precious relationship in Moses's life, given the strained relationships with his wife and siblings. Without his father-in-law, Moses would have been in trouble.

God says that Israel will become a "kingdom of priests" (19:6) Consider that the only priest the Israelites knew, their role model, would have been Jethro, who had helped and taught Moses. To be a kingdom of priests means that the Jews are to be a kingdom of "Jethros" —a kingdom of helpers and teachers to the world.

CARING FOR GOD, CARING FOR PEOPLE— IT IS ALL THE SAME

Some people think that the real meaning of Judaism is to pay attention to God through ritual. Other people think that the real meaning of Judaism is to pay attention to other people through acting ethically.

Guess what? They are one and the same. When God gave Moses the Ten Commandments, the first five commandments—the "God commandments"—were on the first tablet. The second five commandments—the "people commandments"—were on the second tablet. But it turns out that you can actually read the commandments across the two tablets, linking the first and the sixth, the second and the seventh, and so forth. And when you do that, something interesting happens.

Check it out: "I the Lord am your God . . ." (the first commandment) links to "You shall not murder" (the sixth commandment). Because everyone is made in God's image, anyone who murders another person has destroyed the divine image in that person.

"You shall not make for yourself a sculptured image . . ." (the commandment against idolatry—the second commandment) links to "You shall not commit adultery" (the seventh commandment).

Constantly looking for new partners is like worshiping other gods. To violate one sacred relationship is tantamount to violating the other sacred relationship.

"You shall not swear falsely by the name of the Lord your God . . ." (the third commandment) links to "You shall not steal" (the eighth commandment). Why? Because those who steal will always swear that they didn't do so!

"Remember the sabbath day and keep it holy . . ." (the fourth commandment) links with "You shall not bear false witness against your neighbor" (the ninth commandment)—because if you violate the Sabbath, it is as if you are bearing false witness against God, saying that God did not rest after six days of creation.

And then the best for last. "Honor your father and mother . . ." (the fifth commandment) links to "You shall not covet your neighbor's house . . ." Really? What's the connection there? Because if you covet things, you are saying that you wish you were richer—which is another way of saying that you wish you had been born into a different, wealthier family.

To quote the writer Dennis Prager: "Properly understood and applied, the Ten Commandments are really all humanity needs to make a beautiful world. . . . If people and countries lived by the Ten Commandments, all the great moral problems would disappear."

Connections

ᚦ Have you ever gotten constructive feedback from someone? Have you ever given constructive feedback? What are some examples? How did you grow from either experience? What do you think should be the rules of giving feedback and advice to people?

ᚦ What are some contemporary idols or false gods? How are they worshiped? What is wrong with worshiping them?

ᚦ What does it mean to take God's name in vain? What is wrong with doing that?

ᚦ Some people translate the sixth commandment as "You shall not kill." But it is far more accurate to translate it as "You shall not murder." Is there a difference between killing and murder? Is killing ever justified?

ḃ Why is it important to observe Shabbat? How does your family observe it?

ḃ Why is it important to honor our parents? How is honoring them different from loving, or even liking, them?

ḃ What is wrong with stealing? Has anyone ever stolen something from you? (Remember: not everything that gets stolen is an actual "thing.") What did it feel like?

ḃ What is wrong with coveting? What have you coveted? Did you get what you wanted? What have you learned from that experience?

❖ Mishpatim: Exodus 21:1–24:18

All the biblical stories so far in the Torah have been nice, but now it is time to create a Jewish society. This parashah is also known as "the book of the covenant." It is the first body of Torah legislation, and it is mostly concerned with how Israelite society should function. Some of the laws will seem strange, and even dangerous, to modern ears. That is because they are rooted in ancient Middle Eastern laws. Other laws in this portion are still relevant today.

But here is the basic point: the Israelites have been freed not just from Egyptian slavery, but also from worship of the Egyptian gods. Once, they had worked for Pharaoh, and now they work for God.

Summary

ḃ Hebrew slaves must be set free in the seventh year. (21:2–6)

ḃ If someone injures another person, the penalty must be "life for life, eye for eye, tooth for tooth." (21:23)

ḃ You must act justly and kindly toward strangers in society, as well as toward widows and orphans. (22:20–23)

ḃ You must return the lost property of your enemies, and you must help their animals if they are struggling under a burden. (23:4–5)

ḃ You shall not boil a kid in its mother's milk. (23:19)

The Big Ideas

ḃ **Social change is a process.** The kind of slavery that Mishpatim describes is very different from the brutal slavery that the Israelites endured, and that other peoples endured, and, in many places, still endure. It is more like being an indentured servant—a temporary arrangement in which someone works off his or her debt. The Torah might want to get rid of slavery altogether, but apparently it cannot do so all at once. It starts that process by strictly limiting the amount of time that slaves can serve their masters.

ᚦ **Judaism is not about seeking revenge.** The notion of "eye for eye and tooth for tooth" is one of the Bible's most misunderstood ideas. It doesn't mean that you can go around poking out people's eyes or pulling out their teeth. Rather, it means that the punishment and the penalty must always be appropriate for the crime or the damage that has taken place.

ᚦ **Caring for strangers is one of the most important teachings in the entire Torah.** This teaching is so important that it is repeated no less than thirty-six times—more than any other teaching—and twice in this Torah portion alone! The stranger (*ger*) is not only someone you don't know; it is anyone who is not an Israelite and yet lives within your society and lives by its rules. The reason why Jews must treat strangers with kindness and justice is because they themselves were strangers in the land of Egypt.

ᚦ **Judaism believes in watching out for another person's property—even if that person is an enemy.** This is a major part of the Torah's emphasis on justice. We might not like someone, but we are not allowed to be cruel to that person, or the person's belongings. In particular, we have to help people find things that they have lost.

ᚦ **The Torah cares about what Jews eat, like mixing milk and meat.** There are numerous dietary laws in the Torah such as permitting and forbidding certain animals, and not eating leavened products during Passover. Not boiling a kid in its mother's milk is repeated three times in the Torah, and yet it is one of the most baffling rules. The reasoning behind it is somewhat mysterious, but it might be connected to the necessity of separating life (symbolized by milk) from death (symbolized by meat).

Divrei Torah

WHY NO CHEESEBURGERS?

"You may not boil a kid in its mother's milk" is one of the Bible's more puzzling laws. It has come to mean no milk and meat together in the same dish, or in the same meal—or for some Jews, within hours of eating. It has also come to mean that there should be separate dishes for milk and meat. These are part of the Rabbinic laws of kashrut, or keeping kosher.

Perhaps these laws arose because Jews wanted to maintain their difference from other people—even and especially concerning food. The medieval philosopher Maimonides, who was also a physician, thought that eating milk and meat together was unhealthy. But he was also sure that mixing milk and meat was a Canaanite ritual: "Meat boiled in milk is too filling. But it is also connected with idolatry, perhaps being part of a pagan festival." Maimonides was probably correct. Ancient Canaanite documents actually specify that there was a ritual in which a kid was slaughtered in milk.

But there are other, ethical reasons for the practice of separating milk and meat. To cook a kid in its mother's milk is just plain cruel. The Torah cares about animals' feelings. Later, in Deut. 22:6–7, we will learn that if you are going to take eggs from a nest, you have to shoo the mother bird away to spare her feelings. The contemporary teacher Abraham Joshua Heschel teaches: "The goat provides man with the single most perfect food he possesses: milk. How ungrateful and callous we would be to take the child of an animal to whom we are so indebted and cook it in its mother's very milk."

But there is yet another reason—and it might be one of the most important things that Judaism has ever taught. Meat represents death; after all, the animal is dead. Milk represents life because a mother feeds it to her offspring. Judaism believes in the separation of life and death, and so this might be why Jews traditionally do not mix meat and milk. It may also be why Leviticus prohibits the mixing of wool and cotton in the same garment: wool comes from a lamb, which is not killed when it is sheared; cotton comes from a flax plant, which dies in the process. Judaism also prohibits trying to talk with the dead or commune with the spirits; the dead are dead and we are alive, and the realms of life and death should not mix.

Whew, that's pretty heavy. So let's lighten up by ending this serious discussion with a joke. Moses is on Mount Sinai, receiving the Torah. God says to him: "You shall not boil a kid in its mother's milk." Moses asks: "Does that mean we should not eat cheeseburgers?" God repeats: "You shall not boil a kid in its mother's milk." Moses then asks: "Does that mean we should wait six hours between eating milk and eating dairy?" God repeats: "You shall not boil a kid in its mother's milk." Moses then asks: "Does this mean we should have separate kitchenware for meat and for dairy?" At this, God yells at Moses: "OK, HAVE IT YOUR WAY!"

The point is clear. God told Moses what to do, but Moses had to figure out how to interpret the commandment. That's Judaism—a living interpretation of God's words.

YES, TALK TO STRANGERS

What is one of the first basic rules that kids hear from their parents? "Don't talk to strangers!" American culture wants us to be afraid of strangers. They could harm children. They could be immigrants, coming to take our jobs. Science fiction films are obsessed with aliens, who are usually terrible and threatening (though, like E.T., occasionally loveable). There is a word for the fear of strangers: xenophobia.

But, as is true with many things, Judaism offers the world a different point of view. Yes, some strangers and foreigners are hostile. Jews know this well, for, in Jewish history, this was true more often than not. So you might think that Jews would be wary of strangers and preach distrust. But quite the contrary: Judaism teaches that not every stranger is an object of fear and scorn, and, what is more, we need to be concerned about the stranger.

Ancient Jewish legislation offers us the possibility of an entire class of people who are the subject of our compassion and protection—the *ger* (a non-Israelite who accepted some of the basic commandments of the Torah, that is, who agreed to be law-abiding "almost" citizen). As a reward for doing this, the *ger* could reside in the Land of Israel and enjoy many, if not most, of the privileges of citizenship afforded the

Jewish people. As the object of our concern, the *ger* becomes part of a group that includes the Levite, the fatherless child, and the widow.

What do they all have in common? Their absolute vulnerability and their dependence on public goodwill. The Torah mandates love—*V'ahavta, v'ahavtem*—only three times. The order is remarkable. First, "love your fellow as yourself" (Lev. 19:18); then, "love the stranger as yourself" (Lev. 19:34); and, only later, God—"You shall love the Lord your God with all your heart and with all your soul and with all your might" (Deut. 6:5).

Our ancestors needed to hear this because in the ancient world being kind to strangers was hardly a no brainer. Life in the desert could be very difficult. Rashi understood the commandment about loving strangers this way: "If you oppress him, he can oppress you in return and say to you: 'You too are descended from strangers.' Don't complain about a blemish in your friend when you have the identical problems." Remember: the Jews were once strangers in Egypt.

When people are mistreated, there is a tendency for them to become insensitive to other people's suffering. You might want to say: "Hey, no one helped us when we were slaves, so we are not going to stick our necks out for others either!" That could influence the way you feel about, say, immigrants. But in the words of Bible scholar Nehama Leibowitz: "A history of alienation and slavery, the memory of your own humiliation is by itself no guarantee that you will not oppress the stranger in your own country once you have gained independence and left it all behind you." So the Torah has to spell it out: Learn the right lesson. Have empathy. Don't become an oppressor yourself.

The positive attitude toward strangers was so important that for much of its history Judaism was open to converts. During the Roman period many non-Jews wanted to learn about Judaism, and in those postbiblical times we have accounts that entire synagogues were filled with *yirei elohim* ("God fearers," people who believed in God), who, while not officially Jewish, flocked to learn Torah and to observe some Jewish customs.

That's why the ancient Rabbis interpreted the commandment to be kind to strangers to also mean to be kind to converts—and to welcome those who want to explore Judaism and consider joining the

Jewish people. Today, like then, our doors—all our doors—should be wide open to the stranger who is needy and to those who are curious about Judaism.

Connections

ᵺ Have you had any experience with the kosher rule of not mixing milk and meat? How do you feel about it?

ᵺ How do you feel about strangers? Have you ever tried to help a stranger? What would be some guidelines you could give people about helping strangers?

ᵺ What has been the historic American attitude toward strangers? What do you think it is today?

ᵺ Have you ever lost anything? What was it? How did that make you feel? Have you ever returned a lost object to someone? What was that experience like? How did it feel?

ᵺ Do you know anyone who has converted to Judaism? Why did they do so? What have their experiences been like?

❖ Terumah: Exodus 25:1–27:19

This Torah portion describes the design of the ancient Tabernacle (*mishkan*, "dwelling place," or *mikdash*, "sanctuary"). The Tabernacle was a large tent that the Israelites carried with them through the wilderness. Its purpose was not only to be a place for the sacrifices, but, according to the Torah, a place where God could actually dwell in their midst.

The portion is filled with explicit instructions for constructing every aspect of the Tabernacle, including building materials and dimensions. In it was the Ark of the Covenant, which contained the tablets of the Ten Commandments.

Summary

ᵺ God tells Moses that the Israelites should bring donations for the construction of the Tabernacle and gives specific instructions about what materials to use. Some of them seem pretty predictable—gold, silver, and copper. Others, like dolphin skins, are a bit more unusual. (25:1–7)

ⷮ God tells the Israelites that the purpose of the sanctuary is so that God would have a place to dwell in their midst. God even shows Moses a plan of how the sanctuary should look. (25:8–9)

ⷮ The construction project begins with the Ark of the Covenant, where the tablets are to be kept. The ark should have permanent poles attached to it so that it can be carried. (25:10–16)

ⷮ Cherubim—mysterious, angelic figures—adorn the cover of the ark. Their wings are to be spread out, shielding the ark's cover; and the two figures must face each other. (25:17–22)

ⷮ God gives explicit instructions for the design of the menorah, the seven-branched candelabra. The details of the design remind us of a tree. (25: 31–39)

The Big Ideas

ⷮ **Religious life relies on a willing heart.** God commands the Israelites to bring construction materials as voluntary offerings. Yes, there is a small contradiction here. How can you be commanded to bring something, yet still do so voluntarily—"from every person whose heart so moves him" (25:2)? Yes, God wants us to do certain acts, but we still have to *want* to do those things.

ⷮ **The purpose of the Tabernacle is for God to be able to dwell in among the Israelites.** At the Exodus from Egypt, and at the giving of the Ten Commandments, the Israelites clearly felt God's presence. But God knew that it would be very difficult for them to feel that presence all the time, so God commands the creation of the Tabernacle. This way they would always remember that God is with them.

ⷮ **Judaism is portable.** That is why the ark had to have poles attached to it. Wherever Jews have lived, even and especially when they did not have a Tabernacle or Temple in Jerusalem, they have been able to "carry" Judaism with them.

ⷮ **Children are important to Judaism.** In that sense, the cherubim are a powerful symbol of what Judaism is all about. They are usually imagined as children, who represent hope for the future. But they also are turned toward each other, reminding us that Judaism says we must see each other and we must care for each other.

℔ **The menorah is Judaism's most ancient and most enduring symbol.** The biblical description of the menorah seems to indicate that it resembled a tree, with branches and blossoms. The menorah, therefore, represents a living, growing, blossoming organism—much like the Tree of Life, which is Torah.

Divrei Torah

WHAT WERE THE CHERUBIM
(AND WHY DO THEY MATTER?)

Here is an odd coincidence. Often, Terumah coincides with the American holiday of Valentine's Day. Valentine's Day cards often feature cupids, with bows and arrows. They always look like small, cute children. The word that we use to describe them, and any cute child, is "cherubic."

This brings us to one of those mysteries of the Torah. What, exactly, were the cherubim that adorned the cover of the ark in the ancient Tabernacle, and later in the Holy of Holies of the Temple? They must have been important if they adorned the ark, but what are we to make of these half-human, half-angelic images?

We often imagine that the cherubim had children's faces as well as wings. The origins of the cherubim are buried somewhere in ancient Middle Eastern mythology. Winged creatures stood guard outside the gates of ancient Assyrian and Babylonian temples, and that is probably where the Torah got the idea to have them adorn the ark. In fact, the cherubim show up in other places in the Bible—guarding the Tree of Life in the Garden of Eden (Gen. 3:24) and even carrying God's throne! (Ps. 18:10).

Now that we understand their origin, a big question remains. Why were they over the ark? What were they supposed to represent?

First, let's look at the word that describes how the wings of the cherubim are spread out—*sokh'khim*. It is from the same root as the sukkah, the hut that the Israelites dwelt in during the festival of Sukkot. Among other things, the sukkah represents God's protection of the Israelites. And that is what the spread-out wings represent as well— God's protection of the Jewish people.

Second, notice how the cherubim *stood*—with their faces turned toward each other. This symbolizes the ideal of friendship and relation-ship. To be a friend, you have to really be able to see the other person, to see that person's face and to look into their eyes.

A Hasidic commentary says: "A Jew should stretch forth his or her 'wings,' always striving to move upward to higher levels. But at the same time, his or her face has to face the other's face. You must notice your fellow's distress and always seek to help."

The faces of the cherubim may have been like that of children—a little boy and a little girl, which reminds us that God created humanity as male and female. How did they get to be children? It comes from a pun: "Rav Abbahu said: 'Cherub means "like a child," for in Babylon they call a child *ravia*.'" So, the Hebrew way to say "cherub" is *keruv*, and that creates an Aramaic pun—*k'ravia*, "like a child." And how did children wind up on top of the ark? Children represent youth, inno-cence, future, and hope. When we face each other, and strive to soar as if with wings to our full potential, with the Torah as a guide, it is like being in the Holy of Holies.

WHY DO WE EVEN NEED A TABERNACLE?

Every so often, you hear people complaining about "organized reli-gion." Often, their complaints focus on religious buildings, like syna-gogues, churches, and mosques. "Why do we need these buildings?" they ask. "Why can't we just pray in our own heart? Can't God hear my prayers anywhere?"

When you look at the book of Exodus, you realize something: the building of the Tabernacle is arguably the most important thing that happens in this biblical book—maybe even more important than the Exodus from Egypt and the giving of the Ten Commandments. After all, the Torah devotes far more of its words to the Tabernacle than to anything else. The Jewish thinker Franz Rosenzweig teaches: "The building of the Tabernacle was in fact the high point of the entire To-rah. In Egyptian slavery, the Israelites made buildings for the pha-raohs. Now they were privileged to perform labor for the sake of God."

But why did the Israelites even need a Tabernacle in the first place?

The people may have thought that it was only fair to do this for God. After all, God created this entire physical world as a dwelling place for us. The Israelites created the *mishkan* (the Tabernacle) as a little dwelling place for God. God created for humans; we create for God. We return the favor. And when we did that, we concretized our relationship with God—a relationship that we often describe as a partnership.

But it wasn't only a favor for God. The Israelites also needed to engage in the building of the Tabernacle—for themselves. They had just come out of a very intense period in their relationship with God. They had felt God's intimate presence during the Exodus. God had heard their cries and had seen their suffering, and God brought them out of Egypt and parted the Sea of Reeds for them.

Then the Israelites encountered God at Mount Sinai and encountered God during the giving of the Ten Commandments. It was so intense that they asked Moses not to put them through that again. So God stops speaking. Silence. The Israelites must have thought that the link between them and God had been broken. The building of the Tabernacle restored that broken connection. The medieval commentator Don Isaac Abravanel teaches: "God's intention behind the construction of the Tabernacle was to fight the idea that God had abandoned the world, and that God's throne was in heaven and remote from humanity."

So, that is the purpose of the Tabernacle (and the synagogue today)—to express gratitude, to encounter each other, and to remind people of God's presence.

Connections

ẗ Is there a contradiction between God telling us to do something and our wanting to do it?

ẗ Why do you think God needed a Tabernacle? Do you think God needs a place to "live?" Where do you think God "lives?"

ẗ Do you agree that the cherubim should have looked like children? What other kinds of human (or even nonhuman) figures would you have put over the ark In what way has Judaism been portable?

ẗ What are those moments when you feel that God is present in your synagogue? In your own heart? In nature? Where else and when else have you felt God's presence?

❖ Tetsavveh: Exodus 27:20–30:10

In the last Torah portion we read about what the Tabernacle was supposed to look like; now let's focus on who is supposed to work in it.
Those would be the *kohanim* (priests)—the people in charge of carrying out the rituals, which were mostly sacrifices. Tetsavveh contains
detailed descriptions of the special clothing that the High Priest was
to wear, and how the priests were to have been inducted into their
sacred service to the Jewish people. The portion concludes with a description of the altar for burning incense.

Interesting fact: this is the only Torah portion in Exodus, Leviticus,
Numbers, and Deuteronomy that does not mention Moses. This fac-
toid led commentators to imagine that the reading of this Torah portion always coincides with Moses's yahrzeit (the anniversary of his
death)—as if the absence of Moses in the portion served as an advance
announcement of his death.

Summary

- ቴ The Israelites are to bring beaten olive oil that will be used to kindle the *ner tamid* (the eternal light) in the Tabernacle. (27:20–21)
- ቴ Moses has to bring his brother, Aaron, toward him for induction
  into the priesthood. The garments that Aaron and his sons are to
  wear convey dignity and honor. (28:1–3)
- ቴ These special garments include the ephod (a long vest), with a
  breast piece that was used to determine God's will, a headdress,
  and a sash. Aaron is to wear bells on the hem of his sacred garment. Both Aaron and his sons are to wear linen breeches—
  trousers—when they enter the Tent of Meeting or approach the
  altar. The idea of holy garments survives in the clothing that
  Catholic priests wear, as well as in what Mormons wear. (28:6–42)
- ቴ There are extensive and distinct procedures that have to be followed in order to consecrate the priests. These procedures include sacrificial offerings. (29:1–44)
- ቴ There are explicit instructions for the construction of an incense
  altar. The Israelites need incense so that they will not be overcome by the unpleasant odors of animal sacrifice. (30:1–10)

The Big Ideas

₺ **Judaism relies on continuity from generation to generation.** Just as there was a *ner tamid* in the ancient Tabernacle and in the ancient Temples, there is a *ner tamid* in every contemporary synagogue. This demonstrates the continuity of Jewish tradition across thousands of years.

₺ **Judaism has always recognized different models of religious leadership.** Moses and Aaron represent that diversity. Moses is the prophet and Aaron is the priest. The prophetic role is to be in direct communication with God; the priestly role is to make sure that the rituals are correctly observed. Often these roles are in conflict, just like Moses was sometimes in conflict with Aaron.

₺ **Jewish ritual grows and changes, but it always keeps pieces of the past.** The priestly garments have never disappeared. They appear, in slightly different form, as the "clothing" that is found on Torah scrolls. Even the Torah crowns and the bells that adorn them remind us of the garments of the priests.

₺ **Priests can't just jump into doing important work; there needs to be an official welcome ceremony.** The Torah requires that the priests be ushered into their sacred work with appropriate rituals in order to make them, and the Israelites, aware of the presence of God in their midst.

₺ **Judaism is not only God centered; it is also people centered.** The practical purpose of the incense in the Tabernacle was to make sure that the odor of the sacrifices did not offend the Israelites. Jewish ritual must always be concerned with the feelings of the people who are involved in it.

Divrei Torah
GOD'S "DRESS CODE"

You probably don't like dress codes that much. Most people don't. But what about uniforms? That's the subject of much of this Torah portion—the special clothing that Aaron and his sons must wear in connection with their priestly duties. The Torah states that the *kohanim* had to wear their special clothing "lest they die." Maybe just their priestly roles would have died—at least for the time being. You may have heard the expression, "Clothing makes the man." The Talmud says something similar with regard to the priests: "When they are wearing their appointed garments, they are priests; when they are not wearing their garments, they are not priests."

There are no more Jewish priests, and the garments that the priests wore are now found only on the Torah scroll. Rabbis and cantors have taken the place of the priests (leading prayers, not sacrifices!). But it is interesting that rabbis and cantors are among the few clergy in the world who don't have to wear special clothing. Some will wear robes or a tallit, but these are customs rather than requirements.

Consider what Catholic priests wear. The Torah's descriptions of Aaron's clothing directly influenced priests' clothing. Some Protestant denominations require their ministers to wear special clothing too, like white collars, when they are performing their pastoral duties. The white robes that some rabbis and cantors wear on the Days of Awe symbolize spiritual purity. But the black robes that some might wear on the Sabbath actually derive from academic robes that professors used to wear, and that faculty and students still wear during graduation exercises. Perhaps rabbis and cantors originally started to wear black robes to emphasize the role of the rabbi as a teacher. Or, maybe the black robes come from the judicial robes that judges wear—to show that rabbis must act with solemn judgment.

We wear uniforms in our own lives. Some schools require uniforms. Sports teams require uniforms. Cheerleading squads require them. Camps have special T-shirts and sweatshirts. The clothing that we wear signifies the crowd that we hang out with, the social class that we inhabit, our tastes in clothing, and even how much money we have. The labels we wear label us as well. And the clothing we wear—and the way we wear it—makes statements about our values and our identity, how we view our bodies and our sexuality.

As Rabbi Sue Levi Elwell writes: "Clothing makes a statement. Are the items you wear mass-produced, or made by hand? Are the laborers who make the garments paid a fair wage? Are you intentionally advertising a company, a brand, a designer, an attitude? Are you declaring your connection to a school, a camp, a community, a philosophy? Are you showing off your prosperity or proclaiming your modesty?"

Clothing matters. Maybe even more than we have ever thought.

A DIVISION OF LABOR

Have you ever noticed that in most synagogues there is a division of labor? Rabbis lead, teach, and counsel. Cantors sing. Jewish educators organize educational programs. Executive directors manage the synagogue. Custodians keep the synagogue clean. While there are many overlaps between these roles (cantors teach and some rabbis sing, for instance), that is the typical system.

The Torah also imagines a sacred division of labor—between the priest and the prophet. Aaron is the first High Priest of the Israelites, and Moses, of course, is the prophet. A midrash says that Moses actually would have wanted to become the High Priest, but God told him to appoint someone else. You can imagine how disappointed Moses was. "God said to him: 'Go and appoint Me a High Priest.' Moses replied: 'Lord of the Universe! From which tribe shall I appoint him?' God replied: 'From the tribe of Levi.' Moses was glad, saying, 'At least he will be from my tribe!'"

The priests were in charge of the rituals of the Jewish people, making sure that the sacrifices were done correctly. The prophets, however, were God's spokespeople, communicating God's will and always emphasizing justice and ethics.

But the differences in their roles go much deeper. The priests had to be from the family of Aaron. It was a hereditary position, like royalty. But prophets did not come from special families. In fact, we barely know the name of Moses's father, and his sons are not important at all. Priests have special clothing. Prophets can wear anything. Priests have to be separate from the people. Prophets live among the people.

But the contrasts are even deeper than that, and those contrasts actually define and shape Judaism. The priest's job was to get the rituals right. Those rituals had to be done correctly, and never change. This was to ensure that life would be stable and constant. The ancient priest would have resonated with the modern cliché: "What is, is." He wants things to *stay the same*.

But the prophet has a bigger vision. She or he doesn't really care that much about getting the rituals right. Their job is to remind people that rituals are worthless unless they are accompanied by acts of justice. They want to change society for the better.

In the words of the Zionist thinker Ahad Ha'Am: "A certain moral idea fills his [the prophet's] whole being. . . . His whole life is spent in fighting for this ideal with all his strength. . . . His gaze is fixed always on what ought to be in accordance with his own convictions."

Judaism needs both the priest and the prophet, because Judaism requires both stability and change. But, in the Torah, which role comes first? Moses becomes a prophet before Aaron becomes the priest.

Yes, ritual is important—but justice and ethics comes first.

Connections

ቴ What uniforms (in all senses of the word) do you wear? How are they significant?

ቴ Our Torah portion contains references to almost all the senses. How do you use your senses in your observance and appreciation of Judaism?

ቴ How would you define a modern-day prophet? Who are some of them?

ቴ Which Jewish role—the priest, who does the rituals, or the prophet, who teaches about righteousness—do you believe to be the most important? Why is this?

❖ Ki Tissa': Exodus 30:11–34:35

Things were going so well. Ki Tissa' begins with the commandment to take a census of the Israelites. This seems harmless enough. But then it all goes downhill.

Most of this Torah portion concerns the building of the Golden Calf and what happens as a result of this terrible act of betrayal. The people, impatient for Moses to return to them, look to Aaron and they demand a new god. He gives in to their wishes, with terrible results. Upon seeing the calf, Moses loses it, and smashes the tablets. Moses and God then have to "renegotiate" the covenant, and Moses gets a new set of tablets—which he helps create.

Summary

ᵼ God commands Moses to take a census of the Israelites. The purpose is to establish mandatory dues for the upkeep of the Tabernacle. There is to be absolute equality between rich and poor in the payment of this tax. (30:11–16)

ᵼ The Israelites grow impatient waiting for Moses to return from Mount Sinai with the tablets. They turn to Aaron and demand that he provide them a new god—which turns out to be the Golden Calf. (32:1–8)

ᵼ God wants to destroy the sinful Israelites and start again, by making Moses into a new nation. But Moses argues with God, stating that God's own reputation will be at stake. God had promised the Patriarchs that their offspring would be "as numerous as the stars of heaven." God listens to Moses and abandons the plan of destruction. (32:9–18)

ᵼ When Moses sees the Israelites worshiping the Golden Calf, he becomes enraged, and he breaks the tablets of the covenant. (32:19–24)

ᵼ God makes a new covenant with Moses, and this results in a new set of tablets. (32:17–34:5)

The Big Ideas

ᵼ **It is a mitzvah to support the Jewish community and its religious institutions.** This mitzvah does not depend on one's income level. Everyone should give according to his or her ability.

ᵼ **The making of the Golden Calf is the closest that Judaism comes to the idea of original sin.** It was probably the worst thing that the Israelites ever did. Idolatry still exists. We still worship false gods and make things that are not that important into things that are too important.

ᵼ **Arguing with God is an important part of the Jewish relationship with God.** When Moses argues with God, he is acting just like Abraham, who argued with God over the destruction of Sodom and Gomorrah (Genesis 18). In fact, Moses is even more successful than Abraham, because he actually persuades God not to destroy the people.

߸ **Moses has anger issues, always striking something or someone.**
Early on, Moses strikes and kills an Egyptian who was harassing an Israelite (Exod. 2:12). He struck a rock to bring forth water
(17:6; Num. 20:11). And here, he casts the tablets down in anger.
Moses, like all biblical heroes, is human. Part of being human is
feeling anger and frustration.

߸ **After the incident of the Golden Calf, Moses and God have a
new kind of encounter.** Moses gets a quick but powerful lesson
about God's inner personality. God and Moses make a new covenant, which results in a new set of tablets and a restatement of
some of the Torah's basic ritual laws. Moses learns that the covenant with God means that there is always the possibility of forgiveness and the ability to start all over again. (Exod. 33:12–34:35)

Divrei Torah

GETTING OUT OF TROUBLE

"It's not my fault!" How many times have you said this to someone?
It would be nice to believe that when we grow up we won't have to
try to make excuses for ourselves anymore. But that's not how it's going to work out. We never really outgrow the need to explain and justify our actions. We can imagine our biblical heroes never outgrow-
ing this either.

No one comes off well in the story of the Golden Calf. The Israelites
get impatient and grumpy, demanding a new god. They are like rebellious teenagers. As Rabbi Ellen Lippman writes: "Israel is coming into
its own, following the childhood of Genesis, and is on the verge of accepting adult responsibility, symbolized by the Ten Commandments.
At just that moment, the teenager pulls off one last, great rebellion,
one that will get the parents' attention." Aaron gives in to the people's
wishes. Moses loses it and breaks the tablets. Can we look at them—
the Israelites, Aaron, and Moses—a little differently? In a kinder light?

First, the Israelites. They missed Moses. They wanted someone or
something that would substitute for him—like how children use stuffed
toys to substitute for their parents. They had come out of Egypt, and
the Egyptians worshiped animal gods. Let's cut them some slack. The
worship of animal gods was precisely what they knew. An invisible

god—that was much harder to figure out. Making a golden calf was like their security blanket.

Second, Aaron. Sure, he built the calf. Maybe he was afraid that the people would rise up and kill him. But let's look more closely at the biblical text. What did Aaron think was going on? In 32:5, Aaron tells the people that the next day would be a "festival to the Lord." Did you notice that? He didn't say that the festival was for the Calf. Maybe Aaron thought that the calf was a harmless symbol and the people still had faith in God.

And, finally, Moses. It was a bad move to shatter the tablets. But can we get Moses out of trouble? Remember—the tablets contained the Ten Commandments—including and especially the commandment not to worship idols. It might be a stretch, but maybe Moses was thinking this: If I don't give them the tablets, they won't know that they shouldn't worship idols. So, I will smash the tablets, and they will be free and clear! It wasn't that Moses was angry. No, he was being compassionate.

Or, perhaps Moses didn't really smash them; he dropped them. Here's a fanciful midrash: "When God gave Moses the tablets, they carried themselves. But when Moses descended and approached the camp, and saw the calf, the writing on the tablets flew off, and the tablets became too heavy for him to carry."

As bad as the story of the Golden Calf is, if we try hard enough (or not even that hard), we can find reasons for the behavior of the key players in the story.

You don't like this way of thinking? Okay. But haven't you ever tried to justify your own actions? It's easy to rush to judgment about others, but natural to come to our own defense. Maybe we should switch that around sometimes. Can't we show some understanding for the Israelites, and for Aaron and Moses?

TAKE TWO TABLETS—PLEASE!

There are times when your computer is so screwed up that the only thing you can do is hit control-alt-delete, or reboot it. That was precisely what happened between God, Moses, and the Israelites. The Israelites had betrayed the covenant by worshiping the Golden Calf.

Moses had betrayed the covenant by shattering the tablets. Time to reboot. Moses and God renegotiate the covenant, and Moses gets (more
on this "gets" thing later) a new set of tablets.

Question: which set of tablets was better—the old, shattered set, or
the new set? It's not an easy question to answer. We are accustomed
to thinking that newer is always better, but it's not always true. Some
people, for example, really do prefer their old phones or devices to the
upgraded versions. And, yes—some people will just always want to
get something new; the American economy depends on it.

The first possibility: the first set of tablets was better. They contained
a perfect, pure text of the Torah, because God is said to have carved
that first set. God and Moses together collaborated on the second set
of tablets (see 34:1 and 34:4, where it says that Moses did the carving
and God did the inscribing). So the second set was not perfect in the
sense of being completely made by God; it was subject to the imper-
fection of the human hand. As the scholar David Weiss Halivni has
taught: "Ever since the breaking of the Tablets, we have been trying to
figure out the real meaning of the Torah that was once revealed to us."

The second possibility is that the second set was better. Why? One
explanation is that they were more complete; they contained the rest
of the Hebrew Bible, and not just the Torah (the first five books). By
some Rabbinic accounts the new tablets also contained the entire
later Rabbinic tradition, what is known as the Oral Torah. "God said
to Moses: 'Do not be distressed over the first tablets, which contained
only the Ten Commandments. In the second tablets, I am giving you
also *halakhah* [Jewish law], midrash [interpretation], and *aggadah* [leg-
ends].'" According to this understanding, the first set was just the beginning of Judaism—just the basic Ten Commandments. A very ab-
breviated Torah! The second set of tablets contained everything else.

Remember something else about the second set of tablets and how
they differed from the first set: God wrote the first set of tablets, and Moses and God, together, wrote the second set. The new tablets represent
the Jewish people's partnership with God—a partnership that emerges
because God was able to forgive not only Moses, but the Israelites as well.

One last thing: what ever happened to that first set of tablets—the
ones that Moses broke? Did they just lie there and crumble in the des-

ert? No. A well-known midrash says that Moses picked them up and put them in the ark, and carried them along with the new set of tablets.

We always travel with our past. It is very hard to give up—as well it should be.

Connections

ђ Do you agree that every Jew should have to support the Jewish community?

ђ Should synagogues have mandatory dues? Besides financial, what are other kinds of support that people can give to their synagogues and to the Jewish community?

ђ Idolatry did not disappear after the Golden Calf incident. It still exists today. How do you define idolatry? What kinds of idols do we worship today?

ђ What kind of character and inner strength did Moses need to have in order to argue with God? Do you agree with the reasoning that Moses employed in order to convince God not to destroy the Israelites? Have you ever argued with God?

ђ Do you believe that Moses should have thrown down the tablets? Have you ever had issues with anger and frustration? How have you dealt with them?

ђ Have you ever had a fight with a friend and then made up? Did you have to renegotiate the terms of your relationship? What was it like? How did it work out?

ђ Which set of tablets do you think was better? Why? What lessons can we derive from the ultimate fate of the first set of tablets? What does it mean for us to carry broken tablets as well as intact tablets? One interpretation compares the broken pieces of the tablets to elderly people who have forgotten their learning or who are suffering from dementia or Alzheimer's disease. What is this interpretation trying to teach us?

❖ Va-yakhel: Exodus 35:1–38:20

Parashat Terumah gave the instructions for the design of the Tabernacle, and Va-yakhel now follows through on those plans.

It emphasizes that the Israelites enthusiastically (we might even say too enthusiastically!) brought the materials for the building of the Tabernacle. The text singles out two Israelites, Bezalel and Oholiab, as the master craftsmen whose work went into the Tabernacle's construction.

Summary

꜀ Moses expands upon the earlier commandment regarding Shabbat, as found in the Ten Commandments. Whoever does any work shall be put to death, and kindling fire is considered a violation of Shabbat. (35:1–3)

꜀ Moses reminds the Israelites that they should bring donations for the construction of the Tabernacle, and he gives specific instructions about the materials. Moses's directions emphasize the role of the heart: gifts must come from "everyone whose heart so moves him" and those who are skilled (*chakham lev*, "wise of heart") should be involved in the project. There is a particular role for women as well—as spinners and weavers. (35:4–29)

꜀ Moses showcases the talent of Bezalel and Oholiab, who are the master craftsmen of the Tabernacle. (35:30–35)

꜀ The people bring an overabundance of gifts to the building of the Tabernacle, and their gift giving has to be stopped. (36:5–6)

The Big Ideas

꜀ **The building of the Tabernacle might have been an act of atonement for having built the Golden Calf.** It follows right after the building of the calf, and some commentators believe the purpose of the Tabernacle is for God to demonstrate that the Divine Presence is still in the midst of the people and that they need not resort to an idol.

꜀ **Shabbat and the construction of the Tabernacle seem to be linked together.** It is hardly an accident that the observance of Shabbat is mentioned in the same breath as the design of the Tabernacle. When later generations of sages tried to figure out exactly what kind of work would be prohibited on Shabbat, they decided that any kind of labor that was involved in the building of the Tabernacle would be a violation of Shabbat.

ᚻ **While the building of the Tabernacle is a mitzvah, the Israelites must contribute to its building with willing hearts.** It is not enough for God to simply demand that the Israelites do something. Their emotions have to be involved. They have to feel connected to what was going on. The text makes it clear that everyone was involved in some way. The building of the Tabernacle symbolizes the unity of the Jewish people.

ᚻ **Judaism believes that there should be sacred roles for artists and craftspeople.** Because Jews and Judaism are often associated with words and abstract thinking, it is important to remember the gifts of those who are artistically inclined and those who work with their hands. Israel's most prominent arts academy, the Bezalel Academy of Arts and Design, in Jerusalem, is named for one of the Jewish people's ancient craftsmen. It is also significant that Bezalel is from the tribe of Judah (the most powerful tribe) and Oholiab is from the tribe of Dan (the weakest tribe). In the building of the Tabernacle, the strong and the weak work together.

ᚻ **The people actually brought too much to the building of the Tabernacle.** While this would probably be every Jewish leader's greatest dream, it teaches us that too much enthusiasm for a project—even a sacred project—could become dangerous.

Divrei Torah

STOP GIVING—PLEASE!

Here's the scene: You are raising money for your youth group or your sports team. It starts with people giving you a dollar or two, and then people start coming back and giving you five dollars, then twenty dollars, then fifty dollars. You cannot believe all the money that is coming in! You start to get uneasy and at some point even begin to wish that people would just stop already.

Hard to imagine, right? What would be wrong with all that money coming in? That people might go nuts giving? That people might get competitive with each other?

That is exactly what happens in the Torah portion. There is a collection of materials for the building of the Tabernacle. The people keep giving and giving, but at a certain point Moses says that they bring too much. The artisans who are getting the materials protest that there's no room for everything. Moses tells the people to stop bringing those precious materials.

But why do they go overboard? After all, think of the last time this happened. The Israelites had been equally enthusiastic in bringing their donations to the building of the Golden Calf.

Now it could be that the Israelites decide that the way to make up for the sin of the Golden Calf is to use their energies to do something better. In the words of Bible scholar Nehama Leibowitz: "They made amends with the very same thing with which they had sinned. It was their gold earrings that gilded the calf and again their 'earrings and every kind of gold ornaments' that they contributed to the Tabernacle."

There is another major difference besides the ultimate destination of the gifts. When the people brought donations of gold to the building of the Golden Calf, they just deposited their donations. The Torah doesn't say anything about how the people felt about what they were doing. On the other hand, the building of the Tabernacle explicitly calls for a willing heart. As the medieval commentator Isaac Abravanel teaches: "for the sake of the Lord and not for any other motive." So what could be bad about all this enthusiastic giving? Interesting: in Jewish law you are not supposed to give too much *tzedakah* (charity), lest you put yourself in a shaky financial position. You are supposed to be generous, but not go overboard (most often defined as giving away more than 20 percent of your income).

The bottom line: there are limits to everything. By all means, give charity. Support worthy causes. But make sure that you don't turn it into too much of a good thing. The making of the Tabernacle calls for self-discipline—like most things in life.

THE WORK OF OUR HANDS

One of the greatest educational institutions in the State of Israel is the Bezalel Academy of Arts and Design, in Jerusalem. Some of the most creative people in the Jewish world have studied there. The origin of the name comes from this week's Torah portion, where we learn that Bezalel was the chief artisan of the ancient Tabernacle. (Note: Bezalel had a colleague, Oholiab. But there is no Oholiab Academy in Jerusalem.) All that those art and design students probably know about Bezalel is that he was the boss.

Who could blame them? Frankly, the Bible doesn't have that much else to say about Bezalel. We know the name of his father—Uri. Was Bezalel married? Did he have children? Was he gifted as a child? Who did he study with? We don't know. Bible scholar Avivah Zornberg writes: "Just as the Golden Calf emerged suddenly from the flames, so did Bezalel's talent. He enters the world without explanation."

Yet Bezalel's talent is nothing short of miraculous. How could he have learned his great skill? Certainly not in Egypt! The medieval sage Nachmanides teaches: "When Israel was in Egypt, they were crushed under the work of mortar and brick, and they had acquired no knowledge of how to work in silver and gold. It was therefore a wonder that there could be found among them someone as skillful as Bezalel. For even among those who study from experts, you cannot find one who is proficient in all these crafts."

No wonder that the biblical text says that Bezalel was filled with "skill, ability, and knowledge" (35:31). It was the only way that he could have pulled off such a wonderful artistic feat.

What do we learn from Bezalel? Judaism is not just about books and studying; it is also about the creative arts. Starting in the Middle Ages, there were beautiful *Haggadot* and illuminated manuscripts. Today, there is more creativity in Jewish ritual objects than at almost any time in history. Just go to any Judaica store or Jewish museum and you will see beautiful synagogue art, Kiddush cups, *tallitot, mezuzot, Havdalah* sets, *etrog* boxes, seder plates, and more. Sure—you can make *Kiddush* with a paper cup, but why should you? Judaism teaches the concept of *hiddur mitzvah,* that you should adorn or beautify a mitzvah whenever you can.

At the founding ceremonies of the Bezalel school, the first chief rabbi of prestate Israel, Rabbi Abraham Kook, said: "The desire for the beginnings of an art institution in the Land of Israel is in essence a sign of life, a sign of hope, salvation and comfort. Our nation looks well upon the sweet beauty of art which is expressed through human creativity." Let's remember the artists who have enriched Jewish life in our time by the wonderful work that they do. And if you have skills like that, put them to work for the Jewish people.

Connections

- ✝ What things do you think that modern Jews should not do on Shabbat?
- ✝ In what things do you invest your heart? In other words, what are those things that move your heart, and that you want to excel in?
- ✝ What skills do you have? How have you made them work for Judaism?
- ✝ A midrash says that Bezalel was thirteen years old when he built the Tabernacle. Why do you think the ancient sages assigned that age to that great feat? What might this have to do with thirteen being the age of bar and bat mitzvah?
- ✝ Can you think of times when people have become overenthusiastic in doing a good thing?

❖ Pekudei: Exodus 38:21–40:38

And, now, the book of Exodus comes to an end. Despite the fact that this book takes its name from the Exodus from Egypt, leaving Egypt is not the most important thing that happens in that biblical book. Judging from the sheer amount of ink that the ancient scribes used in writing the book, the most important thing that happens in Exodus is that the Israelites receive the "blueprint" for the Tabernacle, and then they build it. Pekudei contains a tally of all the precious metals that were used in its construction, along with detailed descriptions of how the priestly garments were made. It contains explicit instructions for how to set up the Tabernacle, with the refrain "just as the Lord had commanded Moses."

Finally, we read that God's presence filled the Tabernacle. Only when the cloud of God's presence lifted could the Israelites continue on their journeys.

Summary

- ✝ There is a detailed account of the weight and value of all the gold and silver used in the construction of the Tabernacle. (38:21–25)
- ✝ There is a detailed description of all the materials used in the priestly garments. (39:1–30)

Ⓣ Moses sets up the Tabernacle as God had commanded. The language used in describing this project—"work," "completed," and "blessed"—echoes the language that the book of Genesis used when God created the world. (40:17–33)

Ⓣ God's cloud, the visible sign of God's presence, descends upon the Tabernacle and becomes a signal for the People of Israel to move forward on their journey through the wilderness. (40:34–38)

The Big Ideas

Ⓣ **Judaism demands accountability from both leaders and regular people.** Moses demands exact records of all the precious metals used in the building of the Tabernacle because he wanted to be sure no one would think he had taken some of the precious metals and kept them for himself. This teaches us that leaders must be exacting and deliberate in their public dealings, so that they will always remain above suspicion of corruption. The same goes for all of us.

Ⓣ **Religious leadership is special, but not overly special.** Just as there needed to be an exact accounting of all the materials used in the construction of the Tabernacle, there needed to be an accounting of all the materials used in the design of the priests' garments. The garments themselves were considered holy, just as the priests were holy. By describing the garments in such detail, perhaps the authors of the Torah were trying to ensure that later generations would not decide to make the priestly garments even more special than they were intended to be. That is why the text keeps repeating "just as the Lord had commanded Moses."

Ⓣ **There is a linkage between the creation of the Tabernacle and the creation of the world.** The Tabernacle is actually a model for the way that the world should exist—a place where people join together in community and show their gratitude to God. It is, or at least it was at that time, the only place where everything can unfold according to God's plan.

Ⓣ **God is not stationary, sitting on a throne in heaven.** God wanders with the Jewish people. This idea sustained the Jewish people through centuries of exile. Wherever Jews have gone, wherever Jews have lived, no matter what: God has been in exile with us. God will not abandon us.

Jewish Living Can Be In-Tents

That was a bad pun. Sorry about that. But it does have something to teach us.

The place where the Israelites encountered God was called the *ohel mo'ed*, the Tent of Meeting. Not a house. Not a palace. But a tent.

This makes total sense. When you read the stories of Genesis, you see that the ancestors of the Jewish people were nomads who wandered from place to place, much like modern-day Bedouins in the Middle East. When you read the stories of Exodus, Leviticus, Numbers, and Deuteronomy, you get the same notion: the Israelites are always wandering, always on a journey. You might have heard the term "the wandering Jew." Actually, it is not a nice term. It was meant as an insult. It comes from an old Christian belief that God condemned the Jews to wander the earth.

Jews certainly don't believe that. And yet, for much of Jewish history, in many places and times, it has been true.

So, what is the significance that the place where God meets the Israelites is called a tent? By definition a tent is a temporary dwelling (just like the sukkah). That's the point. God doesn't simply "sit" in one place. God "wanders" with the Jewish people.

Throughout Jewish history, Jews have believed that *shekhinta bagaluta,* "the presence of God," is somehow in exile with them. Ever since the destruction of the Temples in Jerusalem, first by the Babylonians and then by the Romans, God has been in exile with the Jews. That idea sustained the Jews and comforted them through their years of wandering. God will not abandon them. In several midrashim, God not only wanders with the Jews; God shares in their pain and even (if you can imagine this) weeps with the Jews. Our religious structures are not always permanent. But our relationship with God is permanent. And God is with us in our distress and in our triumphs as well.

In our tradition God's presence is also likened to a fire. God is said to speak with Moses out of a burning bush, which burned and was not consumed. God is said to speak with the people at Sinai, which the Torah says burned with fire. Think of all the candles of Jewish living that we light: Shabbat candles, *Havdalah* candles, Hanukkah candles, and yahrzeit candles, and most of all, the *ner tamid*, the "eternal light." They all symbolize God's presence among us.

In the words of renowned contemporary commentator Avivah Zornberg: "The Book of Exodus ends with the people contemplating that fire. They see it as the fire of the Presence of God, a version of the fire of Sinai. The couple—God and the people—needs no candle, for the pillar of fire accompanies them in their exits and entrances."

Creation—Or Re-Creation?

You have probably had this experience: your parents or teachers speak to you about something, and then, a week later or so, they repeat the same thing. And you probably find that boring.

But not every repetition is boring. Sometimes, we can learn a lot from it.

Consider this last portion of the book of Exodus. It describes the building of the ancient Tabernacle in painstaking detail. But when we read it, we realize something. The language of the instructions sounds familiar. We read similar language at the very beginning of the Torah when we read the account of the world's creation.

Follow the parallels: Moses examines the handiwork of the Tabernacle. In the creation story, God sees all that God has made and finds it very good. God finds creation to be meaningful, just like the Tabernacle will be meaningful.

There is more: "And when Moses saw [*vayar*] that they had performed all the tasks [*kol ha-melakhah*]—as the Lord had commanded, so they had done [*asu*]—Moses blessed them" (39:43). To the attentive reader, the links to the creation story are unmistakable: "And God saw [*vayar*] all [*kol*] that God had done [*asah*], and it was very good" (Gen. 1:31). In the one case, God looks and sees, while in the other Moses does; in both cases, everything has been completed, just as God wants.

So, are the creation of the world and the creation of the Tabernacle exactly the same? No. God single-handedly created the world. But God gives human beings the task of building the Tabernacle. This is similar to the Jewish mystical idea of *tzimtzum*, which means "to limit" or "to reduce." If God fills all space, how could the world have come to be? God had to "shrink" in order to make room for the world to exist. In a similar way, leaders must make themselves "smaller" in order for their followers to actually do the right thing. It is true of teachers, coaches—and especially parents. In modern psychological terms, we must limit our ego in order to let others grow.

As the contemporary Jewish thinker Eugene B. Borowitz teaches: "Take the case of a parent who has the power to insist upon a given decision and a good deal of experience upon which to base that judgment. In such an instance, the urge to compel is almost irresistible. Yet if it is a matter the parent feels the child can handle—better, if making this decision and taking responsibility for it will help the child grow—then the mature parent withdraws and makes it possible for the child to choose."

So, just as God didn't build the Tabernacle, but let Moses do it, sometimes human beings have to step back and let others learn and grow. Your parents will do this for you, and you will do it for others.

Connections

- ᑫ In what way does God "wander" the world with the Jewish people?
- ᑫ What are some of the places where God "lives?"
- ᑫ In what ways have you had to be accountable—to parents, teachers, and yourself?
- ᑫ Have you ever had the experience of *tzimtzum*—of parents, teachers, or coaches "withdrawing" from a task in order for you (or others) to grow? What was it like?

LEVITICUS

❖ Va-yikra': Leviticus 1:1–5:26

Hard as it might be to imagine, traditionally Leviticus was the first book of the Torah that Jewish children learned. That is how important it is—a handbook of what "Judaism" was like for the ancient Israelites.

This first Torah portion of Leviticus focuses, specifically, on the various kinds of sacrifices (*korbanot*) that the ancient Israelites brought to the *mishkan*, the ancient Tabernacle in the desert (and, after that, the Temple in Jerusalem). Each kind of sacrifice had its own purpose, and those purposes can help us understand exactly what motivated the ancient Israelite worshiper to want to approach God. The sacrifices were not for God; they were ways to elevate the individual and to help the individual in his or her quest for holiness.

Summary

- ẗ God tells Moses about the sacrificial offerings (*korbanot*) that are to be offered. (1:1)
- ẗ Sacrificial offerings should come from either the herd or the flock. (1:2)
- ẗ But not all sacrifices need come from the herd or the flock; the worshiper can also bring birds and grain as offerings. (1:14–2:16)
- ẗ Worshipers can also bring a *zevach shelamim*, an offering of well-being, of *shalom*. (3:1–17)
- ẗ And they can bring a *chattat* offering, an offering that expresses regret for sin. The Torah speaks of two ways of understanding sin: what happens *if* a "regular" person sins, and what happens *when* a leader sins. (4:1–35)

The Big Ideas

- ẗ **Sacrifices were a way for the ancient Israelite worshiper to get close to God.** That is the meaning of the word *korban*. It comes from the Hebrew root *k-r-v*, which means "to get close." Worship, in whatever form it takes, is a way of achieving some kind of intimacy with God.

ᵫ **The sacrifices came from the herd or the flock—which means from domesticated animals.** In an ancient agricultural society, the most important things that the worshiper owned were animals. Animals, like sheep, goats, or cattle, were almost like money. To offer an animal meant that you were offering something that had real value.

ᵫ **Bird and grain offerings were the "economy" sacrifice.** Not everyone could afford to bring offerings like sheep, goats, or cattle; they were simply too valuable. So the sacrificial system allowed for less-expensive alternatives: birds and grain. Burning grain smells good, not so burning feathers, but to God those burning feathers smelled just fine. God cares about the dignity of the poor. Everyone has a role in Jewish life.

ᵫ **A major part of sacrificial offerings—and all worship—is being grateful for shalom.** That was the purpose of the *zevach shelamim*—to express gratitude for a sense of being at peace with your family, with the priests in the Tabernacle, and with God.

ᵫ **Everyone sins sometimes, but rulers and leaders are almost guaranteed to sin.** This is not only a statement about human nature (after all, no one is perfect). It is not only a cynical statement about how power corrupts. It is also a statement of absolute realism: it is almost impossible to be a leader without making mistakes. The best leaders are those who are able to own up to their errors, apologize, and then do things better.

Divrei Torah

IS THIS GOD'S BARBECUE?

Yuck. That's probably what you're thinking about this Torah portion, and maybe the entire book of Leviticus. Bringing animals to the altar and killing them, and then burning them? Who would do such a thing?

Well, actually, what do you think happens when you order meat in a restaurant? True, you don't actually kill the animal on the spot. No, you don't—but someone else slaughtered that animal before it showed up in the restaurant. So, unless you're a vegetarian, don't think that the ancient sacrifices were that disgusting.

But why did Judaism have to have animal sacrifices in the first place? The great medieval philosopher Maimonides suggests that it was necessary because this was what the Jews had experienced in Egypt: "God could not expect us to utterly abandon this mode of worship, for that would have gone against human nature. God therefore allowed these practices to continue but transformed them from idolatrous associations . . . that their purpose should be directed toward Him."

So, God was like a patient teacher, trying to move the Jews away from pagan sacrifice to making offerings for God. Maimonides understood that the ideal form of serving God was prayer, but it took some time for the Israelites to get there.

But on the way to that goal, did sacrifice have anything to teach the Jews?

Yes. We can learn something from the animals that are required as sacrifices. They are all domesticated animals; you have to bring what belongs to you. Those animals are not up in the mountains somewhere. God only asks the possible from us, not the impossible.

What kinds of animals are required? Oxen, sheep, and goats. Each animal is the prey of another animal. The ox is pursued by the lion, the sheep by the wolf, the goat by the leopard. In this way, the sages thought that God was telling the ancient Israelites that many nations would pursue them as well. That was their way of learning what their future history would be.

But what does it really mean to sacrifice? Rabbi David Wolpe writes: "In every relationship, part of the measure of love is the willingness to forgo; I will sacrifice sleep, food, time, money, almost anything for someone whom I love. In ancient Israel, offering the products of labor—crops, animals—showed deep connection to God." So, were the sacrifices disgusting? Maybe.

Did they have something to teach? Definitely.

WHEN LEADERS SIN

It happens. It will always happen. Rulers sin. They make mistakes, sometimes terrible mistakes.

Sure, we know all about the horrible leaders, the tyrants and killers like Hitler, Stalin, Idi Amin, Saddam Hussein, and others. But what about the good leaders? Moses, the greatest leader the Jews ever had, killed a man in Egypt. King David, the true founder of the kingdom of Israel and the greatest king in the Bible, killed a man and then stole his wife. Many American presidents, like Franklin Roosevelt, Dwight Eisenhower, John F. Kennedy, and Bill Clinton, were sometimes unfaithful to their wives. Sometimes political leaders make even worse mistakes—like waging wars that turn out to be less than absolutely necessary.

Judaism understands that this sort of thing happens. Look at what Leviticus says about the sin offering that sinners have to bring. When it comes to "regular" people, the text says "if a person sins." *If.* It might happen; it might not (it probably does, because no one is perfect). But when it comes to rulers, Leviticus does not say *if* they sin. It's *when* they sin. It is going to happen. Be ready for it. As the talmudic sage Yochanan ben Zakkai said: "Fortunate is the generation whose leader recognizes having sinned and brings an offering of purification."

And here is what is even cooler: Biblical Judaism brought a radical revolution to political thinking: the ruler is not above the law. In ancient times, and in non-Jewish nations, if you criticized the ruler you could get yourself killed. The ruler or king was a god. But when King David sinned, the prophet Nathan stood before him and openly criticized him. When King Ahab and Queen Jezebel sinned, the prophet Elijah stood before them and openly criticized them. That was what prophets were supposed to do. True, it didn't win them any popularity contests. And it was also true that it was dangerous; Elijah had to flee from Queen Jezebel, who threatened to kill him. But here's the bottom line: no prophet in ancient Israel was ever put to death by a king for telling the truth to the king.

The Israeli statesman Avraham Burg writes: "The role of the prophet and man of spirit is to stand always at the side of the oppressed and downtrodden, the 'average citizen,' and defend him or her against an unjust regime. Our tradition understands that there is no government that is without injustice."

Connections

ᵬ Why do you think that Jewish children used to start their Jewish education by learning the book of Leviticus?

ᵬ Why does Leviticus make special mention of the sins of rulers? What would be some examples of those kinds of sins?

ᵬ How does Judaism show concern for the dignity of the poor? How do you yourself do this?

ᵬ For what are you grateful? How do you show your gratitude?

ᵬ What kinds of offerings do you "bring" to God?

ᵬ What are your ways of getting close to God?

❖ Tsav: Leviticus 6:1–8:36

The "yuck" theme continues: the ancient Israelite sacrificial system. In this Torah portion we read about the burnt offering (*olah*), the grain offering (*minchah*), the offering that would purify the worshiper of sin (*chattat*), the offering of reparation (*asham*), and the offering of well-being (*zevach shelamim*).

The portion concludes with a description of the way that the priests (*kohanim*) are inducted into their sacred duties.

There are important themes that emerge from all this description of sacrifices and priests.

Summary

ᵬ The burnt offering (*olah*, sometimes translated as "holocaust") must be burned entirely. It must be kept burning on the altar all night long, and the fire of the altar must burn perpetually. Moreover, the priest is responsible for carrying the ashes of the sacrifice outside the camp to a pure place. (6:1–6)

ᵬ The grain offering (*minchah*) is presented to the Lord, but Aaron and his sons eat what is left over from the offering. (6:7–11)

ᵬ The reparation offering (*asham*) is intended as a way to purify the worshiper of the wrongs that he or she has committed. (7:1–10)

ᵬ The elaborate rituals of investiture (ordaining) of the priests are filled with sacrificial offerings. An important part of the rit-

ual is to put the blood of a sacrifice on Aaron's right ear, his right
thumb, and the big toe of his right foot. (8:1–36)

The Big Ideas

꠸ **The fire that burns perpetually on the altar symbolizes
Judaism—and the Jewish people.** In this way, the perpetual fire
is like the burning bush that Moses saw, and the eternal light (*ner
tamid*) in synagogues. These are all sources of warmth and light
that will last forever—like Judaism and the Jews.

꠸ **No one is too special to be involved in small things.** The priest
is not exempt from the "dirty work" of Jewish living. He, and not
a subordinate, is responsible for cleaning up from the sacrifice.
This ensures that the priests will always remember to be holy.

꠸ **We need to love the Jewish past.** The leftover ashes of the sacrifice are also holy. The Jewish past, even though it is history, is as
important as the Jewish present and the Jewish future.

꠸ **Judaism is about community.** The sacrifices are not only for God.
In fact, they are mostly connected with our acts of eating. Eating
is a way for people to feel a sense of community.

꠸ **Judaism says that you can move on from doing something
wrong.** Judaism does not believe in simply feeling guilty, it
teaches that you can make restitution. In ancient days, that was in
the form of a sacrificial offering. Nowadays, it can take the form of
an apology and/or somehow making up for what you have done.

꠸ **Judaism is connected to the body.** The ritual of investiture of the
priests involves three parts of the body: the ear, the thumb, and
the big toe. Each body part symbolizes an essential part of living:
hearing, action, and walking.

Divrei Torah
DOING THE CHORES

Chores. Who needs them? And yet we all have them: doing the dishes,
taking out the garbage, walking the dog, shoveling snow, cleaning our
rooms. Doing chores is one of the most basic aspects of living as part
of a family. No one can do it all, and everyone needs to pitch in.

It turns out that there were chores—even in the ancient Tabernacle. And just wait until you learn who had to do them.

There was a sacrificial offering called the *olah*, the burnt offering. The priest, dressed in his fancy linen garments, took the ashes and placed them next to the altar. He then took off his garments, changed into other clothing, and carried the ashes outside the camp (6:2–4).

Your synagogue probably has a custodian who cleans up after people. (Quick: what's his or her name?) We tend to think of janitors and custodians as, well, "lowly" people, and we sometimes look down on them. This, of course, is wrong. The Bible, too, mentions the "wood choppers and water drawers." But when it came to the Tabernacle the cleanup crew consisted not of the lowliest Israelites, but of the holiest—the priests themselves.

What do we learn from this? No matter how important the priest might have been, he still had to get "down and dirty." It was a lesson in humility. In fact, the priests actually competed to do this work! There was so much competition that two priests once ran up the ramp of the ancient Temple, fighting to get to the top, and one of them pushed the other and he broke his leg. Here's how the early sages said the problem was fixed: "There was a daily lottery to see who would have the privilege of climbing up the ramp to the top of the altar and carrying away the ashes."

We tend to distrust religious leaders who live in big mansions, have fancy cars and vacation homes, and dress a little too well. We want to see humility, not arrogance. After all, "to walk humbly" is the famous teaching of the prophets, and a prime characteristic of Moses.

During the Holocaust, the great German rabbi Leo Baeck was a prisoner in the Theresienstadt concentration camp. He was the undisputed leader of all German Jewry—a man so respected that even Nazis officers showed deference to him. Rabbi Baeck stayed with his community in Berlin, even though he had a chance to leave, and then accompanied them to that awful place.

And yet, what did he do in the concentration camp? He became a "horse," pulling a garbage wagon, like other prisoners. Rabbi Baeck said: "I was quite happy doing this. The other 'horse' harnessed to the same cart was a distinguished philosopher. We had wonderful conversations about ethics and religion as we dragged the refuse through the mud."

Rabbi Baeck knew that there was dignity even in demeaning work. It is a lesson that we can all learn.

A JEWISH ANATOMY LESSON

Ask any rabbi or cantor about the ceremony in which he or she became a rabbi or cantor. They will probably tell you something like this: There was a huge ordination ceremony, perhaps in a large, prominent synagogue. A seminary official called each candidate up by name. The president or chancellor said some private words to the candidate, blessed him or her, and that's it. That person then became a rabbi or a cantor. Mazel tov!

Not bad, especially when you compare it to the way that the priests were ordained in biblical times. An animal was slaughtered, and a little bit of blood was placed on the middle part of Aaron's right ear, and the thumb of his right hand, and then the big toe of his right foot—and then he was a priest. His sons went through the same ordination rituals.

If you're left handed, you're probably feeling a little "left out" right now. Yes, the Bible seems to be discriminating against left-handed people. Equality and inclusion as we know it was not fully developed back then. But, getting past the bias, an important lesson is to be learned from this ancient ceremony: the three body parts—the ear, thumb, and toe—are essential to being a Jew, and being human.

Let's start with the ear. Remember that the central statement of Jewish faith begins this way: *Shema Yisrael* (Hear, Israel). You need to be able to listen to people and really hear what they are saying. This does not mean that you have to agree with everything that everyone says; sometimes it is simply enough to pay attention to others. And we not only have to train ourselves to really listen; we also have to train ourselves to hear—to hear the right things, not to listen to gossip, and to learn how to figure out the truth.

Next, there is the thumb. Having a thumb is one of those things that make us human and able to function as humans. The thumb stands for the ability to act.

Finally, there is the big toe. Funny thing about the big toe; we usually ignore it, unless someone steps on it or we stub it. Without our big toes, we would not be able to balance ourselves. But, more than this, pay attention to how you walk. What's the first part of the body that moves when you move forward? Right—the big toe. Movement and balance.

So, yes, in order to be a fully functional Jewish person you need those body parts. The ancient Jewish philosopher Philo teaches: "The fully consecrated must be pure in words and actions and in life; for words are judged by hearing, the hand is the symbol of action, and the foot symbolizes the pilgrimage of life."

But, beyond that, those body parts are necessary for being human. As contemporary Jewish educator Sorel Goldberg Loeb writes: "The priest is smeared with blood to remind him of his bond with all life. But the parts of his body that are marked are those that distinguish him from and elevate him above the animals."

Connections

- What do you do that is considered menial? Why is it important?
- How can we make sure that Judaism lasts forever?
- What ways can you show loyalty to the Jewish past, present, and future?
- What are some ways that you have felt a sense of community in eating with others?
- What are ways that you have made up for some wrongs you have done?
- In what ways do you use your ears, thumbs, and toes "Jewishly"?

❖ Shemini: Leviticus 9:1–11:47

Okay, we have set up the Tabernacle. We have figured out the rules for sacrificial offerings. It's time to get this whole thing going. Shemini contains the account of the beginning of the sacrificial offerings. But something goes terribly wrong. In the midst of the dedication, Aaron's sons, Nadab and Abihu, are mysteriously killed.

As Aaron continues to mourn for them, God commands the Israelites regarding the animals that they will be permitted to eat and those that will be forbidden. These laws contain the basis for the laws of kashrut (dietary laws), also known as "keeping kosher."

Summary

ᚼ On the eighth day of the priests' dedication ceremony, the Israelites are ready to begin the sacrificial offerings. In some ways, this is where Judaism starts, at least biblical Judaism—with its system of sacrifices. (9:24)

ᚼ Something awful happens. Aaron's sons, Nadab and Abihu, bring offerings that God had not commanded. Fire consumes them. Moses makes an attempt to explain what has happened to them, but Aaron is simply frozen in silent grief. (10:1–7)

ᚼ God prohibits the use of intoxicating beverages by those who bring offerings. This is one way of making a distinction between "the sacred and the profane," which is a major theme of the book of Leviticus. (10:8–11)

ᚼ God gives Moses and Aaron the rules for permitted and forbidden animals. These animals are permitted: land animals that have cloven hoofs and that chew their cud; fish that have fins and scales and are not scavengers; birds that fly and that are not birds of prey. And these animals are prohibited: land animals that *either* have cloven hooves *or* chew their cud, *but not both;* water animals that crawl rather than swim; birds that don't fly; birds of prey. Animals that have died on their own rather than being slaughtered are also prohibited. These laws form the basis of the laws of kashrut. (11:1–47)

The Big Ideas

ᚼ **Eight is a sacred number in Judaism.** It seems to be the number connected to "dedication." Ritual circumcision happens on the eighth day. The festival of Hanukkah lasts for eight nights. And the process of dedication of the priests in this Torah portion lasts for eight days. Why eight? Perhaps because eight is the number of notes that brings us to the octave—the completion of the musical cycle. Eight means wholeness and holiness.

ᚼ **Biblical Judaism expected conformity.** The deaths of Nadab and

Abihu remain a much-debated mystery. But one thing is clear: they brought offerings that God had not commanded. In other words, they innovated and got "creative." While many modern Jews value the idea of creativity and innovation in worship and Jewish life, this is not the biblical model. Those who stray from the rules can sometimes suffer.

Ꞧ **Ritual life requires clearheadedness.** That is why God prohibits the drinking of alcoholic beverages in the ancient Tabernacle. You cannot be drunk and do your religious duties. While wine and alcohol are enjoyable (when you are of the proper age!), we should avoid getting drunk. It not only blocks clear thinking; in certain situations (like driving), it can be dangerous, even fatal.

Ꞧ **Jewish life requires some kind of regulation of what we eat.** Some people choose to observe biblical kashrut—eating only the animals that are permitted and not those forbidden by the Torah. Some people choose to only eat animals that have been ritually slaughtered. Some people choose to separate meat and dairy. These are all acceptable Jewish choices because they remind us that Judaism allows us to sanctify everyday acts, especially eating.

Divrei Torah

THE NADAB AND ABIHU MURDER CASE

It is time for this week's episode of "Law and Order: svu [Sacrificial Victims Unit]."

But, in all seriousness, a real tragedy happens in a flash. Here's the scene: The Israelites have built and dedicated the Tabernacle. There has been a full description of the sacrificial system and a seven-day ordination ceremony for the priests. Now the sacrifices can begin. On the eighth day, the people will use the sacred altar for the first time. It's like taking the whole system out of the box, setting it up, and plugging it in. What could possibly go wrong?

This is what goes wrong: Nadab and Abihu, Aaron's sons, decide to offer incense—"alien fire" that God has not commanded. Then fire flares from God and consumes them.

Who did it, and why? In the words of the classic movie *Casablanca*: "Let's round up the usual suspects." But let's first admit that the Torah itself suggests that this is divine punishment for a breach of protocol, as harsh and as inexplicable as it may seem to us.

So perhaps God did it. Nadab and Abihu were violating the sanctity of the Tabernacle, and God punished them for not following exact instructions, and perhaps to set an example.

The sages try very hard to find fault with Aaron's sons, since the Torah has little to say about what happened. They were drunkards. They were rebellious sons. A passage in the Talmud even suggests that "they were eager for Moses and Aaron to die so that they could take over as priests."

Does the punishment fit the crime? Perhaps we are trying too hard to explain what went wrong. It was simply an accident. You know what they say: "stuff happens."

But another problem is the harsh way that Moses reacts to the tragedy. "Then Moses said to Aaron, 'This is what the Lord meant when He said: Through those near to Me I show Myself holy, and gain glory before all the people'" (10:3).

Gee, Moses, you have a nice way of comforting people. First of all: When had God said that? And what does it mean—that those who are chosen for responsibility have to adhere to strict standards? Can't people make mistakes? And what is this thing about "gaining glory"?

"And Aaron was silent" (10:3). Aaron cannot, or will not, say anything to his brother. How shall we interpret Aaron's silence? Was he just numb with grief, still in a state of shock and not able to respond? Was he merely submitting to the divine will? Or were Moses's words simply too much for him to bear?

The contemporary author André Neher writes: "People can accept that God keeps silent, but not that others should deign to speak in His place."

Sometimes in the face of tragedy, truly, there are no words.

WARNING: PORK-FREE ZONE!

One of the greatest American Jewish heroes was Rabbi Joachim Prinz. He gave the opening address right before the Reverend Martin Luther King Jr. spoke at the famous March on Washington. But here's a quote of his that never made the history books. Rabbi Prinz once explained why he refrained from eating pork: "It is a dietary predilection of my ancestors for which they frequently gave their lives."

No doubt about it: pork has a negative reputation among Jews. What's one of the worst ways to insult a Jew? Call him or her a *chazir* (pig). Tyrants used to torture Jews by forcing them to eat pig. In Maccabean times, "the armies of Antiochus, ruler of the Syria's Greek dynasty, the Seleucids," splashed pig's blood in the Temple to desecrate it. Jews in Spain were called Marranos, "pigs."

So, yes, one reason for not eating pork is that Jews were tortured and forced to eat it.

But there's more. Avoiding pork helps establish controls and boundaries in life. Not every appetite is worthy of being satiated. In this sense, kashrut becomes a metaphor for life. The whole world is not mine. I cannot always spend money the way I want, say anything I want, abuse the earth according to what I think I want. Judaism is about making what we do every day into something holy. It is about our minds and it is about our stomachs. Jewish life means sacrifice. It means the conscious curbing of our appetites.

One last thing: Is there a deeper reason why certain kinds of animals are forbidden? A kosher animal must have cloven (split) hooves, and it must chew its cud. Why is this important? Although many people have wondered and many theories abound, the historical reasons are lost to antiquity. That, of course, does not stop the Rabbis from providing explanations.

Foods are symbolic. The split hoof reminds us that Judaism recognizes division—land/heavens; light/darkness; humanity/God; Isaac/Ishmael; Jacob/Esau; Rachel/Leah; Joseph/his brothers; Moses/Aaron; Israel/the nations; Shabbat/the workday week; holy/profane.

And the chewing of the cud? Animals that chew their cud are called ruminants, and a similar word, ruminate, means thinking things over and over again. (We often say: "Here's something to chew on" or "I'm having trouble swallowing that idea" or even "Do you have to bring that up again?") The ancient Jewish philosopher Philo writes: "Just as a cud-chewing animal draws up food and chews on it, so the student, after receiving wisdom from the teacher, constantly calls up each thing that he has heard."

There you have it. Jews are ruminants. Jews take wisdom and think about it and bring it back up again and chew on it, never happy with what we have learned, always looking for a way to better understand it and to refine it. We even ruminate on what we eat.

Connections

ᛒ What do you think happened to Nadab and Abihu? How would you solve this murder mystery?

ᛒ What is your opinion of what Moses said to Aaron? Do you agree with his words? Do you think they were comforting?

ᛒ In what kinds of situations have you chosen to be silent and not say anything?

ᛒ There has been a resurgence of popularity in various forms of kashrut. Why do you think this is so?

ᛒ How compelling do you find the historical argument regarding kashrut—that it is a way of responding to the pain of our ancestors? What other traditional practices or prohibitions might fall into this category—things we do or don't do because of our ancestors' suffering?

ᛒ One theory of the origin of kashrut was that it separated the ancient Israelites from the other nations of the world. Is that reason still valid today? If that reason is still desirable, what other ways might we adopt that would make us distinct from other peoples today? If it isn't desirable, what has changed in modern Jewish identity that has rendered it less so?

ᛒ What do you ruminate on?

❖ Tazria': Leviticus 12:1–13:59

We now shift away from sacrifices to something much more intensely personal—the human body. Tazria' makes it clear: the body is a place where holiness happens. The portion teaches about the various ritual impurities that a mother experiences after childbirth.

It then moves into a lengthy discussion of *tzara'at,* a kind of skin disease that was prevalent in ancient times, and how that disease made its sufferers ritually impure. Such a condition not only occurred in the human body; it could also show up in cloth and on other surfaces.

Summary

ቴ A woman who gives birth to a male infant is ritually impure for seven days. The boy is circumcised on the eighth day of his life. If she gives birth to a female, she is impure for two weeks. At the end of her period of impurity she makes an offering at the entrance of the Tent of Meeting. (12:1–8)

ቴ There are many verses dealing with *tzara'at*, the infectious skin disease that is mentioned so many times in the book of Leviticus. Leviticus describes the nature of the skin affliction, the role of the priest in its diagnosis, the isolation of the victim, and how the victim ultimately returns to the Israelite camp. (13:1–46)

ቴ The affliction could also appear in cloth or clothing; nowadays, we would call that "mildew." (13:46–59)

The Big Ideas

ቴ **Impurity means something other than dirty.** Today "dirty" would be our normal and natural way of understanding the notion of something being impure. The biblical term *tamei*, however, means something deeper. It signifies an altered or different condition. Being *tamei* is not necessary bad; it could be something so miraculous or awesome that it leaves you in an unnatural state. For that reason, the person who is *tamei* needs to go through a ritual that makes him or her *tahor*, "pure." Some things (like childbirth) are so big that they leave an indelible mark on us.

ቴ **We need ways to handle our fear of certain illnesses.** It is true that certain illnesses like skin diseases aroused fear in ancient peoples. Before we write off those fears as being primitive, we should remember that we still find certain illnesses to be unattractive and frightening. Leviticus is honest in its portrayal of such conditions, their diagnosis, and the role of the priest in being part of the healing process.

ቴ **Our clothing is like a second skin.** We might find it bizarre that the Torah devotes space to the appearance of mildew in fabric or leather. People wear clothing made from those products, and the clothing we wear lies against our skin, and, in many ways, it reflects our identities. (When we wear dirty or stained clothing, we believe that it reflects on us and could send the message that we're slovenly.)

Divrei Torah
BIRTH IS A BIG DEAL

Here's what probably happened when you were born: Your mother began to feel changes in her body. Perhaps her water broke. Perhaps she had labor pains. She went to the hospital or perhaps a birthing center, and she was coached through delivery—with someone helping her breathe and stay calm. Then you were born. It was a big deal. Your mother and father were grateful that everything was okay, and they wanted to celebrate their joy. At some point, there is a ceremony and party (a *brit milah* or a baby naming) to welcome the new baby into the family and into the Jewish people.

Back in biblical times any celebrating took place later because a mother was ritually unclean after giving birth and had to bring a purification offering to the Tent of Meeting.

Why? Why did the mother have to bring an offering? In the ancient world, bringing an offering at a joyous time was the equivalent of what we do today—offering a prayer of thanksgiving. It might have been a moment of thanksgiving for having survived the whole experience of childbirth. Bear in mind that, until fairly recently, many women died in childbirth. To have come through it okay was a big deal. So there was an offering.

Moreover, Judaism teaches that to look at a newborn child is to experience the divine. God, after all, is involved in the miracle of birth. "There are three partners in procreation: God, the father, and the mother." No doubt about it; when a child is born, it is a moment that is truly awesome. Ask any parent.

But why, of all things, did the mother need to be a sin offering (*chattat*)? What's the sin in the joyous event of bringing a new person into the world? We really don't know, but the sages have speculated. One line of thought is that the mother may have said something inappropriate during childbirth. She was going through a very difficult and painful labor. She might have screamed: "I swear that I will never go through this again!" That would have meant that any woman who said that was swearing that she would have no more children. Having no more children would not be good for the Jewish future. So there had to be a way to absolve her of what she had thought and sworn —and the sin offering was the way she could do that.

Another answer comes from someone trying to understand the psychology of what a mother goes through at birth. The modern biblical teacher Nehama Leibowitz explains: "Childbirth makes the mother deeply conscious of the greatness of the Creator, and at the same time of her insignificance that she can only feel herself a sinner." (In other words: childbirth was such a big "wow" that anyone experiencing it must have felt small and unworthy. And with the huge task of raising the baby in front of her, perhaps mother and community wanted to make sure she was free of any burden of sin.)

We tend to overuse the word "awesome," but when it comes to birth it's no understatement at all.

THE SICK ARE PEOPLE TOO

The word "gnarly" could have been invented for just one reason: to describe a disease from biblical times called *tzara'at*. While the usual translation of *tzara'at* is "leprosy," this is not really accurate. Leprosy (or Hansen's disease) is a terrible, disfiguring disease in which limbs dry up and fall off. It is also usually quite contagious, which is why lepers were sent to live in leper colonies.

Tzara'at was more akin to psoriasis, that ailment in which skin becomes scaly and irritated. The biblical authors believed that *tzara'at* was more than skin deep. They believed that it could affect one's clothing (mildew) and one's house (mold). *Tzara'at* was the biblical disease par excellence, the very symbol and metaphor of yuck. In the words of Rabbi Asher Lopatin: "This is a portion about everything going wrong with the way we look. Our skin breaks out in weird ways, we lose some hairs, or they start showing up in a different color."

Not all diseases are scary to onlookers. Take, for example, illnesses like heart disease or high blood pressure. We are not usually scared by people who have those illnesses, mostly because we can't really see the disease.

But *tzara'at* was frightening to people in biblical times. Why? Because it affected the skin, and skin ailments contain their own drama and dread. If you've ever been afflicted by really bad acne you know that this is true. And, from there, fear of skin diseases only gets worse— all the way up the fear ladder to skin cancer and Kaposi's sarcoma in people afflicted with AIDS.

The person who suffered from *tzara'at* must have appeared to be under attack by an invisible and pernicious enemy. *Tzara'at* left its victims with scaly patches on the skin, which must have made the victims look as if they were already dead and decomposing.

Why is this Torah portion so important? Because it reminds us of the ancient Rabbinic adage about the Torah: "Turn it, turn it, for everything is in it." (Just think of those illnesses that still scare us. We fear cancer. Some people can't even say the word. In recent times, we have lived through the dread of AIDS and Ebola.

People also fear those who struggle with mental illness. The emotional and cognitive challenges can be painful and embarrassing for the one who is afflicted and for their family and community

Like those who struggled with *tzara'at* in ancient times, these illnesses of body and mind can be isolating. Ultimately, this Torah portion tells us that we need to move beyond fear. Those inflicted do not remain outside the camp; after treatment there is a path for their return. And while people are sick, Judaism teaches that it is a mitzvah to visit them (*bikkur cholim*).

We must make room for those who are ill—in our families, synagogues, society—and in our hearts.

Connections

℔ Do you think that childbirth is "awesome?" What are some of the ways we mark that event nowadays?

℔ What do you think of the various explanations for the mother having to make a sin offering after childbirth? Do those reasons make sense to you? What other reasons might there be?

ß Are you frightened by any diseases? Which ones? How have you begun to conquer your fear of them?

ß What can your synagogue do that will make people who suffer from various diseases and conditions feel more at home?

❖ Metsora': Leviticus 14:1–15:33

You could call this portion Yuck Alert, Part 2 (or Part 3 or 4, but who's counting?). Metsora' is mostly concerned with that skin disease called *tzara'at*. But this portion is actually hopeful. It teaches about how the person who was afflicted with *tzara'at* and is now healed is reintegrated into the Israelite camp.

In last week's portion, we learned that this ailment could affect one's clothing (mildew). This week, however, it goes even further, telling us that it could even invade our houses.

Summary

ß The priest is responsible for the rituals that accompany the re-acceptance of the *metsora'* (the one afflicted with *tzara'at*) into the community. The sacrificial offerings that are mentioned are among the most elaborate and complicated in the entire Torah. (14:1–20)

ß If the person who was afflicted cannot afford the "standard" sacrificial offerings, then he or she can bring "less expensive" offerings: one lamb, flour, oil, or turtledoves or pigeons. (14:21–32)

ß *Tzara'at* could show up on the bricks of a house. Today, we would refer to this as "mold." (14:34–57)

The Big Ideas

ß **The priest's role is not only to deal with ritual.** Biblical Judaism had a very big sense of the priestly role. It was not only to offer sacrifices, but also to pay attention to the health of the Israelites and be part of the healing process for those who were ill. People with *tzara'at* were removed from the community (probably because of the fear of contagion), but they had to be accepted back in when they were healed.

꜉ **Judaism is for the poor, as well as for those who are more prosperous.** The person who suffers from *tzara'at* did not have to bring an elaborate sacrifice if he or she could not afford it. Other arrangements were made. Judaism is not only for the prosperous; the poor also have dignity and the ability to serve God.

꜉ **Impurity can affect our homes.** Because the home is one's personal domain, we have to make sure that the various "illnesses" that are part of the outside world are prevented from entering these holy spaces of our lives.

Divrei Torah
WE DON'T HAVE ALL THE ANSWERS

In our Torah portion, it says that a plague of *tzara'at* could come into your house (14:34). We would call that mold, and no doubt about it—it is nasty. When it gets into a house, it can make the inhabitants sick. Bad stuff.

But here's the intriguing part back in biblical times: the person who owned the house had to come to the priest to report the problem. In that sense, the priest was like a public health official. And the homeowner had to say: *"K'nega nireh li ba-bayit"*—roughly translated, "Something like a plague, it appears to me, is in the house."

The homeowner didn't go to the priest and say: "Excuse me, Mr. Kohen [priest], you need to come. There is a plague in my house!" He was to say it in a much softer tone: "It appears to me that there is something like a plague in my house." The person may be sure that the plague has struck, but is instructed not to say it that way.

Why was that? Because it was the job of the priest, not the homeowner, to determine if there was something going on in the house, and to take the steps to correct it. The priest was the expert.

We often think that we are the experts and that we know it all. We may be right; we may be wrong, but that is not the point. Rabbi Eliyahu Mizrahi, a Turkish sage of the fifteenth century, writes: "This serves as a moral lesson. Even in the event of certainty about an impurity, one should declare it as doubtful. Thus our sages have stated, 'Teach your tongue to say, "I do not know."'"

The Torah is trying to teach us a very important value—humility.

While we are tempted to boast about the things we know, it is much more important to be tentative about the things we don't know. Sometimes that can be hard to admit, especially when it might appear that we are not as knowledgeable or competent as we think we should be.

Rabbi Gil Steinlauf has written: "I love not knowing! When people come up to me and ask me a question about Judaism—or anything— I'm happy to admit when I don't know the answer. I'm grateful. That person has given me an opportunity to look something up and to learn. How else can I find the Truth? How else can I be ultimately right?"

It is humbling, and so liberating to admit that you don't have all the answers.

GOSSIP IS CONTAGIOUS

Nowadays when people get sick they assume that it's because of germs, or viruses, or just bad luck. Even when people get sick as a direct or indirect result of something that they might have done (like smoking cigarettes), we wouldn't bring those underlying reasons up as part of the conversation. Too cruel. Unnecessary.

But back in ancient times when people got sick, they often thought that it was because of something they had done; they thought that it was direct punishment for moral sins. Knowing that, it's not surprising to learn the ancient sages' response to why people got afflicted with *tzara'at*. They took the word for the one who is afflicted—*metsora'*— and turned it into a pun. They said that the *metsora'* is the person who is *motzi ra*, someone who says bad things about other people.

So you could say that a *motzi ra* is a gossip. In Hebrew, there are numerous words for this kind of sin—for example, *lashon ha-ra* (the evil tongue) or *rekhilut* (tale bearing). And for Jews this is a very big deal. Look how many sins in the High Holy Day prayer book refer to sins of the mouth. "For the sin we have committed against God by gossip, and by tale-bearing, and by mocking and scoffing, and by falsehood, and by needlessly judging other people."

Lashon ha-ra means saying anything bad about anyone, even and especially if it's true. *Lashon ha-ra* means insults, ridicule, and jest, and denigrating someone's possessions, or work, or merchandise. It means commenting on someone's body, mind, money, or medical history; saying anything that might cause another person harm, embarrassment, or displeasure. "Did you hear what he did?" "Did you hear what she said?" "I heard that he actually . . ." "I really shouldn't say, but . . ."

Language is a very powerful thing; it has within it the power of life and death. According to the Talmud, to shame another person in public is tantamount to shedding blood. God created the world through language. God said, "Let there be light, and there was light" (Gen. 1:3).

Rabbi Judah Loew of sixteenth-century Prague was the creator of the Golem, the famous Jewish "Frankenstein" who protected the Jews from their enemies. Rabbi Loew taught: "Consider the Hebrew word for language, *lashon.* The first letter, *lamed,* points upward—to remind us that language can bring us to the heavens. But the last letter, *nun,* points downward—to remind us that language can sink us into the abyss."

Gossip doesn't only exist in verbal form. It exists in social media, where it can spread even faster than a biblical contagious disease. Whenever you hear gossip about someone, turn the conversation around to other things. Just say: "Let's talk about something else." Gossip may not cause you to get a skin disease, but it can do plenty of damage. And it is contagious!

Connections

- ℔ What lessons can we learn from people who think they know it all?
- ℔ What are some things that you don't know about and would be curious to learn about?
- ℔ When have you admitted that you were wrong about something? What does it feel like?
- ℔ Can you think of times when people have been hurt by gossip?
- ℔ What can you do to prevent yourself and others you know from gossiping?

❖ 'Aḥarei Mot: Leviticus 16:1–18:30

Nowadays, when you go to synagogue for Yom Kippur, you sit in services, pray, sing, think of your sins, and fast. That's not how it was back in ancient times, though. 'Aḥarei Mot deals with the rituals that were part of the ancient observance of Yom Kippur. It specifies that the High Priest should choose two goats, sacrifice one of them, and send the other one, carrying the sins of the people, into the wilderness.

It also deals with various kinds of sexual acts, which ancient Israelites considered to be unholy.

Summary

ᚦ The Torah describes the ancient rituals of Yom Kippur. The High Priest symbolically transfers the people's sins to a goat and sends that goat (the scapegoat) into the wilderness. He also purges the ancient sanctuary itself of the people's sins. (16:1–34)

ᚦ The Israelites are commanded regarding sacrifices, with the explicit instruction not to consume blood when they eat the sacrificial animals. (17:1–16)

ᚦ Don't be an Egyptian (or a Canaanite)! The Israelites are commanded regarding various ancient Canaanite practices, including child sacrifice. They also learn the laws of sexual behavior. (18:1–30)

The Big Ideas

ᚦ **The ancient Israelites believed that sins had a physical reality.** The sins were not just something that was spiritual. And the Israelites believed that the scapegoat actually carried real sins away. And the sins of the people actually stained the sanctuary itself.

ᚦ **To the ancient Israelites, blood was not just blood.** It was symbolic of life itself. The ancient commandment regarding the blood of sacrificial animals went on to become a major aspect of the kashrut rules. Animals that have been ritually slaughtered must have all blood drained from them before they are acceptable for eating.

ᚦ **The personal affects the public, and all of society.** The ancient laws of sexuality were not only important for their own sake; they helped maintain the proper boundaries of intimacy within families. They still do. And back then these laws were another means of keeping the Israelites separate from their neighbors. Apparently the Egyptians and the Canaanites engaged in these sexual practices, and one of the most important lessons of the Torah is that the Israelites remain distinct from the surrounding peoples. Such separation is one of the most essential elements of being holy (*kadosh*), and is a major theme of the book of Leviticus.

Divrei Torah
IT'S ALL YOUR FAULT!

Ryan is in the middle-school musical, and, in his big number, his voice cracks. Right after the play, his fellow actors accost him: "You screwed up the whole show for us!" Of course one of them missed his cue, and another one forgot one of his lines. It doesn't matter. They blame Ryan for the play's failure.

It's called "scapegoating"—putting all the blame on someone or something. The concept of the scapegoat comes from this Torah portion. The High Priest would take two goats and cast lots (like throwing dice). According to the way that the dice fell, he would know which goat to sacrifice to God and which he would send into the wilderness after placing the sins of the people on it. That goat "escaped," and that's how we get the word "scapegoat."

Scapegoating happens all the time. It happens in school plays and on sports teams (let's blame the manager for our losses!). It happens in families ("Grandma is the problem!"), and in businesses ("We are not doing as well as we should because of the marketing people!"), and in religious organizations ("No one comes to services because the music stinks!").

Sadly, as we know, all too often in history the Jew has been the scapegoat. The early Christians blamed the death of Jesus of Nazareth on the Jewish people, even though he died at the hands of the Romans. Throughout history, Jews have been the scapegoats for plagues, economic distress, capitalism, atheism, the theory of evolution (even though it was formulated by Darwin, a non-Jew), the media, bad movies, problems in the Middle East—even, at times in history, bad weather!

In some ways we have misinterpreted the ancient scapegoat ritual. It's not that we are *blaming* the goat for our sins. Hardly. The medieval commentator Nachmanides reminds us: "The goat simply bears away the transgressions of the Israelites"—transgressions that everyone in the community had to own up to. In the words of Rabbi Brad Hirschfield: "The success of the scapegoating ritual hinges on individuals' willingness to take responsibility for the wrongs they have done—just the opposite of the way we usually think about making a scapegoat of someone."

What's the lesson? Take responsibility for your own failings. Don't blame others. And don't even bother looking for a goat to carry your sins away.

YOU CALL THAT RELIGION?

We think that religion should be a source of comfort and peace, don't we? That it's about affirming life and feeling good about ourselves and about the community, right?

The ancient Canaanites apparently had other ideas

Leviticus 18:21 instructs the Israelites not to offer any children to Molech, and thus to avoid profaning the name of God. Who was Molech? It was the name of a Canaanite god. The name sounds like *melech*, the Hebrew word for "king," and it was probably based on the fact that "king" was a common name for ancient gods.

Did child sacrifice really happen? Sadly, probably so. The Bible mentions this horrible practice many times. It even occurred in Jerusalem, in the valley of Gehinnom, at a place called Tofet—and the name of that place became *Geihinnom*, the closest Hebrew equivalent for "hell." Archeologists, digging in the Middle East and in North Africa (especially in places that had been settled by the Canaanites or by people who lived in Canaanite colonies), have found remains of child sacrifice.

And why did they do this? We are not sure. Perhaps to guarantee fertility, or to ward off danger. There can be no doubt: The ancient Canaanite cult of Molech was a horrible, devastating way of doing religion. And, sadly, the Canaanites were not the only ancient culture to do this.

The Torah has only one response to this awful practice: NO! The Israelites had to keep themselves as a separate and holy people, and not imitate the ways of the nations that surrounded them—Canaan (the land that they would inherit) and Egypt (the land that they had just left).

To quote Rabbi David Polish: "Those gods stood for the insatiable demands of human blood made upon their worshippers. Men must offer up their children to please the gods. To this, beginning with Abraham, the Jew responded with a mocking question, 'This is religion?' and for this question he has paid a heavy price down through the ages."

Remember that it is Abraham who is dramatically taught the lesson not to sacrifice his son Isaac. At the decisive moment the angel of the Lord says, "Do not raise your hand against the boy, or do anything to him" (Gen. 22:12). This story and the laws of Leviticus reinforce the fundamental notion that Judaism is about life, not death. "Choose life" says the Torah, and when Jews lift a glass to offer a toast, what do they say? "*L'chayyim!* To life!"

It has not always been easy for Jews to be different. In fact, many Jews have rebelled against the idea of being different. But it is essential, especially when it means the difference between life and death.

Connections

℔ Have you ever scapegoated someone? Have you ever been scapegoated? What was it like?

℔ Are Jews still scapegoated today? Do you think Israel is scapegoated?

℔ How have you taken responsibility for your own weaknesses? How have you learned to overcome them?

℔ Does child sacrifice still exist anywhere in the world? Is terrorism through suicide bombing, for example, a form of child sacrifice?

℔ In what ways are Jews different from other people and from other religious cultures? Are those differences important?

❖ Kedoshim: Leviticus 19:1–20:27

If you could look at the location of Parashat Kedoshim in the Torah scroll, you would notice that the parchment is pretty much evenly balanced on each side. That's because Kedoshim is the "spine" of the entire Torah. It's simply that important. Kedoshim comprises the Holiness Code, the handbook for what Jews must do in order to be a holy people.

While much of the book of Leviticus is addressed only to the priests, the text makes it clear that the Holiness Code's commandments are addressed to "the whole Israelite community." Kedoshim is the most systematic understanding of Jewish ethics to be found in the Torah, and in many places contains parallels with the Ten Commandments.

Summary

ᚦ The Israelites are to be holy, as God is holy. Through ethical and communal action, all Jews can potentially achieve holiness. (19:1–2)

ᚦ The Israelites are commanded to leave the corners of their fields unharvested, and to leave any fallen fruit for the poor and the stranger. (19:9–10)

ᚦ The commandment not to steal and not to defraud immediately leads to the commandment to pay workers on time. To not pay workers on time is the same as stealing from them. (19:13)

ᚦ It is forbidden to curse the deaf or to put a stumbling block before the blind. (19:14)

ᚦ It is forbidden to hold a grudge or to exact vengeance against people. That is one way that you will "love your neighbor [or fellow] as yourself." (19:18)

The Big Ideas

ᚦ **Holiness is one of the most precious ideas that Judaism gave to the world.** Holiness means something that is distinct, set apart, lofty. It is an attribute that "belongs" to God, but human beings can become holy in the ways that we interact with others and by the kind of society that we choose to create. Holiness, in fact, is the only quality of God to which human beings can aspire.

ᚦ **Judaism believes in *tzedakah* (righteous giving).** The Torah makes it clear that we must take care of the poor and the vulnerable in our midst, and that those actions must become public policy.

ᚦ **People should not compromise their dignity by having to wait for something that is owed to them.** That is the rationale for paying workers on time. So, too, the corners of the field "belong" to the poor; they should not have to beg for *tzedakah*.

ᚦ **Putting a stumbling block before the blind does not necessarily mean putting something in front of a blind person so that he**

or she will fall over it. It is usually interpreted to mean that you should not deceive people and not take advantage of their ignorance or lack of awareness.

ზ **"Love your neighbor as yourself" is perhaps the best-known verse in the entire Torah, and is sometimes also known as the Golden Rule.** Some old Jewish prayer books had this commandment printed on the first page; it was considered to be the *sha'ar tefilah,* the gateway to prayer itself. But love is not primarily an emotional response to our fellow human beings. It is love in the form of action—specifically, the understanding that our neighbors are, in deep ways, just like us, and that we should treat them as we want to be treated.

Divrei Torah
GIVING IS ALL WE'VE GOT

Everyone knows that *tzedakah* is an essential Jewish value. Sooner or later, every Jew learns that the proper translation of *tzedakah* is not "charity," but "justice." There is a big difference between these two terms. "Charity" comes from the Latin word *caritas,* which means "to love." Charity, therefore, means giving as an act of love. *Tzedakah* comes from the Hebrew *tzedek,* which means "justice." It means giving because it is the right thing to do. It's a mitzvah, a commandment (not just a good deed) that you perform out of a sense of obligation, whether you are feeling "charitable" or not.

But have you ever wondered when and where the idea of *tzedakah* came from? From right here, in Parashat Kedoshim. The Torah portion actually offers the ancient Israelites two ways to do *tzedakah,* and both have to do with agriculture. The first (*peah*) is to leave the corners of the field unharvested so that the poor can help themselves. The Mishnah says: "These are the obligations without measure, whose reward lasts into eternity"—and the first item on the list is *peah.* The second is *leket,* letting the poor take anything that falls to the ground during the gleaning (harvesting) of the field.

Yes, we care about the dignity of the poor. But it's not as if you are giving away what is yours, because you don't own it in the first place! According to Jewish law, if you own a field, the corners of that field are really not yours; they belong to those who are not as fortunate as you. In fact, if you don't give to the poor, it's as if you are actually stealing from them! *Tzedakah* is the mandatory sharing of your field or your income.

Tzedakah is part of the Holiness Code; it's a way of becoming holy. It is based on the still-radical notion that you can't have it all. You don't own all your stuff (whether it's a field or money); the poor get a share of it. You don't own all of your time; Shabbat is a day of the week when you don't think about what you own (which is one good reason why traditional Jews don't go shopping on Shabbat). Ideally, on Shabbat you don't think about what you have, or about what you can consume, or about what you can buy. You think about relationships, which are themselves holy. You think about your responsibility to others, especially those in need.

The contemporary scholar and teacher Micah Goodman teaches: "The holiest word in Hebrew is a word we cannot pronounce: the four-letter Name of God, the vowels of which have disappeared. The holiest place in the world (the Holy of Holies) is a place that we cannot enter. The holy is about what is beyond you and not accessible. It is about what I cannot control."

This is perhaps the most beautiful thing about *tzedakah*. It means giving of yourself. But it also means giving up something that is part of yourself—your money, your time, your efforts. Because you don't fully own or control anything. And because God wants us to share.

Not only that: some of the happiest people you'll ever meet are those who give *tzedakah*. Try it.

THE GREATEST MITZVAH

Quick joke: A rabbi and an astronomer sat next to each other on a plane. The astronomer said to the rabbi: "I don't know much about Judaism, but wouldn't you say that the essence of Judaism is 'you shall love your neighbor as yourself'?" To which the rabbi responded: "I don't know much about astronomy, but wouldn't you say that the essence of astronomy is 'twinkle, twinkle, little star'?"

The point of the joke: one should be very careful about not oversimplifying things—including Judaism. And yet, we can forgive the astronomer for thinking that loving your neighbor is the essence of Judaism. No less an authority than the great Rabbi Akiba said: "'Love your neighbor as yourself' is the great principle [*k'lal gadol*] of the Torah."

This great principle culminates the Holiness Code in this Torah portion, and is one of the most commonly quoted verses of the entire Bible.

But wait a second. It's a commandment. How can you command someone to love? For that matter, how can you command someone to feel anything?

The clue is right there in the Hebrew. "Love your neighbor as yourself" is *ve-ahavta le-rei'akha kamokha*. Most of the time, when the Torah speaks of loving, it's more like *ve-ahavta et* . . . The *et* is a small Hebrew word indicating that the object of the sentence is coming up. Here, it's "you should love—*to* your neighbor." This doesn't even make sense. How do you love *to* someone?

That's the whole point. Love is not only a way that you feel; love is an action. Love is therefore something that you do *to* your neighbor. In fact, in the Bible, quite often *ahavah*, which means "love," doesn't really mean love as an emotion, but as a way of saying that you live in a sacred relationship with someone—that there are responsibilities. We are commanded to love the stranger, which means that we have responsibilities to him or her. We are commanded to love God, which means that we have sacred responsibilities. And, yes, our love for our neighbor is based on taking care of that person as well.

And because love is more than just a feeling, because "love" means that you have to act in certain ways, it takes practice. If you want to be a great baseball player or guitarist or dancer or artist, you have to work at it. In the same way, if you want to be a good Jew and a mensch, you have to work on it as well. Many of the mitzvot are actually part of an exercise program to make people better.

In an old *Peanuts* cartoon, Snoopy says: "I love humanity; it's people I can't stand." Martin Luther King Jr. once said of a senator who believed that blacks and whites should be completely separated: "I do not like Senator Eastland, but I must learn to love him."

The great Jewish theologian and social activist Abraham Joshua

Heschel (and a friend of King) writes: "The basic dignity of man is not made up of his achievements, virtues, or special talents. It is inherent in his very being. The commandment, 'Love your neighbor as yourself' (Lev.19:18) calls upon us to love not only the virtuous and the wise, but also the vicious and the stupid person."

You love humanity, in the abstract? Great. You love your family, and your friends? Wonderful. But how are you going to love the neighbor you don't like, the classmate you don't care for, or the coworker who is a pain?

Try treating them as you would want to be treated. That's where you start.

Connections

Ⅎ What is your definition of holiness? What things, places, times, and relationships are holy for you?

Ⅎ What kind of *tzedakah* do you and your family support? Why are those causes important to you?

Ⅎ In what ways do you try to fulfill the mitzvah of "love your neighbor"?

Ⅎ Do you agree that "loving your neighbor" is a difficult commandment?

❖ 'Emor: Leviticus 21:1–24:23

Priests and holidays—that's what this portion is all about. Parashat 'Emor returns to a big theme in Leviticus: the rules connected to the ancient priesthood. It contains descriptions of the various limitations placed on the priests, such as remaining separate from dead bodies, not marrying divorced women, and not having any physical defects.

The rest of the portion is concerned primarily with the ancient sacred calendar of the Israelites, listing the festivals, and detailing when and how they are to be observed.

But a curious thing happens at the end of the portion: two people get in a fight, one curses—and boy, is that a mistake.

Summary

ᛏ The Torah text outlines certain rules that priests had to follow—
the primary one being that they cannot have contact with the
dead, except for their closest relatives. (21:1–4)

ᛏ Priests are prohibited from marrying women who had been prostitutes, or divorced women. Neither can they shave the corners of
their heads, or their beards, or have any physical defects. (21:5–24)

ᛏ The Torah presents the festival calendar of the ancient Israelites:
Pesach; the feast of unleavened bread (which, apparently, was a
separate holiday from Pesach); the offerings of the Omer to mark
the barley harvest; a holiday with "loud blasts" (the earliest reference to the holy day that would become known as Rosh Hashanah); the day of atonement (Yom Kippur); the feast of booths
(Sukkot); a "mini-festival" on the eighth day of Sukkot (Shemini
Atzeret). The text devotes the majority of its words to the observance of Sukkot.

ᛏ In one of the few incidents to actually happen in Leviticus, a
"half-Israelite" (the son of an Israelite mother and an Egyptian
father) and an Israelite get into a fight. In the middle of the fight,
the "half-Israelite" pronounces the Name of God in a blasphe-
mous way (perhaps the way some people would now say "God-
damn it!"). The punishment for the blasphemer is to be stoned to
death. Moses takes that opportunity to remind the Israelites that
not only will blasphemers be put to death, but so will those who
have taken a human life. (24:10–23)

The Big Ideas

ᛏ **For the ancient Israelites, life and death had to remain strictly
separate.** That is why the priests were prohibited from having
contact with the dead, with the exception of their closest relatives. The priest represented life, a living tradition, contact with
the living God, and therefore had to be completely separated
from anything that was connected to death.

ᛏ **Being a priest, like all Jewish obligations, comes with certain
limitations.** While it was undoubtedly a great honor to be a

member of the priestly class, there were certain things that the priests could not do (in addition to no contact with the dead, they couldn't marry divorcées or women of questionable reputation; shave the corners of their heads; be blind or lame; or have other physical disabilities). While we find these rules offensive today, they remind us that ancient Israelite religion believed in the striving for perfection, and that the priests were expected to be "perfect."

ᛒ **For the ancient Israelites, the experience of gratitude for the harvest seems to have been of paramount importance.** That would explain why so much of Leviticus 23 is devoted to a very detailed description of the festival of Sukkot. It is also the holiday whose description here most closely resembles the way it is observed in modern times.

ᛒ **The Name of God contains great power, and you don't mess with it.** The ancient Israelites took the Name of God very seriously. That Name of God contained the Hebrew letters *yud heh vav heh* (YHVH). The vowels have become lost to us, and therefore the Name is now pronounced Adonai. To this day, many traditional Jews refuse both to say and to write "Adonai" (preferring *ha-Shem,* "the Name").

Divrei Torah
DEALING WITH DEATH

Ever notice how many terms we have for death? We talk about people "passing away," or simply "passing." Sometimes people talk about "going to a better place." Or: "he's gone." "She's left us." "He kicked the bucket." Here's an interesting one: "He bought the farm"—which apparently refers to the fact that if a farmer had purchased life insurance, his or her death would allow the survivors to "cash in," and help them, well, "buy the farm." The Bible has its own share of euphemisms for death. There's "going the way of all flesh," "going the way of all the earth," "sleeping with one's fathers." And *niftar,* which means to be "released" from obligation.

No doubt about it: we don't like to talk about death.

Does that have anything to do with a particular passage that we find at the very beginning of our Torah portion? "Speak to the priests, the sons of Aaron, and say to them: None shall defile himself for any [dead] person among his kin" (21:1–2). The text then goes on to give the exceptions to that rule, which includes close relatives.

Why are the priests forbidden from having contact with the dead? (By the way, among traditional Jews, this is still the case. Traditional Jews who believe themselves to be descended from the ancient priests [*kohanim*] do not enter cemeteries or have any other contact with the dead.)

First, you have to understand that much of the Torah was an attempt to teach the Israelites what not to do—and, in particular, that meant: don't act like they used to act in Egypt! In Egypt, the job of dealing with the dead was given, specifically, to the priests. Much of Egyptian religion was centered on death. The pyramids were huge tombs in which Pharaohs were buried with all their belongings, including their slaves! One of the most important books in ancient Egypt was *The Egyptian Book of the Dead*.

Judaism accepts the reality of death, but it constantly affirms life. Traditionally, Jews are buried in linen shrouds that have no pockets, which reminds us that we take nothing with us into death. The Torah prohibits trying to gain access to the dead and talking to them. While Judaism believes that the soul goes on after death, traditional Jewish texts don't discuss this very much.

Judaism is the only religion in the world where priests cannot come into contact with the dead. Rabbi Shlomo Riskin teaches: "Our religious leadership must deal with the living and not the dead: must spend its time teaching Torah and accessing Jewish experiences . . . must be dedicated primarily to this world rather than the world to come."

Are the priests therefore forbidden from any dealing with any dead people? Not exactly. Rashi teaches: "None shall defile himself for any dead person among his kin. But for a dead person who is not 'among his kin'—if there are not other Jews who can see to the burial—he may do so." When compassion is necessary, the priest is always there. Today, rabbis regularly perform funerals and are trained to do so. And all of us are taught to observe the commandments of *k'vod ha-met*, honoring the deceased, and *nichum aveilim*, comforting the mourners. No, we don't glorify or fixate on death, but, yes, we show compassion for the dead as well as the living.

DEALING WITH DISABILITY

Jason is about twelve-and-a-half years old. He's a great kid, a good athlete, a fine Hebrew student. He walks with a slight limp because his left leg is slightly shorter than his right. The cantor assigns him his bar mitzvah Torah portion—this week's portion, 'Emor. As Jason is going through the text with the cantor, he reads the passage that says: certain physical defects disqualify a person from bringing offerings to the ancient altar—among them, someone "who . . . has a limb too short or too long" (21:18). Jason is really upset. "Does this mean that I can't read the Torah?" he asks, almost at the point of tears.

No doubt about it: this passage from 'Emor is pretty troubling. The text says that people with certain disabilities or characteristics could not offer the sacrificial animals on the altar: people who are blind, lame, or have a limb too short or too long; someone with a broken leg or broken arm; a hunchback; a dwarf; someone with a growth in his eye, or with a boil, or with damaged genitalia. Ouch, ouch, ouch. It seems very cruel and heartless, doesn't it?

This is a constant theme of Leviticus: everything that is offered on the ancient altar had to be perfect and unblemished, and, by extension, everyone who did the offering had to be unblemished as well. How are we to understand this?

Perhaps it meant that you should always present your best, and be your best, when you approach God. That's what Maimonides thought: "Everything that is done for the sake of God must be the finest and best. If one builds a house of prayer it should be finer than his private dwelling. If he feeds the hungry, he should give them the best and sweetest of his table. If he clothes the naked, he should give him the finest of his garments."

Perhaps there was a little bit of psychology going on here. Perhaps the authors of the text were worried that a priest with some kind of deformity would distract the worshipers from their sacred duties.

Our sensibilities and sensitivities have evolved. Nowadays, most synagogues and Jewish community centers pride themselves on being accessible to the handicapped. There have even been blind and deaf rabbis. We no longer disqualify someone from service to the Jewish people based on how they look, or the various physical challenges that they encounter—or, at least, we shouldn't.

The search for perfection can be dangerous. Some boys use steroids. Some girls want to be very thin, and this sometimes results in eating disorders. As Shulamit Reinharz has written: "While the priest's bodily perfection may no longer be a Jewish necessity, the idea and expectations of bodily perfection have become a cultural goal of the wider American Jewish population, with terrible consequences—particularly for women, regardless of age."

Leave perfection to the ancient priests. Don't bother trying to be perfect. No one is perfect on the inside or the outside. While we care about who we are and how we look, remember last week's Torah portion and its great principle, to love our neighbor as yourself. We have to be good, not perfect.

Connections

ᵬ What do you think of the various limitations imposed on the priests? Do any of them make sense to you? What would be their modern equivalents?

ᵬ What are some other ways that Judaism teaches us about the separation of life from death?

ᵬ Do you agree with the Torah portion's interest in physical perfection?

ᵬ How should synagogues treat people with disabilities? What do synagogues do in this regard? How about your synagogue?

❖ Be-har: Leviticus 25:1–26:2

The book of Leviticus has been a wild ride: from details about sacrifices, to laws about animals that you can and cannot eat; to skin diseases and other bodily issues; to laws about priests and the sacred days of the ancient Jewish calendar . . . and, now, to the way that Jews must treat the Land of Israel. Just as the Israelites must observe the Sabbath, the land itself needs a Sabbath—"resting" after six years of sowing and pruning. Then, every fifty years, the land has to return to its original owners, who might have lost their land due to financial difficulty.

Leviticus began with an exhausting description of offerings to God, offerings that actually came from God and belong to God. It turns out that the Land of Israel itself is like a sacred offering, which also belongs to God.

Summary

- ℔ Every seven years the Land of Israel must observe a Sabbath. Like people, the land must be allowed to "rest." This is known as the *shemitah,* or sabbatical, year. (25:1–7)
- ℔ Every fifty years people who had lost their land due to economic disaster are allowed to reclaim their property. The Hebrew term for this is *dror* (release from economic servitude) and the fiftieth year is known as the *yovel* year. It is proclaimed on Yom Kippur, and it begins with the blast of the shofar.
- ℔ If someone is in economic trouble and has to sell part of his or her property, that person's nearest relative must redeem what his relative has sold. (25:25–28)
- ℔ If your kinsman becomes poor, do not loan money to him or her on interest, or treat him or her as a slave. (25:35–46)

The Big Ideas

- ℔ **The Land of Israel—indeed, the entire earth—belongs to God.** Human beings are only the stewards, or managers, of the land. It is therefore human responsibility to take care of God's gift to human beings, and to make sure that it is not abused and that it is allowed to replenish itself. In that sense, the land is like a human being—it, too, needs a Sabbath.
- ℔ **Owning is temporary.** This may be the most radical text in the entire Torah. Imagine: if a family becomes impoverished and has to sell its land, it can reclaim that land after the fiftieth year. This is so important that it is actually written on the Liberty Bell: "Proclaim liberty throughout the land unto all the inhabitants thereof" (25:10). But "liberty" doesn't only mean freedom from political oppression; it means freedom from eternal economic op-

pression. That is what the Torah wants to abolish—the idea that people would always be poor.

ᛒ *Tzedakah* **begins with those who are closest to us.** Many people care passionately about poor people who live on the other side of the world, and people they will never meet. While this is noble, it is far nobler to pay attention to those who are closest to you—your immediate relatives.

ᛒ **Family is family.** Yes, our moral responsibilities begin with those who are closest to us—our relatives. And yet, sometimes we have to fight the temptation to be cruel to them, and to take advantage of their weaknesses, maybe even their impoverished state. That is why the laws about taking care of your relatives end with the proclamation: "I the Lord am your God, who brought you of the land of Egypt" (25:38). Don't become a Pharaoh to your family!

Divrei Torah
JEWISH MATH CLASS

Quick, math whizzes: what "base" is our mathematical system based on? Right: base ten.

Okay, now for the Jewish math class: what numerical "base" is Judaism based on?

Answer: Seven.

It turns out that all of Judaism is based on the number seven. Here goes: The seventh day of the week is holy—Shabbat. And the seventh month of the year is especially holy—Tishrei, which is when Rosh Hashanah, Yom Kippur, and Sukkot occur. (That's if you start counting the year with the first month, Nisan. But what if you start counting the year with Tishrei? Then the seventh month becomes Nisan—which is when Pesach occurs. Also deeply holy.) We can call either of these seventh months the "expanded Shabbat." As Rabbi Saul Berman notes: "God's creation of the universe in seven periods of time is celebrated not only on the seventh day, but on the seventh of every natural time period."

Okay, a Shabbat of days, and a Shabbat of months. And in this Torah portion, we meet a Shabbat of years. Every seventh year, the land lies fallow—the *shemitah* year. (By the way, sometimes teachers and spiritual leaders get their own *shemitah* year. It's called a sabbatical—from the word "Sabbath.") It's not only that the land lies fallow; there's something else that happens, or doesn't happen. Deut. 15:2 adds something to the *shemitah* observance: during this time you can't collect debts from those who owe you money!

Oh, wait—there's more. Multiply seven times seven (which gets you forty-nine), and then add one—which gets you fifty. Every fifty years, property must return to its original inhabitants, who might have lost it because of economic hardship. That's the *yovel*—which we sometimes translate as "jubilee." Was it ever really observed? Probably not. But that didn't stop American blacks from declaring that the year of Lincoln's Emancipation Proclamation (1863) was, in fact, a jubilee year.

The Torah portion begins by telling us that these laws were given on Mount Sinai, a big deal. But why? you might ask. That's exactly what some ancient sages asked: "'The Lord spoke to Moses on Mount Sinai': Why is *shemitah* connected with Mount Sinai? Weren't all the commandments said from Sinai?"

Why is this big? Because the Exodus from Egypt was not just a bunch of Hebrew slaves escaping from Pharaoh. It was intended to create a social revolution. It's as if God were saying to the Israelites: First, I am going to bring you into the Land of Israel. This is my gift to you. Be good to it. Don't abuse it. And not only that. Every seventh year you have to cancel debts! And every fifty years, all economic injustices are healed! People are not meant to be physically or economically oppressed forever.

True freedom means equality and responsibility. Every once in a while society needs a reset. A radical notion and a lofty goal, then— and now.

WHOSE POOR COME FIRST?

The imaginary synagogue Congregation Or Tzedek (Light of justice) requires that all candidates complete a mitzvah project as part of their preparation for becoming bar or bat mitzvah. This is pretty much standard operating procedure for many synagogues. The purpose is to teach kids that acts of giving are an essential part of Jewish life. The old joke is that it's not just about the "bar" it's also about the "mitzvah."

Three kids from our imaginary synagogue are having a discussion about their projects.

Ivan: "I'm giving a portion of my bar mitzvah gift money to our local Jewish Federation. After all, they help elderly Jews in our community. Plus, they give money to Jewish kids to go to summer camp. I feel like I owe them."

Jennifer: "That is so narrow-minded! I am donating a portion of my bat mitzvah money to our local symphony. After all, all kinds of people love music."

Alex: "I'm giving a portion to the needy in Africa. After all, they need it the most."

Conversations like these actually happen—a lot. Some Jews are *universalists*—"we should take care of everyone." And some are *particularists*—"we should take of ourselves." Some people think that Jews should be saving the rain forests, or helping animals. And others believe that Jews should only give to specifically Jewish causes.

And it all gets a little bit more complicated because the "non-Jewish" causes that some Jews support—environment, helping animals, curing illnesses—are all connected to Jewish values. Judaism talks about both *tikkun olam* (healing the world) and *k'lal Yisrael* (caring for your own).

Let's go back to the Torah portion. It clearly says that if your relatives become poor you are to take care of them. This becomes a core Jewish principle. According to the Shulhan Arukh, the most important compilation of Jewish law: "The poor of your city take precedence over the poor of another city. The needy of Israel receive priority over the poor of the Diaspora. Obligations to local resident poor precede those owed to transient poor who have just come into the city. One's impoverished family members come before another poor person."

Judaism teaches that you best learn how to take care of other people, and the wider world, when you "practice" on your own people. While the expression "charity begins at home" is not a Jewish one, it might be; however, Judaism would add, "so long as it doesn't end at home."

Israeli Prime Minister Menachem Begin cared passionately about his own people but sometimes it seemed that he was disinterested in the rest of the world. Yet Rabbi Daniel Gordis writes: "In 1977, when desperate Vietnamese boat people were plucked from the high seas by an Israeli freighter, after ships from other countries had ignored them, Begin, in what was essentially his first act as prime minister, ordered that they be brought to Israel, where he made them citizens."

Yes, we should care about our fellow Jews first. And when we get good at it, we should care about others too.

Connections

🕭 What do you think of the idea of letting the land lie fallow (*shemitah*)?

🕭 How about returning land to its original owners (*yovel*)?

🕭 What could be some problems associated with these concepts?

🕭 Why do you think that the *yovel* was never put into practice?

🕭 If the *yovel*, or jubilee year, probably never really happened, why continue to learn about it?

🕭 Do you agree that supporting one's own poor takes precedence over supporting other people? What could be some of the problems in doing so?

❖ Be-ḥukkotai: Leviticus 26:3–27:34

Just in case you were looking forward to this, the last portion of Leviticus, you should know that it's a bit of a downer. Actually, make that a major downer. God tells the Israelites what will happen if they follow God's laws. That part is okay—but the part about what will happen if they don't obey God's laws—oy.

This parashah, and all of Leviticus, ends with a somewhat anticlimactic piece about the funding of the ancient sanctuary.

Summary

🕭 God promises that if the Israelites observe God's commandments to observe the *shemitah* and the *yovel*, then God will bless the land with prosperity. (26:3–13)

🕭 Big "but" coming: if the Israelites do not observe God's commandments, they are entering into a "world of pain." Illnesses, wild beasts, military defeat, the destruction of the Land of Israel—even cannibalism!—will follow. (26:14–45)

🕭 God tells Moses details about the funding of the ancient

Tabernacle—specific amounts people should give based on age and gender. There are also provisions for those who vow to donate animals that would be converted into money in support of the sanctuary, or who vow to donate land or tithe produce. (27:1–34)

The Big Ideas

 ♄ **Following God's commandments is a social good.** It's not that if you do God's will everything will be fine with you. It's not about "you"—in the singular. This passage tells us that if the Jewish people obey God, then good things will happen in their land. While this idea of reward and punishment is debatable (and many find it, frankly, ethically questionable, if not offensive), it is clearly what the biblical writers believed.

 ♄ **Actions have consequences.** If you are troubled by all the threat and punishment passages in Leviticus, join the club. It even has a name—the "reproof" (*tokhecha*). It is such a horrible section that in synagogue it is read quickly and in a low voice. You just want to get through it and get over it. But if you read the passage carefully, you will notice that it is saying something important: societies collapse when justice is not done.

 ♄ **It is a mitzvah to support the institutions of the Jewish community.** Many people complain that "religion costs too much!" If that is true, then it has always been the case. The Torah specifies the amounts that people should give, based on age and gender, as well as other details of giving. These passages seem quite relevant to modern Jews, because people still argue about the best way to support synagogues and other Jewish institutions.

Divrei Torah
IS GOD A BULLY?

Bullies. Don't you hate them? But who ever expected that God would become The Supreme Bully? God seems to be threatening the Israelites with the ultimatum "Do what I say, or else . . ." Just read the list of curses that this Torah portion contains—everything from threatening to shut down the rain to (gulp) forcing the Israelites to "devour" their children.

Okay, let's figure this one out. Nachmanides, the medieval commentator, teaches: "You must know and understand that everything in this chapter actually took place during the First Temple period and its aftermath, including both the exile to Babylonia and the redemption from there, for that is when they worshiped idols and did all these evil things."

Then came the punishments, which seemed to be a fulfillment of the dire warnings of Leviticus. When the Assyrians destroyed the Northern Kingdom of Israel in 722 BCE, they did horrible things to the Jewish people and to the Land of Israel. The same sort of things happened two centuries later, when the Babylonians destroyed the Southern Kingdom of Judah.

Did God actually bring all those curses upon the Jewish people? Let's imagine it this way: perhaps the people were trying to figure out why all these terrible things had happened to them. In ancient times, the only real answer to that question would be: God. God was punishing the people for their sins. The Jews of ancient times believed that God "used" the enemies of the Jews as a way of disciplining God's people for their sins.

What were those sins? The list is long, and includes the sin of failing to let the land rest for one year out of every seven (*shemitah*). The Torah warns that if the people don't observe *shemitah* they will be expelled from the land, and they won't be permitted to return until the land has made up for all the missed *shemitah* years (26:34–35). What is so bad about not letting the land rest? Because it has to do with not exploiting the land—and also the most vulnerable people who work the land.

So, God gives the Jewish people laws that help to create a just society. That was the whole purpose of *shemitah* (sabbatical year) and *yovel* (jubilee year, returning the land to its original owner every fifty years). If you don't create a just society, then that society will crumble. You will have people who show only callousness to the poor. That society will wind up in ruins—and you are free to imagine that God, who feels *very* strongly about justice, will punish you.

Cantor Sarah Sager describes the mindset of the final portion of Leviticus: "It is both bribe and promise, exhortation and encouragement. The physical and ethical dimensions of God's creation are dependent upon each other, and we ignore that relationship at our peril."

If we don't create a just society, that society will fall apart.

If you look at the long sweep of human history, societies that ignored social justice did, in fact, crumble—think of medieval Spain, Nazi Germany, the former Soviet Union.

Sometimes God may seem like a bully. The same with our parents. But we need to try to get behind the threats of punishment to the real issue of how we behave. There is definitely more here than meets the eye.

SACRED MONEY

We have come full circle . . . and it's about money! Go back to the end of the book of Exodus, and you will see it: Exodus ended on the subject of "how do we pay for the Tabernacle?" And that's how Leviticus ends as well.

The Torah portion has already figured out what people are "worth" in terms of taxation. A man between the ages of twenty to sixty is worth fifty shekels; a woman of the same age, thirty shekels. Once a man hits the age of sixty, his "value" drops to fifteen shekels, and a woman's drops to ten. Yes, it's sexist and ageist. But we're talking about something from long ago, and that's the way it was back then. (Come to think of it: has it really changed that much? Even nowadays, women earn less than men, and there is rampant age discrimination in the workplace.)

What is the best way to financially support our religious institutions? It's a question that we still wrestle with. Every institution costs money to sustain, and the modern synagogue is no exception. Though most synagogues today expect their members to pay a specific sum, called membership dues, this isn't always the case. Synagogues have all kinds of ways of raising the money they need, including voluntary giving.

Some are experimenting with a "pay what you want" system. Rabbi Rick Jacobs, the president of the Union for Reform Judaism, has supported this new approach and said that voluntary pledging may positively change the way people view their synagogues: "The bond that holds the Jewish people to one another is not primarily and fundamentally a financial arrangement, and when we suggest that it might be, it undermines everything we stand for."

A voluntary pledge seems very different from the ancient model described in our Torah portion. There, what you have to pay is spelled out. In postbiblical times, and in medieval times, the community could force its members to pay community dues. Maimonides teaches: "People of the city can force each other to build a wall, doors, and bolt; and a synagogue, and to buy a Torah scroll, and the Prophets and the Writings for anyone in the community who wants to read."

In other words, there was general agreement—a communal covenant, if you will—that a community needs to be physically secure (cities in the Middle Ages were frequently walled in order to keep out enemies), as well as spiritually vibrant, by having a synagogue, a Torah scroll, and a full Bible that would be available for people to read.

When you think about it, support of the Jewish community and its institutions is entirely voluntary today, since nobody forces you to be a member of a synagogue and pay dues. The fact remains, however: synagogues require money to keep the lights on and to pay salaries. They depend on the goodwill of people who feel a sense of responsibility to support the Jewish community.

Yes, it's another expense, and money is often tight. But if we don't support our synagogue and Jewish community, who will?

Connections

ᵽ How do you feel about the list of blessings and curses? Do they make you afraid? Angry?

ᵽ The tradition says that the curses should be read in synagogue quickly and in a low voice. Do you agree with that tradition? Do you have any other suggestions for dealing with passages in the Torah that seem offensive or frightening?

ᵽ Do you agree that unjust societies are often destroyed, either from the outside or from the inside? Can you give some examples? How could those societies have saved themselves?

ᵽ What do you think is the best way to support synagogues? Dues? Donations? Giving whatever you can?

NUMBERS

❖ Be-midbar: Numbers 1:1–4:20

We start a new book of the Torah: Numbers, which in Hebrew is Be-midbar (In the wilderness). The book gets its English name from the various censuses that are central to this Torah portion. Each census has a different purpose: to determine the number of able-bodied men available to serve as soldiers in a time of war; the number of Levites; and then, the numbers in a Levite subclan, the family of Kohath.

As the Israelites prepare to march into the wilderness, it becomes necessary to determine the positions of the various tribes as they carry the ark and the sacred vessels of the Tabernacle, the Tent of Meeting (*mishkan*).

Summary

ـ God commands Moses to take a census of all men over the age of twenty who are able to bear arms. The text lists the head of each tribe who will assist with the census, and then lists the population of each tribe. The total number of Israelites (or, more accurately, males over the age of twenty) is 603,550. (1:1–54)

ـ God gives Moses and Aaron the details of how the Israelite camp is to be arranged around the Tabernacle—on which side each tribe is to stand—along with the chieftain of the tribe and the number of troops in each tribe. (2:1–14)

ـ God commands Moses to take a census of the Levites, who will be responsible for taking care of the Tabernacle's vessels. The age limit is all males from the age of one month and older. The Levites serve in the place of all Israelite firstborn sons, which is the origin of the traditional ceremony of *pidyon ha-ben* (the redemption of the firstborn) when the child is thirty days old. The Torah then records the census of all the subclans of the Levites: Gershon, Kohath, and Merari—along with the specific duties of those clans. (3:5–39)

ϯ The Kohath clan is assigned the most delicate, and perhaps the most dangerous, work of all. They are to carry the most sacred objects of the Tabernacle, and not by hand. Rather, they had to carry them on their shoulders. (4:1–20)

The Big Ideas

ϯ **Every Jew "counts."** Wherever they have lived, Jews have always been a minority. That is one reason why it has been necessary for every Jew to do the best that he or she can to ensure the vitality of Jewish life. A Hasidic teacher, Levi Yitzchak of Berdichev, taught that there was the same number of Israelites—603,550—as there are letters in the Torah scroll. Just as the Torah scroll would be invalid if a letter were missing, if any Jew slacks off, Judaism itself loses energy.

ϯ **The Tabernacle is at the center of the Israelite camp.** The purpose of the Jewish people is to be a holy people, a people centered around its tradition. The Tabernacle was like a portable version of Mount Sinai. The arrangement of the tribes around the Tabernacle is hardly random. A midrash says that the tribes stood around it in exactly the same pattern as their ancestors stood around Jacob's coffin when they carried him back to Israel for burial. In this way, we learn that Jews always carry their memories with them.

ϯ **For a Levite, one month old is "old enough."** Whereas the age for fighting was twenty, the age for levitical duty—taking care of the Tabernacle—is only one month. What can a one-month-old child do to take care of the Tabernacle? Nothing. But this teaches us that Jewish education must begin when a child is very young. Our earliest memories and experiences help shape the kinds of people we will become.

ϯ **Even the most "menial" tasks can be holy.** The Kohath clan, a subclan of the Levites, was responsible for carrying the holiest objects of the Tabernacle. They were not supposed to carry them by hand; rather, they had to carry them on their shoulders. This is an act of physical exertion. Jewish life requires many kinds of exertions—intellectual, spiritual, and physical.

Divrei Torah

DO YOU COUNT?

If you find this Torah portion somewhat tedious, you're not alone. Generations of Jews would probably agree with you. All those names of obscure people, all those numbers—it is about as exciting as reading the telephone book.

Contemporary Jews like to wonder aloud about how many Jews there really are, and what those numbers mean. They love to argue about who is a Jew, and how many Jews there are in different countries, and where Jews live, and what Jews do. You really can't blame them. After all, for a people that lost six million during the Shoah (Holocaust), numbers matter.

But in biblical times, what good was a census, anyway? And why does God tell Moses to count the Israelites? After all, doesn't God know everything, especially how many Israelites there are?

A medieval sage, Rabbi Isaac Arama, teaches that this was so Moses would know that each Israelite was not just part of the entire people, but that each one had individual worth. "They were all equal in stature, and yet the stature of each one was different." Every Jew has something precious inside of him or her. And if we take seriously the idea that the 603,550 Israelites in the census represent the traditional number of 603,550 letters in the Torah, we can interpret that to mean that every Jew has some Torah not only to learn, but also to teach.

Take another look at that number—603,550. Are those all the Israelites? No way. Think about who wasn't counted. Cantor Rachel Stock Spilker writes: "What about the woman who might have wished to fight? Or how about the 19-year-old man, just months short of his 20th birthday, eager to serve God and his people? How about the 23-year-old male who doesn't have the right number of limbs since one of his was lost in a childhood accident?"

This is always the problem with counting people: often some get omitted. That not only means that the count or the census is inaccurate; it means that people are left out, and they know it. It hurts. That is why the term for "counting" is *se'u rosh*—literally, "lift up the head." The act of counting should lift people's heads, and help them feel that their lives and contributions have dignity and meaning.

That is why some people say that nowadays when we count Jews we should make sure that every Jew counts.

How are you making sure that your Jewish life counts?

WHO'S YOUR DADDY—REALLY?

Is there an omission in this Torah portion? Numbers 3 begins: "This is the line of Aaron and Moses at the time that the Lord spoke with Moses on Mount Sinai." And then, it goes on to list Aaron's sons—but not the sons of Moses. Why does it only list Aaron's sons? What ever happened to the sons of Moses?

Moses did have sons—Gershom and Eliezer. And they are famous for . . . nothing. They disappear from the story. Why? Perhaps it wants to make a very big point: Moses was not a king. It was not his intention, nor was it the Torah's intention, to have him create a dynasty. His sons are, well, just "normal" people.

Why then does it list Aaron's sons? Precisely because Moses was their teacher—Moshe Rabbeinu, "Moses, our rabbi," the master teacher of Israel. Rashi, the great medieval commentator, teaches us: "It lists only the sons of Aaron, but calls them 'the line of Moses'—because he taught them Torah. Teaching Torah to someone is like being their parent."

This reminds us that teaching is so important—that it is like parenting, and that parenting is a form of teaching. Indeed, the Hebrew word for "teacher" (*moreh*) and "parent" (*horeh*) are from the same root. And so is the word Torah! They all mean "instruction" or "teaching" in one form or another.

When Jews remember a departed father, it is traditional to refer to him as *avi mori*, "my father, my teacher." That is the greatest sign of respect, the highest compliment one can utter. The job of a Jewish parent is to be a teacher of Torah. And when people cannot have children, one way that they can be involved in nurturing young people is, in fact, to teach them. If you ask teachers how they feel about what they do, they might just tell you that, at times, they do feel as if they are parenting their students.

Look at all the family names in this Torah portion. The Torah is pretty obsessed with who your father is (much less, sadly, with who your mother is). People are often described as being *ben* . . . (the son of . . .). For the first thousand years of Judaism, during the biblical era, Jewish identity was in fact passed down by the father. (It changed in the Rabbinic period to the mother . . . that is another story.)

But, in later generations, Judaism became less concerned with "who's your daddy?" and more concerned with "who's your teacher?" That is why Rabbinic literature is filled with references to who taught what to whom, and the necessity of quoting your sources accurately (meaning, don't plagiarize! and give credit where credit is due). The ancient sages even said that if both your father and your teacher were taken captive (a sad reality in ancient times) and you only had enough money to ransom one of them the teacher gets priority.

The contemporary teacher Howard Eilberg-Schwartz teaches us: "Just as a son must perpetuate his father's lineage, a disciple must preserve his rabbi's teaching."

So, who are your teachers? What is their Torah? How are you furthering what they have taught you?

Connections

- Do you agree with the way that the census was carried out? Who was left out of the census?
- How do we make sure that every Jew counts? How does your Jewish life count?
- In what way will you make your "letter" of the Torah—your own piece of the Jewish heritage—come alive?
- In what ways are teachers and parents alike? How are they different?
- What are some of the most valuable life lessons that you have learned from your parents? From various teachers? Which lessons do you think you will remember in decades to come?

❖ Naso': Numbers 4:21–7:89

Welcome to the longest parashah in the entire Torah! Moses finishes up the census in order to figure out who is available for various tasks.

Once he finishes with that, he goes back to creating the rules that will guide the future life of the Israelites.

The Torah portion describes two ancient customs that no longer exist: the "trial by ordeal" of women who are suspected of adultery, and the role of the Nazirite, a person who decides to go several steps beyond the usual rules of holiness and live a more ascetic life, cut off from many human temptations.

By the time this Torah portion ends, it is time for the dedication of the Tabernacle, the Tent of Meeting (*mishkan*), with a list of every person who brings gifts to the dedication, and the gifts that they bring. Oddly enough, they all bring the same things.

Summary

ℶ The task of taking the census continues. Moses breaks the Levite clan into further subgroupings, describing the tasks of those responsible for carrying various parts of the Tabernacle—the Gershonites, Merarites, and the Kohathites. (4:21–49)

ℶ The text (be warned; this is offensive to modern readers) specifies the way of putting a woman who is suspected of adultery on trial—the *sotah* ritual. She is forced to drink "bitter waters." If her thigh gets distended and distorted, then she is guilty of adultery. If she remains unharmed, then she is innocent. (5:11–29)

ℶ For those who want to go above and beyond in the holiness department, there is the option of becoming a Nazirite. Nazirites were forbidden to cut their hair; to consume anything alcoholic, or anything that could become intoxicating; and they cannot have any contact with the dead—even their own dead relatives. (6:1–21)

ℶ God dictates the beautiful priestly blessing to Aaron, the same words that are still used in synagogue today, including at b'nai mitzvah ceremonies and when parents bless children. (6:22–26)

ℶ At the dedication of the Tabernacle, the prince of each tribe brings gifts as an offering. Each one brings the same gifts. (7:1–87)

The Big Ideas

ℶ **Every Jew has a sacred task to perform.** In the Torah portion, those duties are specific to various families and clans. That is not the way it works anymore. Nowadays, every Jew has to find a particular duty—a mitzvah—that speaks to the heart and that he or she is ready to do.

ᕮ **Jealousy is a powerful emotion.** It is absolutely true that marriage is a sacred trust between husband and wife. But something far more disturbing is going on in this passage. The text focuses only on women who are suspected of cheating on their spouses. This seems very unfair; what about husbands who have cheated? (Sad to say, but in the ancient world wives were considered the property of their husbands.) The whole thing starts when a husband becomes suspicious of his wife's actions. The Torah understands the power of jealousy, and in its own way it is trying to figure out how to manage that strong emotion.

ᕮ **Holiness should be available to everyone.** The particular characteristics of the Nazirite might seem odd and extreme. But their purpose was to allow the "average" Israelite the same kind of access to holiness as that which was available to the priests. The priesthood was limited to those who were *kohanim,* but anyone could be a *Nazir.* It was "equal opportunity" holiness.

ᕮ **People do not bless; God is the ultimate source of blessing.** This is very important. When people utter blessings over food or other things, they must remember that they are not the ones who are making that moment holy. All blessings come from God. And a priestly blessing that goes down from generation to generation ensures that there will be continuity.

ᕮ **Every person's contribution is important.** Was it merely a coincidence that each gift the princes brought was identical? Perhaps it was necessary so that they would all feel equal in the eyes of God. But while the gifts were identical, we cannot know what was going on in their hearts and minds—and those feelings and thoughts make each gift different.

Divrei Torah

SO, YOU WANT TO BE A NAZIRITE?

Let's say that you're living in biblical times. Let's say that you wake up one day, and you decide that you want to become a priest, or a Levite, or someone who has the honor and responsibility of carrying the sacred objects of the Tabernacle from place to place as the Israelites moved through the desert. Let's say, later on in biblical history, that you decide you want to become a prophet.

Well, forget about it. You can't. Because all those roles and responsibilities have been designated and assigned by God. There is no "application" process. You either are, or you aren't.

But there was one special thing that you could choose to do—and that was to become a Nazirite.

So, how do you do that? First, you get to be a Nazirite because someone like your mother (see the case of the famous Nazirite named Samson in the book of Judges) makes a vow that you'll be a Nazirite, and it lasts for your whole life. There's not much choice in that. But, apparently, you could also choose on your own to be a Nazirite as well, and for varying amounts of time.

What were the obligations of a Nazirite? No haircuts. No alcohol. No contact with the dead. This last rule is similar to one requirement of the priests, except that priests could have contact with their own dead relatives. Not so for the Nazirite. No contact with the dead—period. In this way, they are being even holier than the priests! (And there may have been other restrictions on the Nazirites that we are not told about in the Torah.)

So, was it "good" to be a Nazirite? It depends on whom you ask. By rejecting pleasure, the Nazirite battled temptation, and that can strengthen one's character. Why couldn't they get haircuts? In ancient times uncut hair, especially since most people then probably didn't wash their hair often, could be a little gross. Which is to say: the Nazirite had to make himself deliberately unattractive.

Why is that? There is a story in the Talmud about a young man with beautiful, curly hair. He chose to become a Nazirite for a very specific reason. "In my native town, I was my father's shepherd. When I went down to the well, I used to gaze at my reflection in it. That is when I decided to cut off my locks and let my hair go wild." He was in love with the way he looked, and he sensed that this kind of self-absorption and vanity wasn't right.

But not everyone thought that being a Nazirite was such a good idea. Judaism is in favor of legitimate pleasure. Good food, good wine, being attractive—none of those are bad, as long as they are kept in perspective. There are so many prohibitions and restrictions in the Torah—why go and make new ones? Many people probably thought this, and that may be why the Nazirite movement never really caught on in Judaism.

Rabbi Abba Hillel Silver pointed out that the norm of Judaism is to avoid the extreme: "Not a single one of the 613 mitzvot of the Torah enjoins any form of asceticism or mortification upon man. There is but one public fast day ordained in the Torah—Yom Kippur."

One thing is true: the Nazirite devoted his life to things that were higher than pleasure and self-fulfillment. Going above and beyond is not for everyone, but you have to admire people who are trying to live up to high ideals.

OH, NO! NOT ANOTHER ONE!

The kid who becomes bar or bat mitzvah on this Torah portion is in luck. Why? Let's say that your assigned Torah passage consists of the story of the princes' gifts at the Tabernacle's dedication. The prince of every tribe brought precisely the same gift. Yes, it's repetitious—but, on the other hand, there is that much less Hebrew to learn. Learn one set of gifts, and you've learned them all!

But why should this have been the case? Why should all the princes have given the very same gifts? Even more than this: if they all brought the same gifts, why keep mentioning all those princes, and all their gifts?

Centuries ago, Nachmanides, the Spanish Jewish commentator, said: "The Holy One wished to provide equal honor to all the princes by specifying each one's offering on its day, rather than listing the offering of Nahshon ben Amminadab [the first prince to make an offering] and then adding that each of the others had done the same. This would have affected the honor that was due to the others."

Even though the gifts were identical, the Torah wanted to be sure to give credit where it was due. After all, if the princes were going to make the effort to bring their gifts, the Torah should make note of each and every one of them.

Because even though the gifts were all the same, the *givers* were not.

The German Orthodox rabbi Shlomo Breuer teaches: "The Torah does not repeat the description of the offerings twelve times in order to teach us that each prince brought exactly the same as every other prince. In fact, they were actually twelve different offerings. This is because what a person gives is not important; how a person gives is important."

In other words, the gifts might have been the same, but each giver had a different attitude toward giving it. One prince might have given enthusiastically; another one might have given with an attitude. For one prince, those gifts might have been very easy to give. For another, not so well off, they might have been a hardship. By listing all these gifts separately, and according to the name of the giver, the Torah is making sure that we understand the uniqueness of every individual, and everyone's gifts.

Connections

- Do you think that being a Nazirite was good or bad? Why?
- What kinds of pleasures tempt you? Have you ever tried to fight those temptations?
- Why do you think that Judaism has always been in favor of people enjoying themselves (within reason and propriety)?
- What are the dangers of trying to enjoy yourself too much?
- What do you think of the explanation for why all the gifts are listed repeatedly? Do you agree that this was an important thing to do?
- Have you ever had the courage to do something first, before anyone else? What was it like?
- What are some of the most meaningful gifts that you have given? What are some of the most meaningful gifts that you have received?
- What kinds of gifts are nonmaterial? When have you given those types of gifts, and how did you feel about getting them?

❖ Be-ha'alotekha: Numbers 8:1–12:16

In this Torah portion, the Israelites are finally ready to begin their march into the wilderness and their journey to the Land of Israel. But this people, so newly liberated from Egyptian slavery, shows signs that they are still immature.

There are almost constant complaints about Moses and challenges to his authority, which drives Moses to almost total burnout. Still, Moses emerges as the solid defender of Israel, constantly begging God to maintain patience with the people—even when it seems that his own patience is running out.

Summary

ﬡ The Israelites prepare for their journey into the wilderness. They receive the laws for lighting the menorah in the Tabernacle, or Tent of Meeting (*mishkan*), and the Levites are prepared to perform the service. There is both a minimum age (twenty-five years old) and a maximum age (fifty years old) for service. After the age of fifty, they may assist other Levites in standing guard over the Tabernacle. (8:1–26)

ﬡ A group of Israelites complain that they had not been able to perform the Pesach offering, and so a "second Passover" is created for them. (9:1–14)

ﬡ Moses asks his father-in-law, Hobab (also known as Jethro, among other names that he seems to have in the Torah), to be their guide in the wilderness. Hobab declines and says that he wants to return to his own land. (10:29–32)

ﬡ The criticisms don't stop. The Israelites complain about how boring the manna is to eat. They reminisce about all the great food that they had in Egypt, and say that they want meat. God gives them quail to eat. Moses is distraught, and he complains to God about the burden of leadership that he must carry. God tells Moses to choose seventy elders to help him. (11:1–21)

ﬡ Miriam and Aaron speak against Moses for marrying a non-Israelite. As a result, Miriam is stricken with leprosy. Moses utters the shortest prayer in the Bible to heal her. (12:1–16)

The Big Ideas

ﬡ **Judaism cares about the dignity of the aged.** True, there were strict age limits for priestly service, and there was even a mandatory retirement age of fifty years old. Nevertheless, older Levites still had a valuable role to play; they could stand guard at the

Tabernacle (like retired police officers who stand guard in banks and other places). In this way, the community still honored their contributions.

ᵬ **Sometimes in life there are second chances.** Those who could not offer the Pesach sacrifice at the right time had an opportunity to do it one month later. More than that: God realizes that a change had to be made in that ancient custom, and goes even one step further in allowing latecomers to present their sacrifices. This is a remarkable illustration of how even in the Torah Judaism grew, and it continues to develop.

ᵬ **Judaism cherishes the spiritual contributions of people who are not Jewish.** Hobab is not only Moses's father-in-law; he is also a Midianite priest. Moses has a deep and powerful relationship with Hobab, and the older man serves as a mentor and guide to Moses. Moses's invitation to his father-in-law to journey with them in the wilderness symbolizes the esteem in which Judaism holds sympathetic non-Jews.

ᵬ **Memory is often very selective.** The Israelites miss the delicious food that they had in Egypt, and as a result they become nostalgic about their time there. They must have totally forgotten that they had been slaves in Egypt! In life, sometimes people choose to remember what they want to remember. It is always interesting to note what people choose *not* to remember as well.

ᵬ **Prayer doesn't have to be long to be effective.** When Miriam and Aaron criticize Moses, she (and she alone—not Aaron!) is stricken with *tzara'at* (scaly skin disease). Moses protests her punishment and prays for her healing. This demonstrates Moses's depth of character. Miriam had publicly humiliated him, but he still prayed for her to get better. Moses's prayer was only several words long, which reminds us that even short prayers can be spiritually uplifting and effective.

Divrei Torah

THERE'S ALWAYS ANOTHER DAY

It is August 4. Samantha and her family are busy cooking hotdogs and corn on the cob. They are dressed in red, white, and blue T-shirts. A neighbor walks over and asks them: "What are you doing?" "We are celebrating the Fourth of July," Samantha responds.

"Uh—that was a month ago," the neighbor reminds her. "We know," responds Samantha. "But we were away that day and we couldn't celebrate. So we're doing it now, exactly a month later."

Weird? Maybe not.

Consider what happens in chapter 9. A group of men had become ritually impure because they had been in contact with a dead body. (If even thinking about being in contact with a dead body makes you uncomfortable, then you can understand why the ancient Israelites thought that people could become ritually impure if they had contact with someone who was dead.) Those who were ritually impure could not bring a Pesach offering. "No fair!" they complain to Moses.

Moses doesn't dismiss their complaint. No, he brings it right to God. God states that if anyone has been defiled by a corpse, that person can "do Pesach" on the fourteenth day of the second month instead—a full month after the "real" Pesach. So, second chances sometimes do exist.

But wait—there's more. It's not only those who were ritually impure who were allowed to have a "second Pesach." God also allows those who had been on a long journey. But, if you weren't impure or not on a journey, too bad; you were punished for not having brought the Pesach offering. To fail to participate in Pesach is, in some way, to deny the entire story of the Jewish people. Not good.

And then, God goes even one step further. God now commands strangers who might be staying with the Israelites to participate in Pesach as well. In the first Pesach, when the Israelites first got out of Egypt, non-Israelites could not participate (Exod. 12:48). Now, they not only *can*—they *must*.

Generations later, the sages decide to broaden the list of "Pesach latecomers" even more. The Mishnah says: "An individual who is ritually impure or at a distance and did not perform the first Pesach offering shall perform the second. An individual who otherwise erred or had good reasons not to perform the first Pesach offering shall perform the second."

This is just one example of how Judaism grows. In the words of

Rabbi Reuven Hammer: "Even at the time of Moses it was necessary to find answers to questions concerning the fulfillment of the commandments. Even then they had to be applied to new conditions. Without the ability to expand and be interpreted, Jewish law would be frozen and would lose its relevance to new times and new situations."

Jewish law often finds ways to give us second chances.

WHEN MEMORY FAILS

Sometimes it seems as if the entire book of Numbers is one long complaint. Consider what happens at Kibroth-hattaavah in chapter 11. The people complain about the food they had to eat. They find the manna boring; they want better food. The riffraff among the Israelites (presumably, Egyptians who left Egypt with the Israelites) *hitavu ta'avah*—they "craved a craving"—leading the medieval commentator Nachmanides to write: "They actually did not suffer from want in the wilderness. They had as much manna as they wanted, and they could prepare it to yield gourmet flavors. But they imagined themselves to have gluttonous cravings."

The Israelites reminisce about the great food that they had to eat in Egypt—cucumbers, melons, leeks, onions, and garlic—a regular salad bar. In fact, there was probably some historical accuracy in that memory. The ancient Greek historian Herodotus reported that he saw an inscription on a pyramid that listed the food eaten by the slaves.

Wait a second. How is it possible for these ex-slaves to sit around reminiscing about the "good old days" in Egypt? The Egyptians—generous? Weren't these the same people who didn't even let the Israelites have straw to build bricks? Weren't they brutal taskmasters?

This might have been the first time in Jewish history that Jews remembered things not as they actually were but as they wanted them to have been—but it was certainly not the last time. No matter how grim things get for Jews, there are always some who filter out the bad and who focus on the good. In the late 1930s and 1940s, some German Jewish refugees in America would sigh and reminisce: "Back in Berlin, we had such great chocolate, or coffee, or culture, or whatever." They conveniently forgot the horrors of those times. It's called selective memory.

And some things just get deleted from Jewish memories. You've heard of Masada, the fortress in the Judean Desert where the zealots committed mass suicide? Nowadays, people visit there all the time. It has become a sacred place. But for almost two thousand years, Jews never talked about Masada. The same is true in American history. If you live in the South, chances are that people "remember" the Civil War quite differently than those in the North.

The contemporary teacher Rabbi Donniel Hartman has said: "Judaism is not only what we do or believe; it is what we choose to remember. That's why very few Jews actually leave Judaism or the Jewish people. You cannot cut yourself off from your past and your ancestors."

We remember what we want to remember. This is true not only in history; it is also true with ourselves. Even if we keep a diary or write a personal blog, it's not as if we remember everything. We leave some things out. Sometimes that's not so good, like the Israelites in the desert. But sometimes that's not so bad. It all depends on what we do with our memories.

Connections

℔ When have you wanted to have a second chance?

℔ When have you complained about things being unfair? What were the results?

℔ Why do you think that the rules for Passover changed over time?

℔ What do you want to remember from your Jewish education? From your bar or bat mitzvah preparation? What do you think will be your clearest memories?

℔ Do you ever pray spontaneously? What do you pray for? Are your prayers long or short? Which kind of prayer do you prefer?

℔ Do you think that Miriam's punishment was fair? If not, what would have been more fair?

❖ Shelah Lekha: Numbers 13:1–15:41

Moses, responding to God's command, sends spies into the Land of Israel to determine what the land is like, to see if it's conquerable or not. The twelve spies (one from each tribe) come back with discouraging reports about the inhabitants of the land, and about the land itself. When they hear the spies' report, the Israelites weep, bemoaning their fate and wishing that they could return to Egypt. Finally, two of the spies, Joshua and Caleb, attempt to silence the Israelites. Yes, they admit, the land is scary, but they think it's conquerable.

Because of the negativity of that "generation of the wilderness," God condemns them all to die—with the exception of Joshua and Caleb—before they can enter the land.

To continue the constant theme of rebellion in Numbers, a man gathers wood on the Sabbath and is condemned to death. The parashah ends with God's commandment that the Israelites should wear fringes (tzitzit) on the corners of their garments, "to recall all the commandments of the Lord and observe them."

Summary

- ☙ Moses sends spies into the Land of Israel and asks them to find out something about the inhabitants there, the kinds of towns they live in, what the soil is like, and what kinds of fruit grow there. (13:1–24)

- ☙ The spies return with frightening news about the nature of the land and its inhabitants. They report that the people of the land are very powerful and that the cities are large and fortified. One spy, Caleb, sees things a little differently than the others. While the situation in the land is intimidating, he says, the Israelites will surely be able to conquer it. (13:25–33)

- ☙ The people are demoralized by the spies' reports, and they become afraid of what God has in store for them. They turn against Moses and say that they want to go back to Egypt. At that moment, God determines that the wilderness generation should die off before the people could enter the land. Moses argues with God over this death sentence, appealing to God's conscience and ego, saying that if God were to do this the peoples of the world would say that God was incapable of bringing the People of Israel into the land. (14:1–25)

- ☙ God instructs the Israelites to make fringes on the corners of their garments (tzitzit). To this day, Jews wear tzitzit on the cor-

ners of the tallit and often on the corners of their undergarments
as well. (15:37–41)

The Big Ideas

Ƀ **God needs us to discover things on our own.** This is why the
portion begins with the words *shelaḥ lekha*—literally, send the men
to spy on the land *"for your own sake."* It would not have been
enough for God to simply describe the Promised Land to Moses.
God needed Moses and the people to directly experience the land
so that they could understand the challenges that lay ahead. Faith
in God alone would not have been sufficient. Since God is not going to tell you what to do in life, you will often need to rely on
your own experience in order to make mature decisions.

Ƀ **The majority opinion is not always right.** The majority of the
spies believed that it was impossible to conquer the Land of Israel; a tiny minority (Joshua and Caleb) believed quite the opposite. They advocated for their opinion, and they won; the people
would push on into the wilderness and conquer the land. Many
of the great things in world history have not happened because
the majority was in favor of them; it often takes a creative minority of people to convince others to expand their vision.

Ƀ **Arguing with God is an essential Jewish way of relating to God,
even if it is not always successful.** The tradition of arguing with
God goes all the way back to Abraham, who argued with God
over the fate of Sodom and Gomorrah (Genesis 18). There is also
the incident of the Golden Calf (Exod. 32:9.), when Moses appeals to God's sense of justice: it would be cruel for God to kill
the people off in the wilderness. And now here Moses appeals to
God's ego: if God didn't bring the people into the land, others
would say that God was weak. Moses not only speaks to God; he
tries to appeal to God and calls God to account.

Ƀ **All Jews can be holy.** In the past, God had commanded certain
ritual garments for only the priests to wear. But now it is different. By commanding the Israelite people to wear fringes (tzitzit)
on their garments, God is helping to bring about the day when Israel will truly be a "nation of priests."

Divrei Torah

WHO ARE YOU CALLING A GRASSHOPPER?

It must have been very frightening: Here you have a group of newly freed slaves, people who have not been accustomed to traveling away from their homes in Egypt, thrust into the wilderness and then about to enter an alien land, the Land of Israel, with its big, strong people and fortified cities. We can imagine their awe, wonder, and fear—sort of like what happens when you live in the suburbs, or the country, and you go to the big city for the first time. It's overwhelming. You want to turn around and run home.

That's what it's like for the spies who go into the Land of Israel. Everything there is big—the cities, the fruit (it took two men to carry a cluster of grapes, which has become the logo of Israel's Ministry of Tourism), and especially the people. The spies report that the people of the land are giants, descended from the Nephilim, a mythical tribe of giants (see Gen. 6:1). And then, they say something quite telling: "We looked like grasshoppers to ourselves, and so we must have looked to them" (13:33).

What's wrong with what they just said? Rabbi Menachem Mendel of Kotzk, a great Hasidic teacher, taught: "You are certainly permitted to say that you feel like a grasshopper in your own eyes. But what right do you have to imagine how you appear to someone else? To them, you might have appeared as angels."

Whoever we are, however old we are, wherever we are in life: when we are overwhelmed, we tend to think little of ourselves and to imagine that other people think little of us as well. (Girls, often more than boys, imagine themselves to be "grasshoppers." So do kids with physical disabilities, and LGBT kids.) In fact, often that perception is simply wrong. Sometimes it's all a drama that we are playing out in our heads.

Imagine if the Israelites had listened to the spies. They would have overthrown Moses and Aaron, headed back to Egypt, and either have become slaves once again or been killed. The Torah would have been, at most, not quite four books long—if it had even come to exist at all. The Israelites would have been like any number of almost-forgotten ancient peoples.

The spies were wrong to think of themselves as grasshoppers. Their lack of confidence and self-esteem, not to mention their lack of faith, could have had grave consequences for the community. Our self-perception influences our own actions and the way others see us.

Ironically, just a little later in Numbers, King Balak of Moab is terrified of the Israelites! (22:2). So, who was right—Balak, or the spies? As Dr. Erica Brown teaches: "Why not go with the more encouraging perception? Maybe when others believe that we are strong and beautiful and talented, we will train ourselves to hear them. And maybe, just maybe, when someone else feels small and disempowered, we can help them find their inner giant."

TEAR DOWN THAT WALL!

Things are not always the way they seem. That's one of the great themes of this Torah portion. People think they are grasshoppers—puny and weak—and, in fact, the opposite might be the case. A majority opinion—"we can't conquer the land, so let's go back to Egypt!"—is overturned. And a people who longed for freedom blows it and is condemned to die in the wilderness without being allowed to enter the Land of Israel.

Consider how the spies must interpret the data that they bring back from their mission into the land. Moses asks them: "Are the people who dwell in it strong or weak, few or many? . . . Are the towns they live in open or fortified?" (13:18–19). The assumption must have been: if the towns are fortified, then the people must be strong.

Rashi, the great medieval commentator, says that it was quite the opposite. He imagines Moses saying to the spies: "If the people live in unwalled towns, they are strong enough to rely on their own might, but if they live in fortified cities, they are weak."

Rashi's comment is interesting and provocative. Do you think it is true that countries with the largest armies, or the largest percentage of people serving in the army, are the least secure? We do have to admit that some countries, like Israel, have good reason to be heavily armed, having fought five major wars and several smaller ones in less than seventy years of existence.

Consider, too, those huge apartment buildings or condo developments that have multiple layers of security. Are they secure—at least, in the minds of the people who live there? Contrast that to people who live in rural areas, where there is a much lower crime rate. In those areas, you might find that people never lock their doors. Sometimes, they've even lost the keys to their homes!

You probably know people who are always putting up "walls." They are defensive and have a snappy comeback or put-down of other people. They are bullies who are often picking fights with others. Often it turns out that those people really aren't that secure; they have all sorts of fears.

Do we need to build all the walls in our lives? If the wall is to hide our psychological insecurity or pessimism, maybe the answer is no. The economic historian David Landes writes: "In this world, the optimists have it—not because they are always right, but because they are positive. Even when wrong, they are positive, and that is the way of achievement, correction, improvement, and success."

President Ronald Reagan famously said to former Soviet president Mikhail Gorbachev, "Tear down that wall!" He was speaking of the physical Berlin Wall, but likewise of the psychological iron curtain of insecurity and mistrust between East and West. We too need to take down walls, move forward, and be optimistic!

Connections

- ხ When have you felt discouraged and small? What helped you overcome those feelings?
- ხ Have you ever been afraid of something that might happen in the future? What have you been afraid of? What helped you conquer your fears?
- ხ Have you helped someone overcome his or her fears of failure? How did you do it? Were you successful?
- ხ What do you think is the best way to get over a fear of failure?
- ხ Who are some people from world history who have been afraid of failure? What were the results? What can we learn from their stories?
- ხ When have you chosen not to go along with the majority, and went along with the minority instead? Who are some figures in world history who have done that?

❖ Korah: Numbers 16:1–18:32

In a book that is filled with stories of rebellion against Moses, the greatest rebellion was the one that Korah orchestrated. Korah, a Levite (like Moses and Aaron), insists that the entire Israelite community is holy, and that Moses and Aaron have no right to their positions of authority. God punishes the rebels by having an earthquake swallow them alive.

Perhaps as a way of emphasizing the destructiveness of Korah's behavior, God reemphasizes the sacred duties of the Levites.

Summary

♄ Korah, along with Dathan and Abiram, starts a revolt against Moses and Aaron. He declares that all the Israelites, and not just Moses and Aaron, are holy. Moses counters Korah by reminding him that, as Levites, he and his buddies already have sacred duties. Moses insists on his innocence and on his righteous behavior, and tells the rebels to bring incense offerings in fire pans. But Korah and his band are not convinced, and the whole incident ends badly, with the group being swallowed up by the earth. (16:1–35)

♄ The rebels' fire pans become holy and are hammered into the altar. This is to serve as a warning for those who would rebel in the future. (17:1–7)

♄ God wants to destroy the Israelites, but Aaron puts incense on a fire pan as a way of warding off the plague that would have killed them. (17:8–15)

♄ As a way of demonstrating the ongoing sanctity of Aaron and the entire tribe of Levi, God instructs Moses to tell the people to take a staff from each tribe, as well as one from the Levites, and place the staffs inside the ark. The staff of the tribe that is to be chosen by God will sprout. And the one that sprouts turns out to be the staff of Aaron. (17:17–28)

The Big Ideas

♄ **For Jews, holiness is not a given; you have to work toward it.**
In the Holiness Code in Leviticus, God says to Moses: "Speak

to the whole Israelite community and say to them: 'You shall be holy' (Lev. 19:1)," But that's a big "shall." The Israelites are not yet holy. That was Korah's fundamental problem: he believed that the "shall" was an "already is," that everyone was already holy and that everyone was equal. It is important to have goals, but be careful not to believe something is so just because you want it to be so. Have goals and work on a way to reach those goals.

ᚾ **Even rebellion can become holy.** This seems odd. The text tells us that the fire pans are hammered into the altar as a warning. But in another sense, perhaps they are also part of the altar as a way of saying that rebellion and questioning will become a constant (and, often, necessary) theme in Jewish life. There are even psalms in the Bible that are said to have been written by "the sons of Korah." And so we see that the prayerful contributions of a rebel's descendants are part of Jewish sacred literature.

ᚾ **Spiritual heroism entails speaking out and acting in favor of your people.** This is the true greatness of Moses (and in this particular instance, Aaron)—the willingness to go to bat for the People of Israel. There were many times when God threatened to destroy the Israelites. But Moses, following the example of Abraham at Sodom and Gomorrah, stands up for his people and convinces God to relent.

ᚾ **The task of holiness means ongoing growth and renewal.** There are few things as lifeless as a plain wooden staff, and few things as miraculous as its ability to sprout into a living organism. That is a good way to think about life, and about Judaism itself— renewable spiritual energy.

Divrei Torah

SOMEONE HAS AN ATTITUDE PROBLEM

A kid in religious school walks in wearing a T-shirt that bears the following words: "I LOVE my attitude problem."

That kid could have been Korah. He had an attitude problem.

Korah gathers together a loose confederation of malcontents and launches a rebellion against the authority of Moses. "You have gone too far! For all the community are holy, all of them, and the Lord is in their midst," he challenges Moses. "Why then do you raise yourselves above the Lord's congregation?" (16:3)

Did Korah have a point? Wasn't he trying to be democratic and egalitarian? What was so bad about what he said that led to such a severe punishment? The sages say that it was his attitude, his motive, that was really at fault. They go so far as to claim that Korah (who was a cousin of Moses and Aaron, by the way) was not so much interested in his own argument as he was in grabbing power from his own relatives.

Let's follow part of the ancient argument. The sages imagine Korah asking Moses: "Does a house that is filled with Torah scrolls require a mezuzah on its door? Does a garment that is entirely blue still need to have a blue thread in its fringes?" The questions make sense on one level. After all, the Torah scrolls contain the entire Torah; the mezuzah contains just a brief passage from Deuteronomy. Shouldn't all those Torah scrolls fulfill the mitzvah of having a mezuzah? And an entirely blue garment should be blue enough without the blue thread, right? And yet, Moses responds by saying that yes, even a house that is filled with Torah scrolls requires a mezuzah, and, yes, even an entirely blue garment needs a blue thread in the tzitzit. Korah goes ballistic and accuses Moses of making the whole thing up just to keep power.

Was Korah right? Well, yes and no. Yes, the sages, in their portrayal of Korah, want Judaism to make sense and to be logical. Korah would have agreed with the twentieth-century writer Edmond Fleg, who said: "I am a Jew because Judaism requires no abdication of the mind." And it is certainly logical that a house filled with Torah scrolls should need no mezuzah, and that a garment that is entirely blue should not need a blue thread in its ritual fringes. We get this. But here is where Korah got it wrong: Jewish practices are not entirely logical. In some ways, Judaism is like an elaborate, ancient game, with its own rules. Many things in many cultures have no logic to them. Dressing up on Halloween—how does that make sense? And what about lighting candles on a birthday cake? We have many customs and rituals that help keep the community together though they are not what we would call *rational*.

So, what was up with Korah? Why did he ask, as the Rabbis imagined, whether a blue garment needs a blue thread in the fringes? Korah thinks that all the Jews are already holy. If all the Jews are already holy, then an all-blue garment should be holy as well. That was his logic.

And the deal about the mezuzah and the Torah scrolls? Here is what Korah did not understand. It's not enough to have Torah scrolls on the inside of your house. No—the mezuzah sits on the doorpost, at the precise intersection of the private and the public, at the place where our inner life ends and our outer life begins. It is there to remind us that when we leave the house, we must take Torah out into the world.

Korah made the mistake, in the eyes of the Rabbis, of assuming that people are already holy, when in reality they must strive to be holy. He made the mistake of thinking that everything must be rational, when some things must be taken on faith. But lurking behind this was the most problematic thing of all: Korah may have hid behind his arguments because he wanted to create a rebellion and seize power for himself.

Now that is an attitude problem!

AARON'S MAGICAL STAFF—A MIRACLE!

There was a time when kids liked to learn magic tricks—mostly card tricks, though some got into more advanced stuff.

There's magic—and, then, there's *real* magic, like a magic staff.

Each of the twelve leaders of the ancestral tribes was asked to inscribe his name on a staff, which was then placed in the Holy Ark in the Tent of Meeting, the Tabernacle (*mishkan*). The next day "the staff of Aaron of the house of Levi had sprouted: it had brought forth sprouts, produced blossoms, and borne almonds" (17:23). This sign reassured the people that Aaron was the true representative of God.

Aaron's staff has an interesting history. The ancient Rabbis imagined that it was part of the very act of creation itself, created in the twilight between the sixth day and the Sabbath. The first time it was used was by Jacob, when he crossed the Jordan River. A midrash says: "That same staff was held in the hand of every king until the Temple was destroyed, and then it was divinely hidden away. That same staff also is destined to be held in the hand of the Messiah."

We are talking about a miraculous staff here. First, for it to blossom is a miracle.

Not only that. After a normal fruit (or nut) tree blossoms, its flowers wither and become buds, which then grow and eventually become fruit (or nuts). But Aaron's staff went through all those stages *at the same time:* "it brought forth sprouts, produced blossoms, and bore almonds" (17:23). In some ways, it is like Judaism today. When the Holocaust occurred, there were people who thought that Judaism was a dry, dead stick—like Aaron's staff before it sprouted. But now many can see that the hard, dry stick has, in fact, blossomed. Think of the modern State of Israel—what a miracle that is. Consider that there is more serious Jewish learning going on today, more Jewish culture than ever before, more Jews serving in important government positions, even Jews who have sought the American presidency. In many respects, Judaism and the worldwide Jewish community is sprouting anew and bearing fruit.

Often in life we become like Aaron's staff. Sometimes we feel dead and wooden. And then things change. We learn new skills, make new friends, and we have new adventures. We go through all stages of growth: flowers, buds, and fruit. We feel hopeful again.

Ah, but why does Aaron's staff bring forth, of all things, almonds? Almonds are both bitter and sweet—sort of like life.

Rabbi Israel Salanter once said: "We live by miracles every day, but miracles don't happen every day." There are miracles in our lives and in our shared history—some we recognize and some we don't. To pass through difficult times, to have hope, and to flourish again—this is truly holy and truly a miracle.

Connections

ъ Have you ever been part of a rebellion—at home, in school, on a team, in camp, or in religious school? What was it like? What did you learn from that experience?

ъ Do you think that Korah was right or wrong to rebel against the authority of Moses?

ъ Were the challenges that Korah posed to Moses in the midrash about the mezuzah and the fringes effective? Why or why not?

ъ What are some things in Judaism that make sense to you? Some that don't?

ቴ Why do you think this story of rebellion was included in the Torah?

ቴ How would you define a miracle? Have you experienced any in your life?

❖ Ḥukkat: Numbers 19:1–22:1

Death is scary, and this Torah portion knows it. And death and disappointment are major themes here.

It starts by describing the purification ritual for those who have been in contact with a corpse.

In a moment of deep frustration (made worse, perhaps, by his mourning the death of his sister, Miriam) Moses loses his patience with the Israelites. He hits a rock in order to draw forth water from it. But God had commanded him (and his brother, Aaron) to speak to the rock, not strike it, and so God tells Moses that as punishment for his sin, Moses and Aaron will not be the ones to lead the Israelites into the Land of Israel. As the Israelites continue their march into the wilderness, Aaron also dies.

The Israelites complain about the lack of food and water in the desert, and God sends a plague of serpents against the people. As an antidote to the snakes' poison, Moses makes a statue of a serpent; anyone who looks at it would be healed of any snakebite. (This is the origin of the traditional symbol of medicine—the serpent on the staff.) The Israelites continue their march through the wilderness, on the far side of the Jordan River, and they must constantly negotiate for safe passage with the various tribes they encounter on the way.

Summary

ቴ God instructs Moses and Aaron on the laws of the red cow, also referred to as the red heifer. A red cow with no blemishes is to be ritually slaughtered and burned. Its ashes will be used to purify anyone who has been in contact with the dead. (19:1–21)

ቴ Immediately after the death of Miriam, the sister of Moses and Aaron, the Israelites find themselves with no water. They turn to Moses and Aaron and lament that they had ever left Egypt. God tells Moses to speak to a rock and order it to yield its water. Instead, Moses hits the rock. That action brings forth water, but Moses and Aaron are punished for their lack of trust in God and God's commandment. God tells them their punishment: that they will not lead the Israelites into the Land of Israel. Shortly after this, Aaron dies. (20:2–30)

ხ The Israelites complain about the lack of food and water in the desert, and "spoke against God and against Moses" (20:5). Because of their lack of trust God sends a plague of serpents against them, and many die from the snakebites. Then God tells Moses to make an image of the serpent and put it on his staff as an antidote; anyone who looks at it will recover from the snakebite. (21:4–9)

ხ The Israelites encounter several tribes in the wilderness, and the encounters are not friendly. Sihon, king of the Amorites, attacks the Israelites, even though they had asked politely if they could travel through his territory. The Israelites fight the Amorites, and they are victorious. (21:21–32)

The Big Ideas

ხ **Some laws in Judaism don't seem to have any good reason for being.** The law of the red heifer is a great example. While generations of Jewish teachers and scholars have worked very hard to figure out the deeper meaning of this ritual, it remains a powerful mystery. It was considered one of those biblical laws that the ancient Israelite had to follow on faith—"just because God said so." The red heifer reminds us that we cannot understand everything in life, or in Judaism. Some Jewish customs might not seem to make sense; we call them *chukim*. Ritual circumcision and keeping kosher are two such examples. But they are still an important part of Judaism.

ხ **We don't always get to fulfill our dreams.** Moses and Aaron are not permitted to fulfill their dream of leading the Israelites into the Land of Israel. The story would have been nicer if they had been able to fulfill that dream, but it would also have lacked a certain reality. There have been many leaders who have not been able to complete their missions. Everyone leaves this world with some things left incomplete. But we try our best, and most of the time our legacy is much more powerful than we could have ever imagined.

ᛒ **The rod that Moses carried symbolized both his faith—and his lack of it.** Moses has a long history of using a staff. He kills an Egyptian taskmaster with his staff (Exod. 2:12). He casts his rod to the ground, and it turns into a snake (Exod. 4:3). He uses his staff to strike the Nile to turn it into blood (Exod. 7:20) and to part the Sea of Reeds (or the Red Sea) (Exod. 14:16). Right after the Israelites left Egypt, he uses it to draw forth water in the wilderness (Exod. 17:1–7). And, of course, in this Torah portion, Moses strikes the rock with his staff and later uses it to heal the Israelites. Tools have many uses, but the greatest "tool" is the faith and the inner strength that we bring to what we do.

ᛒ **Judaism is very realistic about issues regarding war and peace.** The story of the Israelites' encounter with the Amorites is a good example of how Jews have responded to threats. In this Torah portion they made expressions of peace to the Amorites. But when their peaceful overtures were ignored and they were attacked, the Israelites fought back. Here we learn: the first "act" of war is to ask for peace. But you must often be prepared to fight if necessary. This is a sad but important lesson that the modern State of Israel has learned many times in its history.

Divrei Torah

WHY THE RED HEIFER?

Go ahead. Reread the whole bit about the red cow (the red heifer). Reread how its ashes are supposed to purify someone after he or she has had contact with the dead. Do you understand it? Does it make sense to you? Probably not.

You are in very good company. King Solomon is said to have been the wisest person in the ancient world. And yet even he could not understand it. According to a midrash, Solomon said: "I succeeded in understanding the whole Torah, but as soon as I reached the chapter about the red heifer, I searched, probed and questioned. 'I said, I will get wisdom, but it was far from me' (Eccles. 7:23)."

So, since you are probably not as smart as King Solomon (no offense!), you can forget about understanding this passage. That said, there is great wisdom here—if you look for it.

Ancient Judaism had this thing about death. The Torah states that coming into contact with the dead made a person impure. It was a deep, powerful fear. Do you think that our sense of death has changed that much? How do you feel when you see a dead squirrel in the road? We demonstrate our fear when we choose not to talk about death. We have all sorts of expressions that we use about someone who has died: "passed," "passed on," "passed away," "is gone." (One of the best is the old-fashioned, rural expression "bought the farm," which means that a dead person's survivors could cash in on the life insurance and therefore be able to buy the family farm.) But to say that someone has simply, *died*—not so common.

Why was ancient Judaism so repulsed by death and dead people?

Judaism is obsessed with life. When we lift a glass in celebration, we say: *"L'chayyim*—to life!" When people are buried in a tallit, the custom is to cut off the tzitzit, the ritual fringes, because they represent the mitzvot, and the dead person is no longer able to do any mitzvot.

The Modern Orthodox teacher Rabbi Joseph B. Soloveitchik tells this story. "Before the late Egyptian prime minister Anwar Sadat attacked Israel in 1973, he predicted that Israel would lose the war. He held up an Israeli newspaper with the photograph of a soldier who had been killed, describing how the entire country was mourning for him. Sadat said: 'A nation like this cannot survive a war for very long. If every individual is so dear to them, and they mourn every person who dies, they will simply not be able to fight.'"

Sadat was wrong. The State of Israel has remained undefeated in battle. But Soloveitchik continued on to say: "When one Jew dies, the world collapses." Death is scary, because life is holy.

TEMPER, TEMPER . . .

"Use your words!" Your parents probably yelled that at you when you were a small child. You were probably having some kind of temper tantrum, getting frustrated, maybe even lashing out—and they wanted you to speak about what was going on. Here is what they were telling you: language is an important tool. Use it.

This brings us to that moment in the Torah portion when Moses really loses his temper. The Israelites are thirsty (again!). They demand water. God tells Moses to speak to a rock, that it will yield water for the Israelites to drink. Instead, Moses hits the rock—not once but twice. Sure, water flows from the rock, but God punishes Moses and Aaron: they will not lead the Israelites into the Land of Israel. That is a huge punishment.

What was so wrong about what Moses did? First, he loses his temper (and not for the first time); this is not a good quality in a leader. And then, he struck the rock rather than speaking to it, as God had commanded. The great eleventh-century Bible commentator Rashi imagines God saying: "Had you spoken to the rock and it produced water, I would have been sanctified in the sight of the whole community, and they would have said: 'This rock, which cannot speak or hear, obeys the word of God. We should do the same!'"

And then, consider exactly what Moses said. "Listen, you rebels, shall we get water for you out of this rock?" (20:10). What do you mean—"we?" Was Moses referring to himself and Aaron? Or, worse, to himself, Aaron, and God? Wasn't it only God who was doing the water thing? Or perhaps the sin was that Moses posed it as a question to God: "Shall we get water for you?" A question? Was Moses doubting God?

At the same time, when Moses calls the people "rebels" he is separating himself from his community. Yes, he is frustrated and tired, but this is hardly their worst offense. Moses has run out of patience, and although it is really hard, a leader has to have endless patience.

So Moses is having either a crisis of faith or of patience. It's clearly not his finest hour. Sure, he doesn't exactly follow instructions, but was what he did really so bad? Does his punishment fit the crime? Many people down through the generations who have read this story have wondered about that.

As Rabbi Morris Adler writes: "Maybe there was a moment of pride, of anger, a careless word. Maybe Moses failed to apply the wisdom of his mind to that particular moment and was satisfied with insights taken from remote yesterdays."

Remember, this is not the first time that Moses hit a rock and got water. In Exodus 17, the Israelites were thirsty. God told Moses to hit a rock—which he did—and water came out. Fast forward forty years. Same situation, same thirsty people. God says, "Speak to the rock," and Moses, remembering how that trick had worked years back, goes into rock-hitting mode again. But Moses forgot that something had happened that was supposed to have changed everything. That was the giving of the Torah on Mount Sinai. Ever since that moment, power was not supposed to be in hitting things, but in speaking words— literally, using your words.

One last thing: Moses called the people "rebels." The Hebrew word for "rebels" is interesting. It's *morim,* which also means "teachers." Even though two different Hebrew roots may be involved here, isn't that an interesting coincidence? And how were those rebels supposed to be teachers? Sometimes, God "gives" us annoying people—in order to teach us patience.

Who's teaching you these days? Are you lashing out, or using your words carefully? Moses messed up and learned his mistake the hard way. What about us?

Connections

ት What are some other examples of *chukim,* laws with no apparent reason, in Judaism? What benefit can a person derive from observing them?

ት What are some American customs that seem to have no apparent reason behind them? Why do you think people still do those things?

ት Do you think death is scary? Can you think of examples of how we talk about death?

ት Who are some other leaders who were not able to finish their work? Think of people like President Franklin Roosevelt, Gandhi, Reverend Martin Luther King Jr., or Prime Minister Yitzhak Rabin of Israel. What were their dreams? How did their work go on, even after their deaths?

ት What do you think of the punishment that God gave to Moses and Aaron? Do you think it was fair? Have you ever been punished in a way you thought was unreasonable? How did you deal with that?

ት What makes you particularly frustrated? How do you deal with it?

❖ Balak: Numbers 22:2–25:9

After years of wandering in the wilderness, the Israelites are finally on their way toward the Promised Land. There have been many obstacles, including nations and tribes who have tried to get in their way.

But the Israelites have been victorious over them. That is why Balak, king of Moab, is frightened of the Israelites. Balak believes that the best way to fight them is not with swords, but with words. He hires a seer, Balaam, to curse Israel. This doesn't work out as well as Balak would have liked.

Summary

ቴ The Israelites' victory over the Amorites has freaked out Balak, king of Moab. He sees that there are a great many Israelites, so he hires a seer, Balaam, to curse the Israelites, thinking that this will be effective in defeating them. God, however, has other plans for Balaam, and tells him not to curse the Israelites. Balaam refuses to go with Balak's emissaries but they are insistent and ultimately he agrees to go with them. (22:2–20)

ቴ As Balaam begins his journey to curse the Israelites, he gets on his she-ass (donkey), who has other ideas about this trip. The donkey has a vision of an angel blocking their way. Balaam beats the animal into submission, and their trip continues. (Then the donkey starts talking!) (22:21–35)

ቴ Balaam tries to curse the Israelites, but instead God forces him to utter blessings in the form of oracles (prophetic statements). In his first oracle, Balaam describes the Israelites as a people that dwells apart. (23:7–10)

ቴ In his second oracle, Balaam says that God cannot be manipulated by magic or sorcery. (23:18–24)

ቴ In his third oracle, Balaam goes one step further: not only will Israel not be cursed, but those who curse that nation will be cursed, and those who bless it will be blessed.

ቴ In his fourth oracle, Balaam expands his view to include Moab and other nations, decreeing their ultimate fate. (24:3–25)

The Big Ideas

℔ **Words have power.** In ancient Judaism, blessings and curses were not just words. Ancient Jews believed that blessings and curses could actually shape the future. That is why Balak hired Balaam; his words could have been as powerful, or even more powerful, than any military actions. This is true sometimes even today; what people say can both heal and hurt.

℔ **To be a Jew means to have vision.** In this sense, Balaam's donkey, who sees the angel even when he cannot, represents the Jew. Throughout their history, Jews have seen and understood things that other peoples have not. This has been a source of blessing to the Jewish people, and often a reason why some have not liked them.

℔ **To be Jewish sometimes means to be separate from other peoples.** Going back to ancient times, the Jewish people have often had to go it alone. Often, this was because other peoples persecuted them; at other times, some Jews have sensed that the best way to maintain their faith and culture was to separate themselves from others. Balaam's vision has, more often than not, been true.

℔ **God is not subject to magic.** The original meaning of "magic" was not the performance of a trick. It was to try to use certain rituals and techniques to manipulate the gods to get them to do what you want them to do. While other ancient peoples practiced this kind of god-manipulation (in fact, this is precisely what Balak hired Balaam to do), one of the unique things about Judaism is that it never relied on these kinds of techniques.

℔ **The fate of the world is wrapped up in the fate of the Jews.** Balaam makes it clear that those who curse the Jews will be cursed and those who bless the Jews will be blessed. This echoes God's promise to Abram (Abraham) (Gen. 12:3). But he does not stop at the Jewish people. He expands his vision to include the nations that surround Israel. This reminds us that no nation is ever truly alone, because its actions always have impact on other countries.

Divrei Torah
LESSONS FROM A TALKING DONKEY

Here is one of the greatest and most wondrous aspects of children's literature: animals talk. Here's a short list: Charlotte, the spider in *Charlotte's Web;* Winnie the Pooh; Bugs Bunny; Donald Duck; Porky Pig; Teenage Mutant Ninja Turtles; Donkey in *Shrek;* and the Cowardly Lion in *The Wizard of Oz.* The list goes on and on. And it's not only in children's literature. Animals talk in mythical stories and folklore as well. And twice in the Torah: the serpent in the story of the Garden of Eden (Genesis 3), and the donkey in this Torah portion's story of Balaam.

And while this might seem a little childish, be careful; there is a great and powerful truth in this story.

Balaam, the Moabite soothsayer, is on his way to curse the Israelites. His mode of transportation is a donkey. God is not terribly interested in Balaam making his journey, and so God sends an angel to block Balaam's way. Here's the problem: Balaam cannot see the angel; only the donkey can. The animal walks off the path to avoid the angel, and Balaam hits her. Then, the angel appears in a narrow lane between two vineyard walls, and as the donkey presses against the wall she smashes Balaam's foot. Balaam hits the animal again. The third time, the angel chooses such a narrow place on the path that the animal has to lie down; and once again Balaam hits her. "Then the Lord opened the ass's mouth, and she said to Balaam, 'What have I done to you that you have beaten me these three times?' Balaam said to the ass, 'You have made a mockery of me! If I had a sword with me, I'd kill you'" (22:28–29).

A talking donkey: was this a miracle? No, said the ancient Rabbis—it was built into the very scheme of creation. "Ten things were created at twilight of the first eve of Shabbat—among them the mouth of Balaam's ass." Fine. But why do we even need the donkey in the story?

It's because the donkey sees the angel and has an understanding of God and the divine will. According to David Hazony: "The she-ass is Israel, possessing a divine truth, silently struggling under the lashes of power, driven by revelation to turn away from the path dictated by the violent overlords, eventually revealed and vindicated. Balaam, in turn, represents the nations of the world—perhaps the Egyptians who kept Israel enslaved through force. When the donkey finally speaks, asking what it has done to deserve being beaten, Balaam answers, 'Because you have mocked me.' Israel will always 'mock' the nations, just by refusing to follow the dictates of power."

There you have it—one of the most fascinating interpretations of any biblical story that you will ever read. The story teaches us that Jews understand that power is not the only way. And that is the truth they will continue to teach.

BEAUTIFUL TENTS

What are the first words Jews traditionally say when they enter a synagogue? "How fair are your tents, O Jacob, your dwellings, O Israel!" (24:5). They are part of the *Mah Tovu* prayer. It's an interesting choice when you consider that these opening words come to us from a Moabite soothsayer, Balaam, who had intended them to be words of cursing, and which God transformed into blessing. (Trivia point: this is the only Hebrew prayer by a non-Jew in the Jewish prayer book.)

But there is another reason why we say (or, as the case may be, sing) those words as we enter the synagogue. This author's own interpretation: Balaam praised the tents of the Jewish people, which were their homes. And Balaam also praised their dwellings, which are the synagogues that would someday exist.

Now, some people believe that you only need one, but not the other. Someday, you will probably meet Jews who say: "Why do I need the synagogue? I can pray in my home." They might say that, and it would be great if they did, in fact, pray in their homes, but they probably don't. And if there are no synagogues, what happens to the Jewish community?

Here's a way of thinking about it: Let's say that you're trying to get into shape, or training for a sport or an athletic competition. Sure, you can work out on your own, but you are more likely to have success if you do it with others, in a gym or outdoors. That's how Jewish communities work as well.

Rabbi David Teutsch writes: "A civilization cannot be handed down in privacy. It cannot be handed down just by reading books. To thrive, culture must be lived. . . . The setting for many important facets of Jewish civilization—eating, child-rearing, and Shabbat observance, for example—is the family. But the family cannot learn and sustain even these aspects of Jewish living by itself, and much of Judaism cannot be experienced just within the family. The only plausible setting for much of Jewish living is the community."

But, by the same token, Judaism cannot just be done in synagogue. It requires something to happen inside our homes as well. In fact, the best Jewish stuff happens around the table: Shabbat dinners, festival dinners, and Passover seders. That's what you remember every time you see a mezuzah on the doorpost of a Jewish house; the mezuzah is on a slant, pointing inside, to remind us that Judaism happens right there—inside the home.

So we need home and synagogue, family and community. A midrash teaches: "All the nations came to Balaam and asked, 'Can we take on this nation of Israel in battle?' He replied: 'Go out and make the rounds of their synagogues and houses of study. If you come upon children within them, chirping away in their childish voices, you will be unable to take on this nation in battle.'" Family *and* community are what make us strong.

Connections

Ḇ How have you come to understand that words have power? What words have been most powerful in your life?

Ḇ In what ways do Jews and the Jewish people remain separate from other peoples? Why has this happened? What are some of the benefits and disadvantages to this?

Ḇ In what ways have Jews and the Jewish people been part of the larger world? What's good about this? And maybe not so good?

Ḇ In what ways are the Jews like the talking animal in the story? What have Jews been able to see that other nations have not?

Ḇ Which do you think is more important and essential for the continuation of Judaism—the synagogue or the home? Why?

❖ Pinḥas: Numbers 25:10–30:1

The Torah portion opens on a disturbing note. Pinḥas the High Priest has gone ballistic over the sexual relations of an Israelite man with a Midianite woman. He kills them both. God rewards Pinḥas for his commitment to public morals and says that Pinḥas will merit an everlasting covenant. The Israelites then retaliate against the Midianites for allowing their women to seduce the Israelite men.

To further punish the Israelites for having relations with Midianites, God sends a plague upon them. Moses and Eleazar, the priest, conduct another census.

Finally, the daughters of Zelophehad protest that their father's death will leave them without property and their father's name will be wiped out.

Summary

Ϧ After the Midianite women convince a number of the Israelite men to participate in pagan orgies, a plague breaks out that takes many lives. Pinḥas, the grandson of Aaron, kills Zimri, an Israelite, and Cozbi, a Moabite woman, as they are having sex at the entrance to the Tent of Meeting, while people are weeping over all who died in the plague. As a result, God's anger is calmed and the plague comes to an end. God makes a "pact of friendship" (*brit shalom*) with Pinḥas so that his descendants will inherit the priesthood. (25:10–16)

Ϧ After the plague, God commands Moses and Eleazar, the son of Aaron, to take another census. They count 601,730 men between the ages of twenty and sixty. Moses learns how the land is to be divided by lottery among the tribes and families of Israel.

Ϧ The five daughters of Zelophehad petition Moses that they be allowed to inherit their father's land and retain their family name. God accepts their claim: "If a man dies without leaving a son, you shall transfer his property to his daughter" (27:8). And this ruling is incorporated into the Torah's laws of inheritance.

Ϧ God reminds Moses that he will not cross over into the Land of Israel, that he will only be able to view the land from afar. Moses empowers Joshua to succeed him and lead the people into the land.

The Big Ideas

Ϧ **Sometimes, decisive action is necessary.** While many commentators have criticized Pinḥas's headstrong action, he demonstrated

at least one characteristic of a strong leader—he saw the severity
of a situation and he acted to remedy it.

ᵷ **The purpose of the second census was to determine how many
men would be available to fight.** This was one of the realities of
the years of wandering in the wilderness. The Israelites were constantly encountering hostile nations, and they needed to be able
to protect themselves. This census also helped Moses figure out
how to divide the Land of Israel among the various tribes. The
census was not only a mathematical exercise; it was a vision for
the future of the people.

ᵷ **The Torah is capable of changing and growing.** The daughters of
Zelophehad appeal to Moses, and Moses brings their case to God.
God's sense of justice and fairness actually grows, and with it, so
does Judaism.

ᵷ **The duty of any good leader is to find a successor.** While Moses
was undoubtedly sad that he would not be able to lead his people
into the Promised Land, he put aside any personal feelings of loss
and moved forward to anoint Joshua as his successor.

Divrei Torah
NO FAN OF FANATICS!

Here is an interesting fact. The word "fan," as in baseball fan, or a fan
of a particular band, or a fan of a particular politician, is a shortened
form of the word "fanatic"—someone who is overly enthusiastic or
devoted to something.

That pretty much defines Pinḥas, the leading character and namesake of this Torah portion. Pinḥas, the grandson of Aaron, sees an
orgy going on between Israelite men and Midianite women. This blatant act of immorality has angered God, and God sent a plague upon
the Israelites. Pinḥas sees an Israelite man and a Midianite woman
together, and he gets really angry, and he kills them both. According
to the plain meaning of the Torah, God is pleased: the plague is over,
and Pinḥas gets rewarded with an eternal covenant of peace (*brit shalom*; literally, "My covenant of peace") with God.

God apparently approved of Pinḥas's action. And we have to admit
that there is certainly a strand of the Jewish tradition that finds Pinḥ

as admirable. Pinḥas demonstrated zealotry, which is an extreme version of fanaticism.

Pinḥas inspired generations of Jewish zealots. In the days of the Maccabees, when Mattathias was dying, he commanded his children: "My children, show zeal for the Torah, and sacrifice your lives for the covenant of our ancestors. Remember the deeds of Abraham, Joseph, and Pinḥas, who was deeply zealous and thus received the covenant of everlasting priesthood" (1 Macc. 2:51–54). Mattathias used the story of Pinḥas as a way of inspiring the Israelites to fight for their rights.

Later in this week's Torah portion, God reminds Moses that he will not live to lead the Israelites into the Land of Israel. God tells Moses to appoint a successor, which turns out to be Joshua. Which leads to a provocative question: Why not Pinḥas? Why couldn't he have succeeded Moses?

Maybe it's because he was a fanatic. True, he was zealous for God and for morality. But he took the law into his own hands and executed two people without a trial. Today we call that vigilante justice. It is illegal and it is dangerous.

But didn't God award Pinḥas a *brit shalom*, a covenant of peace? There has been much discussion about what that means. Was it really a reward, or was it a correction to Pinḥas's violent nature? Some say it was an inner peace, to calm Pinḥas down and prevent him for doing any more harm. Rabbi Naftali Zvi Yehuda Berlin, the principal of the yeshiva of Volozhin in prewar Europe, writes: "In reward for turning away God's wrath, Pinḥas was blessed with the attribute of peace—that he should not be quick-tempered or angry. God promised him peace and tranquility of soul."

One more quirky but interesting thing about that "covenant of peace." If you look into the Torah scroll at the word *shalom* in this context, you will notice that the *vav* in *shalom* is distorted and bent out of shape. Every *sofer* (Torah scribe) has to write it that way; every Torah reflects this strange *vav*. Why this unusually drawn letter? No one really knows. But one view is that the *vav* is distorted because the *shalom* was not really a full *shalom*. Enthusiasm in a sacred mission is great. Passion and zealousness for a cause is admirable. But the temptation to fanaticism is always dangerous. If it leads you beyond the law and into violence, watch out—because your "cure" may be worse than your problem.

WOMAN POWER!

Sometimes, the greatest acts of social change happen in the softest of ways. Think of Rosa Parks, an African American woman who boarded a bus in Montgomery, Alabama, and quietly but firmly refused to go to the back of the bus—and sparked the civil rights revolution.

That's how it was with the daughters of Zelophehad—Mahlah, Noah, Hoglah, Milcah, and Tirzah. Their father was an Israelite who had died in the desert, leaving five daughters but no sons behind. We know nothing more about him, but this unexceptional man had exceptional children. This was not the first time that a man died with no male heirs. But these daughters felt they were about to get cheated out of their inheritance—just because they were female. And they decided to do something about it. The five daughters stated their case to Moses and the community's elders: "Let not our father's name be lost to his clan just because he had no son! Give us a holding among our father's kinsmen!" (27:4).

The daughters saw the injustice and argued for a correction. Rashi, the great medieval commentator, teaches: "Their eyes saw what the eyes of Moses did not see." Moses takes the daughters' case to God, and God decrees: "The plea of Zelophehad's daughters is just: you should give them a hereditary holding among their father's kinsmen; transfer their father's share to them" (27:7). And, in their honor, God adds a new law to the Torah, saying that if there are no sons daughters are permitted to inherit land.

So that's how change can happen—at least, sometimes. Someone realizes that he or she is dealing with an unfair situation. The person protests the injustice, and sometimes there's a change, a correction. Of course, it is rarely, if ever, as quick as it happened with the daughters of Zelophehad. It took decades for African Americans to get anything resembling equal rights, and the battle is not over yet. And women are not always treated—and paid—the same as men for doing the same work. But change has happened. Apartheid in South Africa was ultimately defeated, and same-sex marriage is legal now in all fifty U.S. states, to name just two examples. Things that we thought could never change often do.

But, regarding change, another point is worth making. It can't just be about *you*. Rabbi B. Elka Abrahamson teaches: "The daughters of Zelophehad did not *start* with their own needs. Their claim started with a respect for the past, preserving their father's legacy and name. Nor did it *end* with their own needs. They hoped for a future home among their community in the Promised Land. In every generation we can hear the echoes of these ancient voices." Enduring change is about improving one's standing not at the expense of others, but for all.

This point applies to an interesting twist in the daughters' story. When Moses informs the tribal leaders of the change in law to allow women to inherit, these leaders protest that if a woman who has inherited tribal land marries and then leaves the tribe for her husband's tribe (which was the custom), then the tribe as a whole would lose that land. Moses and God realize that this is a real problem, so together they must come up with a compromise. Women can inherit (if there is no male heir) but they must marry within the tribe.

Even though women were still not equal to men after this change, the daughters' story is a major step forward, especially considering the times. Further, this story from so long ago illustrates that Jewish law is not written in stone. People can change it, especially when there is a larger ethical issue at stake. The Torah admits that God approves how the daughters of Zelophehad challenged authority.

Connections

ᵬ Can you think of some examples of zealotry, or people who have acted out of zealotry? Think about examples in American history, Jewish history, or your own experience. What can you learn from those examples?

ᵬ Have you ever been fanatical about something? What was it? What was good about that, and what was not so good?

ᵬ Was Pinḥas right in doing what he did? How could he have handled things differently?

ᵬ What do you think some of the essential qualities of a leader should be?

☙ What can we learn from the story of the daughters of Zelophehad? What are some other ways that the situation of women has
improved over the centuries?

❖ Mattot: Numbers 30:2–32:42

The Torah portion begins with a description of the power of the personal vow and how it must be fulfilled.

The parashah then moves into an account of the Israelites' war
against the Midianites. As the Land of Israel is divided among the
tribes, the tribes of Reuben and Gad announce that they would rather
stay on the other side of the Jordan River rather than entering the land.

Summary

☙ People must fulfill what they have said that they will do. However, this pertains only to men. If a woman makes a vow, her father or husband has the power to negate it. (30:2–17)

☙ The Israelites enter into a bloody and merciless war against Midian. Among the victims of battle is Balaam, the soothsayer. The
Israelites take captive the Midianite women and children, and
they also take the spoil from the battle, for which an inventory is
given. Moses gets angry because the Israelites have spared every
female. It was the Midianite women, after all, who had induced
the Israelite men into paganism and orgies. (31:1–54)

☙ The tribes of Reuben and Gad ask to be able to settle on the
other side of the Jordan River and not enter the Land of Israel. In
exchange for the granting of this request, they offer to serve as
the shock troops—the advance guard—of the Israelites when they
conquer the land. (32:1–42)

The Big Ideas

☙ **Be careful what you say.** This is a basic Jewish concept, and it
is reflected in our religious lives and in our everyday ethics. The
word for "word" is *devar*, which is also the word for "thing." A
word is a thing, in and of itself. Words, pledges, and vows are so
powerful that the most sacred moment of the Jewish year—Kol

Nidre on the eve of Yom Kippur, the Day of Atonement—is devoted to annulling vows that we could not realistically fulfill.

Ҍ **Not every part of the Torah is nice.** This is a hard truth to accept, especially since we are accustomed to thinking of the Bible as "The Good Book." To be sure, the ancient Israelites did not always act as honorably as we might have wished. Things that would horrify us today, such as a violent war in which women, in particular, are victims, pass almost without comment in the Torah. One of God's greatest gifts to us is the ability to question these texts and to wrestle with their implications.

Ҍ **Solidarity with the Jewish people is a crucial part of Jewish life.** The tribes of Reuben and Gad were content to merely live their comfortable lives on the other side of the Jordan River, outside the Land of Israel. Moses had to remind them that the Jews must remain a single, unified people.

Divrei Torah

PUT FIRST THINGS FIRST!

Everyone has had this experience. You are a member of a sports team, or in a school play, or in a choir, or involved in some kind of big group project. Everyone is really engaged in what they are supposed to be doing. But there is always that one kid (if you are lucky, only one) who is, well, a slacker. He or she just isn't giving their all. And, when that happens, the efforts of everyone else suffer. It just isn't fair.

That's sort of what happens in this Torah portion. The tribes of Reuben and Gad ask to be able to settle on the other side of the Jordan River and not enter the Land of Israel proper. When Moses hears this request, he gets very angry and loses his temper (which is standard operating procedure for Moses). "Are your brothers to go to war while you stay here? Why will you turn the minds of the Israelites from crossing into the land that the Lord has given them?" (32:6).

Moses reminds them of how the spies had brought back bad accounts of the Land of Israel. He accuses the people of Reuben and Gad of basically doing the same thing—demoralizing the rest of the Jewish people. Finally, these two tribes offer Moses a consolation prize—that they will act as the shock troops, an elite force, protecting the land from neighboring tribes.

Let's remember that one of the great themes of the book of Numbers is the amount of almost constant complaining that Moses has to endure. There always seems to be a rebellion going on. And now Moses has to deal with yet another, as he comes near the end of his life. It must have stung badly.

And why did it hurt Moses so much? Because it wasn't only that the tribes of Reuben and Gad preferred the land on the other side of the Jordan. It was because they had a lot of cattle, and the grazing land was better there! Here's a great little Hebrew lesson. The word that the Torah uses for "cattle" is *mikneh*—which is related to the word for "buying" and "shopping." In modern terms, the people of Reuben and Gad were simply materialistic.

Look at how those tribes describe what they want to do. "We will build here sheepfolds for our flocks and towns for our children" (32:16). It is distortion of priorities. They put their animals (i.e., their possessions) before their children. Erica Brown teaches: "These people were willing to let go of a sacred, commanded vision to bolster their own material existence while Moses's own sincere appeals to enter the land were rejected." Rashi teaches: "Notice which they mentioned first— they were more concerned about the flocks than about the children."

Several verses later, Moses tells them: "Build towns for your children and sheepfolds for your flocks" (32:24). Moses reminds them of what is really important. It is a message for all of us: first, people, and creating a future for our people; then, and only then, our "stuff."

WAR—WHAT IS IT GOOD FOR?

There's an old classic rock song that goes like this: "War! What is it good for? Absolutely nothing!" Well, not exactly. Sometimes, war is necessary—for example, when you have to defend your people and your land. But, even when that is true, war stinks. It is a tragic, terrible mess.

That might be what bothers you about chapter 31—the account of the war against the Midianites. Why is it even necessary? According to the Torah the Midianite women had seduced Israelite men into orgies and into worshiping their god—part of a concerted effort to destroy the Israelites from within.

And then Moses gets angry because they spared the women! Kill them! Okay, well, you can spare the women who are virgins, but all the other women have to be killed. Oh, and take their stuff. And make a list of everything that you take, just so we get it straight. And, because you have touched corpses, you have to become purified.

What is going on here? To our modern sensibilities this is hard to comprehend and hard to stomach. Does God really command a war of vengeance? Is there such a thing as a holy war? Is it ever permissible to kill civilians?

Let's focus a little bit more closely on this section. God tells Moses to "avenge the Israelite people on the Midianites; then you shall be gathered to your kin" (31:2). How did that feel to Moses? And what's this "then you shall be gathered to your kin" business? Is God saying that this is Moses's final "project"—that once he has performed this act of brutality he can die?

Hold on a second here; this is Midian! The same Midian that Moses fled to, after he killed the taskmaster in Egypt. Midian was where he met his wife, Zipporah, who was, of course, a Midianite woman. Midian was the place where he met his father-in-law, Jethro, who was so kind to Moses and who taught him so much. Sure, the Midianite women did nasty stuff. But the Midianites were also descended from Abraham. They are a "cousin" people to the Israelites.

If this is troubling to you, then it was even more troubling to Moses. In fact, Moses does not go to war against the Midianites himself; he gets others to do it. As a midrash says: "Why did Moses send others to avenge the Midianites, when God told him to do it himself? Because he was highly regarded in the land of Midian, he thought: It is not right for me to cause distress to a people that has been good to me. As the proverb puts it: 'Do not cast a stone in the well from which you have to drink.'"

As contemporary Israeli leader Avraham Burg notes: "In commanding vengeance upon Midian, Moses is essentially destroying a part of himself, of his essence and identity." So is Moses trying to break free from his own Midianite past? Or is he unable to do so and thus has to find others to lead the effort?

It is strange that God chooses this moment to remind Moses that his time is running out: "then you shall be gathered to your kin" (31:2). In fact, there are a few more problems Moses will have to deal with before he dies, and a few more important speeches he will give to the Israelites.

But Moses is being reminded here that his kin are the Israelites, whom he has led for forty years, and who will frustrate him almost to his very final breath. Family is family, for better or for worse. Sometimes we have to do battle for it in ways that are distasteful and tough to do. Yes, we have to choose our battles, and should do so wisely. But there comes a time when we will have to say: this is difficult; this is messy; but this is worth fighting for.

Connections

- Can you give some examples when you have been careful with your use of words, and when you have not been?
- Do you think that it is bad or good to promise (pledge or vow) that we'll do certain things?
- Why did the tribes of Reuben and Gad settle on the other side of the Jordan River? Do you agree with their reasons?
- What are some examples of wars that have been "good"? Wars that have been "bad"? How do we make those kinds of judgments?
- Is it ever good to take revenge on someone?

❖ Mase'ei: Numbers 33:1–36:13

This is the final portion in the book of Numbers. It tells us about the various places that the Israelites encamped during their wandering in the wilderness.

As the Israelites prepare to enter the Land of Israel, God tells Moses about the boundaries of the land. God commands Moses to set aside cities for the Levites to dwell in. There must be cities of refuge among those cities—special places to which people who have killed someone unintentionally can flee, in order to escape the vengeance of a family member of the deceased.

The portion ends with a revisiting of the case of the daughters of Zelophehad, but this time with a new twist—they must marry within their own tribe, so that their inheritance will stay within the larger family.

Summary

ᵬ The Torah portion contains a list of the forty-two places at which the Israelites stopped during their wanderings. It forms an extensive, intricate itinerary (33:1–49). (Interesting piece of trivia: when these verses are chanted in the synagogue, the chanter uses the same tune that is used at the Song of the Sea.)

ᵬ More geography! The boundaries of the Land of Israel are established. (34:1–12)

ᵬ There are procedures for dealing with those who unintentionally kill others. They can flee to cities of refuge in order to be safe from the victim's relatives who will be seeking vengeance. (35:1–34)

ᵬ Once again, the daughters of Zelophehad push God on an issue of social and communal justice. They had earlier challenged God and Moses on the issue of being able to inherit from their father (Numbers 27). Now, the tribal leaders object that if they marry outside their tribe, their inheritance would pass to their husbands' tribes. God decrees that heiresses must marry within their own tribes. (36:1–12)

The Big Ideas

ᵬ **Jewish history is a journey, and it is crucial to remember all the places that the Jews have lived.** Sure, the Torah account of all those places might seem a little tedious and repetitive; over and over again, the verses tell us: *va-yisu va-yachanu*, they set out from . . . they camped in . . . . But that is an essential piece of Jewish history—wandering from one place to another, staying there for a while, and then moving on, when necessary. That is also the way that our own lives unfold. We stay in one place for a while (literally and figuratively), we move on, we have adventures, things go well, or not so well—and we grow.

ᵬ **There is no Judaism without a love of the Land of Israel. That would account for the careful detail with which the biblical author describes the boundaries of the land.** The boundaries as described in these verses actually go as far south as present-day Egypt; as far north as cities in present-day Lebanon; and as far as

Damascus, which is in present-day Syria! At a time when politicians and everyday people debate what the borders of the State of Israel should be, this biblical "map" does not and cannot reflect current reality. The Jewish love for the Land of Israel does not necessarily rely on the precise biblical boundaries of the land.

ƀ **Judaism requires both justice and mercy.** Yes, Judaism takes murder very seriously. But it also recognizes that not all killing of another person is deliberate homicide. Accidents happen, and while they are tragic those accidents neither require nor merit vengeance. The Torah recognizes the reality that people sometimes kill each other and that there must be a system in place for dealing with homicides—both intentional and unintentional.

ƀ **God responds to human need and human circumstances.** The book of Numbers is filled with complaints, both to Moses and to God, and this latest plea from the daughters of Zelophehad is the final "complaint." God responds to the fear that other tribes would inherit the daughters' inheritances by telling them that they must marry within their own tribe. How is that good? Isn't it just a further restriction on the daughters and on their marital choices? Yes it is, but, luckily for them, their tribe was quite large so we assume there were many marriageable men. The Torah is making it clear: the tribe—the larger family that is at the core of the Jewish people—is sacred.

Divrei Torah
GOD'S GPS SYSTEM

GPS systems (or Google Maps) are among the modern world's greatest inventions. Think of it: back in the "old days," there were very few ways to figure out where you were going. You could look at a road map and try to figure it out, or you could ask someone for directions and hope they knew what they were talking about. Now, all you have to do is type the address of your destination and in a nanosecond you will find the route.

Here is something else about many of these GPS systems—and it is either cool or weird. The GPS stores every address that you have entered. Just scroll through the GPS, and you will find a list of every place that you have gone—or, at the very least, every place that you have used the GPS to find.

That's how this Torah portion works as well. It lists every single place that the Israelites camped in, showing their route to the Land of Israel. (Years ago, a kid who became bar mitzvah actually traveled this route in Israel. Very cool.)

Now, you might think that this is the most boring portion of the Torah—just a list of ancient place names, about as exciting as reading, well, a GPS. Why does the Torah have to include this long list? And, to be fair, there are other accounts of journeys in the Torah that have different place-names, or sometimes are in a different order.

So, what's the big deal? What can we learn from this laundry list of places?

First, the whole chapter has a hidden message: God's love for the Jewish people endures, in spite of everything. A midrash teaches: "It is like the case of a king whose son was ill. He took him to a certain place to cure him. On their return journey, his father began to recount all the stages, saying: "Here we slept; here we cooled ourselves; here you had a headache." So God said to Moses: "Tell them all the places where they provoked Me."

God remembers every step on the Jewish people's journey. It's like your parents keeping old photographs of you from when you were growing up. You were not always an easy child. But your parents like looking at the photographs and remembering, and hopefully you do too.

Second, what goes for the ancient Israelites goes for us. Each of us is a product of a journey that is both ancient and modern. Rabbi Arthur Green offers an example: "They journeyed from Berditchev and camped in Hamburg. They sailed from Hamburg and landed in Ellis Island. They journeyed from Ellis Island and camped on Rivington Street. They journeyed from Rivington Street and camped in the Bronx, on the Grand Concourse. They journeyed from the Grand Concourse and settled in Teaneck."

You didn't just get where you are by accident. You were led. Are you grateful?

"IT WAS JUST AN ACCIDENT!"

This has happened to you. You were hanging out, doing "nothing"—and you: (a) dropped and broke your cell phone; (b) broke a window; or (c) spilled a soft drink onto your mother's laptop computer. Whatever it is, you're in big trouble. And all you can say is: "I didn't mean to do it! It was just an accident!"

But what if (God forbid) a man or woman accidentally ran over someone with a car? The official term for that kind of thing is "manslaughter." What would the person do? Today the answer is easy, even though the situation is tragic. He or she would report this terrible thing to the police, and apologize to the family. There might or might not be criminal charges. But one thing's pretty sure: the family of the dead person would not come after the accidental killer and try to kill him or her. At least, we hope not.

That is the situation that this Torah portion describes: the accidental killer. In ancient times, if someone (even accidentally) killed someone, there was always the danger that the dead person's relatives would pursue the "killer." So, the Torah provides six cities of refuge, to which an accidental killer could flee so that there would be no vengeance taken against him or her.

Now, it's not as if the accidental killer gets a totally free pass. The Torah makes it clear: If you hit someone with a stone or wooden tool and that person dies, then you are a murderer. You should have known what was going to happen. Similarly, if you hate another person and you push that person, or throw something at that person, then you are assumed to have acted with malice, and you are a murderer. And, yes—a family member of the deceased could come after you in cases of intentional homicide.

Terrible, right? Perhaps, but this was a major change from the other societies of the ancient world. In those societies, if you killed someone, you could just pay a fee to the bereaved family, and call it a day. Not in the Torah. According to Bible scholar Moshe Greenberg: "In biblical law, the taking of life cannot be made up for by any amount of property, nor can any property offense be considered as amounting to the value of a life."

But the Torah is also saying that there is a difference between outright murder, which the Ten Commandments prohibit, and killing. Society is responsible for making sure that the accidental killer is safe from vengeance. The great medieval sage Maimonides teaches: "The court is obligated to remove all obstacles to cities of refuge so as not to delay one who is fleeing to one of them. The width of a road to a city of refuge should not be less than thirty-two cubits." "Refuge, Refuge" was written at all crossroads so that the perpetrator of manslaughter would recognize the way and turn there. Keep in mind that the person who flees to the city of refuge is not escaping punishment. He must stay there and not go home until a specified period of time has elapsed.

The bottom line: Judaism believes in justice. But justice is not the same as revenge. Intention matters and the punishment should fit the crime. Sometimes we do bad things we didn't mean to do, but there are consequences nonetheless.

Connections

ᛒ Why do you think that the places listed in this parashah are chanted in the same tune as the song that the Israelites sang when they crossed the sea (Exodus 15)? How are those two experiences the same?

ᛒ Why do you think it is important to record the Israelites' journey in such detail? What can we learn from this?

ᛒ Do you know the places where your own family (and your grandparents, or great-grandparents) lived? Have you ever visited those places? What was that experience like?

ᛒ What do you think of the differences between murder and killing? Do you agree with those differences? What are the implications of this teaching for political refugees—those who have not even killed someone, but are searching for freedom?

DEUTERONOMY

❖ Devarim: Deuteronomy 1:1–3:22

In this first portion of the book of Deuteronomy, the final book of the Torah, Moses reminds the Israelites of their journey from Mount Sinai to the Land of Israel. In particular, he focuses on their constant complaining, and on how he recognized that he needed help in judging their various disputes.

Moses describes how he appointed tribal leaders who would serve as judges, and he recounts the basic principles of fairness and justice.

Summary

ᚦ Moses recalls that he appointed leaders and judges to help him execute justice among the Israelites. He reminds the Israelites that justice entails being impartial in judgment, and treating the rich and the poor alike. (1:1–18)

ᚦ Moses reminds the Israelites of the mission of the spies (Numbers 13)—but, this time, he adds something new to the story. He tells the people that they "sulked in their tents," and that they imagined that God hated them. (1:22–33)

ᚦ Moses positions the Israelites for their entrance into the Land of Israel. They will be entering from the east, passing through the territories of Seir (inhabited by the descendants of Esau, Jacob's brother), Ammon, Moab, and the kingdoms of Sihon and Og. (2:2–37)

ᚦ The Israelites engage in battle with several nations. They are victorious over them and conquer their lands, which are then distributed to various tribes. (3:1–21)

The Big Ideas

ᚦ **Even and especially as the Israelites prepare to enter the Land of Israel, Moses must remind them of the basic principles of** justice. The principles described in the first chapter of Deuteronomy are not new; they appeared previously, with slightly different wording, in Exod. 23:3 and Lev. 19:15. Back then, those laws must have seemed merely theoretical. As the Israelites prepare for life in Israel (a basic theme of this biblical book), those ideals suddenly jump to life.

ᵼ **Being discouraged (sometimes) is part of life.** The Israelites had been depressed over the reports that the spies had brought to them—so much so that they thought God's desire to bring them into such a difficult land was because God hated them. It was an understandable reaction to difficult circumstances back in those days.

ᵼ **The route into the Land of Israel is far from "random."** God brings the Israelites through the domains of the descendants of Esau, Moab, and Ammon. What do they all have in common? Esau was Jacob's brother. Moab and Ammon are descended from Abraham's brother, Lot. As the Israelites enter the land, they must first encounter their "cousin" peoples, so that they can remember their past and where they have come from.

ᵼ **God promised the Land of Israel to the Israelites, but they had to work to possess it.** It would have been better, perhaps, for the Israelites to have been able to simply walk into the Land of Israel and make themselves at home. After all, God had promised it to them. But there were other peoples inhabiting the land, and they had to be conquered. As unpleasant as this might seem to us, it is part of the history of the world. There is no country anywhere that has come into existence without conquest and bloodshed. Even David Ben Gurion, the first Prime Minister of the State of Israel, said: "No nation is every presented to its people on a silver platter."

Divrei Torah
BE FAIR!

It's summer camp. Two kids decide that they are going to cut out of camp at night, head to town, and get some ice cream. They are caught. The camp director wants to throw both of them out of camp. Except . . . one kid is from a wealthy, generous family, in which the kids have attended that camp for generations. The camp director sends the middle-class kid home but only gives the rich kid a strict warning to never do that again. She gets to complete the summer with her friends.

Bad, right? That is what Moses is talking about at the very beginning of this week's Torah portion. "Hear out your brothers and decide justly between any man and a fellow Israelite or stranger. You shall not be partial in judgment; hear out the low as well as the high. Do not be afraid of anyone, for judgment is God's." (1:16–17)

Moses wants us to know that all Israelites are "your brothers," and he especially wants judges to know that as well—so that they will judge fairly and let everyone have an equal say in their own defense. As Bible scholar Jeffrey Tigay points out, "Deuteronomy regularly uses the term 'brothers' to emphasize the equality of all Israelites, whether king or servant, prophet or king." (Regrettably, "sisters" weren't included in this equality. In the male-centric world back then, women didn't have all the rights that men enjoyed.)

When it comes to justice, social class and economic station should be irrelevant. And why even say this? Because it is human nature for people to be swayed and influenced by another person's wealth and status.

But "large" and "small" aren't only about the status of the people. They are also about the amount of money or the value of an item that is being discussed As Rashi teaches: "A case involving a small coin should be as important to you as one involving a lot of money, so that if it comes first, do not put it off until last. Also, do not say: this one is poor and the other rich, and it is a sacred duty to support the poor."

You would think that a religious culture like Judaism, which cares so much about social justice, would automatically favor the poor. Wrong. The key word is "justice." When the text says that we should not be afraid of any person, it doesn't mean afraid as in being scared. No; it means that we should not be afraid to judge any person, no matter who he or she might be. Because if we don't, God will know.

One last thing. The text's message is that we must judge fairly between any Israelite or *stranger* (which here in the Torah means a non-Israelite, but today we know it to mean anyone who is different in any way from us). All people in society are equal. Because we are all brothers and sisters.

DON'T HASSLE ESAU'S PEOPLE

In Deuteronomy Moses begins to look back on his days as the leader of the Israelite nation. He reminds the people of their history and of the desert experience that they have shared for forty years.

Suddenly, he relates these words: "Charge the people as follows: You will be passing through the territory of your kinsmen, the descendants of Esau, who live in Seir. . . . Be very careful not to provoke them. For I will not give you of their land so much as a foot can tread on; I have given the hill county of Seir as a possession to Esau. Whatever food you eat you shall obtain from them for money; even the water you drink you shall procure from them for money" (2:4–6).

Esau. Him again, the Israelites must have muttered to themselves. They had grown up on the stories of how their ancestor Jacob had basically swindled the birthright from his brother, Esau, and then how Jacob had stolen from his father, Isaac, the blessing that had been intended for Esau. Perhaps the Israelites had grown up hearing all sorts of terrible stories about Esau and his descendants (not that anyone had ever met a descendant of Esau, but you know how stories can get passed along).

That is why God needs the Israelites to treat the descendants of Esau in a rather sensitive way.

First, God tells the Israelites to *buy* their food and water from the descendants of Esau. Get it? *Buy* food and water. God remembers that Esau had sold his birthright to Jacob when he was weak and hungry. Had the birthright not been sold, it would have been Esau's descendants in the desert. That is how history and destiny were radically transformed by a simple barter of a bowl of soup.

Centuries before this, Esau, beset by thirst and hunger, sold his birthright to Jacob for a bowl of soup. God is worried: what if the Israelites, threatened by thirst and hunger, try to sell their birthright back to Esau's descendants—just to get something to eat? God remembers how momentary thirst and hunger can cause the birthright to change hands, and God does not want that to happen again.

The Israelites must remember that the children of Esau are, in fact, their kinsmen. The medieval commentator Isaac Abravanel asks: "Why did the Almighty confine His command not to distress or contend in battle to Esau, Ammon, and Moab, giving the reason as 'for I have given . . . for a possession' to them their land? Surely all the other nations have also been granted their land by the Almighty?"

The reason is clear. Esau, Ammon, and Moab are "cousin" peoples to the Israelites. Suddenly, the Israelites are the stronger people. In the words of the modern Bible commentator and teacher Nehama Leibowitz: "The Israelites had to resist the temptation to take advantage of their superior strength by harassing their weaker neighbors." When you enter the land, remember your roots. Remember that you are related to some of your adversaries, and have to deal rightly with them. And remember that you were not always as strong as you are now.

Connections

ᚻ Have you ever delegated a task to anyone? Have you ever had a task delegated to you? How did those situations work out? What are the good things about delegation? And the not-so-good things?

ᚻ What are some qualities of a good leader that you favor most? Who's someone who has such qualities? What qualities would you like to imitate?

ᚻ Have you ever seen people abuse their power? What are some examples—from your own life, or from the news, or from history?

ᚻ Can you recall situations where the rich were favored over the poor—in history, in the news, or in your own experience?

ᚻ Have you ever been discouraged while doing something? What happened? How did you get over it?

❖ Va-'ethannan: Deuteronomy 3:23–7:11

This Torah portion begins with Moses recalling how he had pleaded with God to be allowed to cross over the Jordan River and to enter the Land of Israel. No go, says God. So, knowing that the end is coming sooner rather than later, Moses recounts the history of the Israelites so that they will be able to learn its lessons. He reminds them that God has been merciless to idolaters, and that the Israelites must worship God alone.

Jewish laws and teachings affect the reputation that the Jewish people will have, even though they have been conveyed by a God who has no form and only communicates through a voice. Finally, just so the Jewish people really understand, the parashah repeats the Ten Commandments here (an earlier version of them is in Exodus 20)—with a few minor, but significant changes.

This brings us to the *Shema*, the declaration of God's unity and uniqueness, along with specific ways to demonstrate love for God.

Summary

ቴ Moses remembers how he had begged God to allow him to enter the Land of Israel. God had refused, but God showed him the land from afar. (3:23–29)

ቴ Moses tells the people that God's laws are proof of God's greatness, and will be their way of creating a sacred standing among the nations. (4:6–8)

ቴ Moses recalls the moment of Sinai. He reminds the people that they did not see God but only heard a voice. (4:11–14)

ቴ Moses repeats the Ten Commandments—with a few changes. (5:6–18)

ቴ Moses teaches about the uniqueness of God, and emphasizes that the Israelites must demonstrate their love for God through concrete actions. (6:4–9)

The Big Ideas

ቴ **Arguing with God is an ancient Jewish tradition.** This is a common theme in the Torah and in later Jewish tradition. Abraham, Moses, Job, the various authors of the Psalms, various ancient sages, Hasidic teachers, and even Tevye in *Fiddler on the Roof* all argued with God.

ቴ **Judaism is bigger than just the Jews.** Deuteronomy introduces a new idea: what Jews do has implications for the whole world, and Jewish teachings create the way that the world perceives Jews.

ቴ **You cannot see God.** The People of Israel did not see God at Sinai; they only heard God. If they had seen God, they would have spent more time arguing over what God looked like, rather than arguing about the meaning of God's sacred words.

ъ **The Ten Commandments are so important that they appear twice.**
But there are some minor changes in the Deuteronomy version.
The version of them here in Deuteronomy says that Jews must observe Shabbat, as well as "remember" Shabbat. Moses says that
slaves must also rest on Shabbat—conveying the growing sense
that slaves are human beings, too. There is far more emphasis on
how God took the Israelites out of Egypt—"with a mighty hand and
an outstretched arm." Finally, God says that the Israelites are not
only to refrain from coveting what others have, but are not to crave
those things either. This makes the commandment even stronger.

ъ **Moses teaches that God is *echad*.** As most scholars admit, it is
difficult to figure out what this word really means (in fact, thousands of pages have been written on the meaning of this small
word). Whatever it means, the *Shema* has become "the watchword
of the Jewish faith," and it has inspired Jews throughout history.

ъ **Jews must love God.** Love doesn't mean affection. It means a deep,
powerful connection that binds Jews to God through the mitzvot.

Divrei Torah
THE MOST IMPORTANT SENTENCE IN JUDAISM

It is the most important sentence in the Torah. Okay, make that "in
the entire Hebrew Bible." Come to think of it—make that "in all of
Judaism." We are talking about the *Shema*—six Hebrew words *Shema
Yisrael Adonai Eloheinu Adonai Echad* (6:4) that are sometimes referred
to as "the watchword of the Jewish faith," or what the ancient sages
called *kabbalat ol ha-Shamayim* (the acceptance of the yoke of Heaven).

It is the first sentence in Hebrew that a Jewish child learns. When
Jews pray, they say it at morning worship (*Shacharit*) and at evening
worship (*Ma'ariv*). It's also found in the Torah service. It's said at the
end of Yom Kippur. Observant Jews say it when they go to sleep. And,
just as it is the first Hebrew sentence that a child learns, so, too, it is
the last Hebrew sentence that a Jew says.

The *Shema* is almost like a secret Jewish code. During World War II,
there were many Jewish children who had been rescued by Christians
and undercover Jews and who then spent the war hidden in monasteries. After the war, Rabbi Eliezer Silver went around Europe, look-

ing for those children. He would visit those monasteries and simply say: "*Shema Yisrael* . . ." If a child completed the sentence, he would claim the child as a Jew.

But what does it mean when it says that "The Lord is one," *echad*? The possibilities are almost endless—just like God.

It could mean that there is only one god. Except in this stage of the Bible's development, the Torah itself seems to recognize that there are many nations that have many gods. Pure monotheism that insists that no other gods exist comes later in Judaism.

Second, it could mean that there is only one God, not numerically, but spiritually. Even though God seems "different" at different stages of Jewish history, God is always God. A midrash teaches: "I am the Lord your God—the same one who was in Egypt, the same one who was at the Red Sea, at Sinai, in the past and in the future, in this world and in the world to come."

Or, it could simply mean that Adonai is the only god whom Jews should worship. That increasingly accepted interpretation has led many, including the JPS TANAKH to translate the end of the *Shema* as "the Lord alone."

There is one more, controversial, theory: The whole word is a misprint! In ancient Hebrew, the letter *chet* could sometimes look like the letter *heh*. And the letter *dalet* could sometimes look like the letter *vet*. The Torah text was written by scribes and passed down from generation to generation. It would have been easy to make a mistake in copying the letters.

Professor David Sperling contends that the word *echad* was originally *ahav* (love): "Therefore, the real translation should be: Hear O Israel, Adonai is our God—love Adonai." This makes sense in that the very next words are, "And you shall love Adonai with all your heart."

The *Shema* is the most important line in Judaism, yet the debate on what it means goes on. That's Judaism for you!

LOVE GOD!

As you learned in Hebrew school, you can't have the *Shema* without the *Ve-ahavta*. That's what comes right after the *Shema* in both the worship service and in the Torah itself. The *Ve-ahavta* is also called *kabba-*

lat ol ha-mitzvot (the acceptance of the yoke of the mitzvot). The *Ve-ahavta* tells us that we should not only know that there is a God; we should love God, and that love should be manifest in specific actions.

What actions do we list aloud in the *Ve-ahavta*? One of them, most importantly, is "Teach them to your children." It is not enough to merely know these words; they must be transmitted to future generations. That is the meaning of Jewish continuity. In the words of the Israeli writer Fania Oz-Salzberger: "The great story and its imperatives passed from generation to generation on tablets, parchment and paper. As I check my references on an iPad, I realize that we have come full circle: from tablet to tablet, from scroll to scroll."

"Bind them as a sign upon your hand; let them be symbols before your eyes." Those are the tefillin (leather boxes containing words of Torah) that are worn during morning prayer on the forearm and on the forehead by traditional Jews.

"Inscribe them on the doorposts of your house and on your gates." That is the mezuzah that marks the doorposts of the Jewish home.

But you're probably thinking: okay, those are rituals and actions, but how can the Torah really tell us to love God? Isn't love an emotion? How can you command an emotion? Here, we need to learn from archeologists of the ancient Middle East. They tell us that when ancient kings made treaties (or covenants) with their underlings, the underlings were commanded to "love" the more powerful king. Love wasn't an emotional thing; the word "love" was used to symbolize loyalty.

But the early sages tell us that there is another dimension to love. It's not only to love God; it's also to inspire others to love God. "If someone studies Torah, and is honest in business, and speaks pleasantly to people, what do people say concerning him? 'Happy the father who taught him Torah, happy the teacher who taught him Torah!' But if someone studies Torah, but is dishonest in business, and discourteous in his relations with people, what do people say about him? 'Woe unto his father who taught him Torah; woe unto his teacher who taught him Torah!'"

To be a Jew, therefore, is to have awesome responsibility. It is to love God, and it is to be God's PR agent in the world.

Connections

ቴ Have you ever thought that God was being unfair? What did you do about it? Did you talk to God, or even yell at God?

ቴ Have you ever thought that what you do, as a Jew, affects people who are not Jewish? In what ways do you think Jewish laws and teachings can create a good impression on others?

ቴ Do you agree that God is invisible? What would be the benefits of having a god that you could see? The disadvantages?

ቴ What do you think of the changes that Moses made in the second version of the Ten Commandments? Do you agree with them? If you could make any changes, what would they be?

ቴ What is your own interpretation of the *Shema*?

ቴ What does it mean for you to love God?

❖ 'Ekev: Deuteronomy 7:12–11:25

This portion continues Moses's final orations to the People of Israel. It emphasizes that if the Israelites observe God's laws, God will favor them and bless them, and cause them to be fertile. Repeating an earlier theme in the Torah, Moses reminds the Israelites that they should prevail over idolatrous nations of Canaan, and destroy the places where the Canaanites worship their gods.

Moses recounts the Israelites' long trek through the wilderness, and the times they had been tested by various adversities. In preparation for the people's eventual entry into the Land of Israel, Moses warns them not to be arrogant, believing that their own strength will win them the prosperity that they will one day enjoy; rather, it will be God who will bless the people and make it possible for them to conquer and possess the land.

Summary

ቴ As a reward for observing God's laws and commandments, the Israelites will be blessed—through the gifts of fertility, health, and prosperity. (7:12–15)

ቴ Moses reminds the people that they will conquer the Land of Israel, get rid of the people who live there, and destroy their false gods. (7:16–26)

ቴ Moses goes to great lengths to describe the natural beauty of the Land of Israel. He offers the Israelites a vision of a prosperous future in the land, and tells them to always remember that God is the source of their strength. (8:1–20)

ቴ Moses recalls his experience of having waited on Horeb (another term for Mount Sinai) for the tablets of the commandments, and how the Israelites profoundly disappointed both God and him by building the Golden Calf. Moses remembers how he destroyed the tablets and the Golden Calf. He reminds the Israelites how he interceded for them and for Aaron, who had acquiesced to their demand for a visible god. (9:8–21)

ቴ Moses reminds the Israelites that Canaan (Israel), which they are about to enter, is very different from Egypt. For one thing, Egypt required watering through irrigation in order for it to be fertile, but the Land of Israel gets its water from the rains of heaven. (11:10–17)

The Big Ideas

ቴ **The Torah imagines that the observance of mitzvot comes with tangible rewards.** Nowadays, we are likely to believe that the "rewards" for doing the mitzvot include: being a loving person; strengthening the Jewish people; and feeling good about living disciplined, ethical lives. But the Torah goes one better: God's gift for doing the mitzvot will be material prosperity, symbolized by being fertile and having an abundance of crops.

ቴ **While loving the Torah is an essential part of Judaism, there are certain passages in the Torah that are not "likeable."** Many of the more warlike passages in the Torah are in Deuteronomy, and there are some in this parashah. From a historical point of view, most scholars believe that all the "destroy those people and their idols!" stuff is merely, well, made up. Many archeologists think that the ancient Canaanites had already destroyed their cities in their own internal wars, and that the Israelites had little, if anything, to do with it. These passages give the author an opportunity to be especially fierce about idolatry—and idolatry, as we know, is among the worst things a Jew can do.

ቴ **Gratitude is a fundamental Jewish value.** This value makes its first appearance in this Torah portion. It is too easy to become vain and self-important, and think that you have gotten to where you are all by yourself. American culture celebrates "self-made people," who seemingly do it all by themselves. But Judaism rejects that idea. The Jewish tradition does not see individuals as being separate from their communities, and it recognizes that, ultimately, God is behind and beyond all our achievements.

ᴃ **Memory sometimes plays weird tricks on us.** In the account of the Golden Calf in Exodus 32, there is no mention of Moses interceding with God to spare Aaron; indeed, it doesn't even say that Aaron had been in any danger of being punished by God. But here in Deuteronomy he talks about how he begged God to spare Aaron. Did that really happen, and Moses suddenly remembered it at this moment? Or is Moses, knowing that he is at the end of his life, making up that little detail, wishing that he had really done so? This is not the only time that Deuteronomy adds details to previously told stories and laws; think of the repetition of the Ten Commandments in last week's portion. History is often a book that constantly reveals new pages.

ᴃ **The difference between Egypt and Canaan is not only geographic, and not only about the nature of their agricultural requirements.** It's theological as well. Egypt is watered through irrigation; Israel is watered by rain. But the rain will only come if the people observe the mitzvot. The difference between the two lands is that God is intricately involved with the Land of Israel, and our conduct matters.

Divrei Torah

WHY THIS LAND?

There is an old one-line joke that goes like this: the Israelites wandered for forty years in the wilderness, and they managed to settle in the only place in the Middle East that doesn't have oil! (Actually, there are natural gas preserves in the Mediterranean, which might make the need for oil irrelevant—but you get the point.)

Israel is a great land, but it doesn't have everything. Jews love the Land of Israel, but they would be the first to admit that their love is a little biased. Jerusalem is a beautiful city, but, to be honest, there are many beautiful cities in the world. Tel Aviv is a cool place, but it's not Paris. The beaches of Israel are great, but compared to, say, the beaches of Brazil—not so much.

Natural resources? The land is "a land whose rocks are iron and from whose hills you can mine copper" (8:9). Yes, but no oil. Great food resources? Sure—"wheat and barley, vines, figs, pomegranates . . . olive trees and honey" (8:8)—great, if you're a vegetarian. But there were many famines in the Land of Israel, all of which Abraham, Jacob, and Ruth experienced.

So, what's special about the Land of Israel? Precipitation. In Egypt, there was always enough water. It came from the Nile, and Egyptians watered their crops through the irrigation systems they built. *People* had to do it.

What kind of religious attitude does the Egyptian style of agriculture produce? A modern rabbi, Rabbi Eliahu Ha-Cohen of Casablanca, teaches: "The Egyptians rely on their own labor to water their lands, and therefore it appears to them that they are at the center of all that is done. In the Land of Israel, by contrast, there is a constant relationship between worshipping the Lord and performing the commandments, on one hand, and having rain to make the crops grow, on the other."

In the Land of Israel it's different. You have to pray for rain. As a prayer states: "Remember Abraham, his heart poured out to You like water. You blessed him, as a tree planted near water. You saved him when he went through fire and water. For Abraham's sake, do not withhold water." And it's not as if rain is "always" there; it only rains between Simchat Torah and Pesach (roughly, between October and April). And if you don't observe the mitzvot, God will withhold the rain.

Without God's love, Israel would have no rain, and nothing would grow.

The real spiritual difference between ancient Egypt and the Land of Israel is that in Egypt, people took charge of watering the land, and that meant they might think they were the most important thing. Bottom line: God "looks after" the land (11:12)—just like God looks after the Jewish people.

Living in arid, rain-dependent Israel teaches dependency on God. Sometimes we may be thirsty and hungry . . . but faith makes us stronger.

NO NEED TO STUFF YOURSELF

There used to be a strange custom in summer camps: food-eating contests. Two contestants would sit in front of piles of food (hamburgers, or ice cream, or pie). The buzzer would go off, and whoever could eat the most food in a given period of time would win.

It's gross. We should respect food and not waste it, especially when we consider how many people around the world don't have enough to eat.

Jews sanctify the act of eating by saying *brachot*—blessings. The best-known blessing is the one we say before the meal—*ha-Motzi*. And then there is the long blessing after the meal—*Birkat ha-Mazon*. Now comes the question: How much do you have to have eaten before you say a blessing after the meal? A little? A lot? Do you have to walk away from the table stuffed?

Here is what the Torah says: "When you have eaten your fill, give thanks to the Lord your God for the good land which He has given you" (8:10). In fact, this verse is the entire reason why *Birkat ha-Mazon* became a custom. So, you should say a blessing when you have eaten and are totally satisfied—totally full. Right?

That was certainly the Torah's vision. After all, Deuteronomy imagines the Israelites living in the Land of Israel and everyone having enough to eat. But, the early sages, writing after the Romans had exiled the Jews from the land, had a different answer. They said that you should thank God for your food—even if you have eaten as little as an olive or an egg! Huh? An olive or an egg? How could that possibly fill you up? The sages even imagined God approving of this change. God boasts about the Jewish people: I wrote for them in the Torah: "When you have eaten your fill, give thanks to the Lord"—and they give thanks if the quantity is only as much as an olive or an egg!

Why would God take such pride in the Jewish people for choosing to say a blessing over such a meager meal?

Because it takes courage to say a blessing, even when you're still hungry, or even when you are in difficult circumstances. In the words of the contemporary teacher Rabbi David Hartman: "The ancient Rabbis taught the community to experience God's love in the life of mitzvah even when the community was struggling to survive under foreign domination."

That was what it was like for the Jews after the Romans destroyed Judean independence (when many of the sages we quote actually lived). They had been crushed, but their spirits were still alive. Many lived in poverty, and may not have had enough to eat. Yet they still had the power of gratitude, even for the small things in life.

And if they could live with that kind of spirit, can we do any less?

Connections

- Do you believe that people should observe the mitzvot because they want a reward? What are the best reasons for observing the mitzvot?
- Are there things that happened in your childhood that you now remember differently from the way they really happened? What are some examples?
- What are you most grateful for?
- Why do you think there should be a blessing after the meal as well as before?

❖ Re'eh: Deuteronomy 11:26–16:17

Re'eh continues Moses's second farewell address to the Israelites. It begins by reminding them that they can choose blessing or curse: a blessing if they obey God's commandments, and a curse if they disobey. The parashah continues one of Deuteronomy's major themes—the prohibition of idolatry—and, for the first time, tells the Israelites that they will have to confine all their sacrificial offerings to one specific place. As Jewish history continues to unfold, the Israelites will understand this place to be Jerusalem.

The portion repeats the basic laws of kashrut, by describing which animals can be eaten and which are prohibited. The Israelites are warned not to follow false prophets, and are instructed to observe the three pilgrimage festivals: Pesach, Shavuot, and Sukkot. And it ends with social legislation: property must be shared with Levites, strangers, orphans, and widows.

Summary

- ƀ Moses tells the Israelites that they will always have the ability to decide for themselves between blessings and curses. When they enter the Land of Israel, the tribes will pronounce the blessings on Mount Gerizim and the curses on Mount Ebal, which are opposite each other. (11:26–3)
- ƀ He also tells them that when they enter the Land of Israel, they will no longer be permitted to offer sacrifices at just any convenient site. They will worship God only at the place where God chooses. (12:4–16)
- ƀ Moses expands the "menu options" for the Israelites. Even though they will have to bring their sacrificial offerings to one specific place, they will still be permitted to eat meat anywhere, as long as they do not eat the blood along with the meat. (12:20–28)
- ƀ There is a list of animals that are permitted and those that are forbidden. We find a similar list in Leviticus 11, but there are some significant additions in this version. Here, the list of permitted and forbidden animals comes after very specific prohibitions of idolatry. Further, while the Israelites are not allowed to eat anything that has died a natural death, the text specifies that such meat can be given to the stranger to eat. (14:4–21)
- ƀ Moses reviews how people are to share their harvest and treat the poor. The remission of debts and indentured servitude is discussed, against the backdrop that poverty will always be with us. The description of the three important festivals notes that everyone in society should be included in their observance. (14:22–16:17)

The Big Ideas

- ƀ **The ability to make moral choices is one of Judaism's greatest gifts to the world.** This is one of the most important differences between human beings and animals. Animals will always act based on instinct; people have the ability to think about the consequences of their options and their actions first. It is also one of the many differences between human beings and computers. Computers never choose to do anything; they only perform based on the information that people enter into them. The ability to choose the good is what has created the civilization we have today.

ᵇ **Judaism believes that certain places are holy.** While Judaism has always cared more about sacred *times,* like Shabbat and the festivals, it has hardly ignored the idea that places can be holy as well. Deuteronomy introduces this notion by stating that the Israelites will only be permitted to offer sacrifices at a specific place— which later will be the Temple in Jerusalem.

ᵇ **Life is sacred.** This is the main reason why Israelites were not permitted to eat the blood with their meat—because blood symbolizes life. This still forms the basis of kosher slaughtering. The animal must be slaughtered in a particularly humane way so as to minimize pain to the animal, and all blood must be drained from the meat before it can be declared kosher. Some would say that God would have preferred for human beings to be vegetarians, but God understood that this was a rather lofty goal. So, yes, we can eat meat, but it has restrictions attached to it.

ᵇ **To be a Jew means to be different.** In Deuteronomy, this seems to be the major reason why certain animals can be eaten and others are prohibited. Differentiating Jews from others was not part of the message the last time this list was presented (Leviticus 11). God is telling the Israelites that when they enter the Land of Israel they will have to learn to continue to exert their differences from the native Canaanites in every way—no worshiping idols, not even tolerating anyone who worships idols, and eating differently. That is still a major reason why many Jews observe the tradition of kashrut; it constantly reminds them of their Jewish identity.

Divrei Torah
IT'S YOUR CHOICE, SO CHOOSE WISELY!

If you have been paying attention for the last few years, you will have heard a phrase that gets thrown around a lot: "pro-choice." It means that a woman can choose her own health options, particularly whether she wants to bear and give birth to a baby.

So, here is what you need to know: *Judaism is pro-choice*, in the broad sense of the term. Judaism is filled with the language of *choice*. God chose the Jewish people to do the mitzvot. The Hebrew word for "young person" is *bachur* or *bachurah*—one who can make choices—which is the whole meaning of bar and bat mitzvah: old enough to choose wisely.

That's what makes the opening words of our Torah portion so powerful. God sets before us blessing and curse. What does that mean? Here, "blessing" means material prosperity; if you follow the mitzvot, you (not "you" as an individual; "you" as the entire People of Israel) will have prosperity in the land. But if you don't follow the mitzvot, you get the curse—which means, frankly, disaster.

God is saying: "There are options in life. There are alternatives. You make the choice." God is like a parent who is dealing with a child who is maturing. "You can choose: do your homework and succeed in school, or don't and you won't be able to take advantage of all the learning that school offers you." God, like a wise parent, cannot force us to do anything, but God wants us to know the consequences of our actions.

That's what makes us human. Rabbi Harold Kushner writes: "The distinguishing characteristic of human beings, setting us apart from other animals, is our ability to choose the values by which we live. Other animals are driven by instinct. Human beings have the potential to control instinct." We train our pets to do certain things, and *not* to do certain things. When they obey us, it is not out of their free will; they have simply trained their instincts so that they earn a reward. "Good dog!" does not mean that the dog is morally good; it simply means that the dog has done what we have trained him or her to do.

It goes even further than that. In one sense, this whole notion of free choice explains why there is evil in the world. The great medieval sage Maimonides totally understood this. "All people have the freedom of choice—to either follow God's laws, or not to follow those laws. Only man, with his knowledge and thought, can distinguish good from evil and choose between the two, and no one can stay his hand from doing good or evil."

According to this view, there is evil in the world as a consequence of God giving us free will. We are free to choose to do good or evil. God hopes that we will choose the good, but God cannot force us to do so. God chooses to limit God's own interference with human nature. That is the wonder, and the peril, of free will.

Some say that God gives us our freedom, but when we abuse it God goes to a secret place and cries. Because of what we are doing to ourselves and to each other—and because God has freely chosen not to interfere.

It is a tough choice . . . for God and for us. So the choice is ours, to choose, and to do so wisely.

THIS MUST BE THE PLACE!

"Why do I need to go to a synagogue? I can pray anywhere!" You might have heard people say that. The same people would never say: "I can play baseball anywhere!" (Because, actually, you can't; you need four bases and an outfield.)

This is one of the great themes of Deuteronomy: now that we are about to enter the Land of Israel, we need some rules, people! One God. No idols or false gods. (Deuteronomy goes ballistic on this issue: don't serve other gods; destroy the places where false gods were worshiped; don't even ask how the other groups of people served their gods!) No local prophets with false messages! And there can be only one place where you serve God. You can't make your offerings at your local "sacrifice places" anymore. No—God will choose a place where God's Name will dwell (which, in ancient times, actually meant where God would live).

That particular place for God winds up being the Temple in Jerusalem, even though the text doesn't say this. Many scholars believe that this "one holy place" order in Deuteronomy actually comes from a much later time, when King Josiah decided to get rid of local sacrificial altars and centralize everything in Jerusalem, and ordered the people to come to the Temple in Jerusalem on the three festivals—Pesach, Shavuot, and Sukkot. A midrash teaches: "The world is like a human eye. The white of the eye is like the ocean. The pupil is the Land of Israel. The opening of the pupil is like Jerusalem. The reflection in the eye is like the ancient Temple." That is how sacred Jerusalem has been to the Jewish people.

So, in later biblical times, there was only one place for sacrifice—the Temple in Jerusalem. And you had to make a pilgrimage there on the festivals three times a year. That was it? That was all you had to do to fulfill your religious duties? The pilgrimage was a big deal, but what about the rest of the year?

Contemporary scholar Jeffrey Tigay helps us with this question. "Deuteronomy must have expected that some other religious activities would take the place of sacrifice during the rest of the year. It is likely that prayer and study were expected to fill the gap."

After the Babylonians destroyed the First Temple in 587 BCE, the Jews needed another way of serving God. Perhaps that led to the invention of the synagogue—a place of gathering, study, and prayer. Perhaps the synagogue developed because not everyone could make the trip to Jerusalem, and they stayed home and prayed and studied.

Now, there is no longer one place where God has chosen for the Divine Name to dwell. There are many places. Certainly the synagogue is a very important one. An individual may pray and study almost anywhere, but a community needs a gathering place. That is why the synagogue is called *Beit ha-Tefillah* (the House of prayer), *Beit ha-Midrash* (the House of study), and *Beit ha-Knesset* (the House of gathering). And that is why the synagogue has been the center of Jewish life for two thousand years.

Connections

ᚦ What are some of the most important choices that you have made? Important choices that will affect your future? Your Jewish choices?

ᚦ Why has the Land of Israel been considered holy by Jews? What other places in your life are holy? How do you define "holy"?

ᚦ Do you believe that Jews should distinguish themselves through what they eat? How?

ᚦ Do you believe that it's OKAY to eat meat? In what ways does Judaism protect the dignity of animals?

❖ Shofetim: Deuteronomy 16:18–21:9

Shofetim deals mostly with the administration of justice. The Israelites are commanded to appoint judges and civic officials.

In addition, the Torah portion talks about the way that Israelite kings are supposed to behave—not unlimited in power, as in other ancient and even modern monarchies, but humble and obedient to the Torah.

Finally, the Israelite method of doing justice must extend to the way that the Israelites will fight wars to conquer the Land of Israel.

Summary

ẞ The Israelites are commanded to appoint "magistrates and officials," who are commanded to be impartial in judgment and not to accept bribes. (16:18–20)

ẞ The penalty for worshiping idols is death, but the death penalty can be given only if there are two or more witnesses to the act. (17:2–7)

ẞ The Israelites are permitted to have a king, but there are limits to what that king can do. He must be a fellow Israelite, and he is forbidden to have many horses, wives, or wealth. In addition, the king must write a copy of the Torah and must have it with him at all times. (17:14–20)

ẞ The Israelites are forbidden to engage in the ritual practices of the Canaanites who dwell in the Land of Israel: sacrificing children, engaging in various magical practices, and attempting to communicate with the dead. (18:9–14)

ẞ There are specific laws for the way that wars to conquer the Land of Israel are to be fought and rules for who shall be released from battle. Those who were just starting out in life—building a new house, planting crops, or preparing to get married—are exempt from going to war. So, too, there are specific laws for the way that an Israelite army is to behave in war, first and foremost by offering terms of peace to its enemies, killing only the males who fight, and not destroying trees. (20:1–20)

The Big Ideas

ᚻ **Judaism introduces the idea of a just society.** How the Bible defines a just society is so powerful that it deeply influenced the development of American justice. Deuteronomy imagines a society where justice is impartial, blind to social position, and immune to bribery. The traditional American symbol of justice—a blindfolded woman holding equal scales—reminds us of this biblical ideal.

ᚻ **Human life is sacred.** We are free to disagree with the severity of the death penalty for worshiping idols—or any crime, for that matter. But the Torah is making a valuable point: the death penalty is such a grievous and extreme punishment that it cannot be administered lightly. The court must be absolutely sure of the crime that has been committed, and that assurance can only come when there is a minimum of two witnesses.

ᚻ **Leadership is service, not power or status.** That is the reason why the Torah puts so many limitations on kings and what they are permitted to do—so that the king will treat his subjects with dignity and not have too much power.

ᚻ **The Jews must be different from other people.** This is the essential lesson behind many of the Torah's laws—to ensure that the People of Israel will be an *am kadosh* (holy people). In this particular context, however, it means that the Israelites must reject the ritual elements of the Canaanite religion. It is interesting to note that most of those practices are connected to death—the ritual offering of children, and attempting to speak to the dead. By rejecting those practices, Judaism guaranteed that it would become a religion that celebrates life, not one that glorifies death.

ᚻ **There is a "right" way to fight wars.** Judaism has always rejected the idea that "war is hell" and that soldiers can do whatever they want to do. The Torah lists specific prohibitions on who can fight a war (and who doesn't have to fight), and how to fight a war. For many centuries, when the Jews did not have their own sovereign state, these rules were theoretical. In the modern State of Israel, these rules have new life, and form the basis for the Israeli notion of *tohar ha-neshek,* "purity of arms," which is part of the standard operating procedure for the Israel Defense Forces.

Divrei Torah
KINGS: GOOD OR BAD?

To quote the famous Jewish comedian Mel Brooks: "It's good to be king." Well, sort of.

There aren't that many kings and queens in the contemporary world. While there are still many countries that have royalty (the United Kingdom, the Netherlands, Norway, Sweden, and Saudi Arabia, for example), in many cases, they don't rule. Their countries are constitutional monarchies, which means that there are democratically elected officials, like prime ministers. Being a king or queen is largely ceremonial and symbolic.

But in the ancient world, and right up to the modern era, kings had absolute power of life and death over their subjects, and they could do anything they wanted. As the Israeli scholar Menachem Lorberbaum has written: "In the ancient Near East, the king was believed to be 'the image of God.' In ancient Egypt, the king himself was a god. In ancient Greece, the king had a special relationship with God. Roman emperors referred to themselves as sons of God." The king and only the king was in the image of God. No one else. Talk about power! (Notice how Judaism changed that, and said that all people are made in God's image.)

Deuteronomy changed the entire way that royalty would govern. They had to follow certain rules. The king cannot have a lot of horses, and cannot send people back to Egypt to get them. He cannot have multiple wives. He cannot amass huge riches. The king must write a Torah (or, perhaps just the book of Deuteronomy). The king is not the author of the laws but a student of the laws.

The king cannot be on a "power trip." Maimonides writes: "The king must not exercise his authority in a 'stuck up' manner. He should deal graciously and compassionately with the small and the great, conduct the people's affairs in their best interests, be wary of the honor of even the lowliest. When he addresses the public, he should use gentle language."

This is all good. Except, centuries later, the "wise" King Solomon forgot those laws. 1 Kings 10:21 says that all his vessels were of gold. Well, there goes the rule against amassing great wealth. Solomon had chariots and horses—which he got from Egypt! And as for wives, even Solomon probably didn't know how many wives he had. All of Deuteronomy's rules went out the window.

Solomon enslaved his people in order to build garrison cities. Sound familiar? That is how the ancient Israelites became slaves in Egypt! Solomon became like a Pharaoh! And what happens after Solomon dies? His son becomes king, decides to run things even worse than Solomon did, and the kingdom falls apart.

Mel Brooks might have been right. It might have been "good to be king." But, like everything in Judaism, you have to know your limits as well. Solomon didn't, and look what happened. And look what else has happened when kings and modern-day rulers exercise total power. It never turns out well. So unless a ruler doesn't just look good or sound good, but is truly good, watch out.

WAR IS HELL

That was what an old movie claimed.

The Torah might not go that far, but it requires something of the Israelites that no other ancient people does. It constrains war. Among other things, you have to offer a besieged city terms of peace (20:10), and you cannot destroy fruit-bearing trees (2:19–20). This last point is very important; it would mean that it is wrong to use defoliants (chemicals that will destroy trees and plant life).

The Jewish ideal is peace. Numerous texts and prayers insist that we always pursue peace. A midrash teaches: "Peace is a great thing, for even during war peace is necessary. . . . Great is peace, for God created no fairer attribute than that of peace, which has been given to the righteous. Great is peace, for it was given as a reward for devotion to Torah and good deeds."

What about today? How do we make that vision real? And how do we constrain our actions when we do wage war?

Moshe Halbertal, an important Israeli thinker, teaches about the idea of *tohar ha-neshek,* "the purity of arms," and has written a code of conduct that was adopted by the Israel Defense Forces. He teaches that every soldier should ask himself or herself these questions before engaging in any action:

ቴ Are my actions necessary?

ቴ Am I targeting only those who are combatants? Am I doing everything possible as a soldier to avoid harming civilians—even to the point of risking my own safety? Are my actions proportionate to the danger that I am facing?

This doesn't mean that if the enemy kills only three of your soldiers, you are allowed to kill only three of theirs. In fact, you can kill as many combatants as you have to in order to make them stop killing. Proportionality only applies to the possible danger that noncombatants might face.

Are these ideas too idealistic? Perhaps. But it is the true Jewish way to be idealistic and to put forward ideas that many people might not yet accept, but which are still necessary.

These issues are very real today. Sadly, the United States still fights wars, and so does Israel. Morality in war might be difficult, but it is a goal that is necessary to strive for. As Professor Halbertal has said: "My children and their friends want to come back from their military duty, and they want to be able to look at themselves in the mirror."

Connections

ቴ Why is it so important to have two or three witnesses to a crime, rather than just one?

ቴ How do you define "justice"? Why is justice so important to God and to humanity? Is this a just world? How can you make it more just?

ቴ Have you ever felt like a victim of injustice? How did you react?

ቴ Do you agree that there should be rules for the way wars are fought? What are some reasons why such rules would be unnecessary or ineffective? Do such rules apply to other areas of life where there are conflicts? What other rules should there be for war?

❖ Ki Tetse': Deuteronomy 21:10–25:19

This Torah portion is jammed with seventy-two mitzvot—more than any other Torah portion. While many of them seem to be random, if you look closely you will notice that there is an interesting pattern.

Last week's portion (Shofetim) is mostly about government and affairs of state. Ki Tetse' focuses mostly (but by no means entirely) on family matters—what to do with rebellious teens; parental responsibility; who is in and who is out of the larger Jewish family; even how to treat young birds who are part of a "bird family."

Parashat Ki Tetse' is a treasure trove of laws and teachings—some obscure, some still relevant to how we lead our lives.

Summary

- ℔ If a woman is taken captive during a war, she is allowed to spend a month missing her parents. If, after a month, the captor still wants her to stay, then she can become his wife. If the captor no longer wants her, she must be set free and not be sold as a slave. (21:10–14)
- ℔ If parents have a "wayward and defiant son," they must bring that troublesome child before the authorities of the town, and he can be stoned to death. In reality, this never happened; thank goodness! (21:18–21)
- ℔ If a person sees a friend's (or, even an enemy's) ox or sheep straying, or finds someone's garment, that person must return the lost property to the one who has lost it. (22:1–4)
- ℔ When taking young birds or eggs from a nest, you must first send away the mother bird. (22:6–7)
- ℔ The Israelites, as well as later generations of Jews, must always remember the massive cruelty of Amalek, who attacked the weakest of the Israelites when they were leaving Egypt. (25:17–19)

The Big Ideas

- ℔ **Judaism realizes that people sometimes have strong sexual urges, but they are cautioned not to indulge those urges irresponsibly and cruelly.** Judaism recognizes that each person has a *yetzer ha-ra* (evil inclination) and a *yetzer ha-tov* (good inclination), and that only the mitzvot can keep the *yetzer ha-ra* in check. While human beings might not be totally godlike (at least, not yet), neither are they allowed to descend to the level of animals.
- ℔ **Not everything that is written in the Torah really happened.** This is true of many of the Torah's stories (for example, Adam

and Eve, and most likely some of the stories of the Patriarchs and Matriarchs). But, it is also true that some of the Torah's mitzvot were never carried out. Sometimes, those laws and teachings appear in the Torah simply as warnings and object lessons. Still, in this particular case (the rebellious child) the teaching has some very valuable lessons to teach us about parental responsibility and how young people should behave.

℔ **Moral responsibility extends to other people's property.** Here, the Torah is clear: when it comes to what someone has lost, "you must not remain indifferent" (22:3). Perhaps this is the origin of the custom of the "lost and found." But the idea that we are responsible for other people's stuff is a very different attitude than the one that contemporary society offers us. Sure, we care about people, but their possessions? Yes. Since someone's property usually has economic implications for that person, we have to pay attention to what they have as well as who they are.

℔ **Judaism has high respect for life, even and especially, animal life.** It isn't just about not being physically cruel to animals. The notion of avoiding *tza'ar ba'alei chayyim* (unnecessary cruelty to animals) also extends to avoiding psychological cruelty. That is the reason why someone who is taking the eggs or young birds from a nest must first send away the mother bird—so that the mother bird doesn't have to experience the anguish of seeing her children taken away.

℔ **Evil is real, and it must be remembered and resisted.** The tribe of Amalek is the symbol of genocidal cruelty against Jews. Haman, who plotted the destruction of the Jews of Shushan in the book of Esther, which Jews read on Purim, was descended from the tribe of Amalek. Why did Amalek act with such horrific cruelty? Because he was "undeterred by the fear of God" (*v'lo yareh Elohim*). This doesn't mean that the Amalekites were not religious (we don't know what kind of god they worshiped). In the Torah, to "fear God" meant "to be an ethical person." The tribe of Amalek had no ethical grounding; therefore, they had no reason *not* to commit murder against the Israelites.

Divrei Torah

KIDS, BEWARE!

For many years, parents have relied on experts for advice on how to raise their children. An earlier generation had Dr. Benjamin Spock; a later generation had T. Berry Brazelton and Penelope Leach. But no one ever came up with what we find in this Torah portion.

Consider this teaching: if parents have a "wayward or defiant" son who won't listen to them, they should take the child to the town authorities; the authorities would then stone the child to death in the public square (21:18–21).

Relax, it never happened. The ancient sages said: "There never has been a 'wayward or defiant son,' and there never will be. Why then was the law written? That you may study it and receive reward. The whole purpose of this teaching in the Torah is for people to study it and to learn from it." Obviously, our ancestors were as bothered by this passage as we are. Yet they could not ignore it.

So, what can we learn from it?

First, as bad as it is, Deuteronomy is saying that if your child is rebellious, the community must be involved in his discipline. There has to be some kind of due process. You have to turn the teen over to the authorities. It all has to happen in public; the community is now part of the family, and vice versa.

Second, how old did the teen have to be? The ancient sages said that it pertained to teens from the age of puberty to when the child has stopped growing physically—which can be anywhere between eighteen and twenty-two years old. So, the age of moral responsibility actually starts around what we now know as bar and bat mitzvah age. The text and its commentary is suggesting that you need to start taking responsibility for your actions when you are old enough to understand them.

Third, what was the "crime" that the kid had to have committed? We're not exactly sure what "wayward and defiant" means, but evidently it suggests intentional rebellion that harmed the family. But the Torah goes on to say that the teen is a "glutton and a drunkard." We are talking here about impulse control! Eating too much, and certainly drinking too much, is never good and, as we know, can lead to other self-destructive behaviors.

Notice that the text only speaks about a "son." As Bible scholars Tamara Cohn Eskenazi and Andrea L. Weiss have taught: "This law probably does not apply to daughters, for being a glutton and a drunkard seems to be stereotypically male. If the mother and father cannot control him, it becomes the larger society's responsibility." Certainly we recognize today that young women can also have impulse-control problems and destructive behaviors. But throughout history it has been out-of-control young men who have been the greatest threat to society.

That said, let's remember that a certain type of teen independence and even rebellion has its place. According to a midrash, Judaism was born when Abraham rebelled against his father. The Jewish people was sustained when Pharaoh's daughter rebelled against her father and saved the infant Moses. Spiritual rebellion out of moral concern is one thing. But destructive rebellion for its own sake can wreck families and hurt the community. Though it overstates things, that is the point the Torah is trying to make here.

LOST AND FOUND

This really happened: A woman found a ten-dollar bill on the floor of a crowded store. She brought the bill to the cashier and asked her to announce that someone had lost their money. The cashier could not believe it. "Everyone will come and claim it!" he protested. The woman said: "That might be, but it is still a mitzvah to announce that it has been found." The cashier replied: "Did you say 'mitzvah'? Do you mean that this is a Jewish thing to do? Wow. I'm Jewish and I haven't been in synagogue in years. If that's Judaism, I should check it out again."

Yes. That's Judaism. Returning a lost object to its rightful owner is one of the sweetest, simplest, and most profound mitzvot of the whole set of 613. Yes, the world might say "finders keepers, losers weepers," but that is a childish way of viewing life. It is also not the Jewish way.

Finding and returning lost objects is so important that the ancient sages made it the subject of an entire tractate of the Talmud. In the ancient Temple, there was a Stone of Losses, where people who had lost things and people who had found things would go. There, in the holiest place in the world, the finders would bring what they had found and the losers would find what they had lost.

True, the biblical text seems to focus on lost animals. That was because they were so valuable. (The modern equivalent would be if someone lost his or her car.) But this mitzvah is not only about stuff. It's about anything that gets lost. If someone loses their way in life, you must help them find their way back. If someone loses their health, then you must do what you can to help heal them. This is the essence of the Jewish mitzvah to heal. It is why some Jews become doctors; if health is a lost object, then you have to try to restore it.

Isn't that the natural thing to do? Actually, goodness is not "natural." To paraphrase Rabbi Dov Peretz Elkins: The natural human response is to "hide oneself," to pretend that one did not notice the stray animal or lost object, to shirk responsibility and act as if we have no ethical responsibility.

Judaism doesn't believe that we are all born as wonderful, sweet, and ethical beings. Moses Alshekh, a sixteenth-century commentator, writes: "God wished to implant in the Jew a love of his fellow, by means of the mitzvot, and help him overcome his naturally selfish instincts. What person would normally run after his fellow's stray ox and restore it to him? Mitzvot train and discipline the doer. At first, he performs the mitzvah because the Torah told him to do so. As time goes on, he performs the mitzvah willingly and spontaneously."

No one is born a great baseball player or pianist. It takes practice. So does being a mensch—a good, decent human being. Human character is forged in the small deeds—like returning lost objects.

Connections

- ℔ What other "crimes" would you add to the list of things that rebellious children do?
- ℔ What is your opinion of the fact that here in the Torah girls are omitted from being rebellious children? Are there particular "crimes" that girls are more likely to commit?
- ℔ What is wrong with eating too much and drinking too much? The Talmud says that drinking too much leads to bloodshed. Do you agree? What else does it lead to?

ቴ What are some ways that Judaism teaches people to control their impulses?

ቴ Have you ever lost something and had someone return it to you? Have you ever returned something to someone who has lost it? How did it feel to do that?

ቴ What are some ways that Judaism teaches us to be better people?

ቴ What does it mean for us to remember Amalek, the symbol of evil? What can we do to fight against evil in our world?

❖ Ki Tavo': Deuteronomy 26:1–29:8

Parashat Ki Tavo' continues the theme of social justice that is such a major part of Deuteronomy. It describes three rituals that Israelites, both as individuals and as an entire community, had to perform upon entrance into the Land of Israel. Each of those rituals expresses gratitude at having arrived in the land, but they tie that gratitude to a sense of memory—of where the Israelites have come from, and the circumstances that have produced their history.

The Torah portion ends with a ghastly passage: a list of the catastrophes that would befall the Jewish people if they failed to abide by the covenant.

Summary

ቴ An Israelite must present his or her first fruits from the harvest, put them in a basket, and place it on the altar. He or she must then recite an autobiographical statement, which recounts Israelite history up to that point, and in which the Israelite fully identifies with the experience of slavery in Egypt and in being freed from slavery. This ceremony is known as *vidui bikkurim* (the confession or proclamation of the first fruits) and was originally performed on the ancient *Chag ha-Bikkurim* (The festival of the first fruits), which was the original version of the festival that we know as Shavuot. This whole passage forms the core of the narrative in the Passover Haggadah. (26:1–11)

ቴ A second ritual: every third year, Israelites must set aside the tithe (ten percent) of their yield, and they must give it to the Levite, the stranger, the fatherless, and the widow. (26:12–15)

Ƀ A third ritual: this time to mark the Israelites' eventual entry into the Land of Israel. The Israelites divide up into their individual tribes and stand on two facing mountains—Mount Gerizim and Mount Ebal. They recite a list of things that are to be prohibited and therefore cursed, which is followed by the blessings that will occur if those prohibitions are observed. (27:11–28:14)

Ƀ Now comes one of the worst (if not the worst) passages in the entire Torah: Moses tells the Israelites exactly what will happen to them if they fail to live by the covenant with God. The punishments include exile, pestilence, illness, starvation, blight, mildew, a lack of rain, defeat by Israel's enemies, total despair, and madness. It only gets worse. It is not pretty. (28:15–68)

The Big Ideas

Ƀ **To be Jewish means to locate yourself within the larger Jewish story.** In many ways, wherever Jews go and whatever Jews do, the past walks with them. For that reason, the text of the *vidui bikkurim* forms the central part of the Passover Haggadah. It is the story of a people who have been liberated from slavery and allowed to celebrate in freedom. To quote the Jewish poet A. M. Klein: "generations look through our eyes."

Ƀ **When Jews celebrate, they must remember those who are less fortunate.** The passage from Deuteronomy imagines that the Israelites who tithe have already become prosperous. The tithe reminds us that Jews must give to the most vulnerable in society. While it would be great to imagine a society without those who are poor and on the fringes, the Torah is very realistic about how society works. Such people will always be with us, and therefore we will always have responsibilities to them.

Ƀ **Actions have consequences.** This is one of the most important things that people learn as they grow into maturity, and this is what the ancient Israelites had to learn as well. If you do bad things, bad stuff will happen. If you do good things, good stuff will happen. It is interesting to note that the list of prohibitions

in this Torah portion consists of sins that are mainly committed in private, which reminds us that everything we do is part
of our moral and spiritual makeup. Moreover, while some laws
contained in the list can be found elsewhere in the Torah (especially the laws about sexual behaviors), some are new—like moving a neighbor's landmark, which basically meant trespassing on
someone else's property. Finally, in place of the original Ten Commandments (Exodus 20), here there are twelve—a number that
reminds us of the twelve tribes of ancient Israel.

ƀ **Societies that ignore ethics will inevitably fall apart.** This is a constant theme in the Torah. Noah's generation did evil; it was punished with the Flood. The people of Sodom and Gomorrah did evil;
they were punished by destruction. And so it would be for the People of Israel as well—failure to observe the rules of the Torah would
result in the destruction of their nation. In fact, the catastrophic
things that are described in this Torah portion actually did happen
to the Jewish people during the Assyrian exile (721 BCE) and the
Babylonian exile (586 BCE). Many scholars, therefore, believe that
these passages might have been written in the wake of that latter
disaster, and represent an attempt on the part of the Jewish people
to give reasons for the tragedy. If such a terrible thing happened, it
must have been our fault, so let's clean up our act.

Divrei Torah

WHO ARE YOU, REALLY?

A rabbi in a Philadelphia suburb wants to add the following ritual to
bar and bat mitzvah ceremonies at her synagogue: At the celebration
after the service, each kid must take the first gifts that he or she has
received, put them in a large basket, and put the basket on a centrally
located table. Then, the child must go through his or her entire family
history, as far as he or she knows it. For example: "My great-grandfather
came from Poland, and he left there because the Jews were persecuted.
He came to Philadelphia, and lived in a neighborhood called Straw-
berry Mansion. Then, my grandfather moved out to northeast Philadelphia. And then, my parents moved out to the Main Line. And now,
I am here, and I am grateful for all that I have."

That was essentially what happened in the ancient ritual known as *vidui bikkurim*, the confession or proclamation of the first fruits. The Mishnah describes the joyous ceremony in which people traveled to Jerusalem: "Those who lived near Jerusalem brought fresh figs and grapes, but those from a distance brought dried figs and raisins. An ox with horns bedecked with gold and with an olive crown on its head led the way. The flute was played before them until they got close to Jerusalem. . . . When they reached the Temple Mount, even King Agrippa would take the basket and place it on his shoulder and walk as far as the temple court." Why does it say "even" King Agrippa? Because even though he was a king, he still recalled his humble origins.

For the Jews, memory is key—and no biblical book mentions memory more than Deuteronomy. Memory is mentioned 169 times in the Torah (which is 13 x 13, the age of bar or bat mitzvah, squared). As the author Yosef Hayim Yerushalmi has written: "Only in Israel and nowhere else is the injunction to remember felt as a religious imperative to an entire people."

Memory carries with it a sense of obligation, not merely curiosity and nostalgia. Memory creates identity: it means locating your brief life within a larger context and within a story that gives it meaning and direction.

But, go back to the Torah text and read it again (26:5–9). It talks about the Patriarchs, and about slavery, and about entering the Land of Israel. What is missing from the sacred recitation? The revelation of Torah and the forty years of wandering in the wilderness.

Memory is selective. No history book can include everything that happened, just as no Facebook page can capture the totality of a person's life. As you get older, you will remember many things that happened. But you will also forget many things that happened. Some things you might even want to forget. After all, not everything can be important.

Just remember where you come from, who made you, who you are; and be grateful!

ARE YOU AN ARAMEAN?

There was an old television show called *The Lone Ranger*. The Lone Ranger was a hero in the Old West, and he wore a mask to conceal his identity. Whenever he would leave the scene, people would ask each other: "Who was that masked man?"

It is time to ask that question once again. The declaration of the first fruits begins with the Israelites saying: *Arami oved avi*, "My father was a fugitive Aramean" (26:5). The Rabbis were intrigued: why would the important declaration begin with that strange sentence? What does it mean? Just who was this ancestor?

The region in which the Arameans lived was ancient Mesopotamia, which was where the Jewish nation originated. Abraham was (sort of) an Aramean. So, the "fugitive Aramean" would be Abraham. Abraham's grandson Jacob also came from that region (when he sought refuge from his brother, Esau), and, as the Torah says, he certainly did come down into Egypt and he flourished there. So, the "fugitive Aramean" might also have been Jacob.

Not so fast. This passage from the Torah portion appears prominently in the Passover Haggadah. And, there, the Aramean is actually someone else: Laban—Rebecca's brother, Rachel and Leah's father, and Jacob's father-in-law. The verb *oved*, which means "fugitive" or "wandering," can also mean "destroy." That is how the Haggadah understands it: "Go and learn what Laban the Aramean sought to do to Jacob. Pharaoh only decreed the death of the males. Laban sought to destroy them all."

Why would the Haggadah make such a harsh statement about Laban, who was, after all, a close relative of biblical Matriarchs and a Patriarch?

Recall that when Jacob falls in love with Laban's daughter Rachel Laban tricks Jacob and gives him his older daughter, Leah, instead. Why? "It is not the practice in our place to marry off the younger before the older" (Gen. 29:26). Talk about sleazy! He tricks Jacob, and when his trick is discovered, he invokes local custom and "tradition." He doesn't care at all about Jacob's feelings, or even those of his daughter Rachel (and probably not of Leah either). Jacob must work another seven years in order to marry Rachel.

Years later, Jacob wants to take his family and leave Laban's household. They leave in the middle of the night, and Laban chases after them. Is it because he just wanted to kiss them all goodbye? Actually, no. It was because his household idols were missing and he suspects

Jacob of taking them (actually, it was Rachel who stole them—check out the story in Genesis 31). Laban doesn't really care that much about his family leaving him. He's mostly concerned about his missing idols.

Laban doesn't care that much about people or relationships. And he really doesn't care that much about his family; he's only worried that someone might have taken something from him.

If Jacob thought and acted the way that Laban did, it would have shattered his family, and it would have implanted feelings of selfishness within the Jewish people. Instead, Laban's actions may have reminded Jacob of his own trickery against his brother, and spurred him to do the right thing and reconcile with Esau.

As the modern Bible teacher Nehama Leibowitz teaches: "The Jewish people had a special obligation, to remember with gratitude, that they had been delivered from a foreign soil and had been brought to their own land."

So we need to remember our Aramean origins in more ways than one: Abraham, Jacob, and Laban—the good and the bad.

Connections

- ᖶ Do you know aspects of your family's history, going back beyond your grandparents? Do you know where your family is from? What do you know about them, and what could that mean to you?
- ᖶ Why is it important for people to tithe—giving ten percent to charity or for a good cause that you believe in? Is that ten percent figure still practical today? What charities or causes are you passionate about?
- ᖶ How have you succeeded (or not succeeded) in keeping away from bad influences?
- ᖶ Why do you think that Jews have a particular fondness for (and talent for) memory?
- ᖶ Do you think that gratitude is a good value? What are you most grateful for? How do you demonstrate it?

❖ Nitsavim: Deuteronomy 29:9–30:20

Time is running out for Moses. This Torah portion, which is often combined with the next parashah, Va-yelekh, contains the crucial speech that

Moses delivers on the very last day of his life, and he is feeling a sense of urgency. As the Israelites stand on the steppes of Moab, preparing to enter the Land of Israel, Moses reminds them that it is not only they who are standing there, entering into the covenant, but also all future Jews.

Moses reserves a special contempt for those who would turn away from God and the covenant. But Moses also reminds them that those who turn away can always turn back. Unwilling to allow his final words to be filled with anger, Moses encourages the Israelites and helps them understand that the covenant is not too difficult to follow, and that the Torah presents them with choices—life or death, blessing or curse. When all is said and done, the Israelites must "choose life."

Summary

ᴃ Moses tells the Israelites that they all stand before God, and that they stand before God equally, without regard to age, gender, and the kind of work that they do. God makes the covenant not only with them, but also with those "who are not with us here this day." (29:9–13)

ᴃ Moses warns against those who continue to worship idols. He condemns the way that those idol worshipers think about what they are doing—thinking only about themselves and not about the rest of the community. It is that kind of selfish thinking that deserves terrible punishments. (29:15–27)

ᴃ As bad as things might get with the Jewish people—no matter how much they sin and are punished with exile—Moses reassures them that, ultimately, God will take them back in love, and bring them back to the Land of Israel. (30:1–10)

ᴃ Moses reminds the people that *teshuvah* is not only necessary, it is possible. The Torah is not too hard for people to do. Nevertheless, they still have a choice: between life and death, and blessing and curse. All God can do is ask them to make the right choice. (30:11–20)

The Big Ideas

ᴃ **Judaism is never only about "now." It is also about the future.** This is perhaps one of Deuteronomy's greatest messages: a focus

on the education of children, and the sense that the Jewish people must endure into the future. We might even say that Deuteronomy introduces the idea of a Jewish future. Moreover, the covenant with God is meant to be inclusive—men, women, children,
menial laborers, even non-Jews who live in the midst of the Jewish community.

ß **The individual Jew can never think only about himself or herself.** True, Moses condemns those who still worship the idols of
the surrounding nations. That is bad enough, but what really gets
Moses angry is those who think that they will get away with idol
worship and that they can do whatever they want. In this way,
Moses is being more than a little prophetic. To this day, there are
Jews who only think about themselves and not about the implications of their actions for the Jewish people or on the Jewish future. They are following their "own willful heart." Moses warns
that this attitude, if it continues, will ultimately destroy the Jewish people, and that God ultimately knows what goes on in the
privacy of people's lives.

ß **Without *teshuvah*, Judaism and the Jewish people could not exist.** Of all the Jewish ideas that originated in Deuteronomy—
the love of God, education of subsequent generations, the ability to make moral and spiritual choices, the emphasis on social
justice—perhaps the most important one is *teshuvah*. It is often
translated as "repentance," but it really means "return." In this
particular case in the Torah portion, it means that if the Jews repent they will be able to return from exile to the Land of Israel.
In fact, the verb *shuv*, "to return," appears more often in this Torah portion than in the entire Torah. It is hardly a coincidence
that this portion is always the one that is read in the synagogue
right before the beginning of the Days of Awe. *Teshuvah*, the main
theme of the High Holy Days, is written all over it.

ß **Judaism is doable.** Judaism is not a secret teaching that only a
comparatively few people can figure out. Neither is it overbur-
dened with difficult ritual practices that just the extremely dedicated can perform. It is for all Jews. But God cannot force us
to perform the mitzvot. Neither can God force us to do *teshu-*

vah and return to the right way of living. Those are choices that only we can make.

Divrei Torah
YOU CAN DO IT!

"I can't do it. . . . It's too hard!" How many times have you said that, either to yourself or to others? Perhaps it was a new move or skill in a sport. Perhaps a challenging piece of music. Maybe it was having to move to a new home with your family, or starting at a new camp. Maybe it was learning Hebrew. Whatever it is, we all come up against things that seem to be really hard for us to do.

What about Judaism?

There is a hint of that in this Torah portion, too. Moses tells the People of Israel: "Surely, this Instruction which I enjoin upon you this day is not too baffling for you, nor is it beyond reach" (30:11).

Which mitzvah (commandment) is Moses talking about? If you look at what the passage is talking about immediately before Moses delivers these words of encouragement, you might think that the subject is *teshuvah*, "repentance" or "return."

Moses is saying that the mitzvah of repentance is not too hard for someone to do. And this might well be a surprise to us, because if you've ever been in a position of having to say that you are sorry to someone, or (even harder) having to dig down deep inside yourself and say, "I could be better," or, if you've ever had to reconsider an idea that you first thought was great or had to deal with regrets about something, you know how hard it can be.

But perhaps the mitzvah that the verse is referring to is not the mitzvah of *teshuvah* at all. Perhaps the mitzvah is all the mitzvot—all of Judaism itself.

If this is so, then the verse is teaching us that it's not impossible to understand Judaism and follow its laws and teachings, or to practice Judaism. You don't have to go into the heavens to retrieve Judaism's real meaning. A midrash puts it this way: "Moses told the Israelites that he was not going to bring them another Torah from heaven. Nothing of it has remained in heaven." It is all there, right in front of you. It is real. It is doable.

Jewish observance poses challenges. It's not easy to observe Shabbat in any real and meaningful way; it requires doing certain things (like rituals) and not doing certain things. The same thing is true of kashrut. It can be a challenge to figure out what and how to eat, and that can make going to restaurants difficult; but as generations of Jews will tell you, it is doable. Fasting on Yom Kippur: hard, but doable. Learning Hebrew: sometimes hard, but quite often doable (some people just can't learn a foreign language, no matter how hard they try). And no matter how hard the mitzvot are, throughout history Jews have often sacrificed their lives in order to do them.

Says Bible scholar Avivah Zornberg: "God is like a very patient piano teacher who is constantly introducing us to new ways of playing the sacred music. God doesn't give us any pieces that are too hard for our playing level."

The commandments. Hard? Yes. Too hard? No. Their worth? Priceless!

DO IT TODAY!

Don't you find it irritating when people keep using the same words, over and over again? Some people just have their favorite words or clichés, and, frankly, they can get a little annoying.

That is how Moses was with the word *ha-yom,* "today" or "this day." Moses uses it five times in 29:9–17, and then, again, another seven times in 30:1–19. "You stand this day" (29:9); and then again in 29:12: "to the end that He may establish you this day as His people": and then again in 30:2: "just as I enjoin upon you this day." And then, again in 30:11: "Surely, this Instruction which I enjoin upon you this day." You get the idea.

Why this constant repetition of "today?" In the words of the great medieval commentator Rashi: "This teaches that Moses, on the day of his death, gathered them together before God to bring them into the covenant." Moses is delivering this speech on the final day of his life. "Today," "this day," has very special meaning for him. If Moses did not get this sacred work done *ha-yom,* today, it would not get done.

But, maybe Moses was not simply referring to "today" or "this day" as the particular day when he spoke. Perhaps Moses meant that whenever we read these words we should think of those words being delivered "today"—on the very day that we read them. After all, Moses made the covenant "not with you alone, but both with those who are standing here with us this day . . . and with those who are not here with us this day" (29:13). That's all of us.

Imagine, then, a Jewish science fiction movie in which all time is collapsed. Past, present, and future no longer exist. The late comedian George Carlin once said: "Time is just God's way of making sure that everything doesn't happen all at once." In fact, this is how Jewish ritual works. Every time we read the Torah, it is as if we ourselves are standing on Mount Sinai, or in Moab, becoming part of the covenant. Every time we sit at the Passover seder, it is as if we ourselves are getting out of Egypt. (Some Jews even act out the Exodus at the seder itself—getting up from the table and going outside the house.) At a Jewish wedding, the couple "becomes" Adam and Eve in the Garden of Eden—the first couple in history.

In the words of the contemporary scholar Everett Fox: "'Today' in this Torah portion challenges all hearers of the text to make the moment their own. The book of Deuteronomy, the great example of the Teaching made new, thus begins the Jewish process, as old as the Bible itself, of rehearing and rethinking the tradition."

One last thing about "today." As you get older, you will probably figure this out. Laziness is an unattractive quality. So is procrastination—putting things off. Especially when it comes to observing the commandments and doing good deeds, making amends, honoring your parents, reaching out to friends, paying attention to your grandparents—don't put it off. Do it today!

CONNECTIONS

ℶ What can you do to contribute to the Jewish future?

ℶ Do you believe that Jewish education is important? How can you demonstrate your commitment to Jewish learning?

ℶ In what ways have you shown your commitment to the larger Jewish community?

ℶ Have you ever done *teshuvah* (repented, asked for forgiveness) for something that you've done? What was that experience like? How did it feel?

ъ Are there things that you once thought were difficult that have actually proven to be either easy or, at least, doable?

ъ What are some things that you keep putting off? How can you break yourself of that habit?

❖ Va-yelekh: Deuteronomy 31:1–30

This is a very short Torah portion, and it is often combined with the portion before it, Nitsavim. Moses is feeling the full force of his mortality, and, for the first time, he personalizes his message to the People of Israel, describing his own advanced age. He reminds the People of Israel that Joshua will succeed him as leader of the nation, and he encourages Joshua in his new tasks.

Moses instructs the Israelites that they should gather every seven years at Sukkot to read "this Teaching" (probably the book of Deuteronomy).

God reminds Moses that the Israelites will inevitably stray from the covenant, and will suffer because of it, and they will believe that God is not present for them. God tells Moses to write down "this poem" (which comes in the following portion) and to recite it to the people, so that they will truly understand their history and their responsibilities.

Summary

ъ Moses declares that he is growing old, and he tells the Israelites that Joshua will be their new leader, and that they will be successful in conquering and entering the land of Canaan. (31:1–7)

ъ Moses decrees that the entire book of Deuteronomy must be read every seven years during the festival of Sukkot. (31:10–13)

ъ Moses repeats a theme that appears often in the book of Deuteronomy: that the Israelites will undoubtedly be tempted to worship other gods, and as a result they will be punished for doing so. At that time, they will feel that the Divine Presence is hidden, but God will still be present. (31:16–21)

ъ The Israelites are commanded to write down the poem (or song) that Moses is about to deliver to the people, as a future warning about their potential failures to live up to their sacred obligations. (31:19–22)

The Big Ideas

ẗ **Judaism recognizes the inevitability of aging and death.** Contrary to what we might have expected, Moses does not protest his coming death. Rather, he accepts it as natural and encourages the people to follow his successor, Joshua. So, too, he encourages Joshua in all that he will have to do. This is an excellent model for any leader. It has been said that one of the first duties of a leader is to start preparing a succession plan. This is not only true of aging leaders like Moses. It is also true in a school or youth group setting. If you are called upon to lead, know that this is a temporary responsibility and honor, and begin to look for other, new leaders who will be able to take your place when the time comes.

ẗ **The Torah belongs to all Jews, not just a small, elite group.** The Torah should not be read or studied alone; it requires a community to come together to share its words and wisdom. And this has to happen on a regular basis.

ẗ **Sometimes, God's "face" seems hidden.** When bad things happen, we are tempted to think that God simply doesn't care, or that there is no God, or that God is simply "sleeping on the job." God recognizes this possibility. In fact, God is saying that it is not that God doesn't care or is not involved—quite the contrary! God is saying that God hides "His face" because of embarrassment at the people's actions. Modern Jewish thinkers, like Martin Buber, have taken this idea of the "hiddenness of God" into new directions, suggesting that sometimes, like the sun and the moon, God is in "eclipse"—really there, but not readily perceptible.

ẗ **It is not enough to simply learn the Torah. One must also make sure that the Torah gets transmitted.** While the Torah verses mentioned (31:19–22) refer to the poem that the Israelites must write down, later tradition interpreted this to mean that it is a mitzvah for every Jew to write a personal copy of the Torah. This sounds strenuous, and it is. That is why Jewish law allows for someone to hire a *sofer* (Torah scribe) to write a Torah scroll, and even if that scribe writes only one letter on your behalf, you have fulfilled the commandment. It is, in fact, the last commandment in the Torah.

Divrei Torah
YOUR OWN TORAH

There might come a day when no one will use textbooks in school anymore. Perhaps that day is already coming, as more schools turn to texts that are on tablets or smart boards. While you might look forward to that day (after all, who likes lugging around those thick, heavy history and science books?), you might also feel that something's missing. There is something special about being able to hold a printed text in your hands—the feel of the paper, the smell of the ink, even the way that the book is bound.

As bad as lugging those textbooks might be, imagine if you had to write them out for yourself—by hand. For that is certainly what the Torah portion is saying. As Moses reaches the end of his life, he commands the Israelites to write down the poem that he is about to recite to them. And it is not a short poem. No one had voice recorders back then, so we can imagine that there were probably a lot of people asking each other: "What did he say? I didn't get that."

Over the generations, the sages decided that the commandment was not just to write the poem, but, rather, to write an entire Torah scroll! They were realists, so they modified their decision to say that sponsoring a Torah scroll, or even some part of it, even a letter, fulfills the commandment.

Why was it so necessary for everyone to write or sponsor his or her own copy of the Torah? In its time, this was actually revolutionary. Archeologists excavated the ancient Syrian city of Dura, and what they found in two religious sites reveals a lot about how Jews were different. In an ancient pagan temple, a priest is pictured wearing sacred garments and with a closed scroll in his hand; it is only for him and his fellow priests to read. But in the synagogue in Dura, a regular Jewish layperson is pictured reading an open Torah scroll. As Rabbi Elliot Dorff teaches: "In most ancient religions, only the priest could learn the secret beliefs and practices of the religion. In sharp contrast, the Torah records that God repeatedly told Moses to speak not just to the priests, but to everyone."

Fine. But why you have to write the scroll yourself or pay for someone else to do it? Aren't there already enough Torah scrolls around?

Perhaps the great Maimonides has the answer. He teaches: "It is a positive commandment for every Jew to write a Torah scroll, and, even if one inherited a Torah from their parents, they must still write their own or commission a scribe to have it done."

"Even if one inherited a Torah from their parents." The learning that you have inherited from your parents isn't enough. You have to write your own Torah, and pass it on. It is just like how the Passover Haggadah teaches us that each of us has to see himself or herself as if he or she had personally gotten out of Egypt. When you write your own Torah, or make sure that one is written, it is as if you are standing on Mount Sinai itself. You were there, and it's yours.

COME OUT, GOD—WHEREVER YOU ARE

A terrible rainstorm. Or, a hurricane. The streets are flooded. People lose their homes, their businesses—and some people even lose their lives. And what's one of the first things that people say? They say: "Where was God?"

It is an ancient question. When bad things happen to us, we might be likely to question God.

Back in biblical times (and even today), people assumed that, if bad things happened, people deserved them because they had sinned, and that God must be the perpetrator of the bad things that had happened. That is precisely a message of this Torah portion. The people sin; they suffer—and it is because God has turned the Divine Presence away from them. "I will abandon them and hide my countenance [God's "face"] from them" (31:17). The people would think that God was not in their midst, and that was why those terrible things had happened.

This whole idea of God "hiding the divine face" is very complex (and it doesn't mean that you have to believe, literally, that God has a face). Clearly, the Torah is saying that God hides, because (a) God is "embarrassed" by what we have done, and (b) God doesn't want to have anything to do with us at that point, which (c) allows our enemies to do what they want to us.

But times are different now. People simply cannot tolerate the idea that if bad stuff happens it must be God's will. Some believe that if bad things happen it must be because there is no God. That was the reaction of some who survived the Holocaust. Others are willing to reclaim the whole "God's hidden face" idea and say: No, God exists, but God isn't paying as much attention as we might need. It is kind of like what's happening when a young kid falls off a bicycle with his parents nearby. You don't say that the kid has no parents, but you might well say that the parents simply weren't paying attention at that time.

Perhaps we are living in a time when, for many, God is in "eclipse," like a solar or lunar eclipse. God has not disappeared. God is really here, but is not readily perceptible. A midrash says: "After the destruction of the First Temple, the enemies of the Jews taunted them: 'Your God has hidden from you; God is gone forever!' But when the Jews enter their synagogues and read the Torah, they are comforted." A Jew wrote this; it was the way that he or she really felt about God. Only the ritual moment of reading Torah could bring God back.

Sometimes we have faith in God; sometimes we don't. When bad things happen, it is tempting to stop believing in God. But consider the faith of an anonymous person who wrote these words on a wall during the Holocaust: "I believe in the sun even when it's not shining. I believe in love even when I don't feel it. I believe in God even when He is silent."

So maybe the idea that God, for whatever reasons, is hiding, or eclipsed, does have something to say to us. Because when times are hardest . . . that is when we need faith the most.

Connections

꘠ What have been your favorite moments of learning Judaism together with other people? Do you agree that it is better to learn Judaism this way, or do you prefer to learn on your own?

꘠ What does it mean to you to write your own Torah scroll? Does that mean that everyone has to physically write a Torah? Or commission someone else to write one for them?

ቴ What is the "Torah" that you have received from your parents?

ቴ Have you ever thought that God was in hiding? What were the circumstances? How did you feel about it?

❖ Ha'azinu: Deuteronomy 32:1–52

This Torah portion is essentially a long poem, delivered by Moses, in which he recounts the history of the Jewish people (in a beautiful but quirky way). In it he describes what would happen if and when the People of Israel betray the covenant with God. It contains a number of verses that will be familiar to people who attend services.

The parashah ends with God reminding Moses of his imminent death, and the reason why he will not be able to enter the Land of Israel: he and his brother Aaron broke faith with God at Meribat-Kadesh when Moses disobeyed God and, in an effort to draw forth water from a rock, hit the rock rather than speaking to it. Almost as a "tease," God allows Moses to view the land from a distance but not enter it.

This portion, with its constant reminder of the Jewish people's sins, is usually read on Shabbat Shuvah, the Shabbat of Repentance, which comes between Rosh Hashanah and Yom Kippur.

Summary

ቴ Moses begins by calling on the heavens and the earth to *ha'azinu*—"give ear," listen and pay attention. Moses doesn't really believe that the heavens and the earth can actually hear; his calling out this way is an expression of his desire that the entire cosmos should know what is going on between God and the Jewish people. (32:1–3)

ቴ Moses calls God *"Ha-Tzur,"* the Rock, and proclaims that God's actions are perfect, and that God is never false. If anyone is false, it is the Jewish people, who are portrayed as children who rebel against their parent, God (the "Father"), who created them. (32:1–6)

ቴ Moses reminds the people that they should ask their parents and their elders about the way of the world and that God determined the boundaries of all the nations. (32:7–9)

ቴ Moses describes the early history of the Jewish people in a rather creative way: as an orphan child found by God in the desert and then reared by God. This continues the theme of God as parent. (32:10–14)

ꞔ Moses describes what God's anger will be like when the People of Israel abandon God and worship false gods. God will punish them by unleashing a nation upon them that is as worthless as the gods they have worshiped. God will treat the Israelites exactly as God treated the wicked inhabitants of Sodom and Gomorrah. That will be God's way of proving that God is the only God. (32:15–43)

The Big Ideas

ꞔ **Deuteronomy almost "invents" the idea of listening and hearing.** Well, not quite true, but the various terms for listening and hearing—*shema* and *ha'azinu*—have prominent roles in this final book of the Torah. It is as if Moses is making sure that his words do not go to waste. Hearing and listening do not only mean something that happens with our ears. The best (and perhaps the only) way to listen is to be fully present for another person.

ꞔ **One of Judaism's most powerful images of God is of a parent.** The parent-child image of the Jewish relationship with God is one of the most significant features of the High Holy Day season. Sometimes we refer to God as *Avinu* ("our Father" or "our Parent") and sometimes as *Malkheinu* ("our King" or "our Sovereign"), and sometimes, like on the High Holy Days, we merge these two images together. While most people cannot understand what it means to relate to a king or a monarch, it is easy to think about what it means to relate to a parent. Parents love us, but they also discipline us, because they want the best for us. At the same time, we have a duty to honor God, just as we honor our parents—even when it is very hard to do so.

ꞔ **Idolatry is the worship of gods and of objects that are worthless.** Notice the way that Moses refers to the false gods that the people will worship: "no-gods" (32:17)—gods that are not even the gods that other nations worship, not really gods at all. Those gods are also referred to as "gods they had never known; new

ones, who came but lately." The worst thing about these gods is
that they are "new," and not timeless like God.

Divrei Torah
WATCH GOD MORPH

Do you ever think about God? Maybe; maybe not. A lot of people don't,
or, when they do, they get very confused. That's because the first question they are likely to ask is: Who (or what) is God?

The problem is not that we don't have enough ways to think about
God. Rather, it's the opposite—we might actually have too many.
Just look at the way that God is portrayed in this Torah portion. First,
God is described as a rock. Then, a few verses later, God is portrayed
as a father—but a father who just happens to find the Jewish people
in the desert, like homeless infants, and adopts them. But wait: God
becomes a mother eagle. And then God is like a human mother who
nurses her young. Verses later God is like a warrior.

Please stop, you are probably saying. Can't the biblical author simply make up his or her mind? What is God, anyway?

And it's not as if these are the only images of God that we have.
This Torah portion is read between Rosh Hashanah and Yom Kippur,
when we call God Father and King, and we imagine our relationship
to God as sheep to their shepherd, or grapes to the vine keeper. As the
machzor (High Holy Day prayer book) puts it: "For we are Your people, and You are our father. We are your flock of sheep, and You are
our keeper. We are Your vineyard, and You are our vintner."

This is fine if you get the agricultural images. But, what if you never
saw a sheep in your life? What if you have never seen a vineyard, and
the only grapes you know are the ones that you buy at the grocery store?

Professor Rachel Adler teaches: "God is imaged in rapid succession
as a rock, father, a mother eagle, a birth giver, and a warrior. As long
as we are simply receptive and allow the diverse images to flow past,
we experience no contradictions. But when we stop the flow and try
to reconcile the images logically, we run into trouble." In other words,
when it comes to talking about God, don't look for consistency. It's
not going to happen.

Talking about God is not easy. After all, when Moses first encounters God, Moses asks him: "When the Jews ask me who sent you, what name shall I give them?" God replies, *"Ehyeh asher ehyeh."* Some people like to translate that as "I am what I am." This makes God more than a little arrogant: "You don't like me? Tough." More than that: to say that God is what God is makes the whole notion of God very static and very present tense. "What you see [well, not really] is what you get." And remember: the word *ehyeh* is clearly the future tense for "to be." *Ehyeh* means, in effect, "I will be." God's "future" is unfinished. God is, as they say, a work in progress. And if God is not "done" yet, then neither are we.

THE NEW ISN'T ALWAYS BETTER

Let me guarantee you something, right now. You are going to be getting gifts when you celebrate becoming bar or bat mitzvah. You may be getting money and clothing and, basically, a lot of "stuff." Much of that "stuff," especially if it includes electronics and computer stuff, will be the newest, the best, and the fastest.

Sure. Until something newer, better, and faster comes out.

So, if you don't know already, then it's time you learn about the way the world works. Much of what goes on is based on the fact that you're a consumer. You, and everyone else you know, buy things. But we not only buy things, we "consume" them. "Consume" means to use it up—as in "consuming" resources. The basic idea here is that once we have used something and it is no longer usable we have consumed it—and then we throw it away, waiting for the next great thing to come along. If you don't believe this, check out electronics stores that allow people to donate old cell phones, and music players, and televisions. Last year's model? Who needs it? Even last month's model might be too old.

So, let's go back to the Torah portion. The worst thing that Moses can say about the false gods that the Israelites will no doubt worship is that they are "new ones, who came but lately, who stirred not your fathers' fears" (32:17). There are at least a hundred names for God in Judaism. One of them is the Aramaic term *atika kaddisha*, "the Holy Ancient One," which appears in the biblical book of Daniel. A god—or, at the very least, the Jewish God—should be as old as creation itself.

Our stuff always seems to need an upgrade. But God doesn't need an upgrade (maybe the way we talk about God needs the upgrade, but that's a different story).

How can we focus less on our "stuff"? Take Shabbat. Traditional Jews don't shop on Shabbat because Jewish law forbids the handling of money on the Sabbath. But there is a deeper reason: one day a week we can think about not what we own and must have, but just about who we are and our relationships. Modern Jewish theologian Abraham Joshua Heschel writes: "In regard to gifts, to outward possessions, we can have them and we should be able to do without them. On the Sabbath, handling money is a desecration, on which man avows his independence of that which is the world's chief idol."

Ultimately, we need to focus less on our "stuff" and more on who we are as human beings. As the ancient sage Ben Zoma writes: "Who is rich? The one who is content with what he has."

Connections

ҍ In what way is God like a parent? What kind of parent is God?

ҍ What do you think of all those other images of God? Which one do you like the best?

ҍ How do you imagine God? How have your ideas about God changed as you've gotten older? In what way is God like a rock?

ҍ Do you believe that people concentrate too much on their possessions? Can you offer some examples? What are other, more important things for people to be thinking about? How can you make this happen in your own life?

❖ Ve-zo't ha-berakhah: Deuteronomy 33:1–34:12

Technically, Ve-zo't ha-berakhah is not really a Torah portion. It is simply what we read when we reach the end of the Torah on Simchat Torah. It consists of Moses's blessings of the Jewish people, in which he individually blesses each tribe and speaks of its ultimate destiny (in fact, these blessings reflect the political realities of a much later time).

As the Torah draws to a close, Moses ascends Mount Nebo, which is in the land of Moab on the other side of the Jordan River from the

Land of Israel. God shows him the entire land, and Moses dies on Mount Nebo. God buries Moses at a site that is still unknown. The People of Israel mourn for Moses, and Joshua takes over as the leader of the Jewish people.

Summary

ᛒ Moses begins his poem by describing how God appeared in various places in the wilderness to the Israelites. He tells the people that when he (Moses) conveyed the Torah to them, God became king. "When Moses charged us with the Teaching, as the heritage of the congregation of Jacob" is traditionally the first verse from the Torah that a young Jewish child learns. (33:1–5)

ᛒ The blessing of the tribe of Levi indicates that the traditional role of the Levites is to consult the urim and tumim, the ancient stones that will tell them God's decisions. It also indicates that the Levites' role is to teach the people, and that they are to make the sacrificial offerings on the altar. There is also an odd reference to Levi failing to consider his father and mother, disregarding his own brothers, and ignoring his children. (33:8–11)

ᛒ Moses climbs Mount Nebo for what will be his final journey, even though he is still reasonably strong and vigorous. God shows Moses the entire Land of Israel, and reminds him, once again, that, while Moses can see the land, he will not be able to enter it. (34:1–4)

ᛒ God buries Moses in a place that is still unknown. (34:6)

The Big Ideas

ᛒ **God "rules."** When the Jewish tradition refers to God as "King," it simply means that God is more important than anything else and that God's teachings and laws are, ultimately, more important than those of any human ruler. We can interpret this to mean that God's rule over the earth means that all people will live their lives by the ethical teachings of the Torah. Note, by the way, that God only becomes king *after* Moses teaches the laws to the Israelites. God cannot impose kingship. It must happen after the people freely choose to live by God's laws.

ᛒ **Sacred duty often requires that one show no favoritism to one's** family. A passage in this portion reads: "who said of his father and mother, 'I consider them not.' His brothers he disregarded, ignored his own children" (33:9). Does that mean that the Levites had to ignore their own families? Certainly not. Judaism believes in the centrality and the sanctity of the family unit. The best way to interpret this verse is that when the Levites made their decisions they did not take their own families into consideration. They did not play favorites. That is one of the most important principles of true leadership.

ṭ **Death is an essential and inescapable part of life.** This seems to be why the text suggests that Moses accepts his own death without struggle or protest. But the ancient Rabbis were not satisfied with his passivity, and they created legends that teach a different view of Moses's last moments—that he struggled with God and argued for his life to be spared. But, ultimately, even the legends end with Moses accepting his fate. While there is something inherently human about the desire to prolong one's life and the lives of others whom we love, ultimately death is the reality that no one can escape.

ṭ **The dead are to be respected, but not venerated.** This seems to be the reason why the Torah text makes it very clear that no one knows where Moses is buried. True, his burial place is in the mountains of Moab (modern-day Jordan), and therefore outside the Land of Israel, and somewhat inaccessible. But the deeper reason is that the Torah did not want Moses's burial place to become a shrine of pilgrimage. The authors of the Torah were quite familiar with the Egyptian way of death, in which people were mummified and placed in pyramids, along with all their possessions. The Torah is saying a loud "no" to that—and making it clear that the best tribute to Moses is to study the Torah that he proclaimed to the Jewish people.

Divrei Torah
AND IN THE END . . .

If there were to be a contest for the most moving passage in the Bible, it might be this one: the death of Moses. It is so moving that the Reverend Dr. Martin Luther King Jr. used its imagery in the last speech of his life, delivered the night before he was assassinated: "Well, I don't know what will happen now; we've got some difficult days ahead. But it really doesn't matter with me now, because I've been to the mountaintop. And I don't mind. Like anybody, I would like to live a long life—longevity has its place. But I'm not concerned about that now. I just want to do God's will. And He's allowed me to go up to the mountain. And I've looked over and I've seen the Promised Land. I may not get there with you. But I want you to know tonight, that we, as a people, will get to the Promised Land."

Dr. King was like Moses. He freed his people. He knew that he would die (perhaps not as soon as he did). And, like Moses, he knew that he was not in control of his fate.

The ancient Rabbis had trouble with this. They knew that Moses had spent much of his life fighting for his people's freedom. Moses had not even been afraid to fight with God. How could he have simply said. "Okay, I'm done"?

They invented a new way to look at Moses's final moments:

When Moses saw that the decree against him had been sealed, he decided to fast, and he drew a small circle and stood in it, and exclaimed: "I will not move from here until You cancel that decree." Moses stood in prayer before God, until the heavens and the order of nature were shaken. What did God do? God proclaimed that the prayers of Moses would not be heard on high, and that the gates of heaven would be closed to them.

Moses then said: God, if you will not bring me into the Land of Israel, let me be like a beast or a bird, so that I might live and enjoy the world. God said: "Moses, you have spoken enough."

At the end, a heavenly voice was heard, declaring: "The time of your death has come." Moses said to God: "Remember when I stayed on Mount Sinai for forty days and forty nights. I beg You: do not hand me over to the Angel of Death." At that moment, a heavenly voice said to him: "Fear not—I myself will attend to you and your burial."

Moses's prayers were so powerful that God had to keep them out of the heavens. Moses asked to become an animal rather than a human being, and God had to remind him that human beings don't have the option of becoming animals. And, finally, God says that God would bury Moses, as a final act of gratitude and respect for all that Moses had done. Perhaps that is why Moses finally accepted his fate in peace.

The poet and freedom fighter Hannah Senesh once wrote: "There are stars up above, so far away we only see their light long, long after the star itself is gone. And so it is with people that we loved— their memories keep shining ever brightly though their time with us is done." . . . That was Moses. His legacy keeps on shining.

WHERE IS MOSES BURIED?

If you spend enough time channel surfing, sooner or later you will come to a TV program that deals with biblical mysteries. Those shows always feature a team of archeologists and adventurers who take a trip to the Middle East in search of answers to persistent questions. Those questions always tend to be of the "Where?" variety. The most popular "Where?" question is: "Where is Noah's ark?" (Answer: if it really existed, and if it is still discoverable, it is somewhere in the mountains of Armenia near the Black Sea.)

And yet, with all those shows, you never see one that asks the question "Where is Moses buried?"

It is really interesting, isn't it? Think of all the biblical heroes whose burial places are known (sort of). You can actually visit the graves of the following people: the Patriarchs and Matriarchs (with the exception of Rachel) in the cave of Machpelah. Rachel's tomb is between Jerusalem and Bethlehem. King David's tomb is on Mount Zion in Jerusalem. The prophet Jonah's tomb is in Iraq. But Moses's tomb? Not a clue.

Well, not exactly. The Torah says that Moses was buried "near Beth-peor." Why there? This was where the Israelites had an orgy with Moabite women and worshiped the Moabite god (Num. 25:1–9). In fact, there is a tradition that Moses's burial place had been created long before Moses ever existed! Rashi quoted an old tradition from Mishnah *Avot* 5, and taught: "Moses's burial place was created on the sixth day of creation, right before Shabbat. It would serve as a way to cleanse that place from what the Israelites had done there."

But, in fact, no one really knows where Moses is buried. Perhaps it's best this way. First of all, the Israelites had just come out of Egypt, and they were very familiar with how the Egyptians dealt with death. The Egyptians mummified their kings, so that they would live forever. They buried their kings in pyramids. Egypt's holiest book was *The Book of the Dead*. Egypt was all about death. The People of Israel didn't want to recreate that kind of culture; Judaism was to be all about life.

But there was another reason as well. Perhaps there had been the fear that if people knew exactly where Moses was buried they would come to visit his grave. They might even come to worship him. That would not only be idolatry, which is bad enough; it would also be a distraction from the real tasks of Judaism—study, worship, and mitzvot.

The late Nobel laureate Elie Wiesel taught: "Moses's resting place has become neither temple nor museum. He lives on inside of us. For as long as one child of Israel, somewhere, proclaims his Law and his truth, Moses lives on through him, in turn, as does the burning bush, which consumes man's heart without consuming his faith. You don't need to visit Moses's grave. Just study Moses's words."

Connections

ᚦ Do you know of any situations where people have had to make decisions or do things that are unfair to their families, as the Levites had to do?

ᚦ Do you know where your relatives are buried? Do you visit their graves? What is that like?

ᚦ Do you think that Moses was too passive in his death? Do you agree with the midrash that says Moses fought back against God's decree?

ᚦ Have you ever experienced something that you thought was unfair? What did you do about it?

PART 2 ❖ The Haftarot

GENESIS

❖ Bere'shit: Isaiah 42:5–43:10

There is no time like the very beginning of the Torah reading cycle to remember exactly why we Jews have to do what we do.

But, first, let's clear up a little confusion. There were two prophets named Isaiah. The first one preached in the Southern Kingdom of Judah in the second half of the eighth century BCE. The second one, usually called Second Isaiah, was actually an anonymous prophet who preached during the sixth century BCE during the Babylonian exile. (A little history lesson: in the year 586 BCE, Babylonian armies destroyed Jerusalem, burned the Temple, and deported the Judeans to Babylonia, thus beginning the period known as the Babylonian exile.) Actually, the second prophet's name wasn't really Isaiah; someone simply added his teachings to the end of the book of the original Isaiah.

The prophet known as Second Isaiah delivered a speech to the Judeans who were in exile in Babylonia, and in it he reminds them that while God is the creator of the earth (which is the connection to the Torah portion Bere'shit), God also has a direct, loving, and personal relationship with the Jewish people.

"A Light to the Nations"

Along with this relationship comes a special responsibility—the Jewish people are to be, in the memorable language of Isaiah, a "covenant people" and "a light of nations." To be "a light of nations" means that the Jews have a responsibility not only to themselves, but to the world as well. These obligations are not ritual obligations; it is not that the Jews have to go to other peoples and talk to them about Shabbat. It means that the Jewish message is one of social justice—one of the great themes of the prophetic writings. In modern terms, Isaiah is challenging us to be role models to the world, by practicing what we preach and inspiring others.

According to the Torah, God has a very personal relationship with the Jewish people—so much so that God is furious over their continued oppression and exile in Babylonia. God promises to respond to their pain and to redeem them—to bring the Jews from all directions and restore them to their homeland of Israel.

Finally, God reminds the Judean exiles that God is, in fact, the only God: "I am the Lord, that is My name; I will not yield My glory to another, nor My renown to idols" (42:8). This is the major theological event in Second Isaiah—the "invention" of pure monotheism. Before that time, the Jews certainly believed in God, but the intense insistence of Second Isaiah that God is the only god was certainly unique for a time when the belief in polytheism (many gods) was still prevalent.

God needs the Jewish people to be God's "witnesses"—as if the entire world is a courtroom and the Jews are there to testify to God's uniqueness. Isaiah is in effect saying: "We are on a mission."

Every so often, a television station will feature a rerun of the movie *The Blues Brothers,* in which Dan Aykroyd and the late John Belushi play a pair of brothers, Jake and Elwood, who are blues singers. Elwood and Jake take on an important project: to save the Catholic orphanage in which they grew up from foreclosure. To quote Elwood: "We're on a mission from God."

The movie is a classic. So is Elwood's line about being on a mission from God. And, when you read this week's haftarah, you will notice something: the Jews invented the idea of being "on a mission from God." Second Isaiah puts it this way:

I the Lord, in My grace, have summoned you,
And I have grasped you by the hand.
I created you, and appointed you
A covenant people, a light of nations.
Opening eyes deprived of light,
Rescuing prisoners from confinement,
From the dungeon those who sit in darkness. (42:6–7)

That is the clearest statement of the biblical concept that the Jews have a sacred mission. But what does that mission really entail?

Some of the prophet's words are easy to understand. God has a covenant with the Jewish people. They need to live up to that covenant by observing the commandments of the Torah. Many of these relate to doing justice. Isaiah calls upon us to rescue prisoners from their dungeons, to free those who are unjustly "imprisoned." In other words, to help the oppressed of the world.

The most famous phrase in the prophet's teaching, that the Jews are to be "a light of nations," has been the subject of much commentary. The medieval Spanish Jewish philosopher Rabbeinu Bachya understands it to mean that the Jews would need to be dispersed among the nations and that "it is the task of the Jews to teach the nations about God" (*Kad ha-Kemah*, 22). Claude Montefiore, a British Reform thinker, teaches: "Until the earth is filled with the knowledge of the One God—the God of Israel—the Jews will be his witnesses."

Most contemporary Jews agree that the phrase "a light of nations" means that Jews should teach the world about God and about ethics. Whenever Jews are involved in social justice, and influence others to do the same, that light shines brightly.

But perhaps "light to the nations" means something else as well. Throughout their history, the Jews have experienced much of the "darkness" of the world's hatred, culminating in the Holocaust. According to Israeli writer and statesman Avi Beker, "the Jews had to raise a light, and remind the world about the darkness of hatred that is still present." Like the Hanukkah candles, kindling light against the dark reminds us of our past history and our ongoing mission.

❖ Noaḥ: Isaiah 54:1–55:5

The Babylonian exile was one of the bleakest times in Jewish history. That's the bad news. The good news is that it didn't last forever (about seventy years). During their exile the Judeans were always preparing themselves, spiritually, to return to the Land of Israel. Even still, they needed assurances from God, and that need was fulfilled more than anybody else by Second Isaiah, who spoke in God's name.

This haftarah contains those promises and reassurances. Isaiah proclaimed that while it seemed that God had hidden the Divine Presence from the Jewish people and had even "sent" them into exile in Babylon, in reality God had never withdrawn love from them. Just as God restored humanity after the Flood in the time of Noah (which is the link with the Torah portion), so, too, God will restore the Jewish people to their land.

Are You a Builder?

Second Isaiah envisioned a time of restoration for the Jewish people, not only physically to the Land of Israel, but spiritually to a state of peace and happiness.

We all have a role in bringing that about, but need to know how, which is one reason why Judaism puts such an emphasis on education.

Quick: why do you attend religious school? To learn about Judaism? To learn the history of the Jewish people? To learn Hebrew—or, at least, enough Hebrew for your bar or bat mitzvah ceremony? To be with friends? Because your parents say so?

Those are all decent answers. But here's one that maybe you've never considered: to learn how to think. Jewish education is great preparation for how to think like an adult. When many people discuss controversial subjects, they can get very worked up, not really listening to their opponents' views, and seeing them in the worst possible light.

But that is not how Judaism views the world. And we find proof of this in one verse of this week's haftarah: "And all your children shall be disciples of the Lord, and great shall be the happiness [*shalom*, which also means "peace"] of your children" (54:13).

The study of Torah should lead to peace between Jews who are learning Judaism together. It is written in the Talmud, "Rabbi Eleazar said in the name of Rabbi Chanina: Those who study Torah help to build peace in the world. Do not read *banayikh,* 'your children,' but rather *bonayikh,* 'your builders.' Those who learn and teach Torah are the builders of the world."

Builders—not destroyers through cruel and harsh language. The best way that you can build the world is through people learning together. That is why Judaism believes that we should study many different opinions.

Here is one example. Traditional medieval commentaries on the Hebrew Bible have a very interesting page layout. The Bible text is in the middle and commentary, or interpretations of the text, from across the centuries surround it. All those teachers "live together" on the same page, in shalom. Or, look at the mezuzah on a door. It is slanted. Rashi, the great sage of twelfth-century France, said that the mezuzah should be vertical. His grandson, Rabbeinu Tam, said that it should be horizontal. A generation later, Rabbi Jacob ben Asher said that it should be a little of both; it should be slanted—as a way of keeping shalom.

That is why Rav Kook, the first chief rabbi of prestate Israel, said: "When Torah scholars broaden knowledge and provide new insights, they contribute to the increase of peace." All views, even those that seem contradictory, in fact help reveal knowledge and truth. For this reason, the early sage Rabbi Chanina emphasized that scholars are like builders. A building is erected from all sides, using a variety of materials and skills. So too, the whole truth is constructed from diverse views, opinions, and methods of analysis.

An important lesson—be a student; be a builder.

❖ Lekh Lekha: Isaiah 40:27–41:16

For someone who was anonymous, the prophet known as Second Isaiah certainly gets a lot of ink in the *haftarot*. Here he is again, speaking to the Judeans. His message is clear: despite the fact that they are in exile in Babylonia, they will soon be able to return to the Land of Israel—a move from despair to triumph. This will demonstrate God's power over history and over all the nations. God is the creator, the great victor, and the redeemer of Israel. God's power is revealed everywhere: in nature, in international affairs, and in the life of the Jewish people

Second Isaiah reminds Israel that they are the "seed of Abraham" (41:8), which forms the connection to the Torah portion. The Jews who were listening to Isaiah knew that God had made a great promise to Abraham. Believing that God would keep that promise and return them to the land of their ancestors gave the people hope in their time of exile.

Coming Home Again (or Why Jews Love Baseball)

How is the Bible like baseball? (Please don't say that they both start in the "big-inning"!) The purpose of baseball is that you start at home, and come home again.

And that is the message of Isaiah and a big lesson of the entire Hebrew Bible as well.

Let's review our history. In the year 586 BCE, Babylonian armies destroyed Jerusalem, burned the Temple, and deported the Judeans to Babylonia, thus beginning that period known as the Babylonian exile. Some years afterward, the Persian King Cyrus conquered Babylonia, and he let a group of Judeans return to the Land of Israel and rebuild the Temple. So, if you were wondering about the identity of the mysterious "victor from the East" in Isa. 41:2, it would be Cyrus, king of Persia, who was about to conquer Babylonia. That's the way it was in the ancient Middle East: every few hundred years the borders changed and you wound up living in a different empire.

According to the Bible: "The Lord roused the spirit of King Cyrus of Persia to issue a proclamation throughout his realm. . . . "The Lord God of Heaven has given me all the kingdoms of the earth and has charged me with building Him a house in Jerusalem, which is in Judah. Anyone of you of all His people—may his God be with him, and let him go up to Jerusalem that is in Judah . . . ; and all who stay behind, wherever he may be living, let the people of his place assist him with silver, gold, goods" (Ezra 1:1–4).

Cyrus asks everyone to help the Jews return to their land—with silver, gold, and goods. Where have we read that before? It is an echo of the Exodus from Egypt, when the Israelites asked their former Egyptian neighbors for silver and gold to take with them on their journey. The return to the Land of Israel is like an exodus from "another" Egypt—this time, from the Babylonian exile.

For Jews, Cyrus wins the award for Best Loved Foreign Ruler in the Ancient Middle East (though there wasn't that much competition). The Talmud notes that in Hebrew, Cyrus's name is Koresh (*kaph resh shin*), which contains the same letters as the word *kasher* (*kaph shin resh*), meaning "ritually fit and proper." Cyrus was kosher! Second Isaiah predicted that a Cyrus-like figure would help the Jews come home, although he probably did not live long enough to greet Cyrus as a hero. In our day, another hero helped the Jews return home. President Harry S. Truman gave crucial support to the Zionist cause and directed the United States to recognize the new Jewish state when the United Nations set it to a vote. Truman certainly helped create the State of Israel, but he thought that his role was even bigger than that. "What do you mean, 'helped create'? I am Cyrus, I am Cyrus!"

With those stirring words, Truman demonstrated that he was not only in favor of the creation of a Jewish state, but that he grounded that support in his belief in the ultimate truth of the ancient narrative. Truman read the Bible! He saw himself as the modern-day reincarnation of King Cyrus of Persia. And that was good news for the Jews who wanted to come home.

❖ Va-yera': 2 Kings 4:1–37

Sometimes miracles do happen. Take the story from this week's haftarah, for example. Elisha is a prophet and a "man of God"—a wonder-worker in ancient Israel. Elisha visits a widow who is facing one of the worst situations imaginable. She has borrowed money and put her sons up as collateral for the loan. She cannot repay her debt, and the creditor is coming to take her sons. Elisha "magically" takes some of her oil and multiplies it for her, so that she can sell the oil to pay her debt.

Elisha then visits a childless woman and her elderly husband in Shunem. She offers him hospitality (actually, she builds him a room to use whenever he is in town). In gratitude for their hospitality, Elisha promises her that she will have a child—and she does. Sometime later, her child falls ill and dies, but Elisha brings the child back to life.

This story is a flashback to the Torah portion. Abraham and Sarah were too old to have children. They offer hospitality to three men, who turn out to be angels. Then, amazingly, Sarah becomes pregnant and Isaac is born. Birth is a miracle; how much more so when a couple thinks they cannot conceive a child and then do.

Seen Any Miracles Lately?

The theologian and social activist Abraham Joshua Heschel used to begin his lectures with the following words: "My friends, a great miracle happened this morning!" When people asked, "What? What was the miracle?" Heschel would answer, "The sun came up." While it may not seem like a miracle that the sun comes up every day, Rabbi Heschel was making the following point: wondrous and dramatic things happen all the time—if you choose to notice them.

But, seriously, what kinds of miracles did Elisha "really" perform? Look at the first story. It is about economic justice and injustice. The woman must leave her children with a debt collector as collateral on a loan. Elisha comes and mysteriously increases the amount of oil that she has. She sells the vessels of oil, which brings her enough money so that she can buy her children out of debt slavery. (Sounds like the famous Hanukkah miracle—the "one night of oil that lasts for eight nights" miracle—doesn't it?)

Yes, the "one vessel of oil producing many vessels of oil" bit seems like magic. But the far more interesting miracle in the story is this one: "Go, he said, and borrow vessels outside, from all your neighbors, empty vessels, as many as you can. . . . They kept bringing [vessels] to her and she kept pouring" (4:3–4). The "miracle" is that the woman was not left alone. Her community—her neighbors—helped her. They brought the vessels to her, and the vessels became filled. And why is that a sort of miracle (or at least a great blessing)? Because they could have simply decided to do nothing, but instead an entire community rallied around the woman in need.

And then, the two miracles for the woman in Shunem. Elisha promises her that she will have a child, even though her husband is very old. That certainly seems miraculous.

What about bringing the child back to life? There is a very old and powerful idea that God will, someday at the end of history, revive the dead. In the *Gevurot* prayer in the traditional Conservative and Orthodox liturgy, we find: "Your might, O Lord, is boundless. You give life to the dead; great is Your saving power." Yes, many contemporary

Jews believe that God can revive the dead. But Elisha also acted—by performing an ancient form of CPR! (4:34).

As the Talmud teaches: "Don't rely on miracles." You have to make them happen.

❖ Ḥayyei Sarah: 1 Kings 1:1–31

King David was the greatest of the Israelite kings, as well as arguably the most complicated character in the entire Bible. He was a warrior, romantic figure, musician, poet—a man of deep emotions, a man who loved and lost. He was a man of great accomplishments and grave mistakes. More is remembered and written about David than anybody else in the Bible.

As in the Torah portion, which speaks of the final days of Abraham, David is now dying, and it's not pretty. The warrior-king is so feeble that he is now lying in bed, unable to get warm. Back then they didn't have electric blankets or portable heaters, so his courtiers bring him a young girl, Abishag, whose job it is to keep the old king warm. And, as feeble as he is, David is forced to confront the rebellion of one of his sons and the need to establish his true successor.

David's son Solomon was to have succeeded his father, but David's arrogant younger son Adonijah runs around and starts boasting that he will be king. He gets Joab, the commander of David's forces, and Abiathar, the priest who had been his father's lifelong friend, on his side. Adonijah throws a huge feast, but doesn't invite Nathan the prophet, nor Solomon. Nathan tells David's wife Bathsheba that her son Solomon was to have been king, and Bathsheba then tells the dying David that if Adonijah is proclaimed king, she and Solomon will be killed as traitors. David sees that this is true and ultimately Solomon is proclaimed king.

Abishag

Imagine: God summons a huge group of people together and says: "You are going to be characters in the Jewish Bible." God starts giving out parts, and a very sweet, shy, young girl raises her hand, timidly, and asks, "Do you have any *really* small parts?"

"Sure," says God. "You can be Abishag. King David will get old and feeble. All you will need to do is get in bed with him and . . . ." "Wait!" Abishag says. "Hold on right there!" God smiles: "Relax. There won't be any 'funny stuff.'" "Well, okay, then," says Abishag, still a little tentative.

So, let's wonder aloud about Abishag; this minor character who is almost forgotten, but not quite. The question that naturally comes to mind: did King David and Abishag not "do it" because he was too old? No, said the ancient sages: Abishag took charge of the situation. Abishag did not want to be alone with the king unless he married her. As it is written in the Talmud, "Abishag said to King David, 'Let us marry,' but he said, 'You are forbidden to me.'" Perhaps David didn't want any more children who could then demand that they were in line for the throne. He had had enough of that already. The sages believe that both parties acted responsibly and that Abishag was more like a caretaker.

Poets have been attracted to Abishag's character. The Yiddish poet Yitzhak Manger imagines Abishag missing her family and angry at how she is being used:

Abishag sits in her room
And writes a letter home:
Greetings to the calves and sheep—
She writes, sighing deeply . . .
King David is old and pious
And she herself is, 'oh, well'—
She's the king's hot water bottle
Against the bedroom chill . . .
More than once a night
She softly mourned her fate.
True, wise people say
She's being charitable.
They even promise her
A line in the Bible.

The great American poet Robert Frost imagines her later years:

The witch that came (the withered hag)
To wash the steps with pail and rag
Was once the beauty Abishag.

Except maybe that wasn't how it really turned out. Remember, Abishag came from Shunem. Some sages said that the woman in Shunem who offered hospitality to the prophet Elisha was, in fact, Abishag. While far-fetched, this is the way of the sages saying that Abishag turned out okay and went on to live a full life.

It's all too easy to pass over minor characters in the Bible, and in life. But every person has a story; every person has feelings and needs and their own unique contribution. Even the young caretaker of an old man.

❖ Toledot: Malachi 1:1–2:7

No one ever said that a prophet had to be a nice person. In fact, in this haftarah the prophet Malachi might have gotten the nomination for the "king of snark." Malachi was the last of the prophets. He lived in the middle of fifth century BCE, at the time when Persia permitted the Judeans to return to Judah, to re-create their own independent state, and to rebuild the Temple in Jerusalem. You would have thought that the rebuilding of the Temple would have created some kind of increased religious enthusiasm.

No. Very few Judeans were taking their religious obligations seriously, and Malachi spoke out against this neglect. By contrast, however, the prophet imagines that the other nations of the world would bring pure sacrifices to God, that they would actually treat God better than the Judeans do!

So how is this haftarah connected to the Torah portion? The Torah portion, Toledot, contains the story of the brothers Jacob and Esau. They appear in this haftarah—with a twist. The prophet knows that Esau was the ancestor of the kingdom of Edom, which was a long-time enemy of Judea. Just as Esau loses his birthright in the Torah portion, his descendants (the kingdom of Edom) ultimately lose their power as well.

But there is a second connection, and it is very easy to miss it. It hangs on just one word. Malachi refers to the priests "who scorn My name" (1:6). The use of the term "scorn" echoes what Esau did to the birthright when he sold it to Jacob; he spurned it.

Bringing Your Best

Have you ever attended a synagogue worship service where few people are actually praying, or singing? Many people are just sitting around, catching peeks at their cell phones, whispering to their neighbor, or just gazing around. It's as if they aren't engaged at all. It's like being at a baseball game and hardly anyone is cheering, or at a rock concert and nobody is listening.

That's what the prophet Malachi is describing. Back in his day, the religious life of the Jewish people revolved around bringing sacrifices. When people brought the best of their offerings, it symbolized that they had great respect for God. But if they brought a blemished offering, it was considered disrespectful. It was as if the people were saying: we have to go through the motions but we don't care that much about God or what we are doing.

The prophets were concerned with such religious hypocrisy. They were angry when people brought second-rate offerings to God and could care less about the poor. Malachi is angry that people aren't taking God seriously. They are bringing God less-than-great offerings.

And why should Malachi have cared so much about this? The Judeans were returning from exile. The Persians were allowing them to rebuild the Temple in Jerusalem. This was an amazing moment in Jewish history. It should have been filled with power and majesty. The Jews should have realized that they were living in the midst of a great happening. But they certainly didn't show it.

There is a Hasidic tale that also talks about passionless worship. "Once, the Baal Shem Tov, the founder of Hasidism, visited a synagogue but refused to enter the sanctuary. And why? Because, he said, it was too full. Too many people? No, he said. Too many prayers—dead prayers that had been said without feeling, and had not ascended to the heavens, and were just piling up on the floor without going anywhere!"

Back to our modern synagogue where people just seem to be going through the motions. The problem that Malachi first observed still goes on today. It is about people who don't take Judaism seriously, and kind of sleepwalk through the service. They lack *kavanah*—the ability to spiritually connect with what is going on.

The Czech Jewish writer Franz Kafka resented how his father observed Judaism. When he went to synagogue, he was more interested in pointing out the wealthy people who were there, paying more attention to them than to God. This is what Kafka provocatively said to his father: "You went to temple four days a year. You got through the prayers patiently, as a formality; sometimes I was astonished that you were able to find the passage in the prayer book that was just being recited. Getting rid of this kind of Judaism seemed to me itself to be the most reverent act of all."

Kafka rebelled. Some of us rebel. While some just walk away, others take a different path. These young people have decided to take Judaism more seriously than their parents, and maybe even their grandparents, and not be like the Jews in Malachi's time. They have decided to bring their best offerings to God.

❖ Va-yetse': Hosea 12:13–14:10

Imagine yourself in a hot-air balloon, sailing across all of biblical history. That would be a good way of understanding this haftarah. The prophet Hosea lived in the Northern Kingdom of Israel, which was also called Ephraim (after one of Joseph's sons). Hosea reminds the People of Israel that Jacob fled back to Aram and guarded the sheep of his father-in-law, Laban (the link to the Torah portion). As a parallel, it was another prophet—Moses—who guarded the Jewish people on their way out of Egypt.

Hosea then takes us on a whirlwind tour: through the wilderness experience, when the Israelites worshiped the idol Baal and suffered a plague as punishment; through the people's desire for a king in the time of the prophet Samuel (Hosea 13:10–11)—all the way to the idolatrous, Baal-worshiping practices of the Northern Kingdom. When Hosea mentions how the Israelites died in the wilderness because they worshiped Baal, he means this as a warning to the Israelites of the Northern Kingdom, who were doing the same thing.

Hosea's words are stern, and yet he believes that it is both possible and necessary for the people of the Northern Kingdom to repent (in fact, part of this haftarah is also read on Shabbat Shuvah, the Shabbat of Repentance, which comes between Rosh Hashanah and Yom Kippur). Hosea concludes his words with the hope that the wise will consider his words and heed them.

Human Life

Here's a question: You and your family are in the middle of a terrible storm. Your neighborhood is flooded, and you have a rowboat. You see your dog, Dexter. Then you also see your down-the-street neighbor Mr. Green. You only have room in your boat for one more passenger. You can save either your dog, Dexter, whom you love, or Mr. Green, whom you barely know. What do you do?

While you're thinking about that, let's go back to the haftarah. The prophet Hosea lived and preached in the Northern Kingdom of Israel. During his time many Israelites still worshiped the Canaanite god Baal in the form of an idol of a calf (this is similar to the sin of the Golden Calf, Exodus 32). Hosea criticizes his countrymen for "kissing calves" and adds a very strange statement: "they appoint men to sacrifice" (13:2). While the Hebrew is uncertain, some scholars see this as a reference (likely a warning) about human sacrifice that may have still been carried out by the neighboring Canaanites.

Hosea was horrified at the thought that any society could think about worshiping animals while sacrificing people. Awful.

Back to Dexter and Mr. Green and the raging flood waters. Whom are you going to save?

In a famous study, Professor Richard Topolski asked his students a similar question and discovered: "Everyone would save a sibling, grandparent or close friend rather than a strange dog. But when people considered their own dog versus people less connected with them—a distant cousin or a hometown stranger—votes in favor of saving the dog came rolling in!"

There you go: people who kiss calves (or, love their dogs) might, in a difficult situation, choose to save an animal over a human. It's not "Who do we love more—Dexter or Mr. Green?" Obviously, Dexter will win. But Dexter should not win. Mr. Green should win.

Judaism's point is: People are made in God's image, and animals (even though we love them) are not. And being made in God's image trumps everything else. Every human being is sacred in a way that animals are not. While animals are living beings, and Judaism has laws against cruelty to animals, let's remember that humans come first. Saving a human life, even at the expense of an animal's, is the greatest good. The Talmud teaches that when we save a human life we have saved an entire world.

So, save Mr. Green. It's the right thing to do.

❖ Va-yishlah̠: Obadiah 1:1–21

The prophet Obadiah was a "downer." Everything he said was bleak. The whole book is only one chapter long—the shortest book in the Bible—and it is a denunciation of the ancient nation of Edom, which helped the Babylonians destroy the ancient kingdom of Judea.

As we know, in the Torah portion Jacob and his brother, Esau, are about to be reunited. Remember that Esau had sold his birthright to Jacob. Esau's other name is Edom, which means "red"—both because his complexion and hair were red, and because of the red-colored soup that he bought from Jacob in exchange for the birthright. Esau = Edom.

The kingdom of Edom is descended from Esau. And the kingdom of Judea is descended from Jacob; it's named after Judah, one of his sons. So Obadiah sees the struggle between the ancient Judeans and the kingdom of Edom as a continuation of the struggle between Jacob and Esau.

Every prophetic book of the Bible ends on a note of hope, except Obadiah. This prophet trashes the nation of Edom, and the haftarah (and the book of Obadiah itself) ends with the prophet teaching that Edom will ultimately be defeated. A real downer.

What Ever Happened to Brotherly Love?

The prophet Obadiah is totally angry about what Edom did to Israel. You might be too if you had to deal with an enemy who had helped destroy your country!

It was bad enough that the Edomites (descendants of Esau) helped the enemies of the Jews. But think about this—it was like turning on your family—because they helped defeat the Judeans, who were their distant cousins! True, Jacob and Esau were not exactly close; neither were their descendants. When Jacob cheated Esau out of the blessing that was reserved for him as the oldest son, Esau threatened to kill him. But years later—and in the Torah portion—Jacob and Esau meet again. We cannot say that they totally made up with each other. Each went their separate way. Jacob mumbled something about visiting Esau in Seir, Esau's territory—but he never did. Okay, maybe there were still some lingering bad feelings, but they put an end to their years of alienation.

Obadiah is disappointed. He hoped for better from the descendants of Esau. True—sometimes families have tensions, and sometimes family members don't talk. But, please, you simply don't help in their destruction.

But there may be another intriguing reason why Obadiah is so angry, and it's *personal*.

According to the ancient Rabbis, Obadiah had originally been an Edomite before he became a Jew: "Obadiah was an Edomite who joined the Jewish people." If this is true, then his own people had disappointed him. It is as if his birth family turned on his adopted family, all of whom are related.

No wonder Obadiah is so angry!

Obadiah's rant is a warning that even family can disappoint. But if we remember where we all come from, and how we are connected, then like Jacob and Esau, regaining brotherly love is always possible, if not probable.

❖ Va-yeshev: Amos 2:6–3:8

"It's not just about us." That's what you can imagine the prophet Amos saying. He was a native of Tekoa, a village south of Jerusalem in Judah, but he moved to the Northern Kingdom of Israel. In the passage before the beginning of this haftarah, Amos went on a whirlwind tour of the other nations in the ancient Middle East, criticizing their human rights violations. The kingdoms of Israel and Judah must have thought that they were going to get off easy. No such luck. He scolded them too.

According to Amos the violations of Judah and Israel came about because they had broken the covenant with God. The biggest evidence? They had mistreated the poor. How had they done this? They took garments as collateral for loans. They drank wine that had been purchased with money from fines that they imposed on others. Amos is furious: look at how the people are acting, and compare that to how God had treated them during their wandering in the wilderness. Finally, Amos reminds the Jewish people of the meaning of being a Chosen People—not that they are special, but that God will hold them accountable for their sins.

What's the connection to the Torah portion, which describes how Joseph's brothers sold him into slavery in Egypt? In the haftarah, Amos quotes the Lord saying, "Because they have sold for silver those whose cause is just, and the needy for a pair of sandals" (2:6). Both are about "selling out" for the wrong reason. The brothers turned on one of their own and sold their very own sibling. The people of Amos's time turned on the most vulnerable in their midst. It's been said that when Joseph's brothers sold him, the amount of money they received was enough for each of them to buy a pair of sandals. How sad, especially when history repeats itself.

Chosen—For What?

An English journalist, William Norman Ewer, once wrote this little verse:

How odd
Of God
To choose
The Jews.

To which someone replied:

Not so odd
The Jews chose God.

Welcome to one of the most basic but controversial ideas in Judaism. It's the Chosen People, and it has a starring role in this haftarah.

How basic is it? So basic that Jews affirm it whenever we make *Kiddush* over wine, or say the blessing over the Torah. We say: "who has chosen us from all the peoples. But what does it mean? The verse in the blessing continues "and given us the Torah." The idea is that God chose the Jews to bring Torah into the world. In the words of writer Blu Greenberg: "We are chosen to serve as a witness to the world: how to live as an ethical community, a responsible and kind family, a caring neighbor, a believing spirit."

Being chosen in this sense is a mission; it doesn't mean privilege or that we are better than other people. To the contrary, the prophet Amos (see last week's haftarah) put it this way: "You alone have I singled out of all the families of the earth—that is why I will call you to account for all your iniquities" (3:2). Amos goes on say how God cares for other people too, but that Israel bears a special burden.

Throughout history some people have loathed the Jews for their notion of being chosen, some have admired it, and some have envied it.

Among Jews themselves some have denied it or felt embarrassed by it, while many have embraced it. Mordecai Kaplan and the Jewish Reconstructionist movement dropped the reference to the Chosen People altogether on theological grounds. And other Jews have found it too difficult to bear the burden of being chosen for historical reasons. To be chosen means, sometimes, to be persecuted. As Tevye famously jokes in *Fiddler on the Roof:* "God, I know that we're Your Chosen People. But could you choose another people for a change?"

Yet many if not most Jews find the belief in their chosenness to be a source of comfort and strength. Author Dennis Prager puts it rather starkly: "If I did not believe that the Jews were chosen by God, I would not raise my children as Jews. To bequeath the suffering that may attend being Jewish to my descendants is defensible only if we have a divine calling."

Some Jews prefer to call themselves "the choosing people" rather than "the Chosen People." Either way, it's a big responsibility—and the choice is ours!

❖ Mikkets: 1 Kings 3:15–28; 4:1

What is up with the way that people in the Bible treat children? First, Abraham almost sacrifices his son Isaac. And, now, Solomon almost kills an infant!

Well, not exactly. This haftarah opens with a king awakening from a dream—just like the Torah portion, in which Pharaoh had a disturbing dream and needed to find out its meaning. Here, King Solomon has just become king of Israel, after the death of his father, David, and he dreams that he is being blessed with wisdom. Now he has to prove it.

Two women—prostitutes, actually—bring two infants to the king—one alive and the other dead. Each woman claims that the live child is hers. Solomon orders that a sword be brought to him, so that he can cut the live child in half and give half to each woman. At this, the real mother shouts out: "Please, my lord . . . give her the live child; only don't kill it!" (3:26). That was how Solomon knew who the real mother was—because she would rather see the child live, even with another mother, than die.

This is one of the most famous stories in the Bible. It is the source of the phrase "a Solomonic decision." It may have been a wise decision, but what would have happened if the real mother hadn't spoke up? Wisdom is always put to the test.

Can Solomon "Cut It" as King?

What does it mean to be smart? You probably think that it has something to do with getting good grades—"She's the smartest girl in the class." Okay. But what does it mean to be wise? That's something different. There are probably many smart people who aren't necessarily wise, and some wise people who aren't smart. You can measure smart, perhaps, with an IQ test. Wise is something else.

Solomon was wise. In fact, he is considered the wisest person in the Bible. The Bible itself doesn't give many examples of this wisdom except for his first act as king; Solomon doesn't fight a battle or make a decision about taxes. He acts as a judge, and he really has to use his legendary wisdom.

The two women enter. They have no names; they don't even know each other's names. There is a live child and a dead child. Rabbi Zoe Klein imagines how the woman with the dead child must have felt: "The boy is dead. She believes that she suffocated him in the night by rolling over in her sleep. And so the woman is struck all at once by an enormity of grief and guilt."

How did Solomon know which mother was the real mother? A midrash teaches that a *bat kol* (a heavenly voice) came forth from heaven, identifying the real mother. But, as other sages note, maybe it was his intuition or his careful observation or his listening skills that led him to the truth.

Rabbi Joseph Kara, a medieval commentator, observes that the first woman said that three days separated the boys' births. Perhaps Solomon noticed that the older baby looked just a bit more physically developed.

Another medieval commentator, Isaac Abravanel, suggests that Solomon studied the facial expression, manner of speaking, and body language of each woman, and that was how he knew the answer. In other words, he heard not only the facts of the case; he had the skill to look beyond the facts and to really see into the hearts of the women.

The modern commentator Malbim notices that one woman mentioned the live child first and the dead child second. The real mother would have done that because the live child would have been foremost on her mind. That is why Solomon is said to have a "listening heart."

Wisdom is not only having a high IQ. It's having a heart and not just a brain. It's about knowing the facts but likewise having the ability to judge with fairness. The story concludes, "Solomon was now king over all Israel" (4:1). To win over everyone, a great king must be a wise king.

❖ Shabbat Hanukkah: Zechariah 2:14–4:7

A recap: the Babylonians destroyed the kingdom of Judah and exiled its people to Babylon. Years later, Cyrus, king of Persia, conquered Babylonia and allowed some of the Jews to return to their land. Upon returning to Jerusalem, one of the Jews' first projects was to rebuild the Temple. It wasn't easy. Many of the nations that surrounded Judah were opposed to the reconstruction. And many were less than enthusiastic about the project. The major theme of the haftarah is encouragement: to the people; to Joshua, the High Priest; and to Zerubbabel, whom the Persians had appointed governor over Judah. The prophet Zechariah's main message was: finish the Temple!

Why is this haftarah read on the Shabbat of Hanukkah? First, it is about the rebuilding and (eventual) rededication of the Temple, which is the theme of Hanukkah. Second, it contains a wonderful vision of the menorah, which had adorned the ancient Temple and which, in its nine-branched version (the *hanukkiah*), would become the enduring symbol of Hanukkah. And third . . . well, wait. You will see.

Hanukkah—The Real Story?

If someone were to ask you, "Why do Jews celebrate Hanukkah?" you would probably say something like: "Because there was a jar of oil that was enough for one night and it lasted for eight nights." Really?

In the third century BCE, the entire Middle East fell under the influence of Greek culture—Hellenism. There were many Jews who wanted to be like the Greeks, admiring their learning and their success in building empires. Their social position was strengthened by the decrees of the Hellenistic Syrian King Antiochus. But Antiochus went too far by insisting on the worship of Greek gods in Jerusalem and defiling the Temple. Jewish loyalists, aroused by a priestly family in Modi'in known as the Maccabees, fought against the Syrians. They recaptured Jerusalem and rededicated the Temple.

Here is what happened, according to the ancient book of Maccabees: "When Judah Maccabee and his companions had recovered the Temple and the city of Jerusalem, they destroyed the altars erected by the gentiles in the marketplace and the sacred enclosures. After purifying the Temple, they made a new altar. Then with fire struck from flint, they offered sacrifice for the first time in two years, burned incense and lit the lamps. . . . The Jews celebrated joyfully for eight days as on Sukkot, remembering how, a little while before, they had spent Sukkot living like wild animals in caves on the mountains."

Any mention of oil there? No. So why do we celebrate eight days of Hanukkah? Because the Maccabees had been so busy fighting that they couldn't celebrate Sukkot, an eight-day festival. Hanukkah began as a belated Sukkot!

There is no mention of a jar of oil until the Talmud—written about *six hundred* years after the events of Hanukkah. "When the Greeks entered the Temple, they defiled all the oils therein. When the Hasmonean dynasty [the Maccabees] defeated them, they found only one cruse of oil with the seal of the High Priest, but which contained sufficient oil for only one day's lighting; yet there was a miracle and they lit the lamp for eight days."

The Hasmoneans, descended from the Maccabees, were terrible kings. The Rabbis of the Talmud didn't like them nor their power politics . . . so, most scholars say they invented the jar of oil story to take military credit away from the Maccabees. And when they needed a haftarah for the Shabbat of Hanukkah, they found one with the words that downplayed military might and emphasized faith: "Not by might, nor by power, but by My spirit—said the Lord of Hosts" (3:6).

Were the Rabbis right? Or were the Maccabees right? While we might like the Rabbis' message of peace and nonviolence, that is not always the way things work. Jewish history, in both ancient Israel and modern Israel, has shown that in order to survive you sometimes need physical power as much as spiritual power.

And by the way, there is an international Jewish sporting event that you may have heard of: the Maccabiah Games, sometimes called the Jewish Olympics. Consider that every time young people play in the Maccabiah Games, named for the Maccabees, they are demonstrating the physical fitness and competitive courage that are part of their heritage. Hanukkah and the haftarah teach that we should strive to be strong in body and spirit.

❖ Va-yiggash: Ezekiel 37:15–28

Imagine this: instead of delivering his famous Gettysburg Address, President Abraham Lincoln took a bunch of sticks, wrote the names of the states on them—both Union and the Confederate states—and then held up the sticks in his hand, and declared: "Our people must be united!"

That is just what happens in this week's haftarah. The prophet Ezekiel, who lived in the time of the Babylonian exile, has a revelation from God. He takes a stick with the name "Judah" on it and combines it with a stick with the name "Joseph," and he brings those sticks together.

Years before this, King Solomon's kingdom split in two—into the Southern Kingdom of Judah and the Northern Kingdom of Israel, which was sometimes called "Joseph" or "Ephraim" (Joseph's son), because the Northern Kingdom contained the tribal territory of Ephraim. The Assyrians destroyed the kingdom of Israel, and exiled its tribes (the Ten Lost Tribes). By combining sticks inscribed with the names of those kingdoms, the prophet Ezekiel was demonstrating that the lost tribes would be found and that the Jewish nation would once again become whole.

The connection to the Torah portion is obvious. Jacob's sons, led by Judah, reunite with their brother Joseph in Egypt. That reunion was a family event; Ezekiel imagines that their descendants, the entire Jewish people, would one day reenact that reunion.

Are the Jews One People?

Perhaps you have noticed something in your own Jewish community. Depending on its size, you might have synagogues that are Reform, Conservative, and Orthodox. There might be a Reconstructionist synagogue in the mix, and perhaps even a Chabad one.

Jewish denominations disagree on many things. Did God give the Torah directly to Moses? Is Jewish law the word of God? Is it absolutely binding? Are Jews allowed to change Jewish law? Can non-Jewish synagogue members vote on congregational matters? Do both Jewish and interfaith couples have the option of being married by the rabbi in the synagogue? If so, who has the right to make those decisions? How "modern" should Jews be?

And then, there are Jews who don't relate to Judaism primarily as a religion, but mostly as a culture. They might not belong to a synagogue, but they go to the local JCC and learn Jewish cooking or play basketball. Some Jews think that helping other Jews is their religion; they might be active in their local Federation or other groups that support Jews in need.

Let's go one step further. Many Jews are Ashkenazim, descended from central and eastern European Jews. But there are also many Jews who are Sephardim, descended from Jews whose ancestors originally came from Portugal or Spain. Add to the mix: Jews from Middle Eastern countries, like Iraq and Syria; Persian Jews from Iran; black Jews; Asian Jews; Jews who converted to Judaism and whose ancestors were not Jewish at all.

It is very confusing. This is why it is so hard to really understand the Jews. They're divided into so many groups that believe different things and that focus on different things. Are the Jews, in fact, one people?

The famous song says, "Am Yisrael Chai," the People of Israel live. There is a unity within our diversity. We have a shared history, a shared book of our origins and beliefs (the Torah), a shared language (Hebrew), and a shared ancient-turned-modern homeland (Israel). As Rabbi Joseph Soloveitchik teaches: "A Jew who flees from a hostile country now knows that he can find a secure refuge in the land of his ancestors. . . . Jews who have been uprooted from their homes can find lodging in the Holy Land."

Yet our diversity is in itself a blessing. It results in different ideas, customs, synagogues, prayers, and even foods. When we agree to disagree on interpretations of Judaism, let's remember that the early sages said that the Torah could be interpreted seventy different ways. Let's remember that there are wonderful Jewish communities all over the world. Let's remember that there are Jews who speak Yiddish and Ladino, not to mention English, Spanish, French, Russian—and every other major language.

A Jew can walk into a synagogue anywhere in the world and be welcome. Whether we agree or disagree with fellow Jews, we care about their well-being. For many Jews who read the news, their eyes automatically focus on Jewish-related stories. Once again, Rabbi Soloveitchik: "There is a covenant of faith that unites all Jews." When a Jew in Jerusalem bleeds, the Jew in, say, New York, feels his or her pain. And that is what Ezekiel would have wanted to happen.

❖ Va-yeḥi: 1 Kings 2:1–12

King David is dying, and he is conveying his final wishes to his son Solomon, who will succeed him as king. There is a clear link to the Torah portion, in which the Patriarch Jacob is dying, and he blesses each of his sons, often foretelling their future and the future of the tribes that will descend from them. We really can't say that David "blesses" Solomon; more accurately, he gives him a small laundry list of things that he wants his son to do after he dies—and they aren't exactly the most pleasant things.

Even though this is not King David's finest hour, let's remember that he ruled for forty years, and was a leader of great accomplishment. He unified the tribes and made Jerusalem the capital. He brought the ark to Jerusalem and laid the foundation for the great Temple that his son would build. David secured the borders of Israel. According to tradition the poet-king even authored many of the beautiful Psalms of the Hebrew Bible. Last but not least, he founded a dynasty, the House of David, that would rule for generations.

But as the king lies dying, the biblical text does not refer to him as "King David," but merely as "David," without his title and without his crown. This teaches us that death comes to everyone, even and especially kings, and that in the final hour it doesn't matter what title you had. Death makes everyone equal.

Manning Up, David Style

There's an odd expression that men sometimes use with other men: "Man up." It's a way of saying: "Hey, do what you have to do, and, while you're at it, show some courage."

That is precisely what King David is saying in this haftarah. He counsels Solomon to be strong and "to be a man," and to follow God's commandments and to pay attention to God's laws.

The great king made his share of mistakes, however. None was greater than his affair with Bathsheba and the cover-up he ordered. And just before he dies there is that "hit list"; David then goes through a list of his enemies and friends, and he tells Solomon what the fate of each one should be.

Did David really want the people who may have insulted or opposed him killed? Was he out for revenge, pure and simple? The medieval commentator Isaac Abravanel says: "David wanted Solomon to know how Joab and Shimei had acted against him so that his son would not appoint them to high office." Perhaps David is urging his son to look carefully at a person's character. Or maybe he uses such strong language to teach Solomon about the value of loyalty: to reward those who have been loyal, and to keep an eye on those who have been disloyal.

Like many leaders whose accomplishments are real, David is far from perfect. Shimon Peres, the Israeli statesman, once said: "Not everything King David did on land [fighting battles] or on roofs [spying on Bathsheba bathing, and then sending her husband to die in battle] appears to me to be Judaism!"

But, in fact, one could argue that all of what King David did, the good and the bad, is part of Jewish history even if not the highest ideals of Judaism. David is a human being, who struggles with his passions and his sins. David did own up to at least some of his biggest mistakes. On a smaller scale than the king, we all do what David did. We sometimes let our passions get the best of us; we are vengeful or petty. Yet we love, dream, and do plenty of good. As Rabbi David Wolpe writes: "David is great because of his complexity, not in spite of it. We see ourselves in this man, and we see this man in ourselves."

EXODUS

❖ Shemot: Isaiah 27:6–28:13; 29:22–23

One little word—that's all it takes to link this week's haftarah with its Torah portion. The reading in the Torah begins with a report of the Israelites who had come (*ha-ba'im*) into Egypt and become slaves. That occurrence of *ha-ba'im* was not so good. Here in the haftarah the prophet Isaiah also begins with *ha-ba'im*: "in days to come [or, in coming days] Israel shall sprout and blossom." Much better.

In the year 722 BCE, the Assyrian Empire conquered the Northern Kingdom of Israel and scattered its inhabitants, who subsequently came to be known as the "Ten Lost Tribes." Isaiah predicts the day will come when the lost tribes will come home. And not only the tribes whom the Assyrians had exiled, but also those exiles who had somehow wound up in Egypt.

This will be like a new exodus from Egypt—yet another link with the Torah portion, in which God promises Moses that the Israelites will be redeemed from Egypt. Those who are faithful to God will become solidly rooted in the Land of Israel; those who are not will be uprooted.

The Mystery of the Ten Lost Tribes

You probably don't know this, because you have probably been asleep in the middle of the night, when there are television shows with names like "The Bible's Mysteries Revealed." One of the favorite topics is: "Whatever happened to the Ten Lost Tribes of Israel?"

Here's what happened to them: When the Assyrians destroyed the Northern Kingdom of Israel, they carried away the inhabitants and scattered them. And no one knows who and where they are. The Ten Lost Tribes disappeared from history. A legend arose that the tribes went on to live on the other side of the mysterious Sambatyon River (which was said to have stopped flowing in honor of Shabbat). Rumors of other sightings continued throughout history and are rather amazing. One traveler in the 1600s reported that he had found an Indian tribe in South America that could say the *Shema*.

The Jews of Ethiopia have long maintained that they are descended from the ancient tribe of Dan. And there are three groups in India that observe Jewish customs and believe they are descended from the lost tribes: the Bene Ephraim of Telugu in southern India, the Bnei Menashe in northern India, and the Bene Israel. There is also the Lemba, a tribe in Zimbabwe and South Africa; they observe certain Jewish customs, and a DNA study shows that there may be some Jewish linkages.

Some people thought that Native Americans were part of the lost tribes, and that that is why Columbus may have brought along an interpreter who spoke Hebrew. Others believed that the British are descended from the lost tribes, and that the British royal family is directly descended from King David. There is even a legend that the Coronation Stone on which British monarchs were crowned was actually the stone that Jacob slept on when he dreamed of the ladder of angels!

Chances are, no one is ever going to find the Ten Lost Tribes of the Northern Kingdom of Israel. They were probably scattered among other peoples in the ancient Near East. In 1889, Jewish scholar Adolf Neubauer wrote: "Where are the ten tribes? We can only answer—nowhere."

So you might ask: why have people been so fascinated by this subject? Perhaps because to claim that you are a descendant of the people of the Bible is a powerful idea. Jewish teachings, as expressed by the Hebrew Bible, are important to many around the globe, and some have wanted to stake their claim to being part of this remarkable people.

The Talmud teaches: "The Ten [Lost] Tribes will enter the future world, as it is said: 'And in that day, a great ram's horn shall be sounded; and the strayed who are in the land of Assyria and the expelled who are in the land of Egypt shall come and worship the Lord on the holy mount, in Jerusalem.'"

While this has not actually come to pass, think of all the "lost" Jews who have returned to modern Israel. You could say that this miracle has come true.

❖ Va'era': Ezekiel 28:25–29:21

Some people say that the prophet Ezekiel was, well, crazy. He had all sorts of wild visions, including imagining that God was traveling across the heavens in a chariot. But one thing is for sure: he really understood the international situation in the world he lived in. Ezekiel was a prophet who started making prophecies in the final days of the kingdom of Judah, and who went with the Judeans into exile in Babylonia. The people of Judah hoped that if they made an alliance with Egypt they would avoid destruction at the hands of the Babylonians.

Ezekiel knew that this was the wrong decision. He knew that Egypt was an untrustworthy ally, and that it would itself be destroyed. So, he engaged in a loud, bitter rant against the Egyptians. But here's the interesting part: when Ezekiel was screaming about the Egyptian problem of his own day, he was thinking about another earlier Egyptian problem— the arrogance of the ancient Pharaoh in the time of the Exodus from Egypt. So, we can read this haftarah not only as a criticism of the Egypt of Ezekiel's time, but also a criticism of the Egypt of the time of Moses.

Jerk Alert

Yes, I know "jerk" is a strong word, and I do not take name-calling lightly. But do you know any jerks? You probably do. And what, exactly, is a jerk? The Merriam-Webster Dictionary defines "jerk" as "a stupid person or a person who is not well-liked or who treats other people badly."

If you read the Bible, here is what you will discover: the overwhelming majority of non-Israelite kings are jerks. (And, to be fair, there are also a few kings of Israel who fit that description). King Nebuchadnezzar of Babylon, who destroyed the ancient kingdom of Judah during Ezekiel's time, certainly treated people badly. In the Bible he was not well liked and is portrayed as not only evil, but, despite his power, also as a helpless, pitiful, broken man.

Then there's King Ahasuerus, in the book of Esther and a famous character in the Purim story. He is hardly the brightest candle in the menorah. In fact, the Rabbinic tradition refers to him as *ha-melekh ha-tipeish*, "the foolish king." He is something of a buffoon and party animal who fortunately has the good sense to listen to Esther.

But, the winner of the Greatest Biblical Jerk Contest is none other than Pharaoh, king of Egypt. The Pharaoh portrayed in the Torah portion is a guy who simply cannot get it right. Somewhere in the back of his mind, he knows that he should be letting the ancient Israelites go, but he simply cannot do so. God has hardened his heart, and then he hardens his own heart—which does not mean an overdose of cholesterol, but implies a stubbornness so severe that he is actually unable to do what is right. That's why God has to bring the plagues on Egypt.

It turns out that "jerkitude" ran in the Pharaoh family. Centuries later, the prophet Ezekiel yells at the Israelites: Don't put any trust in Egypt! And then, to make it even better, Ezekiel turns his attention on the Pharaoh of his time and disses him, big time. "In the tenth year, on the twelfth day of the tenth month, the word of the Lord came to me: O mortal, turn your face against Pharaoh king of Egypt, and prophesy against him and against all Egypt. Speak these words: Thus said the Lord God: I am going to deal with you, O Pharaoh king of Egypt, mighty monster, sprawling in your channels, who said, My Nile is my own; I made it for myself" (29:1–3).

In particular, what disturbs Ezekiel about this Pharaoh? (You might rightly ask at this point: have we ever met a Pharaoh that we've liked?) Ezekiel compares Pharaoh to a crocodile, a reptilian creature that prowls the Nile. That is bad enough, but what else does Ezekiel say about this Pharaoh?

When Pharaoh said, "My Nile is my own; I made it for myself," he is saying that he is a god—and that he created the Nile—for himself! Like the original Pharaoh this ruler is clueless. The guy simply doesn't understand the words of Proverbs: "Pride goes before ruin; arrogance, before failure" (Prov. 16:18).

But even more than that: you can read the Hebrew version of Pharaoh's boast, "I made it [the Nile] for myself," as meaning "I made myself." When you think that you are so great, so powerful, so successful, that you have made yourself—you are so full of yourself, so arrogant, that you will care nothing for others. As Rabbi Andrea Carol Steinberger teaches: "It is as if the haftarah is warning Pharaoh: 'Do not see yourself as the definer of life, of what is possible and impossible to do.'"

Ezekiel compares Pharaoh to a monster, and that's bad enough. But

Ezekiel's audience would have known that in the story of creation, God created the great sea monsters; they didn't create themselves. If only the Pharaohs of history knew that, that nobody is God and nobody creates themselves. A little humility can go a long way.

❖ Bo': Jeremiah 46:13–28

Pharaoh just doesn't get it, whether it was the Pharaoh who lived in the time of Moses, or the Pharaoh who lived in the time of Jeremiah. The later Pharaoh has a starring role in this haftarah. In this week's Torah portion the earlier Pharaoh cannot make the right decisions, and here the later Pharaoh has the same problem.

The prophet Jeremiah who (like Ezekiel) preached in the time before the Babylonians destroyed the kingdom of Judah, counsels the Judeans not to make an alliance with Egypt against Babylon. He's concerned about his fellow Judeans' flight to Egypt. It won't work, he says. He predicts that the Egyptians will be unstable allies, and that their kingdom—like the regime of the Pharaoh of Moses's time—will fall to ruin.

Jerk Alert, Part Two

In last week's haftarah, the prophet Ezekiel warned the Judeans that it was no use trying to make an alliance with the Egyptians. This week, the prophet Jeremiah is saying pretty much the same thing about the Pharaoh of his time.

The Pharaoh who rules during Moses's time was totally arrogant because he thought that he was divine—that he had actually created the Nile for himself. And, this week, we see another symptom of Pharaoh's inability to get it. Jeremiah calls the Pharaoh of his time a "braggart who let the hour go by" (46:17). Actually, "braggart" is only an approximate translation of the Hebrew word *sha'on*. Rashi, the great medieval commentator, teaches: "Pharaoh was a big noisemaker who raised his voice." He was the loudmouth who never shut up. Pharaoh was, as they say, all hot air—a really big disappointment as a leader.

This should not surprise us. Go back to the Pharaoh of Moses's time. First, God hardened his heart and made him refuse to let the Israelites go, thus bringing on more and more plagues, each one worse than the last. It is as if Pharaoh encounters each plague as the first one. It is as if he has no memory of what has already happened to his land and to his people. More than that, he is so convinced of his own power—after all, he thinks he is a god—that he just lets the time slip away from him. He thinks that he has all the time in the world—and then, Egypt falls apart. That is the way it is with the Pharaoh of Jeremiah's time as well. In the process, they hurt not just themselves, but everyone and everything around them.

You probably know people like Pharaoh. There is always that kid who thinks she is so great—such a great athlete, such a great student— that she gets lazy. Sure, she brags a lot. But while she brags she wastes time that she could have devoted to becoming even better. She misses crucial opportunities. She is the "braggart who let the hour go by."

But there is something else going on here as well. Jeremiah knows something that all the Egyptians and the Judeans should have known as well. "Been there, done that." The Israelites had a bad experience with Egypt and Pharaoh (to put it mildly). They should know better than to think that Egypt is all-powerful. Back in the days of Moses, the plagues were a way of fighting the power of the Egyptian gods. That same battle is going on in the haftarah portion: "The Lord of Hosts, the God of Israel, has said: I will inflict punishment on Amon of No and on Pharaoh—on Egypt, her gods, and her kings" (46:25). And the Egyptians themselves should have learned from their historical experience. But they didn't.

When it comes to the Jews, nations don't learn their lessons. Nations that have oppressed the Jews, from ancient Egypt to medieval England and Spain, have come to regret it. Sir Winston Churchill expressed this in strong terms: "Some people like Jews and some do not, but no thoughtful man can doubt the fact that they are beyond all question the most formidable and the most remarkable race which has ever appeared in the world."

Nations and peoples need to stay humble, guard against arrogance, and guard against the tendency to belittle others and become aloof and cruel. Nobody wants to be a jerk, but it can happen. And that can be dangerous for your country, your community, and yourself.

❖ Be-shallaḥ: Judges 4:4–5:31

If you ever cruise through radio stations, you might discover that some are devoted totally to oldies, classic rock songs, usually from the 1970s and earlier. This week's Torah portion contains one of the oldest songs in human history—*Shirat ha-Yam,* the song at the Sea of Reeds (or Red Sea) that Moses, Miriam, and the Israelites sang after the waters of the sea parted and they were able to cross victoriously. It is read on Shabbat Shirah, the Shabbat of Song. The poem, scholars tell us, is a very old form of Hebrew, and may have been written within a few generations of the Exodus.

The song, or poem that appears in this haftarah is likely as old as the one in Exodus, if not older. It is the song of Deborah. This poem is also in archaic Hebrew, and may have been written immediately after the events described, or soon thereafter.

The story of Deborah takes place during the era in Israel's early history known as the period of the judges, and the stories of that time are found in the biblical book of Judges. The judges were actually tribal chieftains and military leaders who welded the tribes of Israel into loose and temporary confederations, largely for the purpose of fighting the Philistines. Deborah was not only a chieftain and a warrior; she was also a prophetess, just like Miriam in this week's corresponding Torah portion. She counsels the Israelite general Barak to draw the Canaanite general Sisera into battle, and, due to Deborah's help, Barak is victorious. The song of Deborah commemorates that victory.

Women Power

There have been many famous lines by American politicians, and here's one of them. In a presidential debate, someone asked a candidate why he had not hired more women for top positions. He responded that if he were president he would turn to the "binders full of women" for candidates to fill cabinet positions.

This week, both the Torah and the haftarah are like binders full of women. In the Torah portion, we have Miriam leading the women of Israel in song at the crossing of the Sea of Reeds (or Red Sea). And, in the haftarah, you have Deborah, the military leader.

The late Jewish singer-composer Debbie Friedman, who notably sang about Miriam, also sang a great song about Deborah: "Devorah the prophet, a woman of fire, her torch in hand. She led the Israelites to victory. Barak said, 'Devorah, I cannot fight, unless you are standing right by my side!'" Friedman based her own song on Deborah's, which states, "But Barak said to her, 'If you will go with me, I will go; if not, I will not go.' 'Very well, I will go with you,' she answered. 'However, there will be no glory for you in the course you are taking, for then the Lord will deliver Sisera into the hands of a woman" (4:8–9).

There are two more women you need to meet.

The first is Jael, the wife of Heber the Kenite (4:17–21). She happens not to be an Israelite, but she is sympathetic to them. She is one tough lady. Sisera, the Canaanite general, flees to her tent, and Jael invites him to enter. She feeds him, which makes him sleepy, and, as he begins to snooze, Jael assassinates him. And, because of this, Israel is victorious over the Canaanite army. The song of Deborah praises her actions.

And there is one more woman whom the song of Deborah mentions. She shows up at the end, and it is easy to miss her. But don't. She is very important.

But first, let's think about the sound of the shofar (the ram's horn) on the High Holy Days. Have you ever noticed that it sounds like a cry? It is written in the Talmud, "One authority thought that this means that it sounds like a long sigh, and the other that it sounds like short, piercing cries."

Whose cries? A woman's. Fine, but which woman? The Talmud says: the mother of Sisera.

Let's recall the scene. Sisera's mother is waiting for him to come home. "Where is that boy? He must be out pillaging." A few hours later: "He must have stopped off with the others to get a drink." A few hours later: "Where could he be? Why hasn't he called?"

As the poem relates,

Through the window peered Sisera's mother,
Behind the lattice she whined:
"Why is his chariot so long in coming?
Why so late the clatter of his wheels?"

The wisest of her ladies give answer;
She, too, replies to herself:
"They must be dividing the spoil they have found:
A damsel or two for each man,
Spoil of dyed cloths for Sisera,
Spoil of embroidered cloths,
A couple of embroidered cloths
Round every neck as spoil.
  (5:28–30)

But Sisera is not coming home. When his mother discovers that her son is dead, she wails—and the ancient Rabbis connect her wails to the origins of the shofar blasts.

Why should we care about this mother of a barbaric Canaanite general? Because, even though she is "the enemy," we can empathize with her. Her son has died. The ability to empathize, even with our enemies, is a major Jewish character trait.

❖ Yitro: Isaiah 6:1–7:6; 9:5–6

If you know someone who is a doctor, or lawyer, or hairdresser (or whatever profession), they probably wanted to become a doctor, lawyer, or hairdresser. That's the way it is with professions. You have to want to do it. The same thing is true with rabbis, cantors, and Jewish educators: those people are involved with that work because they want to do it.

Being a prophet was different. The biblical prophets rarely wanted to be prophets. Moses, Amos, Jeremiah, Jonah—none of them really wanted the job. God called to them (which is where we get the idea of a "calling" or a "vocation"), and told them that they had to speak God's words, and much of the time they weren't very thrilled about it.

The same thing is true for the prophet Isaiah. In this haftarah, he describes the precise moment when God calls him to do prophetic work. He protests. He says that he is "a man of unclean lips" (6:4; we are still not sure what he means—does it mean that he is deceitful, or uses foul language?). Isaiah can complain all he wants but he still has to do what God wants him to do—to speak to the people of Judea.

Even before he begins his calling, Isaiah figures that the people won't understand his message, because they won't want to hear that God wants them to be punished! That's how badly they have sinned. And yet, with it all, Isaiah finally relents. Okay, he says, I'm ready.

Isaiah has a vision of God seated on the divine throne, surrounded by seraphim (angelic figures). For Isaiah this moment of personal revelation is huge—as huge as the moment in the Torah portion at Mount Sinai, when God revealed the Ten Commandments to all the Jewish people. That is why this haftarah is linked to the moment at Sinai: they were both ultimate moments of feeling God's presence.

Awesome

There is a word that almost every kid uses: "awesome." It's used to describe something that is totally cool, almost beyond-belief cool, but also sometimes a bit nerve wracking or scary. Think of how Dorothy and her friends felt while approaching the Wizard of Oz.

That was probably the word that the prophet Isaiah used to describe his experience in this haftarah. "In the year that King Uzziah died, I beheld my Lord seated on a high and lofty throne; and the skirts of His robe filled the Temple. Seraphs stood in attendance on Him. Each of them had six wings: with two he covered his face, with two he covered his legs, and with two he would fly. And one would call to the other, 'Holy, holy, holy! The Lord of Hosts! His presence fills all the earth!'" (6:1–3).

Seeing God, seated on a throne in a heavenly temple, with God's robe filling the entire temple and seraphim (more on them later) singing God's praises. . . . Well, there is simply no other word for that than "awesome." Except maybe "insane," right? Because, seriously, no one can see God, right? And what's with God's robes and feet? God doesn't have a body, right?

Well . . . let's just say that nowadays most people agree that you can't see God, and that God has no body. And it could be that the language describing God was meant by the authors to be taken symbolically. But, back in ancient times, some people really did think that God had a body, and that you could see God. Or, at least Isaiah could. Moses could, too; he saw God's back—in a vision, at least.

Okay, let's deal with perhaps the oddest piece of this story. Isaiah not only caught a glimpse of God; he also saw the seraphim. They seem to be depicted as semidivine beings who surround the divine throne. Some people think they were actually stars. Bible scholar James Kugel writes, "Many people identified these heavenly bodies with gods and goddesses; their path through the heavens was seen as containing clues as to what these deities were planning for people down below." Why are the seraphim up there? They seem to have had only one job: to praise God. And not all at once either. They formed a kind of heavenly choir. According to Rashi, they invite each other to praise God.

Isaiah's vision has a starring role in the Jewish worship service: the *Kedushah* (Sanctification). The congregation echoes the seraphim, singing *"Kadosh, Kadosh, Kadosh,"* rising on their toes as if they were angels flying up to the divine throne. The Kotzker Rebbe comments: "God says, 'I need you to be holy as human beings. I have enough angels.'" So, as we say "Holy, Holy, Holy," we rise up on our heels. But, when the prayer ends, we are back on earth, trying to live an imperfect, aspiring life of mitzvot.

Any way you look at it, Isaiah's experience was, well, awesome. That's how religious feeling starts, but it does not end there. Abraham Joshua Heschel writes: "The root of religion is the question of what to do with the feeling for the mystery. Religion begins with a consciousness that something is asked of us." After his vision Isaiah knows that he is being called, that something is being asked of him. He responds, "Then I heard the voice of my Lord saying, 'Whom shall I send? Who will go for us?' And I said, 'Here am I; send me'" (6:8).

Something is, in fact, asked of us. Prayer, study, mitzvot: all these are ways that we can respond to that feeling of "awesome."

❖ Mishpatim: Jeremiah 34:8–22; 33:25–26

When bad stuff happens, you need to figure out why it is happening. That pretty much sums up the ancient Jewish response to catastrophe. The prophet Jeremiah, preaching in the years leading up to the destruction of Judea by the Babylonians, has his own reason for why the destruction is coming.

It is simply this: in this week's Torah portion, we read that the Israelites were supposed to set free their Judean slaves at the end of the sixth year of service. Yes, the Judean ruling class did that—but, then, they took back the slaves that they had previously released! A bad decision, and God will punish them with exile.

Free Your Slaves: Or Else!

Jeremiah is not a happy camper. No way.

Of course, that is usually the way it is with Jeremiah. None of the prophets were particularly sweet people, but Jeremiah was, in some ways, the most thunderous of them all. There is a term for a long literary work in which the author laments what is going on in society. The term is "jeremiad." You guessed it: it comes from the prophet Jeremiah.

So, here's Jeremiah's "jeremiad du jour." He is angry—and, frankly, who can blame him? He knows that God commanded something very specific about Hebrew slaves: they had to be released after six years. Six years of working, and then set free in the seventh year. Get it? Just like Shabbat.

Now, let's be clear about what we are talking about here. You read the word "slave," and what's the first thing that comes to mind? Probably Israelite slaves in Egypt, and maybe African American slaves in the Old South. But that's really not what this passage is talking about. When it refers to Hebrew slaves, it is actually referring to people who sold themselves into temporary servitude in order to pay off their debts. They were more like indentured servants. But, for the period of time they served, these servants were owned by someone else, which is why we refer to them as slaves.

And why did the Israelites have to free their slaves? Because they knew what it was like to be slaves themselves, in Egypt! How could they have done anything else? As Rabbi Lori Cohen writes: "After having been recently released from bondage in Egypt, the Israelites were commanded by God to be especially sensitive to the needs of the slave. The slave was both a human being with feelings and insights, as well as property, having monetary value." So they had to be sensitive to the feelings of their slaves (which was totally not what happened in Egypt), and they had to set their slaves free after a set period of time (which was also totally not what happened in Egypt).

No wonder Jeremiah is so angry. This violated the covenant that King Zedekiah had made with the people of Jerusalem: he had promised to set free the Hebrew slaves. And it also violated an earlier, even more important covenant: the covenant that God made with the Israelites when God took them out of Egypt. The wealthy Judeans cheated. Yes, they freed their workers—but then they took them back. As punishment, God cut the Israelite kingdom into shreds. As Jeremiah proclaimed, "But afterward they turned about and brought back the men and women they had set free, and forced them into slavery again" (34:11).

Jeremiah then quotes God's response. "Assuredly, thus said the Lord: You would not obey Me and proclaim a release, each to his kinsman and countryman. Lo! I proclaim your release—declares the Lord—to the sword, to pestilence, and to famine; and I will make you a horror to all the kingdoms of the earth" (34:17).

The ancient philosopher Philo writes: "The Hebrew legislation concerning the Hebrew bondsman breathes kindness and humanity throughout." And, by refusing to live that way, the Judeans had profaned God's name (34:16). That act of refusing to set slaves free, according to Jeremiah, was the reason why the Judeans were forced to go into exile—not because of a "religious" sin, like idolatry, but because they failed to observe the divine laws of social justice.

The lesson? God cares about so much more than simply "religion" as ritual; justice is supremely important. And it should be essential to us too. For some reason, the Torah did not completely abolish slavery, despite its ambivalence about it. Even in an imperfect world, always pursue justice.

❖ Terumah: 1 Kings 5:26–6:13

First, God told the Israelites how to construct the ancient *mikdash* or *mishkan* (sanctuary) that they would carry with them through the wilderness. That was in the Torah portion. But it turns out that the *mishkan* was nothing less than a scale model—a trial run, if you will—for a far greater building project: the construction of the Temple in Jerusalem by King Solomon, which happened around 958 BCE.

Now, it wasn't that the two building projects were exactly the same.

Hardly. When God told the Israelites to build the *mikdash/mishkan*, they were to do so willingly. That was not the way that Solomon did it, however. The biblical text says that he "imposed forced labor on all Israel"—sort of like Pharaoh had done in Egypt! Not only that: when the Israelites built the *mikdash/mishkan*, they did it themselves. That was not the way that Solomon had done it, however. He had help—and that is the sweetest part of the story.

Bring in the Outside Contractor!

It wasn't always this good for Jews in America. Once upon a time Jewish medical students could not practice in many hospitals. In order to solve that problem, Jewish communities built their own hospitals. Here are some of their names: Cedars of Lebanon Hospital in Lebanon, Ohio; another is called Cedars of Lebanon in Miami, Florida (nowadays it is simply called Cedars Miami Medical Center); in Los Angeles is the Mount Sinai Home for the Incurables (uplifting name!)—it merged with Cedars of Lebanon and became Cedars-Sinai.

What's up with all those hospitals called "cedars?" They remind us that when King Solomon built the first Temple in Jerusalem, he built it out of those powerful trees that had been imported from the land of Phoenicia, just to the north of the land of Israel, the land which is now Lebanon. Who sent him those cedars? King Hiram of Tyre, a city-state on the Mediterranean coast.

Solomon and Hiram had a great relationship. The biblical text says that there was "friendship" (*shalom*) between them. But a better translation would be that there was "peace" between them. It says that "the two of them made a treaty [*brit*]," but we all know that *brit* really means "covenant." This was no ordinary friendship; it was a deep partnership. Hiram had been friends with Solomon's father, King David. Friends? Actually, the text says that Hiram *oheiv* David—he loved him. In fact, he had built David's palace for him! (2 Samuel 5: 11). So we are talking about a "bromance" that lasted for two generations!

But here's the big question: Hiram was not an Israelite. Why would he have been so enthusiastic about building the Temple for Solomon's god?

Before Hiram became king of Tyre, the ancient Phoenicians had worshiped many gods. Hiram changed that. He made sure that each Phoenician city had, at most, a pair of gods—a god and a goddess. Hiram had built beautiful temples to his gods. The Greek historian Herodotus would write of them: "I visited the temple and found that the offerings which adorned it were numerous and valuable, not the least remarkable being two pillars, one of pure gold, the other of emerald which gleamed in the dark with a strange radiance."

So there's the answer to why Hiram liked David and Solomon so much. The building of the Temple meant that the Israelites could no longer worship at various local cultic places, and it was certainly part of the ongoing Israelite war against idolatry. Hiram looked south toward Israel and saw Solomon—and there may have been something within his soul that really responded to what Solomon was doing. Hiram wanted to help.

One more thing about Hiram. Because the Bible doesn't mention his death, some sages thought that Hiram, in fact, never died—just like the prophet Elijah. As this author, Rabbi Jeffrey Salkin, writes: "In the World to Come, Hiram looks down upon earth, and upon Jerusalem, and he smiles inwardly at all that the Jewish people has done in that place and on that Land."

❖ Tetsavveh: Ezekiel 43:10–27

In order to be a Jew, you need a good imagination. And that is precisely what the prophet Ezekiel has. This week's Torah portion ends with a description of the incense altar that will be used in the ancient Tabernacle (*mishkan*). Generations later, the prophet Ezekiel has accompanied his people into exile in Babylonia, and he imagines aloud what the someday-to-be-rebuilt Temple in Jerusalem will look like.

But before he tells them about that grand plan, he must get them to repent of the sins that forced them to go into exile in the first place. Ezekiel mixes hope and responsibility.

The Vision Thing

The prophet Ezekiel, writing from exile in Babylonia, has a vision of how the rebuilt Temple will look, focusing on the altar. This makes sense because the altar, where sacrifices will be offered, is certainly a central place in the Temple. But he makes something very clear: he will only tell the exiled Judeans about the Temple's design after they have acknowledged their sins. Because Ezekiel, like the other prophets, believed that it was those sins that got them into Babylon in the first place. The siddur (prayer book) agrees with this, reminding Jewish worshipers: "Because of our sins, we were exiled from our land."

If sins could result in exile from the land, sins could also lead to the destruction of Judea and the First Temple in Jerusalem. Which sins were responsible for these? Take your pick. The Mishnah says, "It was because of idol worship, prohibited sexual relations, bloodshed, and neglect of the agricultural sabbatical year." We can understand the first three. Idolatry means worshiping other gods. Prohibited sexual relations destroy the fabric of the family. Bloodshed is, well, bloodshed—destroying the very image of God within every human being. But the Mishnah goes one step further: neglecting the sabbatical year of the land, refusing to let the land lie fallow for one year in seven—disrespecting the Land of Israel and, with it, the earth itself.

But wait. There's more. It's written in the Talmud, "Jerusalem was destroyed only because they desecrated the Sabbath," . . . "only because they neglected reading the *Shema,* morning and evening," . . . "only because they neglected the education of school children." These are religious failings, though we might also think that the punishment—destruction and exile—doesn't fit the crime. And here is another: "Jerusalem was destroyed only because the small and the great were made equal." This means that there was no longer any authority in the land. We're no longer talking about religious issues now; we are talking about what happens in a society that falls into anarchy.

But if there is to be a real reason for exile, this quote from the Talmud might be it. "Because there was baseless hatred." Simply put: the Jews hated each other for no particular reason, and could not get along—and, for that reason, destruction resulted. To which Rabbi Abraham Isaac Kook, the first chief rabbi of prestate Israel, replies: "There is no such thing as 'baseless love.' Why baseless? This other person is a Jew, and I am obligated to honor him. There is only 'baseless hatred'—but 'baseless love'? No!" Hatred without cause will tear apart a society, and this internal weakness will make it vulnerable.

The obligation to love our fellow human, on the other hand, confers a strong and caring society that is much more cohesive and strong, able to withstand external challenges.

Here is another Talmudic teaching, in the form of a legend about the destruction of Judea and the First Temple: "When the First Temple was about to be destroyed, bands of young priests took the keys of the Temple and mounted the roof of the Temple and exclaimed: 'Master of the Universe, we did a bad job guarding the Temple. We are returning the keys to you.' They then threw the keys up toward heaven. And the figure of a hand emerged, and took the keys from them."

Perhaps God still has the keys to the ancient Temple. Perhaps it is time for modern Jews to ask God: "Can we have the keys back? We are ready to practice Judaism even better than our ancestors did. We are ready to let go of hate and let love prevail." Wouldn't that be a wonderful vision?

❖ Ki Tissa': 1 Kings 18:1–39

Here's the deal with Moses and the prophet Elijah, who stars in this week's haftarah portion: they are basically the same person. Moses gathered all Israel around a mountain (Sinai); Elijah gathered all (of the Northern Kingdom of) Israel around a mountain (Carmel). Moses dies mysteriously (no one knows where he is buried); Elijah dies mysteriously (swept into the heavens by horses and chariots of fire). Moses went ballistic over idolatry (the Golden Calf, in this week's Torah portion); Elijah goes ballistic over idolatry (the worship of Baal, in the haftarah).

Elijah is totally bummed. It seemed to him that the entire people of the Northern Kingdom of Israel have abandoned God and are worshiping the Canaanite god Baal. That's because Queen Jezebel, who came from ancient Phoenicia, brought Baal worship into the kingdom, along with a bunch of Baal prophets. So Elijah sets up a contest on Mount Carmel. Its purpose: to see which god was more powerful—the Jewish God, or Baal.

No doubt about it, the Baal religion was weird. The prophets of Baal offered up sacrifices to their god. They cut themselves with knives and lances until the blood gushed out! (Why? Who knows? Perhaps they thought that this was what their god wanted. Perhaps they believed that blood, being the essential life force, should be offered to their god.) The prophets of Baal set up a sacrifice to Baal; Elijah set up a sacrifice to God. Fire descended from heaven, consuming Elijah's burnt sacrifice. All the People of Israel present fell on their faces, chanting, "The Lord alone is God, the Lord alone is God."

Make a Choice

Elijah senses that all the people of the Northern Kingdom of Israel are now worshiping the foreign god Baal. He knows that this idolatry is a betrayal of Judaism and it will lead to all kinds of sinful behavior associated with the Canaanites. Elijah may have also been afraid that the Israelites would give up their own identity and assimilate into the surrounding culture.

So Elijah needs to force the issue. He summons the prophets of Baal to a showdown on Mount Carmel, near modern-day Haifa. Here's the test: who will consume the sacrifice that has been laid out—Baal or Adonai?

Elijah wants the People of Israel to be clear with themselves as well. "Elijah approached all the people and said, 'How long will you keep hopping between two opinions? If the Lord is God, follow God; and if Baal, follow Baal!' But the people answered him not a word" (18:21). Make up your minds already! As playwright David Mamet said: "Every sin contains within it the kernel of the sin of the Golden Calf." Elijah learned from Moses that idolatry is an old and persistent problem. It's a betrayal of what Israel stands for. It cannot be tolerated.

The episode on Mount Carmel is one of the most important moments in all of Jewish history. Although most people don't notice, it so important that it reappears at what might be the holiest moment of the Jewish year. Every time we observe Yom Kippur we are recalling the drama of Elijah and the people at the mountain.

The confrontation at Mount Carmel was an all-day event—starting in the morning, and ending in late afternoon—at the time of the "grain offering" (*minchah*). That was the moment when the People of Israel saw that God had accepted the sacrifice and that Baal had not done so. God won! And then the people cry out: "The Lord alone is God, The Lord alone is God!" (*Adonai hu ha-Elohim*). Bible scholar Alex Israel writes: "Elijah has achieved his objective: The people have made their commitment to God. In that twilight hour—the Ne'ilah hour at the end of the day—Israel proclaims its undivided religious allegiance."

The *Ne'ilah* service is the final service on Yom Kippur. It happens late in the afternoon—just when the confrontation on Mount Carmel moves to its exciting climax. It is as if the entire day of Yom Kippur is a playing out of the day on Mount Carmel. Every Jew imagines himself or herself standing not only at Sinai, but at Mount Carmel too. Who is the true god—Adonai, the god of sacred relationships, or the false god, Baal, the god of power and control?

At the end of Yom Kippur, Jews imagine that God (Adonai) has, once again, won. And they proclaim the same words that the People of Israel proclaimed back on Mount Carmel: "The Lord alone is God, The Lord alone is God!" (*Adonai hu ha-Elohim*). These are the words that are dramatically repeated seven times just before the blast of the shofar that signals the end of Yom Kippur.

A final thought: After Baal failed to consume the sacrifice, we read that Elijah "repaired the damaged altar of the Lord" (18:30). Actually, the text says that the altar was *va-yirape*, healed. Why does the prophet repair, or heal, the altar, rather than build a new one? Because he wants to demonstrate that when our relationship with God becomes disrupted, we can fix it. We can heal it. In fact, God wants us to do precisely that, and it all begins with making a choice.

❖ Va-yakhel–Pekudei: 1 Kings 7:40–50

Despite the fact that the second book of the Torah is called Exodus (or, in Hebrew, Shemot, "Names"), the greatest number of words in the book of Exodus is devoted, not to names, but to the construction of the ancient Tabernacle (the *mishkan*). It's not because religious buildings are the most important thing in the world; it's because those buildings make community possible. That is why there are several *haftarot* about the construction of the ancient Temple in Jerusalem, which was the successor to the desert Tabernacle and King Solomon's biggest project.

In this haftarah, we meet a talented bronze worker named Hiram (in Hebrew, Hirom). (That name may sound familiar to you, but he's not to be confused with Hiram in Haftarat Terumah, who is King Hiram of Tyre, a city-state in modern-day Lebanon, who helped King Solomon build the ancient Temple.)

In this haftarah, we read about Hiram the artisan. His bronze contributions were so heavy that King Solomon could not weigh them. We also read about the gold furnishings that Solomon made for the Temple: altar, candelabra, basins, ladles, and doors. All these details of the Temple parallel the description of the Tabernacle.

Call Me Hiram/Hirom

How many ways can you spell the name Deborah. Yes, there's Deborah—or is it spelled Debra? And her nickname: Debbie, or Debbi, or Debi, or Debby?

The same thing is true with Hiram. It's spelled two different ways in Hebrew. So sometimes it is more like Hirom. To make matters worse, there are two different people with the two variations of the same name!

First, as mentioned above, there is King Hiram of Tyre, who helped King Solomon build the ancient Temple in Jerusalem. And now, in this haftarah, we read of another person with the same name, and he also helped with the building of the ancient Temple.

King Hiram was mostly involved in sending building materials—notably, those majestic trees known as the cedars of Lebanon—to Solomon to use in the construction of the Temple. This other Hiram is involved in the same project but from a different angle. He is a talented bronze worker. It seems that his major talent is in crafting huge, rounded pieces made of bronze. He comes from Tyre, like King Hiram. But he definitely is not a king, because he does not come from anything resembling royal lineage. We read that Hiram's father was a craftsman of Tyre, and that his mother was a widow of the tribe of Naphtali. That would make him half-Israelite on his mother's side. Whether he considered himself Jewish is unclear, since in those days lineage passed from the father.

Shall we imagine a backstory for this "new" Hiram? Where did he come from? How did he get his name? How did he learn his trade?

As I have written: "It would start with a nameless Israelite widow. She meets a nameless Tyrian craftsman, and they fall in love. She gives birth to an infant whom she names Hiram, and, as fathers will often do, his father teaches him everything he knows about metalworking and other kinds of craftsmanship." As for Hiram's mother, perhaps she also taught him things. Perhaps she taught him of her own people— their stories, dreams, and songs.

And so, Hiram became a craftsman. A rather good craftsman. Perhaps the actions of his royal namesake had inspired him, and he willingly and enthusiastically made the trip to Jerusalem to become part of the holy process of building the Temple. Perhaps—just perhaps— Solomon's request sparked something inside this Hiram's soul, just like the spark in the king that led to his collaboration with Solomon. True, he had not been raised in the Land of Israel. True, he had been cut off from his people. But he knew one thing: when Solomon called him, he wanted to help.

Rabbi W. Gunther Plaut writes: "In the Torah, God chose Bezalel to do the work on the Tabernacle; in the haftarah, Solomon chose Hiram to help." I wonder what Solomon thought of the coincidence that the king and the key craftsman had (almost) the same name. Maybe it wasn't just a coincidence . . .

LEVITICUS

❖ Va-yikra': Isaiah 43:21–44:23

To review: there are two biblical prophets named Isaiah. The first was a prophet who lived in the eighth century BCE. Then, there was a prophet who was called Second Isaiah. That wasn't actually his name (no one ever called him Isaiah 2). He was actually an anonymous prophet who preached during the sixth century BCE at the time when the Babylonian exile was about to end. (Sometimes, he is called Deutero-Isaiah; "deutero" means "repeat.") Everything in the book of Isaiah that comes after chapter 40 is the work of this anonymous prophet. (Some scholars say that there was even a third Isaiah, but we won't get into that now.)

The Second Isaiah was perhaps the most optimistic prophet in Jewish history. And why wouldn't he be? He felt sure he was about to witness one of the great moments in history—the coming return of the Jews to their homeland. His messages were always about hope.

According to Isaiah, God is upset that the Jews haven't brought offerings to God (that's the connection with the Torah portion Va-yikra', which is all about the sacrificial system), and haven't remembered their ethical obligations. No doubt, many Jews turned to the worship of Babylonian gods, and the prophet finds that both stupid and upsetting.

But then Isaiah's tone radically changes. Hey, Jews! We can reestablish our relationship with God! It's time to come home! We can do it!

What's Wrong with Idolatry, Anyway?

If there is one thing that made the prophets go ballistic, it was idolatry. Worshiping false gods is prohibited in the Ten Commandments. Over and over again, the Torah condemns those who worship the gods of ancient Canaan. The prophets hammer that message home: idolatry is bad.

But what was really so wrong about idolatry? Was it simply the worship of gods who didn't happen to be Adonai? Was it the worship of many gods, rather than the one true God? Was it the kind of worship that those false gods demanded—human sacrifice and other disgusting, terrible things? Or was there something much more basic?

The prophets objected to idolatry for all the reasons above, and we find an additional reason in this haftarah. Several times, the prophet known as Second Isaiah goes on a rant against those who make idols. "The makers of idols all work to no purpose; and the things they treasure can do no good, as they themselves can testify" (44:9). That's his biggest issue with idolatry: It's the issue of what the idolater worships! He or she is worshiping an object that someone created. And even if the idol is symbolic of some god, it's preposterous to bow down to an object itself.

Oh, sure, the craftsman who made the idol was very good at his or her work, and the prophet even gives credit where credit is due: "The craftsman in iron, with his tools, works it over charcoal and fashions it by hammering, working with the strength of his arm" (44:12).

But the prophet also has to laugh at that workmanship. Let's say that the idol maker uses a tree to make a wooden idol. The craftsman uses part of the tree to make the idol, and the other part of that same tree simply as firewood to use for roasting meat! How "holy" could the wooden god actually be, then?

You probably already know the famous legend about how thirteen-year-old Abram (Abraham) broke the idols that his father had made. "Abram seized a stick, smashed all the images, and placed the stick in the hand of the biggest of them. When his father came, he asked: 'Who did this to the gods?' Abram answered: 'A woman came with a bowl of fine flour and said: "Here, offer it up to them." When I offered it, one god said, "I will eat first," and another said, "No, I will eat first." Then the biggest of them rose up and smashed all the others.' His father replied: 'Are you messing around with me? They cannot do anything!' Abram answered: 'You say they cannot. Let your ears hear what your mouth is saying!'" Young Abram figured out that if you make something, that means you actually have power over it. And if you have power over something, then that "something" cannot be a god. Because you created it, it is actually a part of you.

Rabbi Ed Feinstein teaches: "An idol is . . . a projection of my desires, my fears, my needs. . . . So . . . I flatter and sweet talk the idol. I bring gifts to the idol and I beg the idol to do what I need done in the world. And if the idol complies, I become its loyal servant. And if not, . . . I'll shop my needs around until I find a god who's interested in helping me in exchange for my devotion. Cosmic room service."

That's why idols cannot be gods. Because they are simply projections of our own desires. So idolatry is a form of self-worship. And God is always much bigger than that.

❖ Tsav: Jeremiah 7:21–8:3; 9:22–23

Let's remember the word "jeremiad." A "jeremiad" is a hot, angry, rant that someone delivers in the hope of changing society. The word comes from the prophet Jeremiah. Jeremiah, who preached during the final days of the Southern Kingdom of Judah, was sure of many things. Among them was his belief that sacrifices alone could not make God happy. Rather, those sacrifices had to be accompanied by acts of justice.

It's the subject of sacrifice that links this haftarah back to the Torah portion, which is a continuation of Leviticus's description of the ancient sacrificial system. Jeremiah is warning the people: if you keep worshiping idols in the Temple, and if you keep sacrificing your children to idols in the valleys of Jerusalem, God will destroy Jerusalem, and you will all be destroyed as well.

It gets even worse. Jeremiah tells the people that even after they have been killed, their bodies will be pulled from their graves and left to rot under the sun and the stars—under the "hosts of heaven," which they have worshiped.

Now, you know why they call these kinds of proclamations "jeremiads." Jeremiah was angry. He must have believed in shock therapy. Although not all his message is so negative, much of it is—just like political advertising today!

Idols Are More Than Statues

The prophets were soldiers in a war—and that war was against idolatry. As the writer Norman Podhoretz said: "This was a war to establish the truth of the great revelation—namely, that there was only one God, not many gods, that you couldn't see him, you couldn't make a picture of him, you couldn't make a statue of him to which you would then bow down."

Yes, making a god with your own hands was surely idolatry. But it didn't end there. Jeremiah didn't like the way that the Judeans were worshiping God. He and the other prophets thought that the worship of *anything* other than God was idolatry.

Jeremiah says: "Thus said the Lord: Let not the wise man glory in his wisdom; let not the strong man glory in his strength; let not the rich man glory in his riches" (Jer. 9:23). It's a continuation of the theme in last week's haftarah portion, on the danger of self-worship.

Sometimes, people think their intellect is the most important thing there is, and that leads to abuses of knowledge. Sometimes, people think power is the most important thing, and that leads to abuses of power. It's not only nations that do this; individuals do it as well. (Think of the athletic coach who abuses his or her power over team members.) And, sometimes, people think that their money and what it can buy is the most important thing. (Think of how much some families spend on bar or bat mitzvah celebrations!)

Rabbi Dini Lewittes puts it this way: "Are we not guilty of making academic achievement, political power and material wealth the ultimate values of our Jewish community? Perhaps if we listen carefully to Jeremiah's moving words, we can create a community that reflects the most cherished values of our people: justice, kindness and equity."

So, what is the real way to worship God, asks Jeremiah? To reject idolatry. The Talmud teaches: "Whoever rejects idolatry has already observed the entire Torah." We worship God by knowing that "I the Lord act with kindness, justice, and equity in the world; for in these I delight—declares the Lord" (9:22–23).

Act that way; that is all that God really wants us to do.

❖ Shemini: 2 Samuel 6:1–7:17

Do not, do not! mess around with holy stuff. That seems to be one of the messages of this week's Torah portion. Nadab and Abihu fail to take their sacred responsibilities seriously, and they are consumed by fire. A similar thing happens here in 2 Samuel (which is how the haftarah is linked to the Torah portion): King David is bringing the ark to Jerusalem, the city that he conquered from the Jebusites. By bringing the ark to Jerusalem, David was solidifying his control over the city and establishing it as his political and religious capital.

What a wild celebration it is, complete with music and dancing! But in the midst of the festivities, something terrible happens. One of the oxen pulling the cart with the ark in it stumbles, and it looks as if the ark is going to fall. (If you have ever seen someone almost drop a Torah scroll, then you know how scary this can be.) A well-meaning man, Uzzah, reaches out to steady the ark, and God strikes him down. Like the story in the Torah portion, we are hard pressed to understand the tragedy, but the lesson about breaching boundaries seems clear, if brutal.

(Let's not forget that the ancient Israelites believed the ark had magical powers. There is a famous scene in the movie *Raiders of the Lost Ark* in which Nazis who steal the ancient ark actually melt!)

Three months later, David decides to move the ark again, and once again, there is music and dancing. This time, however, King David gets so wrapped up in the dancing that his robe opens up, giving everyone a glimpse of, well, you know. . . . David's wife Michal scolds him over this breach of dignity, with sad results. David does not take kindly to her criticism. Their relationship is never the same; in fact David apparently has little to do with Michal from then on.

King David: The Dancing Fool

In 1987, songwriters Susanna Clark and Richard Leigh wrote a song, "Come from the Heart," which contained the following lyrics: "You've got to sing like you don't need the money, love like you'll never get hurt. You've gotta dance like nobody's watchin', It's gotta come from the heart if you want it to work."

If anything could summarize the life and soul of King David, that song would be it. David was probably the most complex character in the entire Hebrew Bible—a king, warrior, lover, poet, musician, and, apparently, a spirited dancer as well.

David is so enthusiastic about bringing the ark to Jerusalem that he just goes wild. The music is loud. The spirit is contagious. David dances. He actually whirls around in circles, which is a mystical kind of dance, the kind of dance that Sufi Muslim whirling dervishes do. It's not just a dance to show that you're happy; it's a dance that makes you want to jump up and touch God (if that could be possible).

And then, along comes David's wife Michal, and she gets real sarcastic with him. She feels it is beneath the king's dignity to make a spectacle of himself in front of everyone. By the way, although the Bible says little about her, according to the sages she was one tough woman. The Talmud says: "Michal wore tefillin [which traditionally women did not do] and the sages did not attempt to prevent her."

David retorts that he was happy to do what he did, that he would do it again—and, by the way, "I'm the king now—and your father, the late King Saul—isn't." Ouch. (And, by the way, notice that the text never identifies Michal as being David's wife, only as the daughter of Saul—King Saul, who had been insanely jealous of David. Perhaps that was more important to her identity than being David's wife. You think that maybe Michal was perhaps carrying a grudge on behalf of her late father?)

The story ends sadly. It says that Michal didn't have children. We don't know why. Was it because David refused to sleep with her again after that incident? We hear nothing more about Michal, even though much is said about David's other wives.

Even though he was the king, David showed passion. He could let go of his role and simply have fun. This is very rare, even and especially today. For example, Queen Elizabeth of Great Britain is known for her stiff upper lip and not showing much emotion—neither joy nor sorrow. But not so David. Zvi Kolitz writes: "David had both the ability to transform a nation and the power to be himself. As a king he knew the importance of decorum, but he also knew the power of simplicity and the sincerity of true passion."

But there is something else about David that we learn in this portion. Let's remember that his motive for bringing the ark to Jerusalem was pure, as was his wanting to build a temple for God. "Here I am dwelling in a house of cedar, while the Ark of the Lord abides in a tent" (7:2). For all his grandeur and power, David was actually humble. He did not think it proper that his house should be greater than a house for God. While God, through the prophet Nathan, conveys to David that his request to build a temple for God will be denied (although granted to his son Solomon), God establishes a covenant with David that his line will rule Judah for generations.

You have to love David. He is a mighty king and yet he is perhaps the most human person in the entire Bible. His accomplishments, and his mistakes, were huge . . . and he never forgot how to dance.

❖ Tazria': 2 Kings 4:42–5:19

Poor Naaman, the Syrian commander who features prominently in our haftarah. "Naaman, commander of the army of the king of Aram, was important to his lord and high in his favor, for through him the Lord had granted victory to Aram. But the man, though a great warrior, was a leper" (5:1).

Not: "He has leprosy." Not: "He's afflicted with leprosy." It's not that he *has* a disease. The disease has *him*. He *is* the disease. He's a leper. (That is the connection with this week's Torah portion, even though, *tzara'at* was not, in fact, leprosy, as the commentary on the parashah in this book explains.) Hardly anyone would refer to President Franklin D. Roosevelt as a cripple; rather, we think of him as a great man and a great president who was a victim of polio. But Naaman is simply referred to as a leper. The disease has hijacked his identity.

Naaman seeks healing from the prophet Elisha. And he not only gets healed; he is so impressed with what the prophet seems to have done for him that he even begins to worship God, rather than his Syrian gods. In the words of Jewish liturgy, Naaman experiences *refuat ha-guf* (healing of the body) and *refuat ha-nefesh* (healing of the soul).

You Gotta Heal Yourself

Naaman was a great general—brave, and loyal to his king. That's the good news.

The bad news is this: No matter how many battles Naaman won, the most difficult war that he fought was the war against his nasty skin ailment *tzara'at*. And he is willing to do almost anything to get rid of it.

Why did he get *tzara'at* in the first place? We really don't know; it was not his fault. But remember that the sages saw things differently; they looked for a flaw in people's character that might explain their "punishment." A midrash teaches: "Naaman was arrogant on account of his being a great warrior, and this is why he was afflicted with leprosy." But Naaman has more than a problem with *tzara'at*. He has a bit of an attitude problem. And that might be even harder to cure.

Naaman learns that the best way for him to get relief from his *tzara'at* is to visit Elisha, "the prophet in Samaria," who will heal him. He is so desperate for a cure that he seeks to cross enemy lines. While the king of Israel initially refuses the request of the Syrian commanding general, thinking it's a ruse, he is eventually persuaded to allow Naaman to cross into his territory (a humanitarian gesture).

Naaman travels to the prophet's house with his horses and chariots. He is fighting a war against his illness (we still speak this way; think of the "war on cancer"). Elisha tells Naaman to go bathe in the Jordan River seven times, and he will be healed. Naaman is not a good patient. Most likely he was thinking, "What do I need this for? We have perfectly good rivers back in my country!" Not only that: he thought that Elisha would simply wipe his illness away: "I thought . . . he would . . . wave his hand toward the spot, and cure the affected part" (5:11).

What was Naaman's attitude problem? Did he think that the prophet can do all the work for him? There are many people who believe this, even today. They think that you can be healed by prayer. And there might some truth in that. It is possible that when people know that they are the subject of prayers, their emotional and mental outlooks improve and this can help in the healing process. Often, though, there is more involved, like getting medical care. Doctors can play a big role, but no doctor can heal someone on his or her own. People have to be active partners in their own treatment—taking medication if needed, exercising, watching their diet, getting enough rest, and the like.

Naaman, too, had to take an active part in his own healing. Fortunately he listened to the advice of his servants, who told him to calm down, be cooperative, and do what the prophet told him to do. As I have written: "Naaman needs to learn that no prophet can do for him what he needs to do for himself. He had to take responsibility for his own affliction and he had to physically take himself to the Jordan River and immerse himself seven times—seven times representing the seven days of the week, the gift of time from the Creator God."

Naaman is healed. In gratitude, he embraces the God of Israel, like so many people who have joined the Jewish people over the ages. The prophet Elisha tells him to go home *l'shalom,* "to peace." Maybe he then had inner peace, and maybe he, as a great general, would return to his country to work toward outer peace, for his people.

Naaman has learned a valuable lesson: if you want to be healed—from an illness, or even a bad attitude—you cannot expect that others will do it for you. You have to do it for yourself.

❖ Metsora': 2 Kings 7:3–20

To be Jewish means to be have hope. And here is why.

In this haftarah the Northern Kingdom of Israel (also known as Samaria) is at war with Syria (also known as Aram). The conditions are terrible. A famine breaks out that is so severe that people actually resort to cannibalism. Four Israelite lepers (leprosy, or some kind of skin disease, is the connection to the Torah portion) are sitting outside the gates of Samaria. They believe that they are on the verge of death, and so they decide to go over to the Arameans—after all, they have nothing to lose. When they get to the Aramean camp, they find it deserted, because God had frightened the soldiers away.

The lepers find enough provisions in the Aramean camp to feed and equip themselves and others in Samaria. The Israelite army goes out and finds supplies that the Aramean army has left by the side of the road, and they bring these things into the Israelite camp.

The prophet Elisha ("the man of God," 7:18) had prophesized that there would be enough food for everyone, and that the price of barley and flour would therefore come down. An officer expressed his doubts about that happening. But it did, and people rushed out of the city of Samaria for the food—and in the process, trampled the officer to death.

The moral of the story: don't lose hope; things can always get better.

We Will Survive!

Call it a coincidence if you want, but this Torah portion and its accompanying haftarah often appear right around Yom ha-Shoah (the commemoration of the Holocaust), or sometimes a week later, at Yom ha-Atzmaut (Israel Independence Day).

So, even though you might find the whole topic of leprosy, or *tzara'at*, to be profoundly unappealing, pay attention. There is much that we can learn.

Think back to Samaria at the time that this haftarah takes place. Consider the conditions there. The Samarians are at war. People are starving. And then this group of four lepers—who are already the lowest of the low, because lepers were always ostracized from society—take a look at each other and say, in essence: "Just what are we doing here? Yes, we might die. But why should we wait for death? Let's do something outrageous. Let's join the Arameans!"

An act of treason? Probably. Admirable? Probably not. An act of desperation? You bet. The point is: they refuse to simply sit around and die. They have to do something. And they do. And luckily for them, God had scared the daylights out of the Aramean army, who had run away and left all their stuff behind, and the famine lifted.

And what does this have to do with Yom ha-Shoah, or Yom ha-Atzmaut?

Imagine what those four lepers looked like. Pretty bad, right? Actually, probably pretty gruesome—emaciated, with their skin peeling? That is exactly what the survivors of the Shoah, the Holocaust, were like. And like the people of ancient Samaria, they had managed to survive. True: unlike the lepers in our story, none of them went over to the German army. But here's the major point: they refused to die. They refused to give up hope. They believed that they could live again and make new lives. And that is precisely what they did.

The modern Jewish thinker Emil Fackenheim said: "We are forbidden to hand Hitler any posthumous victories." What he meant was that Jews have to maintain hope and keep on living. That is what the Jews did after the Shoah, and because of that faith in life the State of Israel came into being. Remember the national anthem of the Jewish people— "Hatikvah" (The hope), which says "Our hope is not yet lost—the hope of two thousand years. To be a free people in our land, in Zion, and in Jerusalem."

The book of Job expresses this hope in another way, comparing us to trees that are cut down but survive because of their roots. "There is hope for a tree; if it is cut down it will renew itself; its shoots will not cease. If its roots are old in the earth, and its stump dies in the ground, at the scent of water it will bud and produce branches like a sapling" (Job 14: 7–9). Life may cut us down; but hope springs eternal.

❖ 'Aḥarei Mot: Ezekiel 22:1–19

Have you ever wondered why the ancient prophets were not exactly the most popular people? If they had something to say, they didn't hold back—and this haftarah is perhaps the most blatant example of that. Ezekiel, who prophesied as the Southern Kingdom of Judah was being destroyed (and who went into exile in Babylonia with his people), comes up with a list of all the sins the Judeans had committed that would result in their being sent into exile. The corresponding Torah portion contains a list of various sexual sins that Jews should not commit—and this haftarah contains them all, and then some.

But it wasn't just sexual sins that upset Ezekiel; there were other sins as well that would send the Judeans into exile, including total failures of social justice. The lesson: total moral failure can destroy a society just as easily as a military defeat.

That Bad? Really?

There are many jokes about Jewish guilt—the notion that Jews tend to feel guilty over things that they have done. Jews seem to have an uncanny ability to blame themselves—as a people—for things that have gone wrong in Jewish history.

If you don't believe this, go no further than this week's haftarah portion. Take a look at the catalog of sins that the prophet Ezekiel enumerates: bloodshed (22:2); idolatry (22:3—"fetishes" are idols); abuse of power (22:6); dishonoring parents, abusing strangers, wronging orphans and widows (22:7); dishonoring holy things and the Sabbath (22:8); committing incest with one's father and raping menstruating women (22:10); committing adultery and incest with family members (22:11). . . . Yes, the traditional liturgy says: "Because of our sins, we were expelled from our land. . . . But, please, enough is enough.

This list caused Bible scholar Harry Orlinsky to write: "If one reads the book of Ezekiel, one gathers that the government and the people of Judah were on the greatest sinning binge in the history of Judah and Israel, if not in all of history."

Really? Were the ancient Judeans really that bad? That's hard to believe, considering the other people that surrounded the ancient Judeans. Or, perhaps Ezekiel was laying it on a little thick (prophets had a way of doing that, to get people's attention).

Let's make it relevant to today. Many supporters of Israel get upset when Israel's critics point out Israel's flaws. They ask: Why don't people look at what is happening in, say, Rwanda or Somalia? And they are not wrong. For many complex reasons, it often looks like the world magnifies things that Israel seems to do wrong. And yes, the world doesn't criticize other countries nearly as much as it criticizes Israel. For instance, many of the United Nations resolutions are anti-Israel.

From a strictly biblical point of view, there is a reason why Jews are so self-critical—especially about the Jewish state. God has a covenant with the Jews—and Jews therefore need to set high standards for their actions.

That's why Ezekiel is piling it on. He holds a microscope up to the people, and he wants them to repent.

Did you notice something in that list of sins? There are only three "religious" sins in there: idolatry, profaning holy things, and violating the Sabbath. All the rest are ethical sins that go to the very heart of family life, like honoring parents, adultery, and incest. And what are the last of those sins on the list? Taking bribes, charging exorbitant interest on loans, and committing fraud (22:12). As bad as all the other sins are (and they are bad), the prophet saves the worst for last—economic sins, failures to treat the poor with dignity. They are the worst because they represent real abuses of power. They perpetuate societal injustice.

But there is always hope. Ezekiel compares the people to dross—metal with impurities. When the people repent, they will become like pure metal again, and God will bring them back to their land.

Yes, we hold ourselves to the highest standards. Yes, we fall short repeatedly. But yes, we have the power make good choices and turn ourselves around. Ultimately we can go forward in the right way, and that will make all the difference.

❖ Kedoshim: Amos 9:7–15

Judaism believes that Jews can be holy, and that's the topic of this week's Torah portion. But that doesn't mean that you are an angel, and it certainly doesn't mean that you can imagine yourself to be morally superior. The haftarah, from the book of Amos, warns us about that.

Amos was a native of Tekoa, a village south of Jerusalem, in the Southern Kingdom of Judah, who lived in the eighth century BCE. At a certain point in his life he moved to the Northern Kingdom of Israel. The Northern Kingdom was far wealthier than its southern neighbor, and the people tended to act in inappropriate ways. They were heavily into idolatry. The old Canaanite kingdom of Phoenicia was just over the border, in the territory that we call Lebanon, and elements of the ancient Canaanite religion heavily influenced the people of the Northern Kingdom. More than that, because Israel was fairly prosperous, the people there became materialistic and morally lazy.

Amos has to get the people off their high horse. He reminds them that although God made a covenant with them, God's activity is also evident in the history of other nations. And, specifically because God made a covenant with them, God will hold them responsible for all their shortcomings.

But prophetic words never end on a negative note. While Amos foresees that the kingdom of Israel will be destroyed, he also predicts that it will be rebuilt, and that this will be a sign of God's favor.

Get Over Yourselves!

"My child is special." Of course, every parent thinks that his or her child is special (and no doubt, your parents feel that way about you). But the biggest problem with "specialness" is that you might think that you are, in fact, special—and that never ends well.

That's what the prophet Amos is talking about. "To Me, O Israelites, you are just like the Ethiopians—declares the Lord. True, I brought Israel up from the land of Egypt, but also the Philistines from Caphtor and the Arameans from Kir" (9:7). In other words, God is telling the Israelites, "Get over yourselves. You are not that special."

Wait a second. Of course Israel is a special people for God. God brought them out of Egypt, right? God gave them the commandments, right? God chose them, right?

Yes, but . . .

Let's take a deeper look at what Amos is saying. "You are just like the Ethiopians." Amos is telling the people that, in God's eyes, the People of Israel are no different than a faraway people in Africa. And then God says that the Israelites shouldn't go overboard in thinking about the "specialness" of the Exodus from Egypt—because God is also present in the lives of other nations.

Take the Philistines, for example. In biblical times, they were the hereditary enemies of the nation of Israel. They were probably from Asia Minor (contemporary Turkey), and they lived on Caphtor (Crete, in the Mediterranean Sea), and God brought them out of Caphtor. And the Arameans? (The ancient Syrians, not exactly the best friends of the Israelites.) But, there again, God moved them out of Kir. God is involved with other nations as well as Israel. So much for "specialness."

The Ethiopians are sub-Saharan Africans. They are black skinned. You got a problem with that? The Talmud states, "Only one person was created at the dawn of creation, so that no one can say, 'my ancestors are better than your ancestors!'" We are all human beings with a common ancestor. Remember that.

The great sage and activist Rabbi Abraham Joshua Heschel comments: "The nations chosen for this comparison were not distinguished for might and prestige, but rather, nations which were despised and disliked. The Ethiopians were black, and in those days many of them were sold on the slave markets. The Philistines were the arch-enemies of Israel, and the Syrians continued to be a menace to the Northern Kingdom. The God of Israel is the God of all nations, and all men's history is His concern."

Rabbi Heschel was firmly committed to civil rights (he was a friend of Martin Luther King Jr. and marched with him). From that quote you can see why.

Although God has a special relationship with Israel, God also cares about other nations. Jews learn from these prophetic teachings to look at other peoples' experiences and see the similarities. The Armenians, like the Jews, have suffered exile. African Americans, like the Jews, have been persecuted. The list goes on. . . .

God lifted the Jews up again—like a fallen sukkah. And God can do the same for other peoples as well. In the meantime, we're told to lend a hand to help make it happen.

❖ 'Emor: Ezekiel 44:15–31

Some say that the prophet Ezekiel was totally out of his mind. True—he had crazy visions of God streaming across the heavens in a chariot. But there was something else about Ezekiel: he had a plan. Ezekiel was a priest, and he prophesied during the Babylonian exile—in Babylon itself. Ezekiel knew that the Temple in Jerusalem would be rebuilt one day. He knew that the priests would be descended from Zadok, the "proper" ancestral line of priests. He knew that some priests had gone astray, like their fellow Judeans, but that others had kept their faith in God.

He shares his vision of what the priesthood will look like in the rebuilt Temple, and, as he does this, he provides a bridge between the past and the future.

And there's more: Ezekiel has an important understanding of the role of the priests. Their job description has three parts: to offer sacrifices at the altar; to teach the difference between that which is holy and that which is profane; and to act as judges, so that society will be able to maintained. In all this, Ezekiel provides continuity between the Tabernacle in the desert of the Torah portion and the Temple of later biblical Judaism.

You Are Not an Egyptian!

Imagine this scenario: Back in biblical times, a guy decides that he wants to become a priest. (Yes, they were all men; people were not as enlightened then as they are becoming today.) So, he goes for an interview, and the interviewer asks him the following questions: (1) Have you ever offered sacrifices before? (2) Can you explain the difference between the holy and the profane? (3) How do you feel about judging various cases that will come up from time to time?

Those are all good "priest" questions, and that seems to be the basic job description of a priest. But why is this scenario a fantasy? Because, in biblical times, only those who were *kohanim* and from the tribe of Levi could become priests. And, as you know, there are no more priests in Judaism today. Many of the important roles that the priest performed (animal sacrifices aside) became part of the rabbi's job description. (And many of today's rabbis are women.)

Now come the really tough questions: "How do you feel about never having any contact with the dead? And how about never being able to own any land? About existing totally on the people's offerings?" Yes, these were also part of the priest's job description.

Much of what we find in the Torah focuses on the following issue: "You, Jewish people, are not allowed to act like the nations that surround you." What was wrong with those nations? As contemporary commentator Leon Kass writes: "They were the heaven-gazing and heaven-worshiping Babylonians, the earth-worshiping Canaanites, and the technologically sophisticated and masterful Egyptians." The Babylonians relied on heavenly omens to make decisions. The Canaanites focused on fertility. And the Egyptians, who were indeed technologically sophisticated, used their greatest technological expertise to build the pyramids, which stored the mummies; they were "death palaces." The Egyptian priests prepared the dead for their journey to the next world.

So, don't do what the Egyptians did. Don't be "masterful" and enslave other people. And, if you're a priest, don't behave like an Egyptian priest. To this day, traditional Jews who believe themselves to be descended from the ancient *kohanim* will not enter cemeteries or a home containing a dead person (an exception is made for a close relative).

What about "no holding shall be given them [the priests] in Israel"? (44:28). The tribe of Levi—the tribe of the priests—was the only tribe that got no land in the dividing up of the Land of Israel. Why? Perhaps the reason is that, back in Genesis when Joseph was in charge of Egypt, the only people who were allowed to have land were the priests. Therefore, once again—we are not Egyptians.

Our ancestors were a small people struggling to maintain their identity. It was almost as if the Torah is saying: if your neighbors do it, you shouldn't. That is part of what it means to be a holy people—dedicated to a different ideal.

Being different, choosing the road less taken, means to look at what other people are doing, and sometimes saying: "This is not us. We do things differently." And we are proud of it.

❖ Be-har: Jeremiah 32:6–27

Think of any impoverished, desolate, crime-ridden area of a major city. Go there with your parents. Suggest to them: "Hey, we should buy some property here!" Chances are they will tell you that you're crazy.

Now, take your parents and travel to a war zone. Everything has been destroyed. Suggest to your parents: "Hey, let's buy some property here!" If, in fact, they have even agreed to make the trip in the first place, they will tell you to get back in the taxi because we're going home as quickly as we can.

That is precisely the situation that Jeremiah is facing. The Babylonian army has destroyed the city of Jerusalem, and, right then, Jeremiah's cousin Hanamel asks the prophet to help him out. He lost his land due to economic reverses, a situation similar to what this week's Torah portion describes. The Torah makes it clear: relatives have to step in, buy back the land, and put the person back on his feet. That is exactly what Hanamel asks Jeremiah to do—to redeem his portion of land in the Jerusalem suburb of Anathoth.

And Jeremiah does it. To be a prophet is to testify to the power of hope, and that the future will be better than the present. Jeremiah's faith in the land and its future can inspire everyone.

Why Jews Care about Israel

Why do Jews care so much about a piece of land called Israel, and the people who live there?

It should be pretty easy to figure out the answer to that question, shouldn't it? After all, the Land of Israel was the place where the ancestors of the Jewish people lived—ever since the time of Abraham. Even though they were exiled from the land several times (the Assyrians destroyed the Northern Kingdom of Israel; the Babylonians destroyed the Southern Kingdom of Judah; and, centuries later, the Romans exiled the Jews from the land), the Jews never stopped dreaming about the Land of Israel.

When Jews pray, they face Jerusalem. Jewish prayers contain hopes that the Land of Israel will be restored to them—and that God will come back to Zion as well. As it is written in the prayer book, "May our eyes behold Your compassionate return to Zion. Blessed is Adonai, who restores the Divine Presence to Zion."

Jews know that they can move to Israel if they need to, if anti-Semitism becomes intolerable in the countries where they live. Jews take pride in Israel's achievements—in areas such as medical research, science, technology, culture, and education. Jews take pride in Israel's military accomplishments, in its ability to stand up to hostile neighbors. That pride in Israel is powerful, even when Jews disagree over the precise details of how Israel should handle the many societal, political, and military challenges that it faces.

All of that is important, but there is something else about Israel that is central to the way Jews view themselves: Israel embodies their hope in the future.

That's what Jeremiah is talking about. And he put his money where his mouth is. Even as Jerusalem was about to be destroyed, Jeremiah knew that he had the responsibility to redeem his family's land in order to fulfill the Torah portion's commandments of land redemption. It must have seemed crazy, but Jeremiah had a sense that his land purchase was part of Jewish history, for he laid out the entire history of the Jews—going back to the Exodus from Egypt (32:20–22). Jeremiah believed that buying back the land was part of the Jewish history of hope. He knew his act was a symbolic one, so he made sure to publicize it with the help of his media consultant (scribe) Baruch.

And so it is that when Jews get married one of the prayers is this: "Yet again it shall be heard, in the cities of Judah and in the streets of Jerusalem—the sound of joy and gladness, the voice of bride and groom." A wedding is a moment of hope, and the wedding couple brings the ultimate hope—the hope for return to the Land of Israel—into that moment of love.

Jeremiah's example lives for us today. As Rabbi Yitz Greenberg writes: "Today, Jews are back in Israel and facing the prospect of peace and prosperity in the land. This miraculous achievement was made possible by loyalty and love even under fire, by buying and building even in the face of defeat, through hope and trust in God even when it appeared to be hopeless. Thus Jewish history proves that life, love and hope are stronger than death, selfishness and despair."

No wonder that, at the end of the Passover seder, we sing "Next year in Jerusalem!" and that the Israeli national anthem is called "Hatikvah"—The Hope.

❖ Be-ḥukkotai: Jeremiah 16:19–17:14

When it comes to the ancient Israelites, sin can be deadly—literally. That's one of the central ideas of the Hebrew Bible, and the prophet Jeremiah hammers it home for us in this final haftarah of the book of Leviticus.

The Torah portion speaks of the sins that (ancient Israelites believed) were the reason why they might be exiled from their land. The horrific conditions of destruction and exile, described in the Torah portion, had become living realities when the Assyrians and the Babylonians destroyed, respectively, the Northern Kingdom of Israel and the Southern Kingdom of Judah.

Jeremiah, living in the time of the destruction of Judah, has his own take on why it is happening. To the sins of idolatry and of exploitation of the vulnerable, Jeremiah adds one more: the sin of failing to trust in God. Jeremiah believes, therefore, that some of our sins come not from what we actually do; they come from how we feel—from what is going on inside of us.

Actions, Not Feelings

Someday this will happen to you. You will know someone who is wealthy (maybe it will be you!), and that person decides she wants to give a lot of money to a particular project. Let's say that she decides to donate money for the construction of a building on a college campus, or to a project in Israel.

Good, right? But then someone gets up and says: "You know, this woman who wants to give the money—I know that she just wants the honor and respect that comes with giving all that money! It's all about her ego; she doesn't really care that much about this project."

How are you going to react to this? Sure—we would hope that the giver is sincere. But what if she isn't sincere? What if she really doesn't care that much about the project and really just wants her name on the outside of the building?

So, it's time to talk about our inner lives—the stuff that happens inside us.

First, let's get real—very few people give a whole lot of money to things that don't interest them.

Second, and what if they didn't really care that much? Is that our business? Are the inner intentions and feelings of people really that important?

Jeremiah and other prophets did care about what we think. They wanted us to be pure on the inside and the outside. But, to be honest, the weight of Jewish tradition is on our words and our actions, not on our thoughts.

Let's go to an interesting example of this from the great medieval sage Maimonides. He created a famous "ladder of *tzedakah*," in which he explained the best kinds of giving, ranked from highest to lowest. The highest level: "To support a fellow Jew by endowing him with a gift or loan, or entering into a partnership with him, or finding employment for him, in order to strengthen his hand until he need no longer be dependent upon others." Go through all those levels of *tzedakah*, and you will find that secret giving (where the giver and the recipient don't know each other) is way up there as well. The second to lowest step: "When one gives inadequately, but gives gladly and with a smile."

So, according to Maimonides, when it comes to helping people, our own emotions really don't count for that much. What matters most is the actual giving (even if you scowl)!

Jeremiah himself acknowledged that you can never really know what a person is thinking: "Most devious is the heart; it is perverse— who can fathom it? I the Lord probe the heart, search the mind—to repay every man according to his ways, with the proper fruit of his deeds (17:9–10).

We can never be sure of what's going on in other people's hearts; only God knows that. By the way, quite often we ourselves are not totally clear about our own motives for doing something. Do I want to be class president for my personal glory, or because it will look good on my college application, or because I really want to help my school? If you do a good job, does it really matter?

When President Jimmy Carter said famously that he had sinned because he had lusted after another woman in his heart, many Jews were unsure what all the fuss was about. It's not like the president had an affair (unlike many other politicians).

As Rabbi Leonid Feldman writes: "Only God truly understands our motives, and what we humans should focus on are the deeds and not the heart."

Jeremiah and the prophets urged us to have good thoughts on the inside so we have good actions on the outside. But if you can't have both (and we are only human), focus not on the first, but on the second.

NUMBERS

❖ Be-midbar: Hosea 2:1–22

The book of Numbers gets its English name from the fact that it begins with a census of the people. In Hebrew it is Be-midbar, "the book of the wilderness," because it's an account of the wilderness wanderings of the Israelites, as they make their way to the Land of Israel.

In the haftarah, the prophet Hosea relates to both themes (and this is the connection to the Torah portion). He tells the reader that there will come a time when the People of Israel will be as numerous as the "sands of the sea, which cannot be measured or counted." The prophet also refers to the *midbar*, the spiritual wilderness in which the Israelites will find themselves, due to their sinning.

God's Broken Heart

Let's admit it: this is tough stuff—perhaps the toughest haftarah in the entire cycle of the Jewish year. That's because Hosea uses such graphic language and is so critical of his people. But it's easier to understand if we can see just what is going on here. Hosea was a prophet who lived in the Northern Kingdom of Israel in the eighth century BCE. The biggest issue there was that the people were constantly forsaking God and worshiping the Canaanite god, Baal.

According to Hosea, Israel's actions were a major disappointment, and even an insult, to God. It was as if God had a wife (the People of Israel) who had other lovers; the People of Israel was committing adultery! Remember that the Israelites and God have pledged themselves to each other in a covenant going all the way back to Sinai. Like a marriage, that covenant was based on faithfulness. The Jewish theologian Abraham Joshua Heschel writes: "Idolatry is adultery. More than stupidity, it is lewdness. Israel is like a wanton wife; the Lord is like a faithful, loving but forsaken husband."

God wanted Hosea to understand these feelings of betrayal. So, in a radical move, God commanded Hosea to marry Gomer, a prostitute. (Or maybe Hosea just thought he had to do something radical to dramatize his message.) Gomer ran around with other lovers, causing the prophet deep heartache. Then God said to Hosea: Perhaps you'll understand how I feel. Now perhaps you can convince the People of Israel to stop what they are doing and be loyal only to me.

That's where this haftarah comes in. God demands that the prophet send his wife away. According to the Talmud: "God said: 'I will order Hosea: "Go and marry a prostitute and have children with that prostitute." Then, I will order him: "Send her away!" If he will be able to send her away, I will send Israel away, too.'" This is amazing; God is depending on the prophet to help determine whether Israel will be sent away from divine favor: "let her put . . . her adultery from between her breasts. Else I will strip her naked and leave her as on the day she was born" (Hosea 2: 4–5).

If you see something sexist in the way God is acting, you are not alone. In those days, marriages were far from the kind of equal relationships that contemporary couples want. To quote Rabbi Lia Bass: "God has the authority of possession and control over Israel in the same way that a husband has authority over a wife. The people, by definition, are subservient to God's will. Women, therefore, should be subservient to men." While the aim of God and the prophet is worthy—a faithful relationship—the means to achieving it, by exploiting Hosea and Gomer, is questionable.

This haftarah, like other parts of the Bible, has ideas about God that we may find difficult to understand. God is not just a distant God; the supreme ruler God is actually emotionally vulnerable. God had to put the prophet Hosea through this terrible experience just so that the prophet could empathize with God's feelings.

God promises that there will be a renewed, intimate connection with the Jewish people. "I will espouse you forever" (2:21). These are beautiful words and a noble ideal. In fact, traditional Jews say these words as, each day, they put on tefillin, the leather straps wrapped on the arm and head as commanded in the Torah. The relationship of the people with God endures, with its ups and downs, just like in a marriage. Ideally it will be based on mutual trust and affection, not simply on God's power over the relationship. The medieval commentator Rashi says: "You will worship me from love, and not from fear."

A broken marriage—and other broken relationships—can lead to a broken heart. But if we do everything we can, maybe our ties with those we care about, and our hearts, will heal.

❖ Naso': Judges 13:2–25

Quite often, in the Bible, when children are about to be born, unusual things happen. There is a typical pattern that contains at least one of these elements: the mother-to-be has been struggling with infertility; an angel (a messenger of God) comes and tells her that she will have a child and that the child may grow up to be someone special. This is how it worked with Isaac, son of Abraham and Sarah, and with Samuel, son of Hannah.

This is also how it works with the story of Samson's birth, which is found in this week's haftarah. But there is an additional element: the angel tells Manoah and Mrs. Manoah (his wife is, sadly, unnamed) that their child will be a Nazirite—the link to this week's Torah portion. For that reason, Mrs. Manoah learns that she is not allowed to drink alcoholic beverages during her pregnancy (which is actually a good idea), and that the child will never get his hair cut.

The child of this pregnancy is one of the greatest biblical heroes— the judge Samson, who is blessed with almost superhuman strength. And a few weaknesses, as well . . .

Samson, the First Jewish Superhero

Superheroes were a Jewish invention. The creators of Superman were two Jewish guys from Cleveland, Ohio—Joe Shuster and Jerry Siegel. Where did they get the idea for Superman? One interesting theory is that they were inspired by the story of Samson, the star of this week's haftarah.

It is easy to see why this might be the case. Let's start with Samson's birth, which is a little mysterious, to say the least. An angel of God comes to tell his parents that he will be born, and he will grow up to become a mighty hero, with great strength. The writer Elie Wiesel teaches: "Samson laughed at his enemies, whom he effortlessly vanquished. Nothing frightened him. With one hand he could reduce an entire mountain to dust. His only weakness? Women."

Because Samson is a Nazirite, he is not allowed to cut his hair. And his hair becomes the secret source of his great strength. If it is cut, he will become weakened, sort of like the threat of kryptonite to Superman.

Samson is unique; he is a different kind of Jewish hero. Traditionally, Jews identify heroism not in what you are able to do with your physical strength, but with moral and ethical heroism. The Mishnah teaches: "Who is a hero? He who resists his temptations." Even though Jews believe that the body is precious and that we should take care of ourselves to stay healthy, physical strength has never been a big Jewish value. In traditional Jewish life, the only time that you really need physical strength is to lift the Torah—which, when you open it up to reveal the sacred writing on the parchment, is very heavy!

For centuries, Jews thought that mental, moral, and spiritual strength were enough. But the birth of the State of Israel demonstrated that Jews had to be physically strong as well, strong like Samson. The Zionist leader Vladimir (Ze'ev) Jabotinsky wrote a novel about Samson, and in his book Samson derives his physical strength from his hair, but he also admires and learns from the military strength of his enemy, the Philistines. These are Samson's last words, as imagined by Jabotinsky: "Get hold of iron. Give whatever you have for it. The second [thing you need] is a king. One person, at a signal from whom thousands will raise their arms all at once."

Samson's story does not end well. Ultimately, he is betrayed by Delilah, who turns him over to the Philistines. She seduces him and learns his secret; then she cuts his hair. The Philistines imprison and blind him. When his hair starts to grow back, Samson pulls down the pillars of a Philistine temple, killing many Philistines, along with himself.

Samson is physically powerful, but he becomes emotionally and morally blind (by allowing himself to be seduced) before he becomes physically blind. What is the story trying to teach us? Without vision and wisdom, physical strength and power are meaningless—sometimes even lethal. Samson is a hero, but an incomplete hero. He is the first to save Israel from the Philistines, but he's not the last. Samson's end is tragic, and his work is unfinished. Every generation has to do its part. And every person needs to be strong internally, if not externally.

❖ Be-ha'alotekha: Zechariah 2:14–4:7

The Babylonians destroyed the kingdom of Judah and exiled many of its people to Babylon. Years later, Cyrus, king of Persia, conquered Babylonia and allowed some of the Jews to return to their land. Upon returning to Jerusalem, one of the Jews' first projects was to rebuild the Temple. Many of the nations that surrounded Judah were opposed to the reconstruction (as were some Jewish groups, as well), and, after decades of exile, many Judeans themselves were less than enthusiastic about building another Temple. The major theme of this haftarah is the prophet Zechariah's encouragement: to the people; to Joshua, the High Priest; and to Zerubbabel, whom the Persians had appointed governor over Judah.

An interesting figure makes a rare biblical appearance in this passage: Satan, who here is called "the Accuser." The scene is the heavenly court. The charge: Joshua, the High Priest, is unfit for office. Satan, the Accuser, who is the prosecutor, brings the charge against Joshua. The angel of God defends Joshua, saying that he is not only fit for office, but that he could actually become an angel in heaven! In this passage, Satan has no horns, he's not breathing fire or any of that stuff; that image of Satan as the Devil will come years later.

What is the link between this haftarah and the Torah portion? A very simple detail: both passages mention the lighting of the menorah (the ceremonial lamp). Once those ceremonial lamps were in the ancient Tabernacle (Tent of Meeting, or *mishkan*); then they existed in the Temple in Jerusalem. Someday, the prophet is saying, the Temple will be rebuilt and the lamps will be lit once again.

Being a Survivor

We don't know much about Joshua, the High Priest. Apparently, he was in the first group of Jews to return to the Land of Israel after the Babylonian exile. The haftarah portrays him standing before the Accuser (Satan), dressed in filthy garments, with the Accuser ready to charge him. Then God's angel has Joshua's dirty clothes removed and replaced with priestly robes, with a diadem (a sort of crown) placed on his head. God's angel tells the Accuser, in so many words, to leave Joshua alone; that he is like "a brand plucked from the fire" (3:2).

Joshua is a survivor of what had been, until that time, the worst national catastrophe that the Jewish people had ever experienced: the destruction of Jerusalem, the burning of the Temple, and the exile in Babylon. Jerusalem had burned, and Joshua was like a brand—a wooden poker, like you would use in a fireplace, that someone pulled out of the fire. Joshua's father had been exiled from Judah, and his grandfather had been executed by the Babylonians (2 Kings 25:18–21), but Joshua had been saved.

And why were Joshua's garments filthy? They had been scorched by fire. The Talmud says that the Babylonians had condemned three men to die in a furnace. The men wanted Joshua to accompany them into the furnace, thinking that his righteousness would protect them. "So he was brought, and they were all thrown into the furnace. They were burned, but, as to Joshua the High Priest, only his garments were scorched." As we have seen, Joshua was a survivor.

Why did Satan accuse Joshua? We don't really know. His sin could have been doubting whether God really cared about the Jewish people. Perhaps he doubted whether his survival was worth it. Or maybe Joshua, as the High Priest, bore the sin of the people as a whole.

Leave him alone, the angel is saying, Joshua has suffered enough.

Jews living decades after the Shoah (the Holocaust) know how God's angel felt. Just as there was a national awakening after the return from Babylonian exile, there was a national awakening after the Shoah. Rabbi Joseph Soloveitchik wrote: "In the midst of a night of terror filled with the horrors of Maidanek, Treblinka, and Buchenwald, in a night of gas chambers and crematoria, in a night of absolute divine self-concealment, in a night ruled by the satan of doubt . . . in that very night the Beloved appeared." Soloveitchik knew about Satan. For him Satan, or the Accuser, was the one who caused Jews to doubt their faith. But what happened? "The Beloved"—God—showed up again, in the form of the Jewish people's determination to return to Israel and to create a nation.

Many survivors of the Shoah, and their children and grandchildren, could have totally abandoned faith in God, and in life itself. But they didn't. They committed themselves to making the world better. As Rabbi Judith Schindler, herself the daughter and granddaughter of survivors, has written: "I'd love to sleep soundly, but I can't. I pray that I can use my extra hours to honor the memories of those who died by creating a society that honors diversity and by tending to the altar of my people in order to keep the flames of Judaism and Torah vibrant so that they can forever warm and bring light to our world."

Zechariah (through the angel) reminds us that we prevail "Not by might, nor by power but by My spirit" (4:6; words also spoken at Hanukkah and in a popular song). Survivors are the most powerful testimony to that truth.

❖ Shelaḥ-Lekha: Joshua 2:1–24

Everyone loves a good spy story, and this week's Torah portion gives us one of the best—the story of the spies who scout out the Land of Israel in order to see what kind of land it is. They bring back devastating reports to Moses, and those reports have devastating consequences.

Years later, as this week's haftarah tell us, it's time to actually conquer the land, and Joshua sends spies to Jericho to prepare the conquest. But this story ends on a much happier note than the earlier one. The spies in the Torah story show no faith at all; they don't believe that the land can be conquered. They lose faith in themselves, and in God. But in the haftarah, Rahab, a Canaanite prostitute, shows great faith in herself, and even in God. She hides the spies, then helps them escape, and she is spared by Joshua when the conquest occurs.

It just goes to show: sometimes you can't predict who is going to win in the faith department. Let's hear it for Rahab!

The Greatest Prostitute in the Bible

There are many prostitutes in the Hebrew Bible. But the nicest one in the entire Bible has to be Rahab, the prostitute in this haftarah. And why? Her efforts helped guarantee the success of the Israelite conquest of the Land of Israel. By the way, she was supposed to have been gorgeous. According to the Talmud: "There have been four women of surpassing beauty in the world: Sarah, Rahab, Abigail [one of King David's wives], and Esther." (Of course, how they knew that is anyone's guess!)

Rahab lives in Jericho, and she shelters a group of Israelite spies who have secretly entered the land in order to make plans to invade and conquer it. The spies hide on her roof, and, when the king of Jericho comes to find them, Rahab warns them and they are able to escape by climbing down a rope that she hangs out the window. The men are safe to continue their mission. In the words of Bible scholar Tikvah Frymer-Kensky: "Rahab is proactive, smart, tricky and unafraid to disobey and deceive the king."

Rahab knows that when the People of Israel conquer the land, there is going to be widespread destruction. She brings her entire family into her home, and she ties a cord of crimson thread in the window, so that their lives will be spared.

Where have we heard this story before? It happened during the Exodus from Egypt. Remember how the Israelites took a little bit of blood and sprinkled it on their doorposts, in order to protect themselves from the final plague that would kill the firstborn children? Back then, the red blood would ward off the Angel of Death; here, the cord of crimson thread would ward off the human forces of death.

The Rahab story should remind us of something else. We have seen her kind of trickery before, in the story of Shiphrah and Puah, the two midwives who saved Israelite infants in Egypt (Exodus 1:17). They were also deceptive, but with a sacred purpose. Yes, Rahab acted deceptively, but with the purpose of saving life.

Rahab lived in Jericho, which is right on the border of the Land of Israel. And she lived in a house right next to the wall of Jericho, which means that she lived at the edge of Jericho.

Rahab lived "on the edge"—in more ways than one. She rose above her social class, and she showed great courage.

❖ Koraḥ: 1 Samuel 11:14–12:22

Some people have trouble with authority. Korah, who is the star of the Torah portion, was one of those people. Korah, a Levite (and cousin to

Moses and Aaron), insists that the entire Israelite community is holy, and that Moses and Aaron have no right to their positions of authority. Moses retorts, somewhat defensively: "I have not taken the ass of any one of them, nor have I wronged any one of them" (Num. 16:15).

The ancient Rabbis, who chose the *haftarot* for each Torah portion, took the theme of Korah's rebellion, and they associated it with something that happened centuries later, told in this week's haftarah. The People of Israel gang up on the prophet Samuel and demand that he appoint them a king to rule over them. Samuel responds, in much the same way as Moses did: "Whose ox have I taken, or whose ass have I taken?" (12:3).

The link between the Torah portion and the haftarah is clear: both Moses and Samuel, faced with what seemed to be a rebellion, defend themselves, saying that they have behaved justly. Their example is one that all leaders should imitate.

Give Us a King!

Samuel, like Moses, must have had it up to here with the People of Israel. All they seem to do is nag! And what are they nagging about? They want a king, just like all the other nations. (It's like a mother getting fed up with a kid who is constantly bugging her about something that he wants—just because the other kids have it.)

Samuel was not only a prophet; he was also a judge—a chieftain who ruled the People of Israel. He was an excellent leader, but his sons were not. In fact, you might actually say that they were total screwups. The people become fed up with Samuel's sons. That, too, contributed to their demand for change, and in 1 Sam. 8:6, they ask for a king.

This upsets Samuel, but God tells him that it's not as if the people were rejecting him (Samuel); rather, they were really rejecting God, who should be their true king. Samuel then reads the people the riot act. He warns them of all the possible abuses of power that a king might engage in: a king would draft their sons into his army; he would force them to plow his fields and make his weapons; he would take their land; he would make the women perfumers and cooks (8:10–18). These warnings were very much in line with the passage in Deuteronomy 17, which specifies what kings can and cannot do. That chapter is sometimes called "the chapter of the king," and as the Talmud says: "All that is set out in the chapter of the king, the king is permitted to do."

But the people still insist, so Samuel relents and appoints a king: "I have yielded to you in all you have asked of me and have set a king over you" (12:1).

We really cannot blame the people for wanting a king. After all, Samuel's sons have done a terrible job at leadership. More than this: the people realized that the best way for them to be able to defend themselves against their enemies was to have a king.

More than that: in the "old system," every so often, a judge or military ruler would arise. As the sociologist Max Weber writes: "There was only the intermittent, varying sway of the charismatic war heroes." It was chaotic. Even worse—it relied on the charisma—the great personality—of the individual leader.

While it might be nice to have charismatic leaders, it's hard to rely on them actually turning up when you need them. Charismatic leaders can also be dangerous; think of Hitler and Stalin. Kings become kings not because they are charismatic (in fact, often they are not); they become kings because they "inherit" the job. There are also dangers in having a king: he must not be above the law—he must serve the law. That is why the chapter of the king in Deuteronomy ends by commanding that the king have a copy of Torah right by his side at all times. Now that's a powerful visual aid!

Therefore, why do the people want a king? Because kingship would be far more predictable and stable. Sometimes the right choice is not the perfect choice, but the welfare of the majority is what counts the most.

❖ Ḥukkat: Judges 11:1–33

You really have to feel sorry for Jephthah. He had a difficult life: the son of a prostitute, kicked out of his family home, and not allowed to share in his inheritance. He grew up to be a tough guy, surrounded by even tougher guys.

When the People of Israel are fighting the Ammonites, they seek Jephthah out and ask him to be their leader. (This, by the way, is the link with the Torah portion. Moses had negotiated with the Ammonites to be able to pass through their territory; years later, Jephthah winds up in battle against them). After initial attempts to reach a peaceful settlement fail, Jephthah prepares for battle. He rashly vows that if God makes him victorious over the Ammonites he will sacrifice as a burnt offering whatever first greets him upon his return home.

The haftarah ends with Jephthah's military victory—never indicating what, if anything, the consequences of his vow will be. But the next book of the Bible, Judges, goes on to tell us, and it's worse than Jephthah's worst nightmare.

Jephthah's Fatal Mistake

There's an old expression: "Be careful what you wish for; you might just get it." That is probably what Jephthah said to himself—for the rest of his life.

As the haftarah closes, Jephthah is about to go into battle with the Ammonites. He makes a promise to God that if he is victorious he will sacrifice to God the first thing that comes out the doors of his house to meet him. (Since people lived with animals in their courtyards, he was probably thinking that one of them would be the first to appear.)

Here's what the haftarah does not include (because the haftarah ends right before it happens): it's Jephthah's (unnamed) daughter who comes out to meet him, dancing in great delight over the victory. Jephthah tells her that, essentially, a vow is a vow—and she says, essentially, "Oh, well. You gotta do what you gotta do. Just give me some time to hang out with my girlfriends in the mountains, so that we can sit around and cry about the fact that I am going to die before I can get married."

Commentators have long objected to this awful story. The biblical scholar Phyllis Trible calls this one of the Bible's "texts of terror." "Premature, violent, without an heir: all the marks of unnatural death befall this young woman, and she is not even spared the knowledge of them. Hers is premeditated death, a sentence of murder passed upon an innocent victim because of the faithless vow uttered by her foolish father."

Here's the really sad part: It didn't need to happen. Sure, Jephthah had made a vow to sacrifice the first "thing" that he saw. He could have gotten out of that vow. All he had to do was go to the High Priest and ask him to negate the vow.

Why didn't he? A midrash is very harsh about Jephthah and the High Priest, calling them arrogant idiots: "Jephthah said: 'Shall I, a chieftain and ruler in Israel, go to the High Priest? Let him come to me!' The High Priest responded: 'Shall I, the High Priest and the son of a High Priest, go to an ignorant person? Let him come to me!' Because the two of them were arrogant, the poor girl perished, and they were both condemned for her death. Jephthah's punishment was that limb after limb fell away from his body, and he was buried."

The midrash suggests that Jephthah's daughter died because of the egos of those two men. And what was Jephthah's punishment? He literally fell apart.

But, why does the haftarah end before it gets to this terrible part of the story? Professor Ellen Umansky writes: "Perhaps the haftarah stops short of the story's conclusion in order to emphasize Jephthah's heroism [in battle] rather than the foolishness of his actions."

Watch your words. Watch your ego. Watch your family relationships. They all really matter.

❖ Balak: Micah 5:6–6:8

Sometimes memories become distorted. Take the story of Balak, the Moabite king, and Balaam, the soothsayer, which is found in this week's Torah portion. You might think that the historical memory would record that Balaam tried to curse Israel but God transformed his curses into blessings. And, in fact, that is precisely what Jews remember about that incident, because Balaam's words, "How fair are your tents . . ." are the first words that Jews say (or sing) when they enter the synagogue.

But in the time of Micah, a prophet of the eighth century BCE, the "good" memory of that incident had not yet surfaced. No, for Micah, the incident was wholly negative. The prophet recalls "what Balak king of Moab plotted against you" (6:5).

According to Micah, God will not only destroy Israel's enemies, but will also wreak havoc on Israel's own idolatrous practices. This is the essence of the prophet's message: God is not terribly interested in Israel's pious sacrifices. Above everything else, God wants ethical behavior—as expressed in Micah's famous verse: "He has told you, O man, what is good, and what the Lord requires of you: only to do justice, and to love goodness, and to walk modestly with your God" (6:8).

Read That Again, Please

We find these words, written across the doors and *bimahs* of countless synagogues all over the world. "He has told you, O man, what is good, and what the Lord requires of you: only to do justice, and to love goodness, and to walk modestly with your God" (6:8).

It has practically become a cliché, which would be a good reason for us to ask ourselves: What does it really mean, especially the part about walking modestly?

This verse is so important that it was even imagined to be one of the great summaries of all Judaism. "Micah reduced the mitzvot to those three principles . . . [including] 'walking modestly with your God,' that is, walking in funeral and bridal processions." Rabbi Simlai, the talmudic sage and author of this statement, fleshed out the meaning of "walking modestly" in an interesting and unusual way: the mitzvah of attending funerals and weddings—of being with people at sad times and at joyous moments. Taking the time to simply be with people in their hour of need; not necessarily saying anything, but just being there for them, is a true act of humility.

The biblical scholar Professor David Sperling offers another interpretation: "Be aware that, in the presence of God, we are only human." Act with self-restraint. Don't show off. To be modest is to know our limitations.

There is an alternative way to translate and understand the first phrase of Micah's statement: *Higid lekha adam mah tov, u-mah Adonai elohekha doreish mimkha.* This is how it is rendered over the *bimah* at the Liberal Jewish Synagogue in London: "Man might have told you what is good, but what does God require of you?"

That unique translation imagines a dialogue between what people think is important, and what God knows is important. "Man" (human beings) might tell you that sacrifices are important, but God requires ethical behavior.

Or, perhaps it means something even more radical. Don't pay attention to what society says. Know that there are greater ideals out there, a deeper reality. In the words of psychiatrist and author Silvano Arieti: "People continue to see the Jew as an iconoclast, as the one who has destroyed their most cherished beliefs. The Jew not only challenges their ideas, but he places in doubt what for them has counted most."

To be Jewish is to strive for the ethical no matter what the circumstances. To be Jewish is to listen to God, even more than you listen to people. Now, that is a challenge!

❖ Pinḥas: 1 Kings 18:46–19:21

Pinḥas was a hothead; so was Elijah (the more conventional term is "zealot," which can have both positive and negative connotations). That is the basic message of this haftarah and its connection to the Torah portion. The priest Pinḥas lashed out and executed a Jew for having sex with a Midianite woman, which was part of an idolatrous act of worship. Elijah killed the prophets of Baal. The stories are similar; they are about zeal against idolatry.

Based on this, the ancient Rabbis actually believed that Elijah was, in fact, really Pinḥas! Why not? It may be a stretch, but the sages were aware that in the Torah nowhere is the death of Pinḥas mentioned— and nowhere is the birth of Elijah mentioned, either.

Calm Down, Elijah!

What is it about religion, that it keeps producing zealots and extremists?

Pinḥas, the priest in the Torah portion, was one. He went ballistic when he saw an Israelite man having sex with a foreign woman, and he killed both of them. Elijah is another biblical zealot. He challenges the prophets of Baal to a contest. "Whose God is more powerful?" Elijah wins, and then he kills the prophets of Baal.

That's why the midrash says: "Pinḥas is Elijah." It is as if Pinḥas was actually reincarnated as Elijah! Professor Melilah Hellner-Eshed teaches: "The role of the prophet is to engage in anger management with God, to remind God of God's endless mercy." Fine, but first the prophet has to engage in anger management for himself.

If you're overly zealous, you wind up taking stuff very personally. After Elijah kills the prophets of Baal, he has to flee for his life. He escapes to the desert, and travels forty days until he reaches Mount Horeb, which is another name for Sinai. There, in the place where God had revealed the Divine Presence to Moses, God appears to Elijah. God asks him the crucial question: "What are you doing here?" because Elijah had fled to a cave in the midst of the mountain. Elijah responds out of despair—radical despair and loneliness.

A shocking question! It is God who saved Elijah and has presumably brought him to this spot, and now God asks Elijah why he is here?

Actually, God is asking Elijah a bigger question: "Why, Elijah, are you here—here, at Sinai, of all places?" Elijah must have come to Sinai expecting the same kind of thunder and lightning that Moses experienced. Elijah must have come to Sinai expecting that the dramatic sound and light show would inspire him to continue his prophetic mission.

That's not how it worked out, though. Sure, God gives Elijah the whole big deal—wind, earthquake, and fire. But that was not where God was. God was in a "soft murmuring sound," sometimes translated as "the still small voice." In the words of Rabbi Daniel Gordis: "It is the intimate, gentle, almost silent moment in which something happens to Elijah. Something tantalizes and touches him. Something thoroughly non-intellectual enables him not to see or hear—but rather to feel—the awesomeness of God."

God tells Elijah: no more wallowing in self-pity or self-righteousness. Go back to your home and to your work. Anoint kings and, while you're at it, anoint your own successor. And don't think that you are totally and utterly alone. There are far more supporters of God than you think!

Everyone expects moments of faith in God to be like a fireworks show. That's not how it is—at least, not all the time.

Perhaps that is why Sinai has two names: Sinai and Horeb. Perhaps they represent two sides of Sinai—the big sound and the small sound.

The rock duo Simon and Garfunkel sang a famous song called "The Sound of Silence." We need to listen for God in the high notes, the low notes, and the pause between the notes. Then maybe we will become passionate and determined without being overly zealous. That just may be the balance we need.

❖ Mattot: Jeremiah 1:1–2:3

This is how the book of Jeremiah begins. The prophet experiences two omens: an almond tree and a boiling pot tipping away from the north. In particular, that boiling pot will have major significance. The Babylonians, who will destroy Judah, will be coming from the north, and that "boiling pot" will ultimately not only scald the Jewish people; it will burn them, almost beyond recognition.

Don't look for any deep connection between the Torah portion and the haftarah; there isn't any. In fact, between this week's parashah and the end of the Jewish year, there are few connections between the Torah portions and the *haftarot*. The Jewish calendar now marks one of its most interesting periods: the time before the destruction of the Temple by the Babylonians, beginning after the Fast of the Seventeenth of Tammuz, the breaching of Jerusalem's walls by the Babylonians; the destruction itself (Tisha b'Av), and then seven weeks of consolation for the destruction, leading up to Rosh Hashanah.

This is the first of three prophetic readings of admonition that precede Tisha b'Av. Each one is concerned with the direness of the sins that would lead to destruction. It is as if God is saying: "Don't say I didn't warn you."

A Sort of Love Letter

Have you ever thought of the relationship between God and the Jewish people as a kind of wedding?

When God and the Jewish people first met, it was during the time of the Patriarchs and Matriarchs. From time to time, God would talk to individuals, like Abraham, Sarah, and Jacob. From time to time, they would offer sacrifices to God. No big deal. That was a flirtation.

But then came Sinai. God said to the Israelites: "I am your God." The Israelites said: "We are your people." That was the wedding.

Then came the honeymoon, in which God and Israel wandered together in the wilderness. It was like a young married couple who are trying to figure out what they want to do with their lives and their relationship. And yes, there are bumps in the road—arguing over small things, and even big things. It takes commitment to stick with any marriage.

As we have already seen (in the haftarah for Be-midbar), the marital metaphor isn't all that it's cracked up to be. But Jews still used it to describe the relationship between God and Israel. The sages thought that Song of Songs, the erotic love poetry of the Bible, was actually about the love between God and Israel. That's why the early sage Rabbi Akiva cautions: "Whoever sings the Song of Songs in banqueting houses and turns it into a drinking song loses his portion in the world to come." This is no ordinary "song"; it's about God and the Jewish people.

Watch what happens on Shavuot, the holiday that marks the giving of the Torah at Sinai. It's the wedding itself. Some synagogues actually erect a chuppah on Shavuot. Rabbi David Wolpe teaches: "The Torah is the ketubah [wedding contract] between God and the Jewish people. A ketubah enshrines sacred obligations. Sinai was the chuppah [the wedding canopy], and Shavuot is our anniversary."

And, in fact, when we read the Torah, we are encouraged to read it as if it were a love letter. Rabbi Sue Levi Elwell teaches: "Every year, we reopen the Torah scroll, and week after week, we attempt to discover, decipher and decode the words, as well as the desire behind the words that our ancestors have so lovingly handed down to us." We treat the Torah as we would treat a beloved—caressing her, and carrying her close to the heart.

So, yes, the relationship between God and the Jewish people is like a marriage. It has had good days, and bad days. As Ron Wolfson teaches: "As in all relationships, there is constant renegotiation of the terms of agreement, as well as the terms of endearment." But the most important part of a marriage is devotion.

God is glad that we stuck it out together. That's what God is saying in this haftarah: "You followed Me in the wilderness. Thanks for doing that."

❖ Mase'ei: Jeremiah 2:4–28; 3:4

This is the second of the three *haftarot* that are read in synagogue between 17 Tammuz and Tisha b'Av. Jeremiah relates that God is having serious trouble believing the Jewish people have betrayed the covenant with God, thus putting themselves in serious danger.

First, they totally forgot about God. And then, they went and worshiped idols. It just doesn't make sense, God says. But, wait a second, God says, maybe they still do remember me. Maybe all is not lost.

God My Father, God My Companion

Okay, let's admit it: not everyone is in love with the whole "God and Israel" marriage thing (see last week's haftarah). First of all, marriages back in ancient times weren't always so great, especially for wives. And second, if you've never been married (or even had a serious boyfriend or girlfriend), the whole comparison is probably lost on you.

Fine. Luckily, the final words of this haftarah give us another way of thinking about our relationship with God. Actually, two other ways. Try them on.

"Just now you called to Me, 'Father! You are the Companion of my youth'" (3:4). Looking at the first half of that biblical passage, one way is to think of God as Father. Many people don't like attributing the male gender to God, so let's just cut to the chase here: it's not about God as Father, really; it's about God as Parent. Rabbi Richard Levy writes: "How would you like your mother to be? How would you like your father to be? Your parents have the potential to be that way, but God is that way now. The kind of parent-love you want . . . it's there in God."

While God might be the ideal parent, relationships between parents and kids constantly grow and evolve. Sometimes, that relationship means anger—which comes from both sides in fact. You've slammed your share of bedroom doors in your time, haven't you—swearing that you're never going to talk to your parents again? The Jews did that, too, when they got angry with God. Even Moses did it. Seeing into the future at how the great sage Rabbi Akiva would ultimately suffer at the hands of the Romans, Moses cried out: "This is the Torah, and this is its reward?" And just as you ultimately made up with your parents (and they, with you), we can ultimately make up with God, as well.

The second half of the biblical passage gives us a second way to look at our relationship with God: "Companion of my youth." Being God's friend—that's a very sweet and trusted metaphor. Jews actually sing about it on Yom Kippur: "We are your beloved; you are our friend." Abraham was called "the friend of God" (in fact, that is how Abraham is known in Muslim lore).

There are many dimensions of friendship worth mentioning: hanging out, sharing interests, admiration, trust. But what's beautiful in the verse is how it plays out: "You are the Companion *of my youth.*" It's like having a friend, but one you've been out of touch with for a while. Maybe you went to different schools, or different camps—and, suddenly, you rediscover each other, and the friendship is revived.

That's why this haftarah ends on such a joyous note. Yes, the relationship with God had been estranged. The Jews had abandoned the covenant and worshiped idols. But God knew that the people would come back, and they would remember what it was like when they were young, back in the days of Abraham and Sarah, and Moses. . . .

The Jews and God would be back together again—just like old times.

DEUTERONOMY

❖ Devarim: Isaiah 1:1–27

We have been counting down, and it has been a very sad "count."
On the Seventeenth of Tammuz, the Babylonian armies breached the
walls of Jerusalem. That began the period known as "the three weeks."
And, now, it's almost time for Tisha b'Av, the commemoration of the
destruction of the ancient Temple. This is the Shabbat before Tisha
b'Av, which always coincides with Parashat Devarim, and it's called
Shabbat Hazon (Vision), named after the first word of this haftarah.

The prophet Isaiah has a vision—*hazon*—of the future. Isaiah, living
in the eighth century BCE, sees the Assyrian armies ready to pounce.
He warns the people of Judah that their sinful behavior will lead to
national catastrophe. He begs them to repent.

As it turns out, Isaiah was wrong—not about sin and repentance,
but about that catastrophe. The Assyrians destroyed the Northern
Kingdom of Israel. Jerusalem itself was not destroyed, though that
did happen a century later when the Babylonians ravaged the land.

The prophet was wrong, but only temporarily. His calls for repentance
should have made a difference. But ultimately, they fell on deaf ears.

It's More than Ritual

Most of the time, you probably make your parents very proud. But,
sometimes, you might disappoint them. That's how it is in this haftarah.
The prophet Isaiah reminds the people that God has been like a father
to them. And yet, the people continue to rebel against God. Every time
they sink further into sin, they get punished. But they don't learn from
their mistakes; they keep doing wrong. Their sins even spiritually "pol-
lute" the Land of Israel, which later leads to their exile from the land.

And so, the people decide that God simply needs more and better
sacrifices. But those don't work, either. Quite to the contrary: "'What

need have I of all your sacrifices?' says the Lord. 'I am sated with burnt offerings of rams, and suet of fatlings, and blood of bulls; and I have no delight in lambs and he-goats. . . . Your new moons and fixed seasons fill me with loathing" (1:11,14).

Why, according to Isaiah, does God despise their sacrifices? Because the people think that this is all that God requires. But, in fact, it's not their ritual infractions that have caused them to teeter on the edge of disaster. It's the failure to perform acts of social justice; to follow basic rules of ethical behavior

Wait a second. Are you saying that God doesn't care about rituals? Are you saying that God only cares about ethical behavior? (Does that mean that I can stop learning Hebrew and don't need to attend synagogue?)

Let's get a handle on what Isaiah is really saying. As Bible scholar Michael Fishbane writes: "Isaiah does not reject sacrifices. He rejects hypocrisy." Perhaps that is why mitzvah projects for bar and bat mitzvah have become so popular. We know that we cannot merely worship God, while the world continues to suffer. Isaiah taught: "Learn to do good. Devote yourselves to justice; aid the wronged. Uphold the rights of the orphan; defend the cause of the widow" (1:17). Doing these things is at least as important as getting the Hebrew right.

The text says that God is fed up with "your new moons." *Our* new moons? Hold on. Didn't God tell us to celebrate the coming of the new moons (the beginning of every month)? A midrash says: "Had God said 'I hate *My* new moons,' that's one thing. But God said '*your* new moons'–yours, not Mine. If you celebrate them as if they are only 'yours,' without proper devotion, then they are hateful to Me. But if you remember that they are Mine, if you truly celebrate them well, then I will always love them."

As we grow older (and especially when we raise families), we gain new appreciation for ritual. It helps tie us to family and faith, to our heritage and community. But what the prophets teach is that ritual is not enough. Rituals without deeds of compassion and justice will be empty and self-serving. Beware of false piety. Here's the reality check: What have you done for others lately? How have you made your home and your world a better place? How have you "learned to do good"?

❖ Va-ethannan: Isaiah 40:1–26

For most of the Jewish year, there is a thematic connection between the haftarah and the corresponding Torah portion. But starting with this Shabbat, and until we get to Rosh Hashanah, you can forget about such a connection. The *haftarot* for the entire book of Deuteronomy from here on will have almost nothing to do with their Torah portions.

Instead, they will have everything to do with this particular time of year. Start with the "holiday" that Jews observe this week—Tisha b'Av (the commemoration of the destruction of the Temple in Jerusalem). Then, count seven weeks, and we get to Rosh Hashanah. Seven is a special Jewish number, as in seven days of the week, or seven days for sitting shiva. That's exactly what we are doing here—sitting shiva for the independence of ancient Judea, while we imagine that God is visiting us, offering comfort.

That's why these weeks are called *sheva denechemta*—the seven weeks of consolation that follow Tisha b'Av. And it begins with this week, which has a special name: Shabbat Nachamu (Comfort). *Nachamu* is the first word of the haftarah.

During these seven weeks, all the *haftarot* come from the great prophet known as Second Isaiah, whose words appear in the book of Isaiah, chapters 40 through 66. His name was most likely not Isaiah, but his prophecies were added to the book of the earlier prophet Isaiah. This anonymous prophet lived in the period when the Babylonian Empire was coming to an end, and Persia was gaining in power. Second Isaiah sensed that even though the Jews were now in exile, they were about to come home. His words are full of hope for the Jewish people.

Cheer Up

If there were to be a name-recognition contest for prophets, Isaiah would win. He is the most famous of all the prophets, and his name is practically synonymous with the prophetic impulse in Judaism. That is certainly the case with the *haftarot* for *sheva denechemta*. They all come from the book of Isaiah—but remember, from the prophet known as Second Isaiah.

Rabbi Mark Dov Shapiro asks: "If the haftarot following Tisha B'Av are all devoted towards consolation and are taken from the book of Isaiah, on what basis were the specific verses for each of the seven sabbaths selected?" The question arises because the prophetic portions seem to have been chosen with no particular rhyme or reason.

Here's an intriguing answer to Rabbi Shapiro's question: Abudaraham, a commentator in the fourteenth century, believed that if you take the first verse of each of the seven *haftarot*, they form an imaginary conversation between God, the prophet, and the Jewish people.

Let's start with this week's haftarah portion. God tells the prophet: "Comfort, oh comfort my people" (40:1). God wants the people to know that their time of exile in Babylon is coming to an end, and that they will soon be able to return to the Land of Israel.

But, go to next week's haftarah. The people are not so sure that God really will fulfill that promise. "Zion says, 'The Lord has forsaken me, my Lord has forgotten me'" (49:14).

So, in the following week's haftarah, the prophet tells God that the people are "unhappy, storm-tossed one, uncomforted!" (54:11). God has to speak directly with the people. The next week's haftarah begins with God saying: "I, I am He who comforts you!" (51:12).

In the subsequent *haftarot*, God continues with personal reassurances. In the Bible, a woman who cannot have children is a symbol of hopelessness. And yet, in the fifth haftarah of consolation—"Shout, O barren one, you who bore no child!" (54: 1)—a hopeless people will find hope once again! The sixth week features God saying: "Arise, shine, for your light has dawned" (60:1). And by the seventh week, leading up to Rosh Hashanah, the people are emotionally ready to return to Zion: "I greatly rejoice in the Lord, my whole being exults in my God" (61:10).

Notice, by the way: the people cannot comfort themselves (much like infants who need others to comfort them). The prophet cannot do it alone. And God cannot do it alone. That is why these *haftarot* contain both God's words and the prophet's words. A midrash says: "The prophet came to God and said that the people refused to be comforted. God then said: 'Then you and I will go together to comfort them.'"

That's a provocative thought about cheering people up and giving them hope. Telling people to "keep the faith" perhaps is not enough, and being there for someone goes a long way, although maybe that too falls short. But a combination of both approaches just might do it.

❖ 'Ekev: Isaiah 49:14–51:3

A people, long abandoned, living in exile—that is the Jews living in Babylon. They are feeling dejected and depressed. The decades of oppression have taken a toll. Has God totally forgotten them?

No. The prophet known as Second Isaiah tells them that their time of exile is coming to an end, and that they will be able to return home to the Land of Israel. God is still in their midst.

For those of us who are accustomed to imagining God as a male, father, king, the language of this haftarah will come as a surprise. Instead of *Avinu Malkheinu* (our Father, our King), we have the image of God as Mother, and, more precisely, a mother who will never abandon her children. There is no shortage of Jewish ways to think about God. God as "Mother" is a compelling metaphor; then and now.

In Order to Have a Future, You Must Look to the Past

Perhaps you are on a sports team, and you've been losing a lot. Perhaps you've not been working up to your potential in school. Perhaps your Hebrew preparation is not what it should be. And so you get a pep talk. It could be from a coach, or a teacher, or your parents, or your rabbi, cantor, or religious school teachers. What do they say to you? "C'mon—you can do it. You've got to do it! You're better than this! Get your act together!"

But, there is something else they might say. They might say: "You have done this well in the past. You can do it again." The Jews in Babylon need that kind of pep talk. They have been separated from their native land for a long time. Many of them are choosing Babylonian names for their children and assimilating into the ways of the Babylonians.

What do the Jews need to hear? For one thing, a vision of a shining future, which the prophet gives them: "As for your ruins and desolate places and your land laid waste—you shall soon be crowded with settlers, while destroyers stay far from you" (49:19). The Jews will return to their land, and they will rebuild it.

Ironically, the prophet's promise was fulfilled again in the twentieth century, when Jews returned to Israel after two thousand years! Jews turned the Land of Israel into a prosperous and powerful state. Yes, true to the words of Isaiah, even crowding began to happen, and new housing developments have sprung up all over Israel. Regarding those "destroyers" staying far away, that has not proven completely true. While Israel has thankfully not faced a major war with its neighbors, terrorism is still a grim reality.

But let's not forget how true the prophetic promise is. As Rabbi Bradley Shavit Artson has written: "Israel's existence is a miracle: After wandering in exile for almost twenty centuries, the Jewish people have returned to their homeland where they govern a Jewish democracy, speak the ancient language of the Torah and the Mishnah, and conduct their daily routine in the neighborhoods of Isaiah, King David, and Rabbi Judah Ha-Nasi. It is easy to take this collective resurrection for granted. Even after visiting Israel many times, I still forget how astonishing the establishment of Israel really is."

Jews rebuilt Israel by never forgetting the dream that once was. But before you can get to that glorious future, you have to remember your glorious past. That's what will give you the inspiration to continue. As Isaiah reminds the people: "Look back to Abraham your father and to Sarah who brought you forth. For he was only one when I called him, but I blessed him and made him many" (51:1–2).

Why are Abraham and Sarah role models? The great medieval commentator Rashi says: "Because Abraham was alone when he came forth from his homeland and from his father's house." The prophet knew what he was talking about. After all, where had Abraham been born? In Ur, the land of Babylon! The very place where the Jews were sent into exile. If Abraham and Sarah could leave Ur, which means leaving Babylon, and go to the Land of Israel, so could the Jews of the generation of the exile. They looked to Abraham, and they found courage.

❖ Re'eh: Isaiah 54:11–55:5

(Reader note: this haftarah is the same as the haftarah for
Parashat Noaḥ, in the book of Genesis.)

The Jews are now preparing themselves, spiritually, to return to the
Land of Israel. Even still, they need assurances from God, for the
people see themselves as a boat that is being tossed around in a terrible storm (54:11).

But the storm will someday end, and the "boat," which is the Jewish people, will come to a safe harbor. It will not only be a geograph-
ical homecoming, to the Land of Israel, but a spiritual one as well. It
will require that Jews make a renewed commitment to being a people
concerned with *tzedakah*—charity and acts of social justice.

While it seems that God had hidden the Divine Presence from the
Jewish people, and had even sent them into exile in Babylon, in reality, God has never withdrawn love from them.

Are You Making Peace?

I bet you never thought that studying Torah and its varying perspec-
tives leads to peacemaking. It's an amazing lesson—and it is one that
Judaism has tried to teach the world.

Second Isaiah envisioned a time of restoration for the Jewish people, not only physically to the Land of Israel, but spiritually to a state
of peace and happiness. We all have a role in bringing that about, but
need to know how, which is one reason why Judaism puts such an
emphasis on education.

Quick: why do you attend religious school? To learn about Judaism? To learn the history of the Jewish people? To learn Hebrew—or,
at least, enough Hebrew for your bar or bat mitzvah ceremony? To be
with friends? Because your parents say so?

Those are all decent answers. But here's one that maybe you've never
considered: to learn how to think. Jewish education is great preparation for how to think like an adult. When many people discuss controversial subjects, they can get very worked up, not really listening to
their opponents' views, and seeing them in the worst possible light.

But that is not how Judaism views the world. And we find proof of this in one verse of this week's haftarah: "And all your children shall be disciples of the Lord, and great shall be the happiness [*shalom*, which also means 'peace'] of your children" (54:13).

The study of Torah should lead to peace between Jews who are learning Judaism together. It is written in the Talmud, "Rabbi Eleazar said in the name of Rabbi Chanina: Those who study Torah help to build peace in the world. Do not read *banayikh*, 'your children,' but rather '*bonayikh*,' 'your builders.' Those who learn and teach Torah are the builders of the world."

Builders—not destroyers through cruel and harsh language. The best way that you can build the world is through people learning together. That is why Judaism believes that we should study many different opinions.

Here is one example. Traditional medieval commentaries on the Hebrew Bible have a very interesting page layout. The Bible text is in the middle and commentary, or interpretations of the text, from across the centuries surround it. All those teachers "live together" on the same page, in shalom.

Or, look at the mezuzah on a door. It is slanted. Rashi, the great sage of twelfth-century France, said that the mezuzah should be vertical. His grandson, Rabbeinu Tam, said that it should be horizontal. A generation later, Rabbi Jacob ben Asher said that it should be a little of both; it should be slanted—as a way of keeping shalom.

That is why Rav Kook, the first chief rabbi of prestate Israel, said: "When Torah scholars broaden knowledge and provide new insights, they contribute to the increase of peace." All views, even those that seem contradictory, in fact help reveal knowledge and truth. For this reason, the early sage Rabbi Chanina emphasized that scholars are like builders. A building is erected from all sides, using a variety of materials and skills. So too, the whole truth is constructed from diverse views, opinions, and methods of analysis.

An important lesson—be a student; be a builder, be a peacemaker.

❖ Shofetim: Isaiah 51:12–52:12

It hasn't been enough for the prophet, known as Second Isaiah, to issue promises of the future redemption of the Jewish people. No, God
must comfort the people directly. That is why this haftarah begins
with the words "I, I am He who comforts you!" (51:12). It's as if the
people have forgotten all about God, and God jumps in and reminds
them of who God really is.

Interesting to note: God does not identify the Divine Self as the
One who, centuries ago, took them out of Egypt. God does not remind them of the giving of the Ten Commandments (though the first
word of this haftarah—*Anokhi*—"I am"—is an echo of the first words
of the Ten Commandments).

No, God instead reminds the Jews of the creation story. God is the
one "who stretched out the skies and made firm the earth!" (51:13).
This is a major theme for the prophet Second Isaiah. Here's why: The
Jews who were living in exile in Babylonia might have been tempted
to believe that the Babylonian gods were responsible for the Creation.
God (or at least the prophet) is afraid of competition between the
Egyptian gods and God and therefore has to reassert that God alone
was the Creator. For that reason, Second Isaiah is sometimes credited
with originating the idea of monotheism—that only God is God, and
that the so-called other gods don't even exist.

It's not as if God has totally forgotten the Exodus from Egypt. Hardly.
When the Israelites left Egypt, how did they do it? "Hurriedly" (Exod.
12:11); that was why they left Egypt without time for their bread to
rise. But there is about to be a new "exodus"; this time, it will be the
Jews leaving exile in Babylonia. This new "exodus" from Babylonia
will not be like the first Exodus. "For you will not depart in haste, nor
will you leave in flight; for the Lord is marching before you, the God
of Israel is your rear guard" (Isa. 52:12). God is with the Jews. There
is no need to fear.

Jerusalem or Zion?

If someone were to ask you to identify the twin cities, you would probably say Minneapolis and Saint Paul, Minnesota.

It turns out that Jerusalem is also a twin city. There are two Jerusalems. You could figure that out grammatically, because the Hebrew word for Jerusalem—*Yerushalayim*—is actually in the plural form.

Today some people see two Jerusalems in that Jerusalem has an old, walled city, and a new, modern city. Others looks at East Jerusalem, which is predominately Arab, and West Jerusalem, which is predominately Jewish. But there is another way to look at the two Jerusalems; the haftarah constantly refers to the holy city as both "Zion" and "Jerusalem."

Is there a difference between "Zion" and "Jerusalem," or are they simply synonyms for the same place? Rabbis W. Gunther Plaut and Chaim Stern teach: "'Zion' and 'Jerusalem' express two aspects of the city. Zion was predominantly its spiritual identification, and Jerusalem its geographic aspect."

This is crucial to understanding Jerusalem—and probably to understanding the entire State of Israel. There is a geographic reality to the city, but there is also a spiritual reality. Or, think of it this way: In "Jerusalem" there are shopping malls. In "Zion" there are synagogues and yeshivas.

For the ancient Rabbis, it sometimes seemed as if the spiritual Jerusalem had become more important than the "real" Jerusalem. We can understand why; some of those Rabbis were writing after the Romans had destroyed Jerusalem, and they were carrying a sacred memory within their hearts. They liked to imagine that there was a *Yerushalayim shel matah*, an earthly Jerusalem, a Jerusalem of reality—as well as a *Yerushalayim shel ma'alah*, a heavenly Jerusalem, a Jerusalem of the ideal. Zion is the heavenly ideal. Jerusalem is the earthly reality.

What is the heavenly Jerusalem like? The ancient sages imagined Jerusalem to be a place of miracles: "No man ever had an accident in Jerusalem; no fire ever broke out in Jerusalem; no man ever said, 'There is no place for me to sleep in Jerusalem.'" It's the kind of place we wish for in our dreams.

Yes, there is something magical about Jerusalem—a magic that, for the Jew, exists nowhere else on earth. There is a special atmosphere in Jerusalem that some describe as otherworldly. But while it's wonderful to sense that specialness, let's not get carried away.

Jerusalem, and all of Israel, is a very real place, with very real problems and challenges. "Zion" might be the uniquely spiritual aspect of Jerusalem, but there is still "Jerusalem" the capital, with all the realities of a big city.

"Hatikvah," Israel's national anthem, describes the country as the "land of Zion *and* Jerusalem." The ideal can become real. As Rabbi Roland B. Gittelsohn writes: "To survive and develop creatively, a civilization must have a locus, a laboratory or hot-house, if you will, where it can be the primary culture of its people, where new strands and strains may be tested and refined." Israel is the lab for cultivating Jewish ideals, and Jerusalem is a place to dream.

❖ Ki Tetse': Isaiah 54:1–10

As we have said, it is easy to see how the Jews in Babylon could have plunged into deep despair. But the prophet known as Second Isaiah has moved into total encouragement mode. He says that even if the Jewish people (symbolized by a barren woman) feel that they have no hope, because they are still in Babylonian exile, don't worry! She will be healed from her infertility, and she will have lots of children—so many that her house will have to be expanded! That's how the prophet chooses to tell the people: Relax, you will be coming home to the Land of Israel soon.

Can This Marriage Be Saved?

Sometimes, it is difficult to really get into the language of the prophets, especially when they use ideas that seem so outmoded and foreign to us. And yes, sometimes those ideas are not only outmoded and foreign; they are actually offensive to modern ears.

That, frankly, is what happens in this haftarah. How is the Jewish people described? In exclusively feminine terms. But those terms are troublesome. First, the Jews are like a "barren one" (54:1)—a woman who is not able to have children. (Yes, the barren woman will eventually have children—a whole lot of them—but you can imagine how painful it might be for a childless woman to hear these words in synagogue.) Then, the Jews are compared to a "widow" (54:4). The text speaks of the "disgrace" of being a widow. (Since when is it a disgrace to be a widow?) And then, the passage seems to say that the Jewish people are like a divorced woman, who can be brought back to her husband (54:6–8).

How can we make sense of all this? First, we need to remember that, in ancient times, to be childless was to be considered cursed. And not only in ancient times. If you ask people today who have been trying to have children and have not been successful, you will discover that they, too, feel many things—sad, angry, depressed, and perhaps even cursed. In that sense, the Jewish people, exiled in Babylonia, felt as if they were under a curse, and that they were not being "productive." That's why God promises them that they will have many children, and that those children will be triumphant.

What about the "widow"? Rabbis W. Gunther Plaut and Chaim Stern teach: "Isaiah takes 'widow' in a wider sense, as a woman who has been abandoned and divorced by her husband and has thus been publicly shamed."

The most painful image is divorce. This makes sense when we remember that, often, the relationship between God and Israel is imagined to be like a marriage. (The prophet Hosea loved that image.) But if Israel breaks the marital covenant (which usually means "messing around" with false gods), then it leads to a divorce. The biblical system is unfair and one sided: as the "husband," God has the sole power to initiate the divorce.

Even the whole idea of reconciliation seems a little troubling. While one may hope for that, sometimes in a troubled or broken marriage the relationship is too far gone to repaired. Rabbi Vivian Mayer writes: "For us, the scenario of the rejected woman reconciling with her husband may resonate all too well with the familiar domestic reality of battered wives rejoicing in a reunion with their abusers."

And yet, God still loves the Jewish people—and always will. Commenting on the verse "In slight anger, for a moment, I hid My face from you" (54: 8), the medieval commentator David Kimchi teaches: "Even though the days of exile were long, they will feel like only a brief moment compared to the time of redemption."

Isaiah uses the language of marriage and family that we can relate to. Even though it reflects some of the biases of the time, getting personal gets our attention. One's relationship with one's spouse or partner really matters . . . and so does our relationship with God.

❖ Ki Tavo': Isaiah 60:1–22

As the clock ticks, and as it gets closer to Rosh Hashanah, it looks ever more likely that God will keep the divine promise and restore the Jewish people to their homeland. That is the triumphant mood of this haftarah. It is filled with images of light, which in Judaism are always synonymous with Torah, God, and hope itself.

Not only will the Jews be brought back to their land; other nations will come to serve them, and those that refuse to do so will vanish. Things will be so good for the Jews that even nature will conspire to help them; the people will no longer need either the light of the sun, or that of the moon.

The Secret of Judaism's Most Popular Song

Imagine if Judaism had a "greatest hits" list; what would be its most popular song?

The answer: *Lekhah Dodi,* the hymn that is sung on Erev Shabbat. There are thousands of versions of this song, and it seems that Jewish composers are writing new versions every year.

Lekhah Dodi emerged from the city of Safed, in the north of Israel. In the sixteenth century, Safed consisted of a small community of mystical seekers, most of them refugees from Spain. Many of those mystical seekers gathered around a charismatic teacher, Rabbi Isaac Luria.

Solomon ha-Levi Alkabetz was part of Luria's "club," and he was the author of *Lekhah Dodi.* In the song Alkabetz imagines that Shabbat is a bride—and that when Jews observe Shabbat, it is as if they actually "marry" Shabbat. The opening line and refrain is: "Come, my friend, to meet the bride; let us welcome the presence of the Sabbath." As Luria himself wrote: "I sing in hymns to enter the gates of the field of apples of holy ones. A new table we lay for her, a beautiful candelabrum sheds its light upon us. Between right and left the bride approaches in holy jewels and festive garments. . . . Torment and cries are past. Now there are new faces and souls and spirits."

When Alkabetz wrote *Lekhah Dodi,* he freely picked verses from the prophet Second Isaiah—in particular, this week's haftarah portion: "Arise, shine, for your light has dawned; the Presence of the Lord has shone upon you!" (60:1)

What's the connection between Second Isaiah's vision of redemption and Shabbat?

Here's what is happening. As we have seen, Second Isaiah is obsessed with the Jews' return to the Land of Israel, and, in particular, Jerusalem. For Jews, Jerusalem is the holiest place in the world, and Shabbat is the holiest time in the week. It all fits together. The holiness of place combines with the holiness of time—two "Shabbats" coming together. That is why the Talmud teaches: "If only Israel would observe just two *Shabbatot,* then they would immediately be redeemed."

For weeks, the prophet has been urging the Jews: Stop mourning for Jerusalem and the Land of Israel; it's almost time to come home! In the words of Professor Reuven Kimmelman: "The task of the singer of 'Lekhah Dodi' is to comfort the mourning city and to urge her to get up from sitting shivah. He reassures her that the original beloved bridegroom who abandoned her will be back and now it is time to ready herself for his return."

And just as mourning for Jerusalem must end, Shabbat symbolizes the temporary postponing of mourning. You can't mourn on Shabbat. In the synagogue, as the singing of *Lekhah Dodi* ends, it is customary for the community to welcome that week's mourners into the synagogue. The traditional greeting combines personal and national comfort: "May God comfort you, among all those who mourn for Zion and Jerusalem."

So the imminent return of the Jews from exile will be like a never-ending Shabbat. That is also how the sages described the Messianic Era, and the life to come. Hope springs eternal.

❖ Nitsavim–Va-yelekh: Isaiah 61:10–63:9

This haftarah has a double name because it's read along with two *parshiyot,* Nitsavim and Va-yelekh.

Seven weeks ago, it was Tisha b'Av. The Babylonians destroyed Jerusalem and the Temple. The horror was beyond imagining. (Read the book of Lamentations for the eyewitness accounts; it is not pretty.)

For seven weeks, Jews have been reading *haftarot* that ask the following questions: Can God bring us home from Babylon? *Will* God bring us home from Babylon? And the answer is: Yes. Yes, it is time to come home. And this is no mere "coming home." It's like a wedding in which God is the bridegroom and Israel is the bride. "Like a bridegroom adorned with a turban, like a bride bedecked with her finery" (61:10).

More than that: sometimes, when people get married, the bride will take a new name—usually, her husband's last name. (This happens less often these days, but it's still common.) When the Jewish people "marry" God, it's not as if God has a last name for them to take (!). But they do change their names—"Nevermore shall you be called 'Forsaken,' nor shall your land be called 'Desolate'; but you shall be called 'I delight in her,' and your land 'Espoused'" (62:4).

In the Bible, when someone's name is changed—for example, Abram to Abraham, Sarai to Sarah, Jacob to Israel—it means a total change of status. And that is what has happened to the Jewish people. Changing their name, even poetically and temporarily, means that they have changed their status from a demoralized people to a victorious people. Or, think of it this way: there is an old Jewish custom to change the name of someone who is seriously ill, imagining that this will confuse the Angel of Death. The Jewish people have been seriously "ill," suffering from inner despair. So, change their name—let them live again!

When It Comes to Israel, Don't Be Silent

If you were going to look for the verse from the haftarah that has had the most enduring influence, it would be this one: "For the sake of Zion I will not be silent; for the sake of Jerusalem I will not be still, till her victory emerge resplendent and her triumph like a flaming torch" (62:1).

The great Bible commentator Rashi, who lived in the Middle Ages, didn't forget what that verse means. In fact, he had a new understanding of it, because he lived in the days of the Crusades, when armies went to war in Jerusalem: "I shall act, and I shall not be silent about what was done to Jerusalem, and I will not be at peace until her victory emerges."

But, nowadays, what does it mean not to be silent regarding Zion? It means recognizing that Israel is the ancestral home of the Jewish people, and it is part of every Jew's religious identity. It means recognizing that Israel is a refuge from antisemitism, and that it is a place where Jews can go to escape persecution and be safe. Finally, it means recognizing that Israel is an example to the rest of the world for how to engage in *tikkun olam,* repairing the world.

What can you do to support Israel, and to speak up with your own deeds? You can visit Israel; make friends with Israelis and stay in touch with them; improve your knowledge of Hebrew; follow what's happening in the Israeli political arena; buy Israeli products whenever possible, especially food products; write letters to the newspaper supporting and defending Israel; give *tzedakah* to organizations that support Israel; read Israeli newspapers and magazines online; read books about Israel; listen to Israeli rock music; watch Israeli films; follow Israeli sports; learn to cook Israeli or Middle Eastern dishes.

And why should Jews not be silent about Israel? Think about how the Jews in Babylon felt. They had been dreaming about returning to the Land of Israel; now it is becoming a reality. So, too, with modern Jews, who especially after the Holocaust could celebrate a return to the Jewish homeland.

As the late Esther Jungreis writes about her childhood in a Nazi concentration camp: "The nights in Bergen Belsen were very long. I would close my eyes and try to escape by recalling stories from the Bible, stories of our sages, and stories of Jerusalem. We would yet come to Jerusalem, where the sun always shone, where no one ever went hungry, where, my mother assured me, candy bars actually grew on trees, and birds sang the psalms of King David. Never had a nation returned to its land after two thousand years, and we saw it with our very eyes. The ancient prophecy was fulfilled."

How can one be silent or apathetic about the miracle by the Mediterranean that is Israel?

❖ Ha'azinu: 2 Samuel 22:1–51

The drama of "will we return to Israel?" of the last several *haftarot* is now complete. With the coming of Rosh Hashanah, the Jews are "home"—not only geographically, in the Land of Israel during ancient times, but "home" as well in modern times, now that we have a re-established Jewish state, and have synagogues that build and nurture active Jewish communities.

Knowing this, we can now go back to linking the Torah portion thematically with the haftarah portion. Back to finding common themes and language. This week's Torah portion contains Moses's farewell song to the Jewish people. And this week's haftarah presents the song that King David composed in his old age. So the connection between the two is farewell songs.

What rests heavily upon David's memory? It is the fact that when he was younger, King Saul pursued him and tried to kill him. Saul had been jealous of David's growing popularity, and that jealousy pushed him into a murderous madness. But David is not killed, and he thanks God for having saved him.

As we know, King David is considered one of the Jewish people's most important poets. Jewish lore and tradition credit him with writing many of the psalms in the Bible. And, as a poet, David had no shortage of ways of thinking about God. He compares God to many things, and these different images teach us that our ways of thinking about God are hardly frozen; they can and do change.

Meeting God—On Our Own Terms

Let's imagine King David sitting down and coming up with a list of terms for God. But, before he can do that, he has to think about why he is talking to God in the first place. David is grateful to God, whom he credits with saving him. That's why most of his terms for God are about David's own sense of security.

He calls God a "rock" (22:3), which means that he believes God is sturdy and unchanging. He calls God a "shield" (22:3), reminding us that the six-pointed "Jewish star" is sometimes called a Magen David (Shield of David), because David believes that God has defended him from Saul. He calls God a "stronghold" (22:35)—a fortress. (There is a Christian hymn called "A Mighty Fortress Is Our God.") He calls God a "lamp" (22:29). Perhaps it was because David hid from Saul in caves, which tend to be dark, and thinking about God was like shining a little bit of light into that darkness.

And, for good measure, David throws in some God imagery that was popular in his time—images that we have totally abandoned. "Smoke went up from His nostrils, from His mouth came devouring fire; live coals blazed forth from Him. He bent the sky and came down, thick cloud beneath His feet. He mounted a cherub and flew; he was seen on the wings of the wind" (22:10–11). Yes, there were some ancient Jews who thought that God was like, well, a dragon, but a dragon who could bend the sky and who rode on a cherub, a mythical angel-like figure—whom we have already met, because there were representations of the cherubim over the ark in the ancient Tabernacle.

What can we learn from this? If David was not consistent in his way of experiencing God, that means we do not have to be consistent, either. Think of how we experience God on the High Holy Days:

> We are Your people; you are our King.
> We are Your children, You are our Father.
> We are Your possession; You are our Portion.
> We are Your flock; You are our Shepherd.
> We are Your vineyard; You are our Keeper.
> We are Your friend; you are our Beloved." (*Ki Anu Amekha*)

Many of those ways of understanding the God relationship are familiar, but notice: they go from royal terms, to paternal terms, to agricultural terms, and finally to a deep sense of human relationship and affection.

But, let's admit, we can never fully "get" God. Rabbi Abraham Isaac Kook, the first chief rabbi of prestate Palestine, wrote: "All names and titles of God reveal but a small and dim spark of the hidden light toward which the soul really yearns and to which it calls out."

All that we say and think about God, all that we teach and sing about God, all that we think we know about God—these are all radical understatements. They are only sparks of what we think we know and what we think we want to know. But those sparks are there and if you tend them and if you poke them with a stick, they will flame into a fire.

SPECIAL HAFTAROT

❖ Mahar Hodesh: 1 Samuel 20:18–42

Whenever Shabbat falls before the beginning of a new Hebrew month (Rosh Hodesh) many synagogues read a special haftarah. Mahar Hodesh ("Tomorrow is the new month") is a segment from 1 Samuel. Its relationship to the new moon is clear, for the text begins with the words: "And Jonathan said to him [David]: 'Tomorrow will be the new moon'" (20:18).

Jonathan is the son of King Saul, and heir to the throne of Israel. Saul knows that the powerful hero David is a good friend to Jonathan, but that doesn't prevent Saul from seeing David as a threat to the throne. As we know, David does eventually become king of Israel— but only because Jonathan dies in battle against the Philistines, and Saul takes his own life.

It is quite appropriate that we read this passage right before Rosh Hodesh. Months are connected to the cycles of the moon, and, as the new moon approaches, the night skies are almost entirely dark. There is deep darkness within the soul of King Saul, and the friendship between Jonathan and David brings some much-needed light into an otherwise dark story. In fact, this is one of the most powerful stories about friendship in the entire Hebrew Bible. If you have one friend who is as close to you as David was to Jonathan, consider yourself very lucky.

The Mystery of Friendship

Thanks to Facebook, friendship isn't what it used to be.

Back before social networking a friend was someone whom you knew very well; with whom you shared things in common and hung out; and whom you could trust. Today, it's different. People on Facebook can often claim that they have thousands of "friends." Sometimes, but not always, they've actually met some of these "friends" in person!

If you really want to see the ultimate meaning of friendship, you have to know the story of David and Jonathan.

Let's understand the cast of characters. King Saul is the first king of Israel, and, frankly, he's a very difficult person. He has violent mood swings, and sometimes suffers from deep depression. (The Bible doesn't call it that; today, we know more about depression and how to treat it.) King Saul's son is Jonathan, and he's the heir to the throne. David's a young man who's becoming a popular military hero. He has already killed the Philistine giant, Goliath, in battle—armed with only a slingshot. He also has a unique talent: he plays the harp, which soothes Saul's spirits and helps him feel better. Nonetheless, Saul is becoming increasingly jealous of young David's popularity, and increasingly resentful of Jonathan's close attachment to this emerging leader.

The haftarah portion describes an elaborate trick that Jonathan and David devised—a trick that Jonathan uses to warn David if Saul intends to do David harm. Jonathan tells David that he'll shoot three arrows and send a boy to find them. If he tells the boy that "the arrows are on this side of you" (20:21), David will know he's safe. If the arrows are "beyond you," that's the signal for David to flee.

Jonathan and David's friendship is the biblical model for all friendships. "Any loving relationship that depends on something—when that thing is gone, the love is gone. But a relationship that does not depend on something will never come to an end. That is the love of David and Jonathan."

Why does Jonathan love David? We don't really know the mystery of their friendship. But part of Jonathan's admiration for David might be that, despite several opportunities to humiliate his father, Saul, or retaliate against him, David always chose to respect him. For example, when David killed the Philistine giant, Goliath, Saul greeted him in public and said: "Who is this young man?" David could have said: "Hold on. Haven't I been doing 'music therapy' with you? You're a broken, pitiful man. How dare you pretend that you don't know me!"

Here's some insight about this story from a modern author, Andre Neher: "David says, 'I am the son of your servant Jesse of Bethlehem' (1 Sam. 17:58) and he stops there without speaking the word which would have betrayed the king." David refused to humiliate King Saul in public, which only endeared him even more to Jonathan.

To be a friend, you not only have to know what to say. You also have to know what *not* to say.

❖ Shabbat Parah: Ezekiel 36:16–38

Shabbat Parah is a special Shabbat that comes right after Purim. It accompanies the additional Torah reading about the famous red cow (Num. 19:1–22). A red cow with no blemishes is chosen to be ritually slaughtered and its ashes used to purify anyone who has been in contact with the dead.

This special haftarah goes a little bit further because it reminds us that it's not only contact with the dead that can make you impure. Worse kinds of impurity are moral and spiritual impurity, and that is precisely what Ezekiel is prophesying about. Yes, there are special ritual ways of becoming physically pure after experiencing impurity, but becoming morally or spiritually pure—those are much more difficult.

God Has a Reputation

No doubt about it; we all worry about our reputations. Think of the kid who gets bullied or teased on Facebook or Twitter, and how quickly that kind of talk goes viral. "Viral" is the right word for it, because when your reputation suffers it is like a disease—a disease that is very hard to cure. It's tough to get rid of that stuff on the Internet. There are companies that will try to clean up someone's online reputation, but they cost a lot of money and they're often not 100 percent successful.

We tend to think that only people have reputations. But, it turns out, God has a reputation as well. And that's the focus of this haftarah.

Here in the book of Ezekiel God is angry that the Jews have done terrible things. Yes, God has punished them by sending them into exile, but it's not enough. God worries that when the Jews wind up in the nations to which they have been sent, their mere presence there will testify to the fact that they have profaned God's name, that they have damaged God's reputation.

"But when they came to those nations, they caused My holy name to be profaned, in that it was said of them, 'These are the people of the Lord, yet they had to leave His land.' Therefore I am concerned for My holy name, which the House of Israel have caused to be profaned among the nations to which they have come'" (36:20–21). The medieval commentator Rashi explains the real problem: "The nations would say that God had not been able to save His people and His land."

This is called *chillul ha-Shem*—profaning God's name, damaging God's reputation. We like to imagine that God is all powerful (this is much debated in Judaism), but there is one thing over which God has no power: the way that God is perceived. And that power is totally in our hands!

The Talmud teaches: "If someone studies Scripture and Mishnah and attends to the disciples of the wise, but is dishonest in business, and discourteous in his relations with people, what do people say about him? 'Woe unto him who studied the Torah; woe unto his father who taught him Torah; woe unto his teacher who taught him Torah! This man studied the Torah: Look, how corrupt are his deeds, how ugly his ways; of him Scripture says: "In that men said of them: 'These are the people of the Lord, yet they had to leave His land' (Ezek. 36:20)."

The way that Jews behave has public implications. The term *chillul* (desecration) is related to the Hebrew verb that means "to hollow out." When we desecrate God's name, we show that our Judaism is hollow. That is why Jews get so upset when other Jews commit crimes; they imagine that those crimes reflect on the entire Jewish people. While in one sense God is God and need not worry about reputation, we do need to be concerned. How we talk about God reflects on us, and affects the morale of the community. That is why the sages have always been very sensitive about blasphemy and other behavior that reflects poorly in public.

As I have taught: "Jews are God's PR agents in the world." Do your job. Make God beautiful.

❖ Shabbat Shekalim: 2 Kings 12:1–17

How do you get ready for Pesach? Here is what most Jews do: put together the guest list for the Passover seder, choose a Haggadah to use, and start buying special foods for the holiday. Traditional Jews will spend a lot of time cleaning out their houses, disposing of any traces of *chametz*, foods that contain any leavened or fermented ingredients. Preparing for Pesach takes time, and it is best not to leave it for the last minute.

The same kind of process happens during synagogue services—four special Shabbatot in preparation for Pesach, each with a special Torah portion that is added to the weekly Torah reading, and each with a special haftarah.

The first, Shabbat Shekalim, has the wilderness census as its theme. In this haftarah, Jehoash, king of Judah, prepares to make much-needed repairs on the Temple, using money that the people have given as their sacred donations for its upkeep. Imagine how the king felt when he realized that, even though money had been donated, the priests had not made the necessary repairs. Luckily, the priest Jehoida corrected that situation and saw to it that the money was used properly.

Sacred Housekeeping

Imagine the following: you go to synagogue for Shabbat morning services. Your friend Jamie is becoming bat mitzvah. You are sitting in the pews, and you notice that the carpeting in the sanctuary is, well, dirty. This bugs you; after all, a synagogue should look nice, right?

At the end of the service, you mention this to a friend: "Hey, did you see how dirty the carpeting is in the sanctuary?" Your friend responds: "Why does that matter? Why were you even paying attention to that? You should have been paying attention to how awesome Jamie was! Who cares, anyway? Do you think that God cares what the synagogue looks like?"

Who is right—you, or your friend? On the one hand, you can understand your friend's reaction. After all, Jews have prayed in synagogues that have not been, well, elegant; some of them have been a total shambles. Often, Jews have not even had synagogue buildings to pray in. One Jewish man recalled what it was like to pray in the army, when he was serving in Vietnam: "We were in the middle of the jungle. It was pouring rain. We knew that enemy soldiers were all around us. We didn't have a temple, or a synagogue, or even a Torah scroll.

All we had was the chaplain, and the prayers that we had memorized. And we had each other."

So, why not just pray in a synagogue that needs repair, or that isn't totally clean? Does it matter?

Let's go to the haftarah. Jehoash was only seven years old when he became king, but, even at that very young age, he knew what he had to do. The Temple in Jerusalem had become worn out, and he wanted to restore it to its former glory. Money had been collected for that sacred purpose, but it had not been used, and the necessary repairs had not been carried out. As you might expect, he was not happy about this.

Jehoash could have said: "Hey, it doesn't matter. God will accept our sacrifices anyway." But he didn't say that. He knew that there was a sacred obligation to serve God in a place that is visually pleasing. If it was at all possible.

Judaism values *hiddur mitzvah,* the beauty of mitzvot. Maimonides writes: "It was commanded that the priest should be clothed properly with the most splendid and fine clothes, 'holy garments for glory and for beauty' . . . for the multitude does not estimate man by his true form but by . . . the beauty of his garments, and the Temple was to be held in great reverence by all."

This is precisely why synagogue maintenance is important—because the way that our sacred buildings look is part of our statement to God. You might even say that the work of synagogue custodians and maintenance workers is holy work, almost as holy as that of rabbis, cantors, and teachers. We often take their work for granted, but they too are participating in *hiddur mitzvah.* And that is a beautiful thing.

❖ Rosh Ḥodesh: Isaiah 66:1–24

When a worship service occurs on Rosh Hodesh (the first day of the Hebrew month), there is a special haftarah. Like many *haftarot,* this one comes from the prophet known as Second Isaiah. This anonymous prophet lived in the period when the Babylonian Empire was coming to an end and Persia was gaining in power. This prophet sensed that even though the Jews were now in exile, they were about to come home.

What does this haftarah have to do with Rosh Hodesh? Traditionally, Rosh Hodesh was a "woman's holiday." Women, who normally work very hard at a variety of tasks, had Rosh Hodesh as a day off—a mini-Shabbat. It has become customary for some Jewish communities to sponsor special Rosh Hodesh women's prayer groups and study programs.

Appropriately enough, much of the language in this haftarah is feminine and maternal. The prophet imagines that when the Jewish people return to the Land of Israel it will be as if the land itself is giving birth to the people—a newborn people, born into freedom and vast potential.

Happy Birthday!

Ask any mother, and she will tell you: giving birth is hard work. Very hard work. That's why they call it "labor." A woman can be in labor for hours on end before the baby is born. Yes, it's painful, but most mothers will tell you that it's the most joyous pain they have ever experienced.

It is interesting, then, to note that one of the major images in this haftarah is that of "Zion" (the Land of Israel) giving birth—to the Jewish people! "Before she labored, she was delivered; before her birth pangs came, she bore a son. . . . Can a land pass through travail in a single day? Or is a nation born all at once? Yet Zion travailed and at once bore her children! Shall I who bring on labor not bring about birth?—says the Lord" (66: 7–9).

Now, remember, women can often be in labor for hours and hours. And yet the prophet imagines that Zion (whom he visualizes as a mother) actually had a very short labor. There's more: Most of the time, we tend to think of God as a man—and a rather tough man at that. Not here. Second Isaiah imagines that God is like the midwife, attending the birth, like a nurse, standing by to help Zion "give birth."

What can we learn from this? First, a lesson about Jewish history. The prophet compares the emergence of the Jewish people—as a once-again-free people, liberated from Babylonian exile—to the birth of a baby, which usually happens in one day. In the words of the medieval commentator David Altschuler: "All of Zion's children will be gathered to her, as if it happened now—but without the pains of childbirth."

Childbirth is both painful and joyous, and that was the way the liberation of the Jews from Babylonian exile was. That was the way the birth of the State of Israel was as well—painful (consider all of the lives that were lost), but joyous.

Rosh Hodesh comes at the very beginning of the lunar cycle. (Interestingly: many Jewish holidays occur at the full moon, symbolizing completeness and wholeness.) What does this have to do with women? Rabbi Ilene Schneider writes: "The phases of a woman's body were as predictable as the appearances of the phases of the moon. As remarkable and mystical as it seemed to the ancients for the moon to disappear and reappear every month, equally remarkable was the ability of women to bleed without being in mortal danger."

The Jews also go through phases. Sometimes it is dark—the Holocaust, for example. But then things get better. The Jews live in safety and become prosperous—like the moon getting bigger, shedding more light. Such fluctuation is also true of Jewish communities; sometimes they get smaller, sometimes they get larger.

The Jews are a "moon" people—telling time and marking seasons by watching the cycles of the moon. We celebrate Rosh Hodesh to keep track of the calendar. But the deeper meaning is that like the cycles of the moon the Jewish people go through phases, always knowing that a new phase is about to arise.

NOTES

THE TORAH
Genesis

5 **"Beloved are human beings"**: Mishnah, *Avot* 3:14.

5 **"We hold these truths"**: Irving Greenberg, "Covenantal Pluralism," *Journal of Ecumenical Studies* 34, no. 3 (Summer 1997): 427.

6 **"It is not written"**: *Bereshit Rabbah* 22:9.

6 **"True hope is born"**: Marshall Meyer, *You Are My Witness: The Living Words of Rabbi Marshall T. Meyer* (New York: St. Martin's Press, 2014), 44.

10 **"Dispersion is part"**: Daniel Gordis, "The Tower of Babel and the Birth of Nationhood," *Azure* (Spring, 2010).

11 **"If a man fell"**: *Pirkei de-Rabbi Eliezer,* 24.

14 **"Abram seized a stick"**: *Bereshit Rabbah* 38:13.

14 **"There are times"**: Jonathan Sacks, *Covenant & Conversation—Genesis: The Book of Beginnings* (Jerusalem: Koren, 2009), 85.

15 **"All Israel is responsible"**: Talmud, *Shevu'ot* 39a.

15 **"A Jew must feel"**: Joseph B. Soloveitchik, *Abraham's Journey: Reflections on the Life of the Founding Patriarch* (New York: KTAV), 130.

16 **"To Abraham"**: *Bereshit Rabbah* 50:2.

19 **"To welcome a guest"**: Rabbi Judah Loew, *Netivot Olam, Netiv Gemilut Hasadim,* ch. 4, quoted in Shai Held, "The Face of Guests as the Face of God: Abraham's Radical and Traditional Theology," Mechon Hadar, Parashat Vayera 5774, accessed December 1, 2015, http://www.academia .edu/21694107/The_Face_of_Guests_as_the_Face_of_God_Abrahams _Radical_and_Traditional_Theology.

19 **"Abraham said to God"**: *Tanhuma Yelamdenu Vayera* 10.

20 **"There is no Judge"**: Talmud, *Kiddushin* 39b.

20 **"A righteous man"**: Elie Wiesel, "Words from a Witness," *Conservative Judaism* 21 (Spring 1967), 52.

23 **"Machpelah is one of the places"**: *Bereshit Rabbah* 79:7.

24 **"We have come to the land"**: "Anu Banu Artzah" (We have come to the land).

25 God **"auditioned" Moses"**: *Shemot Rabbah* 2:2.

27 **"For thirteen years"**: *Bereshit Rabbah* 63:9.

27 **"God must choose"**: Samuel K. Karff, "The Soul of the Rav," in *The Soul of the Rav: Sermons, Lectures, and Essays* (Austin: Eakin Press, 1999), 282.

29 **"Rabbi Simeon ben Gamaliel"**: *Bereshit Rabbah* 65:15.

29 **"I come from"**: Mordecai Finley, "The Most Serious Thing That Ever Happened to Me, by Esau Isaacson," in *Text Messages: A Torah Commentary for Teens*, ed. Jeffrey K. Salkin (Woodstock VT: Jewish Lights, 2012), 24.

32 **"The first group of angels"**: Solomon B. Freehof, *Preface to Scripture: A Guide to the Understanding of the Bible in Accordance with the Jewish Tradition* (New York: UAHC, 1957), 45–46.

32 **"Life is comparable"**: Philo, *On Dreams*, 1:150,153–56.

33 **"Jacob is the ultimate proof"**: Avraham Burg, *Very Near To You* (Jerusalem: Gefen, 2012), 52.

36 **"He was afraid"**: Rashi on Gen. 32:8.

37 **"We can forgive the Arabs"**: "Quotes on Judaism & Israel: Golda Meir," "On the Palestinians & Violence," Jewish Virtual Library, accessed December 1, 2015, http://www.jewishvirtuallibrary.org/jsource /Quote/meirq.html.

37 **"it was the guardian Prince"**: *Bereshit Rabbah* 77:3.

38 **"This night-time being"**: Shmuel Klitsner, *Wrestling Jacob: Deception, Identity, and Freudian Slips in Genesis* (Jerusalem: Ben Yehuda Press, 2009), 125.

41 **"A parent should never"**: Talmud, *Shabbat* 10b.

41 **"[Joseph's brothers] find themselves"**: Avivah Gottlieb Zornberg, *The Beginning of Desire: Reflections on Genesis*, (Philadelphia: Jewish Publication Society, 1996), 275.

42 **"Tamar refuses"**: Geela-Rayzel Raphael, "Parshat Vayeshev," in *The Women's Torah Commentary: New Insights from Women Rabbis on the 54 Weekly Torah Portions*, ed. Elyse Goldstein (Woodstock VT: Jewish Lights, 2008), 95.

42 **"Why did Judah's descendants"**: *Mekhilta Be-shallah* 5.

45 **"If that name is Egyptian"**: Nachmanides on Gen. 41:45.

46 **"Jews live in two civilizations"**: Mordecai Kaplan, *Judaism as a Civilization: Toward a Reconstruction of American-Jewish Life* (New York: Schocken, 1967. Originally published, 1934), 216.

47 **"Privilege is in danger"**: Morris Adler, *The Voice Still Speaks: Message of the Torah for Contemporary Man* (New York: Bloch, 1969), 101.

47 **"What constitutes complete repentance?"**: Maimonides, *Mishneh Torah*, Laws of Teshuva 2:1.

50 **"True, God used the brothers"**: Nehama Leibowitz, *Studies in Bereshit* (Jerusalem: Eliner Library, n.d., 499). See more at: http://www.reformjuda ism.org/learning/torah-study/vayigash/long-view#sthash.o9dpjJy6.dpuf.

51 **"At its deepest level"**: Lawrence Kushner, *Invisible Lines of Connections: Sacred Stories of the Ordinary* (Woodstock VT: Jewish Lights, 1996), frontispiece.

51 **"Joseph died before his brothers"**: Talmud, *Berakhot* 55a.

52 **"Joseph was the Hebrew"**: Barry Shrage, "Joseph or Moses: Who Do You Want to be?" in *Text Messages: A Torah Commentary for Teens*, ed. Jeffrey Salkin (Woodstock VT: Jewish Lights, 2012), 53.

55 **"*Lu* can mean"**: Rashi on Gen. 50:15.

55 **"In very small doses"**: Lawrence Kushner, *The Book of Words: Talking Spiritual Life, Living Spiritual Talk* (Woodstock VT: Jewish Lights, 1993), 80.

56 **"When Jacob was dying"**: *Bereshit Rabbah* 98:3.

56 **"Having Jewish friends"**: Steven M. Cohen, NEWCAJE webinar, 2010.

Exodus

61 **"for this office was"**: Josephus on Exodus, in *Antiquities of the Jews*, book 2.

63 **"Bonding yourself with your people"**: Jeffrey Salkin, *The Modern Men's Torah Commentary* (Woodstock VT: Jewish Lights, 2009), 85.

63 **"In a place where there are no men"**: Mishnah, *Avot* 2:5.

65 **"God said to Moses"**: *Bereshit Rabbah* 6:4.

66 **"As though it really was"**: Arthur Green, *These Are the Words: A Vocabulary of Jewish Spiritual Life* (Woodstock VT: Jewish Lights, 2001), 5.

67 **"The infant Moses"**: *Shemot Rabbah* 1:26.

67 **"As long as there are those"**: A. I. Greenberg, *Itturei Torah* (Tel Aviv: Yavneh Publishing, 1985), 3:54.

70 **"as long as the Israelites"**: *Shemot Rabbah* 16:2.

70 **"Come tomorrow and its blood"**: Lawrence Kushner, *The River of Light: Spirituality, Judaism, Consciousness* (Woodstock VT: Jewish Lights, 1991), 126.

71 **"It is highly improbable"**: Eli Barnavi, ed. *A Historical Atlas of the Jewish People: From the Time of the Patriarchs to the Present* (New York: Alfred A. Knopf, 1992), 4.

74 **"It was easy to return"**: Rashi on Exod. 13:17.

75 **"Too often we want the shortcut"**: Steven Moskowitz (sermon, Congregation L'Dor V'Dor, Brookville NY, February 1, 2013).

76 **"When Israel stood by the sea"**: *Be-midbar Rabbah* 13:4.

76 **"Maybe you don't believe"**: Sid Schwarz, "Beshalach," in *Text Messages: A Torah Commentary for Teens*, ed. Jeffrey Salkin (Woodstock VT: Jewish Lights, 2012), 81.

79 **"I draw near"**: *Mekhilta Yitro* 1.

79 **"Just before the revelation"**: Shai Held, "Does Everyone Hate the Jews?" Parashat Yitro 5774, Mechon Hadar, accessed June 29, 2016, https://www.mechonhadar.org/torah-resource/does-everyone-hate-jews.

81 **"Properly understood and applied"**: Dennis Prager, accessed June 29, 2015, http://www.dennisprager.com/still-the-only-solution-to-the-worlds-problems/.

84 **"Meat boiled in milk"**: Maimonides, *Guide to the Perplexed* 3:48.

84 "The goat provides man": Samuel H. Dresner, Seymour Siegel, David M. Pollock, *The Jewish Dietary Laws* (New York: United Synagogue, 1980), 32–33.

86 "If you oppress him": Rashi on Exod. 22:20.

86 "A history of alienation": Nehama Leibowitz, *Commentary on Shemot* (Jerusalem: World Zionist Organization, 1980), 384.

90 "A Jew should stretch forth": A. I. Greenberg, *Itturei Torah* (Jerusalem: Yavneh, 1985), 215.

90 "Rav Abbahu said": Talmud, *Sukkah* 5b.

90 "The building of the Tabernacle": Plaut, *The Torah: A Modern Commentary* (New York: UAHC, 1981), 598.

91 "God's intention": Nehama Leibowitz, *New Studies in Shemot* (Jerusalem: World Zionist Organization, 1995), 472.

94 "When they are wearing": Talmud, *Zevachim* 17b.

94 "Clothing makes a statement": Rabbi Sue Levi Elwell, quoted in Jeffrey Salkin, *Text Messages: A Torah Commentary for Teens* (Woodstock VT: Jewish Lights, 2012), 94.

95 "God said to him": *Shemot Rabbah* 37:1.

96 "A certain moral idea": Ahad Ha'Am, "Priest and Prophet," in *Selected Essays by Ahad Ha'Am*, trans. Leon Simon (Philadelphia: Jewish Publication Society, 1912), 125.

98 "Israel is coming into its own": Rabbi Ellen Lippman, in *The Women's Torah Commentary: New Insights from Women Rabbis on the 54 Weekly Torah Portions*, ed. Elyse Goldstein (Woodstock VT: Jewish Lights, 2000), 171.

99 "When God gave Moses": *Tanhuma Ki Tissa'* 26.

100 "Ever since the breaking of the Tablets": David Weiss Halivni, *Breaking the Tablets: Jewish Theology after the Shoah* (London: Rowman and Littlefield, 2007), Kindle edition.

100 "God said to Moses": *Shemot Rabbah* 46:1.

101 A well-known midrash: Talmud, *Berakhot* 8b.

104 "They made amends": Nehama Leibowitz, *New Studies in Shemot* (Jerusalem: World Zionist Organization, 1995), 669.

105 "Just as the Golden Calf": Avivah Gottlieb Zornberg, *The Particulars of Rapture: Reflections on Exodus* (New York: Doubleday, 2001), 475–76.

105 "When Israel was in Egypt": Nachmanides on Exod. 31:2.

105 "The desire for the beginnings": Rabbi Abraham Isaac Kook, *Orot Ha-Kodesh* 3:306, accessed June 29, 2016, http://www.atid.org/resources/art/ravkook.asp.

109 "The Book of Exodus": Avivah Gottlieb Zornberg, *The Particulars of Rapture: Reflections on Exodus* (New York: Doubleday, 2001), 498.

110 "Take the case of a parent": Eugene B. Borowitz, "Tzimtzum: A Mystic Model for Contemporary Leadership," in *Studies in the Meaning of Judaism* (Philadelphia: Jewish Publication Society, 2002), 165.

Leviticus

113 **"God could not expect us"**: Moses Maimonides, *Guide to the Perplexed* 3:32.

113 **"In every relationship"**: David Wolpe, "In Defense of Animal Sacrifice," *Huffington Post*, July 26, 2011, http://www.huffingtonpost.com/rabbi -david-wolpe/animal-sacrifice-defense_b_907405.html.

114 **"Fortunate is the generation"**: Talmud, *Horayot* 10b.

114 **"The role of the prophet"**: Avraham Burg, *Very Near to You* (Jerusalem: Gefen, 2012), 211.

117 **"There was a daily lottery"**: Mishnah, *Tamid* 1:2.

117 **"I was quite happy"**: Joshua Loth Liebman, "The Saintly Rabbi Baeck," *Milwaukee Journal* (June 18, 1948): 15.

119 **"The fully consecrated"**: *The Works of Philo Judaeus, the Contemporary of Josephus,* trans. C. D. Yonge (Ann Arbor: University of Michigan Press, 1855), 2:54.

119 **"The priest is smeared"**: Sorel Goldberg Loeb, "Musings On Opposable Thumbs and Other Body Parts," in *Living Torah: Selections from Seven Years of Torat Chayim,* ed. Elaine Rose Glickman (New York: URJ Press, 2005), 243.

122 **"they were eager"**: Talmud, *Sanhedrin* 52a.

122 **"People can accept"**: Andre Neher, *The Exile of the Word: From the Silence of the Bible to the Silence of Auschwitz* (Philadelphia: Jewish Publication Society, 1980), 35.

123 **"It is a dietary predilection"**: Personal reminiscence of Rabbi Haskell Bernat, Miami, FL, 1988.

123 **"Just as a cud-chewing animal"**: Philo, *Special Laws* 4:106–7.

126 **"There are three partners"**: Talmud, *Niddah* 31a.

127 **"Childbirth makes the mother"**: Nehama Leibowitz, *Studies in Vayikra* (Jerusalem: World Zionist Organization, 1986), 106–7.

127 **"This is a portion"**: Peretz Wolf-Prusan and Asher Lopatin, "Deep and Looking Up: How a Weird Story of Skin Disease Can Tell Us about Life over Death and Seeking Inner Peace," in *Text Messages: A Torah Commentary for Teens,* ed. Jeffrey Salkin (Woodstock VT: Jewish Lights, 2012), 129.

128 **"Turn it, turn it"**: Mishnah, *Avot* 5:22.

130 **"This serves as a moral lesson"**: Nehama Leibowitz, *Studies in Vayikra* (Jerusalem: World Zionist Organization, 1986), 217.

131 **"I love not knowing"**: Rabbi Gil Steinlauf, "Teach Your Tongue to Say, 'I Don't Know'" (Talmud, *Berakhot* 4a), accessed June 4, 2009, http:// rabbisteinlauf.blogspot.com/2009/06/teach-your-tongue-to-say-i-dont -know.html.

132 **"Consider the Hebrew word"**: Rabbi Judah Loew, *Netivot Olam* 2:73.

134 **"The goat simply bears"**: Nachmanides on Lev. 16:21.

135 **"The success of the scapegoating"**: Brad Hirshfield, "In Defense of Scapegoating," accessed April 10, 2014, http://thewisdomdaily.com/in-defense-of-scapegoating-how-to-send-off-your-mistakes/.

135 **Archeologists, digging in the Middle East**: Jon D. Levenson, *The Death and Resurrection of the Beloved Son: The Transformation of Child Sacrifice in Judaism and Christianity* (New Haven: Yale University Press, 1995), 19–20.

136 **"Those gods stood"**: David Polish, *Abraham's Gamble: Selected Sermons for Our Time* (Evanston: Beth Emeth The Free Synagogue, 1988), 157–58.

138 **"These are the obligations"**: Mishnah, *Peah* 1:1.

139 **"The holiest word"**: Micah Goodman, lecture, Shalom Hartman Institute, Jerusalem, July 2013.

140 **"Love your neighbor"**: Jerusalem Talmud, *Nedarim* 9:4.

140 **"I do not like Senator Eastland"**: Martin Luther King Jr., "Facing the Challenge of a New Age," address delivered at the First Annual Institute on Nonviolence and Social Change, Montgomery AL, December 3, 1956.

141 **"The basic dignity of man"**: Abraham J. Heschel, "Sacred Image of Man," in *The Insecurity of Freedom: Essays on Human Existence* (New York: Schocken, 1972), 153.

144 **"Our religious leadership"**: Shlomo Riskin, "The Role of Jewish Priests: A Matter of Life and Death," *New York Jewish Week*, May 15, 2012.

144 **"None shall defile himself"**: Rashi on Lev. 21:1.

145 **"Everything that is done"**: *Mishneh Torah, Issurei Mizbeach* 7:11.

146 **"While the priest's bodily"**: Shulamit Reinharz, "Parashat Emor," in *The Women's Torah Commentary: New Insights from Women Rabbis on the 54 Weekly Torah Portions*, ed. Elyse Goldstein (Woodstock VT: Jewish Lights, 2008), 743.

148 **"God's creation of the universe"**: Saul Berman, "The Extended Notion of the Sabbath," *Judaism* (Summer 1973): 342–52.

149 **"The Lord spoke to Moses"**: *Sifra, Behar* 1.

150 **"The poor of your city"**: Shulḥan Arukh, *Yoreh De'ah* 251:3.

150 **"In 1977"**: Daniel Gordis, *Menachem Begin's Zionist Legacy: Essays* (New York: Mosaic Books, 2014), 411, Kindle edition.

153 **"You must know"**: Nachmanides on Lev. 26:16.

153 **"It is both bribe and promise"**: Sarah Sager, "Parashat Be-hukkotai," in *The Women's Torah Commentary: New Insights from Women Rabbis on the 54 Weekly Torah Portions*, ed. Elyse Goldstein (Woodstock VT: Jewish Lights, 2008), 783.

154 **"The bond that holds"**: Michael Paulson, The 'Pay What You Want' Experiment at Synagogues, *New York Times*, February 2, 2015, http://www.nytimes.com/2015/02/02/us/the-pay-what-you-want-experiment-at-synagogues.html?_r=0.

155 **"People of the city"**: *Mishneh Torah, Hilkhot Shekhenim* 6:1.

Numbers

159 **"They were all equal"**: *Akedat Yitzhak, Be-midbar* 72.

159 **"What about the woman"**: Cantor Rachel Stock Spilker, in *The Torah: A Women's Commentary,* ed. Tamara Cohn Eskenazi and Andrea L. Weiss (New York: URJ Press, 2008), 811.

160 **"It lists only the sons"**: Rashi on Num. 3:1.

161 **"Just as a son"**: Howard Eilberg-Schwartz, *The Savage in Judaism: An Anthropology of Israelite Religion and Ancient Judaism* (Bloomington IN: Indiana University Press, 1990), 230.

164 **"In my native town"**: Talmud, *Nedarim* 9b.

165 **"Not a single one"**: Abba Hillel Silver, *Where Judaism Differed: An Inquiry into the Distinctiveness of Judaism* (New York: Macmillan, 1956), 228.

165 **"The Holy One"**: Nachmanides on Num. 7:12.

166 **"The Torah does not repeat"**: Rabbi Yissocher Frand, "Lessons Learned from Gifts of the Nesiim: Parshas Naso," torah.org, June 7, 2002, http://torah.org/learning/ravfrand/5756/naso.html.

169 **"An individual who is ritually impure"**: Mishnah, *Pesachim* 9:1–4.

170 **"Even at the time"**: Reuven Hammer, *Entering Torah: Prefaces to the Weekly Torah Portion* (Jerusalem: Gefen, 2009), 211.

170 **"They actually did not suffer"**: Nachmanides on Num. 11:4.

171 **"Judaism is not only what we do"**: Donniel Hartman, lecture, Shalom Hartman Center, Jerusalem, July 2006.

174 **"You are certainly permitted"**: Lawrence S. Kushner and Kerry M. Olitzky, *Sparks Beneath the Surface: A Spiritual Commentary on the Torah* (Northvale NJ: Jason Aronson, 1993), 188.

175 **"Why not go"**: Dr. Erica Brown, "They Could Be Giants–So Could You!" in *Text Messages: A Torah Commentary for Teens,* ed. Jeffrey K. Salkin (Woodstock VT: Jewish Lights, 2012), 184.

175 **"If the people live"**: Rashi on Num. 13:18.

176 **"In this world"**: David Landes, *The Wealth and Poverty of Nations: Why Some Are So Rich and Some So Poor* (New York: Norton, 1999), 524.

179 **"Does a house"**: *Be-midbar Rabbah* 18:3.

179 **"I am a Jew"**: Edmond Fleg, "Why I Am a Jew," in *The Zionist Idea: A Historical Analysis and Reader,* ed. Arthur Hertzberg (Philadelphia: Jewish Publication Society, 1997), 483.

180 **"That same staff"**: *Be-midbar Rabbah* 18:23.

181 **"We live by miracles"**: Israel Salanter, *Ohr Yisrael* (Vilna: n.p., 1874), quoted in Irving Greenberg, *The Jewish Way: Living the Holidays* (New York: Summit Books, 1988), 185.

184 **"I succeeded in understanding"**: *Yalkut Shimoni* 759.

185 **"Before the late Egyptian prime minister"**: Aaron Rakeffet-Rothkoff

and Joseph Epstein, eds., *The Rav: The World of Rabbi Joseph B. Soloveitchik* (Hoboken NJ: KTAV, 1999), 126.

186 **"Had you spoken"**: Rashi on Num. 20:12.

186 **"Maybe there was a moment"**: Morris Adler, *The Voice Still Speaks: Message of the Torah for Contemporary Man* (New York: Bloch, 1969), 341–45.

190 **"Ten things were created"**: Mishnah, *Avot* 5:6.

190 **"The she-ass is Israel"**: David Hazony, "On the Side of the Angels," July 6, 2011, http://davidhazony.typepad.com/david-hazony/2011/07/on-the-side-of-the-angels.html#sthash.rGzeyEgm.dpuf.

191 **"A civilization cannot be handed"**: Kerry Olitzky and Rabbi Avi S. Olitzky, *New Membership and Financial Alternatives for the American Synagogue: From Traditional Dues to Fair Share to Gifts from the Heart* (Woodstock VT: Jewish Lights, 2015).

192 **"All the nations came to Balaam"**: *Eikhah Rabbah, Petihah* 10.

195 **"My children, show zeal"**: 1 Macc. 2:51–54.

195 **"In reward for turning away"**: Zvi Yehuda Berlin, *Ha'amek Davar*, quoted in Nehama Leibowitz, *Studies in Bamidbar: Numbers* (Jerusalem: Eliner Library, n.d.), 331.

196 **"Their eyes saw"**: Rashi on Num. 27:7.

197 **"The daughters of Zelophehad"**: Rabbi B. Elka Abrahamson, "It's Not Fair!" in *Text Messages: A Torah Commentary for Teens*, ed. Jeffrey K. Salkin (Woodstock VT: Jewish Lights, 2012), 205.

200 **"Notice which they mentioned first"**: Rashi on Num. 32:16.

205 **"They journeyed from Berditchev"**: Rabbi Arthur Green, "Resting Places on the Journey," in *The Modern Men's Torah Commentary: New Insights from Jewish Men on the 54 Weekly Torah Portions*, ed. Jeffrey K. Salkin (Woodstock VT: Jewish Lights, 2009), 249.

206 **"In biblical law"**: Moshe Greenberg, "The Biblical Conception of Asylum," *Journal of Biblical Literature* 78, no. 2 (June 1959), 125–32.

207 **"The court is obligated"**: *Mishneh Torah, Hilkhot Rotzei'ach* 8:5.

Deuteronomy

211 **"Deuteronomy regularly uses the term"**: Dr. Jeffrey H. Tigay, *The JPS Torah Commentary: Deuteronomy* (Philadelphia: Jewish Publication Society, 2003), 12.

211 **"A case involving a small coin"**: Rashi on Deut. 1:16.

212 **"Why did the Almighty confine"**: Nehama Leibowitz, *Studies in Devarim: Deuteronomy* (Jerusalem: Eliner Library, n.d.), 32.

213 **"The Israelites had to resist"**: Nehama Leibowitz, *Studies in Devarim: Deuteronomy* (Jerusalem: Eliner Library, n.d.), 28.

215 **After the war**: Story from Miriam Swerdov about Rabbi Eliezer Silver, accessed December 1, 2015, http://www.torahtots.com/holocaust/stories.htm.

216 **"I am the Lord your God"**: *Mekhilta Bachodesh* 5.

216 **"Therefore, the real translation"**: David Sperling, "The God We Ought to Love," in *Ehad: The Many Meanings of God Is One*, ed. Eugene B. Borowitz (Port Washington NY: *Sh'ma*, 1988), 85.

217 **"The great story"**: Amos Oz and Fania Oz-Salzberger, *Jews and Words* (New Haven: Yale University Press, 2014), 8.

217 **"If someone studies Torah"**: Talmud, *Yoma* 66a.

221 **"The Egyptians rely on their own labor"**: Shaul Regev, "Not Like the Land of Egypt," Parashat Ekev 5772/August 11, 2012, Lectures on the Torah Reading by the faculty of Bar-Ilan University, http://www.biu.ac.il/JH/Parasha/eng/ekev/ekev.shtml.

221 **"Remember Abraham"**: "Geshem" (prayer for rain), *Musaf* service, in Jules Harlow, ed. *Siddur Sim Shalom: A Prayerbook for Shabbat, Festivals, and Weekdays* (New York: Rabbinical Assembly and United Synagogue of America, 1985), 483.

222 **"When you have eaten your fill"**: Talmud, *Berakhot* 20b.

223 **"The ancient Rabbis"**: David Hartman, *A Living Covenant: The Innovative Spirit in Traditional Judaism* (New York: The Free Press, 1985), 221.

226 **"The distinguishing characteristic of human beings"**: David L. Lieber, ed., *Etz Hayim: Torah and Commentary* (New York: Rabbinical Assembly/The United Synagogue of Conservative Judaism, 2001), 161.

226 **"freedom of choice"**: *Hilkhot Teshuvah* 5:1.

227 **"The world is like a human eye"**: *Derekh Eretz Zuta* 9.

228 **"Deuteronomy must have expected"**: Jeffrey H. Tigay, *The JPS Torah Commentary: Deuteronomy* (Philadelphia: Jewish Publication Society, 2003), 119.

231 **"In the ancient Near East"**: Yair Lorberbaum, *Disempowered King: Monarchy in Classical Jewish Literature* (Jerusalem: Robert and Arlene Kogod Library, 2011), 7–8.

231 **"The king must not exercise"**: *Mishneh Torah*, Laws of Kings 2:6.

232 **"Peace is a great thing"**: *Be-midbar Rabbah* 11:7.

233 **"Are my actions necessary?"**: Moshe Halbertal, lecture, Shalom Hartman Institute, Jerusalem, Israel, July 2010.

233 **"My children and their friends"**: Moshe Halbertal, lecture, Shalom Hartman Institute, Jerusalem, Israel, July 2010.

236 **"There never has been a 'wayward or defiant son,'"**: Talmud, *Sanhedrin* 71a.

237 **"This law probably does not apply"**: Tamara Cohn Eskenazi and Andrea L. Weiss, eds., *The Torah: A Women's Commentary* (New York: URJ Press, 2007), 1168–69.

237 **Finding and returning lost objects**: Talmud, *Bava Metzi'a*.

238 **The natural human response**: Dov Peretz Elkins, *The Torah's Top Fifty*

Ideas: The Essential Concepts Everyone Should Know (New York: Specialist Press, 2006), 290.

238 **"God wished to implant"**: Nehama Leibowitz, *Studies in Devarim: Deuteronomy* (Jerusalem: Eliner Library, n.d.), 215.

240 **"generations look through our eyes"**: A. M. Klein, "A Psalm Touching Genealogy," in *A. M. Klein: Selected Poems*, ed. Zailig Pollock, Seymour Mayne, and Usher Caplan (Toronto: University of Toronto Press, 1997), 77.

242 **"Those who lived near Jerusalem"**: Mishnah, *Bikkurim* 3:4.

242 **"Only in Israel"**: Yosef Hayim Yerushalmi, *Zakhor: Jewish History and Jewish Memory* (Seattle: University of Washington Press, 1982), 9.

244 **"The Jewish people had a special obligation"**: Nehama Leibowitz, *Studies in Devarim: Deuteronomy* (Jerusalem: Eliner Library, n.d.), 261.

247 **"Moses told the Israelites"**: *Devarim Rabbah* 8:6.

248 **"God is like a very patient piano teacher"**: Avivah Gottlieb Zornberg, lecture, Shalom Hartman Institute, Jerusalem, July 2011.

248 **"This teaches that Moses"**: Rashi on Deut. 29:1.

249 **"'Today' in this Torah portion"**: Everett Fox, "Committing to the Torah 'Today,'" TheTorah.com: A Historical and Contextual Approach, accessed September 18, 2014, http://thetorah.com/committing-to-the-covenant-today/.

252 **"In most ancient religions"**: Elliot Dorff, "Parashat Nitzavim/Vayelech," *Learn Torah With . . .* (Los Angeles CA, Torah Aura, 1977).

253 **"It is a positive commandment"**: *Mishneh Torah,* Laws of Sefer Torah 7:1.

254 **"After the destruction of the First Temple"**: *Eikhah Rabbah* 3:7.

257 **"God is imaged in rapid succession"**: Rachel Adler, *Engendering Judaism: An Inclusive Theology and Ethics* (New York: Beacon Press, 1999), 88.

259 **"In regard to gifts"**: Abraham Joshua Heschel, *The Sabbath: Its Meaning for Modern Man* (New York: Farrar, Straus and Giroux, 2005), 28.

259 **"Who is rich?"**: Mishnah, *Avot* 4:1.

262 **"Well, I don't know what will happen"**: Accessed December 1, 2015, https://en.wikipedia.org/wiki/I%27ve_Been_to_the_Mountaintop.

263 **"Remember when I stayed on Mount Sinai"**: *Devarim Rabbah* 11:10.

263 **"There are stars"**: Elyse D. Frishman, ed. *Mishkan T'filah: A Reform Siddur—Shabbat* (New York: Central Conference of American Rabbis, 2007), 291.

263 **"Moses's burial place"**: Rashi on Deut. 34:6.

264 **"Moses's resting place"**: Elie Wiesel, *Messengers of God: Biblical Portraits and Legends* (New York: Touchstone, 1976), 204–5.

THE HAFTAROT

Genesis

269 **"it is the task of the Jews"**: Rabbeinu Bachya, *Kad ha-Kemah* 22.

269 **"Until the earth is filled"**: Michael Meyer, *Response to Modernity: A History of the Reform Movement in Judaism* (Detroit: Wayne State University Press, 1995), 216.

269 **"the Jews had to raise a light"**: Avi Beker, *The Chosen: Anatomy of An Idea* (London: Palgrave Macmillan, 2008), 109–10.

270 **"Rabbi Eleazar said"**: Talmud, *Berakhot* 64a.

271 **"When Torah scholars"**: Rav Kook, "Psalm 122: The Peace of Torah Scholars," Rav Kook Torah, accessed June 29, 2016, http://ravkooktorah .org/shalom59.htm.

272 **The Talmud notes**: Talmud, *Rosh Hashanah* 3b.

273 **"What do you mean"**: President Harry S. Truman, quoted in Michael B. Oren, *Power, Faith, and Fantasy* (New York: W. W. Norton. 1998), 501.

274 **"Your might, O Lord"**: Jules Harlow, ed. *Siddur Sim Shalom: A Prayerbook for Shabbat, Festivals, and Weekdays* (New York: Rabbinical Assembly and United Synagogue of America, 1985), 107.

275 **"Don't rely on miracles"**: Talmud, *Megillah* 7b.

276 **"Abishag said to King David"**: Talmud, *Sanhedrin* 22a.

276 **"Abishag sits in her room"**: Yitzhak Manger, "Abishag Writes a Letter Home," in *Voices from within the Ark: The Modern Jewish Poets*, ed. Howard Schwartz and Anthony Rudolph (New York: Avon, 1980), 304–5. Reprinted with permission.

277 **"The witch that came"**: Robert Frost, "Provide Provide," in *The Poetry of Robert Frost*, ed. Edward Connery Lathem (New York: Holt, Rinehart and Winston, 1969).

277 **Some sages said**: *Pirkei de-Rabbi Eliezer*, 33.

279 **"You went to temple"**: Franz Kafka, "Letter to My Father," trans. Ernst Kaiser and Eithne Wilkins, rev. Arthur S. Wensinger (New York: Schocken, 2013).

280 **"Everyone would save a sibling"**: R. Topolski, J. N. Weaver, Z. Martin, and J. McCoy, "Choosing between the Emotional Dog and the Rational Pal: A Moral Dilemma with a Tail," *Anthrozoos* 26, no. 2 (2013): 253–63.

282 **"Obadiah was an Edomite"**: Talmud, *Sanhedrin* 39b.

283 **"How odd / Of God"**: https://en.wikipedia.org/wiki/William_Norman _Ewer.

284 **"We are chosen to serve"**: Blu Greenberg, "What Do American Jews Believe?" *Commentary* (August 1996): 44.

284 **"If I did not believe"**: Dennis Prager. "What Do American Jews Believe?" *Commentary* (August 1996): 78.

286　**"The boy is dead"**: Zoe Klein, "Haftarat Miketz," in *The Women's Haftarah Commentary: New Insights from Women Rabbis on the 54 Weekly Haftarah Portions, the 5 Megillot and Special Shabbatot*, ed. Elyse Goldstein (Woodstock VT: Jewish Lights, 2004), 46.

286　**A midrash teaches**: Midrash, *Bereshit Rabbah* 85:12.

287　**"When Judah"**: 2 Macc. 10.

288　**"When the Greeks entered the Temple"**: Talmud, *Shabbat* 21.

290　**"A Jew who flees"**: Joseph Soloveitchik, *Kol Dodi Dofek* (Hoboken NJ: KTAV, 2006).

292　**"David wanted Solomon"**: Alex Israel, *I Kings: Torn in Two* (Jerusalem: Maggid Books, 2013), 31.

292　**"David is great"**: David Wolpe, *David: The Divided Heart* (New Haven: Yale University Press), 141.

Exodus

294　**"Where are the ten tribes?"**: Adolf Neubauer, "Where Are the Ten Tribes?" *Jewish Quarterly Review* 1 (1889): 14–28.

296　**"It is as if the haftarah"**: Andrea Carol Steinberger, "Haftarat Va-era," in *The Women's Haftarah Commentary: New Insights from Women Rabbis on the 54 Weekly Haftarah Portions, the 5 Megillot and Special Shabbatot*, ed. Elyse Goldstein (Woodstock VT: Jewish Lights, 2008), 67.

297　**"Pharaoh was a big noisemaker"**: Rashi on Jer. 46:17.

298　**"Some people like Jews"**: Martin Gilbert, *Churchill and the Jews: A Lifelong Friendship* (New York: Holt Paperbacks, 2008), 308.

300　**"Devorah the prophet"**: Debbie Friedman, "Devorah's Song."

300　**"One authority thought"**: Talmud, *Rosh Hashanah* 33b.

303　**"Many people identified"**: James Kugel, *How to Read the Bible: A Guide to Scripture, Then and Now* (New York: Free Press, 2007), 541.

303　**"God says, 'I need you'"**: David Wolpe, "The Angels and Us," *New York Jewish Week*, July 8, 2015.

303　**"The root of religion"**: Abraham Joshua Heschel, *Man Is Not Alone: A Philosophy of Religion* (New York: Farrar, Straus and Giroux, 1976), 68–69.

304　**"After having been recently released"**: Lori Cohen, "Haftarat Mishpatim," in *The Women's Haftarah Commentary: New Insights from Women Rabbis on the 54 Weekly Haftarah Portions, the 5 Megillot and Special Shabbatot*, ed. Elyse Goldstein (Woodstock VT: Jewish Lights, 2008), 85.

305　**"The Hebrew legislation"**: Boaz Cohen, *Jewish and Roman Law: A Comparative Study* (New York: Jewish Theological Seminary, 1966), 176.

307　**The Greek historian Herodotus would write**: *The History of Herodotus: A New English Version* vol. 2, n.d., 69.

307　**"In the World to Come"**: Jeffrey K. Salkin, *Righteous Gentiles in the Hebrew Bible: Ancient Models for Sacred Relationships* (Woodstock VT: Jewish Lights, 2008), 92.

308 "Because of our sins": Prayer book, *Musaf* service for the festivals.

308 "It was because of idol worship": Mishnah, *Avot* 5:8–9.

308 "Jerusalem was destroyed": Talmud, *Shabbat* 119a–b.

308 "Because there was baseless hatred": Talmud, *Yoma* 9a.

308 "There is no such thing": Simcha Raz, *Malachim Kivnei Adam* (u.d.), 484.

309 "When the First Temple": Talmud, *Ta'anit* 29a.

310 "Every sin contains within it": David Mamet, *The Wicked Son: Anti-Semitism, Self-Hatred, and the Jews* (New York: Schocken, 2008), 73.

311 "Elijah has achieved his objective": Alex Israel, *I Kings: Torn in Two* (Jerusalem: Maggid Books, 2013).

312 "It would start": Jeffrey K. Salkin, *Righteous Gentiles in the Hebrew Bible: Ancient Models for Sacred Relationships* (Woodstock VT: Jewish Lights, 2008), 92.

313 "In the Torah": W. Gunther Plaut and Chaim Stern, *The Haftarah Commentary* (New York: URJ Press, 1996), 222.

Leviticus

316 "Abram seized a stick": *Bereshit Rabbah* 38:13.

317 "An idol is . . . a projection": Rabbi Ed Feinstein, Rosh Hashanah sermon, Valley Beth Shalom, Encino CA, September 4, 2013, https://www.vbs.org/worship/meet-our-clergy/rabbi-ed-feinstein/sermons/its-time-we-talk-being-jewish-rosh-hashanah-2013.

317 "This was a war": Norman Podhoretz, "The Prophets' War Is Not Over," Beliefnet, December 2002, http://www.beliefnet.com/Faiths/2002/12/The-Prophets-War-Is-Not-Over.aspx.

318 "Are we not guilty": Dini Lewittes, "Haftarat Tzav," Haftorah This Week, CLAL, accessed November 20, 2015, http://www.clal.org/h28.html.

318 "Whoever rejects idolatry": Talmud, *Megillah* 13a.

320 "Michal wore tefillin": Talmud, *Eruvin* 96a.

320 "David had both the ability": Zvi Kolitz, *The Teacher: An Existential Approach to the Bible* (New York: Jason Aronson, 1977), 20.

322 "Naaman was arrogant": *Be-midbar Rabbah* 7:5.

322 "Naaman needs to learn": Jeffrey K. Salkin, *Righteous Gentiles in the Hebrew Bible: Ancient Role Models for Sacred Relationships* (Woodstock VT: Jewish Lights, 2008), 100.

324 "We are forbidden": Emil Fackenheim, *The Jewish Return into History* (New York: Schocken, 1978), 19–24.

326 "Because of our sins": Festival liturgy, *Musaf Amidah*.

326 "If one reads the book": Harry Orlinsky, *Essays in Biblical Culture and Biblical Translation* (Hoboken NJ: KTAV, 1974), 215.

328 "Only one person was created": Talmud, *Sanhedrin* 37a.

328 "The nations chosen": Abraham Joshua Heschel, *The Prophets* (New York: Harper Perennial, 2001), 40.

330 **"They were the heaven-gazing"**: Leon R. Kass, *The Beginning of Wisdom: Reading Genesis* (Chicago: University of Chicago Press, 2006), 13.

332 **"May our eyes behold"**: Prayer book, *Avodah* prayer.

333 **"Today, Jews are back in Israel"**: Yitz Greenberg, "Haftarat Behar," Haftorah This Week, CLAL, accessed November 20, 2015, http://www.clal.org/h35.html.

334 **"To support a fellow Jew"**: *Mishneh Torah*, Laws of Charity 10:7–14.

335 **"Only God truly understands"**: Leonid Feldman, "Haftarat Bechukotai," Haftorah This Week, CLAL, accessed November 20, 2015, http://www.clal.org/h36.html.

Numbers

337 **"Idolatry is adultery"**: Abraham Joshua Heschel, *The Prophets* (New York: Harper Perennial, 1962), 62.

338 **"God said: 'I will order Hosea'"**: Talmud, *Pesachim* 87a.

338 **"God has the authority"**: Rabbi Lia Bass, sermon, Temple Israel, White Plains, NY, n.d.

339 **"You will worship me"**: Rashi on Isa. 2:22.

340 **"Samson laughed at his enemies"**: Elie Wiesel, *Wise Men and Their Tales: Portraits of Biblical, Talmudic, and Hasidic Masters* (New York: Schocken, 2009), 119.

340 **"Who is a hero?"**: Mishnah, *Avot* 4:1.

340 **"Get hold of iron"**: Hillel Halkin, *Jabotinsky: A Life* (New Haven: Yale University Press, 2014), 156.

342 **"So he was brought"**: Talmud, *Sanhedrin* 93a.

342 **"In the midst of a night"**: Joseph B. Soloveitchik, "Kol Dodi Dofek," in *A Dream of Zion: American Jews Reflect on Why Israel Matters to Them*, ed. Jeffrey Salkin (Woodstock VT: Jewish Lights, 2009), 245–46.

343 **"I'd love to sleep soundly"**: Judith Schindler, in *God, Faith and Identity from the Ashes: Reflections of Children and Grandchildren of Holocaust Survivors*, ed. Menachem Z. Rosensaft (Woodstock VT: Jewish Lights, 2015), 254.

344 **"There have been four women"**: Talmud, *Megillah* 15a.

344 **"Rahab is proactive"**: Tikvah Frymer-Kensky, *Reading the Women of the Bible: A New Interpretation of their Stories* (New York: Schocken, 2002), 35.

346 **"All that is set out"**: Talmud, *Sanhedrin* 20b.

346 **"There was only the intermittent"**: Max Weber, *Ancient Judaism* (New York: The Free Press, 1967), 90.

347 **"Premature, violent, without an heir"**: Phyllis Trible, *Texts of Terror: Literary-Feminist Readings of Biblical Narratives* (Philadelphia: Fortress Press, 1984), 104.

348 **"Jephthah said"**: *Kohelet Rabbah* 10:16.

348 **"Perhaps the haftarah stops short"**: Ellen Umansky, "Haftarat Huk-

kat," Haftorah This Week, CLAL, accessed November 20, 2015, http://www.clal.org/h41.html.

349 **"Micah reduced the mitzvot"**: Talmud, *Makkot* 24a.

350 **"People continue to see the Jew"**: Silvano Arieti, *Abraham and the Contemporary Mind* (New York: Basic Books, 1981), 58.

350 **"Pinḥas is Elijah"**: *Pirkei de-Rabbi Eliezer*, 47.

350 **"The role of the prophet"**: Melilah Hellner-Eshed, lecture, Shalom Hartman Institute, Jerusalem, July 2013.

351 **"It is the intimate"**: Daniel Gordis, *God Was Not in the Fire: The Search for a Spiritual Judaism* (New York: Touchstone, 1997), 56.

353 **"Whoever sings"**: Talmud, *Sanhedrin* 101a.

353 **"The Torah is the ketubah"**: David Wolpe, "Shavuot, When We Became Who We Are," Jewish Telegraphic Agency (JTA), May 27, 2014.

353 **"Every year, we reopen"**: Sue Levi Elwell, "Torah: It's God's Love Letter to All Humanity," *Jewish Exponent*, August 5, 2010.

353 **"As in all relationships"**: Ron Wolfson, *Relational Judaism: Using the Power of Relationships to Transform the Jewish Community* (Woodstock VT: Jewish Lights, 2013), Kindle edition.

354 **"How would you like"**: Richard Levy, *On Wings of Awe: A Machzor for Rosh Hashanah and Yom Kippur* (Washington DC: B'nai B'rith Hillel Foundations, 1985), 276.

354 **"This is the Torah"**: Talmud, *Menachot* 29b.

354 **"We are your beloved"**: High Holy Day *machzor, Ki Anu Amekha*.

Deuteronomy

358 **"Isaiah does not reject"**: David L. Lieber, ed. *Etz Hayim: Torah and Commentary* (New York: Rabbinical Assembly/The United Synagogue of Conservative Judaism, 2001), 1001.

358 **"Had God said"**: *Be-midbar Rabbah* 25:21.

360 **"If the haftarot following Tisha B'Av"**: Mark Dov Shapiro, "The Unfolding of Comfort," *Journal of Reform Judaism* (Spring 1984).

360 **"The prophet came to God"**: *Pesikta de-Rav Kahana* 16:8.

362 **"Israel's existence is a miracle"**: In Jeffrey Salkin, ed., *A Dream of Zion: American Jews Reflect on Why Israel Matters to Them* (Woodstock VT: Jewish Lights, 2009), 120.

364 **"Rabbi Eleazar said"**: Talmud, *Berakhot* 64a.

364 **"When Torah scholars"**: Rav Kook, "Psalm 122: The Peace of Torah Scholars," Rav Kook Torah, accessed June 29, 2016, http://ravkooktorah.org/shalom59.htm.

366 **"'Zion' and 'Jerusalem' express two aspects"**: W. Gunther Plaut and Chaim Stern, eds., *The Haftarah Commentary* (New York: URJ Press, 1996), 477.

366 **"No man ever had an accident"**: Mishnah, *Avot de-Rabbi Natan* 35.

367 **"To survive and develop creatively"**: Jeffrey Salkin, *A Dream of Zion: American Jews Reflect on Why Israel Matters to Them* (Woodstock VT: Jewish Lights, 2009), 225.

368 **"Isaiah takes 'widow' in a wider sense"**: W. Gunther Plaut and Chaim Stern, eds., *The Haftarah Commentary* (New York: URJ Press, 1996), 484.

368 **"For us, the scenario of the rejected woman"**: Rabbi Vivian Mayer, "Haftarat Ki Tetse," in *The Women's Haftarah Commentary: New Insights from Women Rabbis on the 54 Weekly Haftarah Portions, the 5 Megillot and Special Shabbatot*, ed. Elyse Goldstein (Woodstock VT: Jewish Lights, 2004), 233.

368 **"Even though the days of exile"**: Radak on Isa. 54:8.

369 **"I sing in hymns"**: Peter Cole, *The Poetry of Kabbalah: Mystical Verse from the Jewish Tradition* (New Haven: Yale University Press, 2012), 149.

370 **"If only Israel would observe"**: Talmud, *Shabbat* 118a.

370 **"The task of the singer"**: Reuven Kimmelman, lecture, Shalom Hartman Institute, Jerusalem, Israel, July 2007.

371 **"I shall act"**: Rashi on Isa. 62:1.

372 **"The nights in Bergen Belsen"**: In Jeffrey Salkin, *A Dream of Zion: American Jews Reflect on Why Israel Matters to Them* (Woodstock VT: Jewish Lights, 2009), 105–6.

374 **"All names and titles of God"**: Abraham Isaac Kook, *Peraqim Be-Mahashebeth Yisrael*, ed. S. Israeli (Israel, 1952), 77–78, quoted in Louis Jacobs, *Principles of the Jewish Faith: An Analytical Study* (Eugene OR: Wipf and Stock, 1974), 126.

Special Haftarot

376 **"Any loving relationship"**: Mishnah, *Avot* 5:18.

376 **"David says, 'I am the son'"**: Andre Neher, *The Exile of the Word: From the Silence of the Bible to the Silence of Auschwitz* (Philadelphia: Jewish Publication Society, 1980), 14.

378 **"The nations would say"**: Rashi on Ezek. 36:20.

378 **"If someone studies Scripture"**: Talmud, *Yoma* 66a.

379 **"We were in the middle of the jungle"**: Donald Miller, private conversation, Bayonne NJ, May 2014.

380 **"It was commanded"**: Maimonides, *Guide for the Perplexed* 3:45.

381 **"All of Zion's children"**: *Metzudat David* on Isa. 66:7.

382 **"The phases of a woman's body"**: Rabbi Ilene Schneider, "Haftarat Rosh Chodesh," in *The Women's Haftarah Commentary: New Insights from Women Rabbis on the 54 Weekly Haftarah Portions, the 5 Megillot and Special Shabbatot*, ed. Elyse Goldstein (Woodstock VT: Jewish Lights, 2008), 262.